Sabine Hake
The Proletarian Dream

Interdisciplinary German Cultural Studies

Edited by
Irene Kacandes

Volume 23

Sabine Hake
The Proletarian Dream

Socialism, Culture, and Emotion in Germany, 1863–1933

DE GRUYTER

ISBN 978-3-11-064696-2
e-ISBN (PDF) 978-3-11-055086-3
e-ISBN (EPUB) 978-3-11-055020-7
ISSN 1861-8030

Library of Congress Control Number: 2018961807

Bibliographic information published by the Deutsche Nationalbibliothek
The Deutsche Nationalbibliothek lists this publication in the Deutsche Nationalbibliografie;
detailed bibliographic data are available on the Internet at http://dnb.dnb.de.

© 2017 Walter de Gruyter GmbH, Berlin/Boston
This volume is text- and page-identical with the hardback published in 2017.
Paperback reprint with minor corrections. The corresponding hardback was published in 2017.
Cover image: Hans Schmitz, Die Masse/The Mass (1923). Part of a series of nine signed linocuts
published by Werner Kunze (Berlin) in 1972. With permission of Collection Merrill C. Berman.
Printing and binding: CPI books GmbH, Leck

www.degruyter.com

Contents

Acknowledgements —— VII

Abbreviations —— IX

List of Illustrations —— XI

Introduction —— 1

Part One: Imperial Germany

Chapter 1. The Threat of the Proletariat and the Discourse of the Masses —— 33

Chapter 2. Proletarian Dreams: From Marx to Marxism —— 49

Chapter 3. Emotional Socialism and Sentimental Masculinity —— 64

Chapter 4. On Workers Singing in One Voice —— 84

Chapter 5. The Proletarian Prometheus and Socialist Allegory —— 100

Chapter 6. Ferdinand Lassalle, the First Socialist Celebrity —— 120

Chapter 7. Re/Writing Workers' Emotions —— 138

Chapter 8. The Socialist Project of Culture and Education —— 155

Part Two: Weimar Republic

Chapter 9. Revolutionary Fantasy and Proletarian Masculinity —— 177

Chapter 10. The Revolutionary Fantasy Revisited —— 193

Chapter 11. Franz Wilhelm Seiwert's Critical Empathy —— 205

Chapter 12. Social Democracy and the Performance of Community —— 222

Chapter 13. Taking a Stand: The Habitus of Agitprop —— 238

Chapter 14. Marxist Literary Theory and Communist Militant Culture —— 255

Chapter 15. The Emotional Education of the Proletarian Child —— 270

Chapter 16. Wilhelm Reich and the Politics of Proletarian Sexuality —— 288

Chapter 17. John Heartfield's Productive Rage —— 301

Chapter 18. *Kuhle Wampe* and "Those Who Don't Like It" —— 319

Afterword: A Historiography of the Proletarian Dream —— 334

Select Bibliography —— 357

Index —— 362

Acknowledgements

This two-volume book project could not have been conceived without the generous institutional support provided by my home institution, the University of Texas at Austin. Because of the Texas Chair Endowment, I was able to undertake several summer research trips to archives in Europe, including the International Institute of Social History in Amsterdam, the Deutsches Literaturarchiv in Marbach, and the German National Library in Frankfurt am Main and Leipzig. A 2012 DAAD Faculty Research Visit Award allowed me to complete archival research in Berlin, including in the Staatsbibliothek and Kunstbibliothek. The last year of support through a 2011–13 Humanities Research Award paid for a research assistant. A Faculty Research Assignment in Spring 2014 gave me much-needed release time for writing up my initial findings. Throughout the years I benefitted tremendously from the vast holdings of the Perry-Castañeda Library and the remarkable resourcefulness of its interlibrary loan staff. A generous book subvention grant from the Office of the President of The University of Texas at Austin paid for all illustration-related expenses. Last but certainly not least, because of a 2015–16 EURIAS-Marie Curie Fellowship at the Freiburg Institute for Advanced Study (FRIAS), I was able to finish the manuscript in record time; my special thanks to the FRIAS director and staff for an unforgettable year.

During the five years of working on this book, I have benefitted enormously from the feedback of colleagues across the disciplines. Christina Schrör and Benoît Dillet were spirited interlocutors during the Freiburg year. For some time now, the members of my faculty-writing group at UT, Tracie Matysik, Judy Coffin, Ben Brower, and Yoav Di-Capua, have been a supportive intellectual community and provided insightful comments and useful suggestions. My colleague in Germanic Studies, Kit Belgum, shared her expertise in nineteenth century literature. Barbara McCloskey of the University of Pittsburgh read the entire manuscript and offered encouraging feedback. Invited lectures at Vanderbilt University, the University of Miami, the University of Wisconsin at Madison, Texas A&M University, and the Free University of Berlin allowed me to present versions of individual chapters and to benefit from discussions with students and colleagues. Meanwhile, I found new intellectual communities at the annual conferences associated with the journal *Historical Materialism* and the Emotion Studies and German Socialisms Networks of the German Studies Association.

In preparing the manuscript, I have been competently assisted by Karin Maxey who translated the quotations from workers' poems and socialist plays into readable English and by Amanda Frost who completed a first round of copy-editing. Marisol Bayona Roman checked the bibliographical references prior to submission and saved me from many embarrassments. Academic publishing is known for its glacial pace; De Gruyter managed to publish the book in eight short months after initial manuscript submission. The enthusiasm of Irene Kacandes, the editor of the Interdisciplinary German Cultural Studies series at De Gruyter, and the professionalism of its editorial staff, including Manuela Gerlof, Stella Diedrich and Olena Gainulina, made the experience both meaningful and enjoyable; my heartfelt thanks to the two anonymous external readers. As I now return to the archives for primary research on the second volume, tentatively titled *The Workers' States*, I want to express my love and friendship to all those near and far who have been part of this mysterious journey called life, work, and politics; you know who you are.

Abbreviations

AIZ	Arbeiter Illustrierte Zeitung (Workers' Illustrated Newspaper)
AAUE	Allgemeine Arbeiter-Union (General Workers' Union)
ADAV	Allgemeiner Deutscher Arbeiterverein (General German Workers' Association)
ADGB	Allgemeiner Deutscher Gewerkschaftsbund (General German Trade Union Federation)
ASSO	Assoziation revolutionärer bildender Künstler Deutschlands (Association of Revolutionary Visual Artists of Germany)
ATB	Arbeiter-Turnerbund (Workers' Gymnastics Association)
ATBD	Arbeiter-Theaterbund Deutschlands (Workers' Theater League of Germany)
ATSB	Arbeiter-Turn- und Sportbund (Workers' Gymnastics and Sports Association)
AWO	Arbeiterwohlfahrt (Workers' Welfare Institution)
BPRS	Bund proletarisch-revolutionärer Schriftsteller (Association of Proletarian-Revolutionary Writers)
DAS	Deutscher Arbeiter-Sängerbund (German Workers' Choral Association)
DKP	Deutsche Kommunistische Partei (German Communist Party)
DSB	Deutscher Sängerbund (German Choral Association)
FRG	Federal Republic of Germany (Bundesrepublik Deutschland)
GDR	German Democratic Republic (Deutsche Demokratische Republik)
IAH	Internationale Arbeiterhilfe (International Workers' Aid)
IATB	Internationaler Arbeitertheaterbund (International Workers' Theater Association)
IfA	Interessengemeinschaft für Arbeiterkultur (Syndicate for Workers' Culture)
KAPD	Kommunistische Arbeiter-Partei Deutschlands (Communist Workers' Party of Germany)
KdAS	Kampfgemeinschaft der Arbeitersänger (Fighting League of Workers' Singers)
KG	Kampfgemeinschaft für Rote Sporteinheit (Fighting League for Red Sport)
KJI	Kommunistische Jugendinternationale (Communist Youth International)
KJD	Kommunistische Jugend Deutschlands (Communist Youth of Germany)
KJVD	Kommunistischer Jugendverband Deutschlands (Communist Youth Association of Germany)
KPÖ	Kommunistische Partei Österreichs (Communist Party of Austria)
KPD	Kommunistische Partei Deutschlands (Communist Party of Germany)
NSDAP	Nationalsozialistische Arbeiterpartei (National Socialist Workers' Party)
RAG	Reichsarbeitsgemeinschaft der Kinderfreude (National Working Group for the Friends of Children)
RFB	Roter Frontkämpferbund (Red Front Fighters' League)
RGO	Revolutionäre Gewerkschafts-Opposition (Revolutionary Union Opposition)
SAJ	Sozialistische Arbeiterjugend Deutschlands (Socialist Workers' Youth of Germany)
SDAP	Sozialdemokratische Arbeiterpartei Deutschlands (Social Democratic Workers' Party of Germany)
SED	Sozialistische Einheitspartei Deutschlands (Socialist Unity Party of Germany)
SPD	Sozialdemokratische Partei Deutschlands (Social Democratic Party of Germany)
SPÖ	Sozialdemokratische Partei Österreichs (Social Democratic Party of Austria)
USPD	Unabhängige Sozialdemokratische Partei Deutschlands (Independent Social Democratic Party of Germany)

VKPD   Vereinigte Kommunistische Partei Deutschlands (United Communist Party of Germany)

List of Illustrations

Cover: Hans Schmitz, *Die Masse/The Mass* (1923). Part of a series of nine signed linocuts published by Werner Kunze (Berlin) in 1972. With permission of Collection Merrill C. Berman.
Fig 3.1   Wilhelm Liebknecht, August Bebel, Ferdinand Lassalle et al., "Die Befreier des Proletariats/The Liberators of the Proletariat, 1863–1913," 50-Year Celebration of the Founding of the SPD 1913, postcard. With permission of Archiv der sozialen Demokratie der Friedrich-Ebert-Stiftung.
Fig 3.2   August Bebel, "'Ich hämmere jung das alte morsche Ding den Staat./I Am Hammering that Old Decrepit Thing Called the State,' Gruß zur Maifeier!/May Day Greetings," postcard, c. 1905. With permission of Archiv der sozialen Demokratie der Friedrich-Ebert-Stiftung.
Fig 4.1   Bundesfest of the Arbeitersängerbund "Rheinland," Düsseldorf, 13–14 July 1908, postcard. With permission of Archiv der sozialen Demokratie der Friedrich-Ebert-Stiftung.
Fig 4.2   Erstes Deutsches Arbeitersängerbundfest, Hannover, 16–18 June 1928, postcard. With permission of Historische Bildpostkarten, Universität Osnabrück Sammlung Prof. Dr. Sabine Giesbrecht.
Fig 5.1   "Der gefesselte Prometheus/Prometheus Bound," *Der Wahre Jacob* 136 (1891): 1104. With permission of Universitätsbibliothek Heidelberg.
Fig 5.2   "Kapital und Arbeit/Capital and Labor," *Süddeutscher Postillon* 9 (1895): n. p. With permission of Deutsches Historisches Museum, Berlin.
Fig 5.3   "Ich bin ein Proletar!/I Am a Proletarian!," *Süddeutscher Postillon* 21.6 (1902), title page. With permission of Deutsches Historisches Museum, Berlin.
Fig 5.4   Karl Marx as "Der gefesselte Prometheus/Prometheus Bound," 1843. With permission of Heinrich-Heine Institut, Düsseldorf.
Fig 5.5   Max Slevogt, "Wir sind die Kraft/We Are the Power," *Mai-Festzeitung* 1903, back cover. Reprinted in Udo Achten, ed. and intr., *Süddeutscher Postillon. Ein Querschnitt in Faksimiles* (Bonn: Dietz, 1979), 126.
Fig 5.6   Walter Crane, "The Capitalist Vampire," *Mai-Festzeitung* 1901, back cover. Granger, New York. All rights preserved.
Fig 5.7   Hermann Scherenberg, "Hasselmanns Enthüllungen/Hasselmann's Revelations," *Ulk* 42 (1878). With permission of Bayerische Staatsbibliothek München, Signatur 2Z 2008.79–7.
Fig 5.8   Ephraim Moses Lilien, "Die Einheit von Kunst und Arbeit/The Union of Art and Labor," *Mai-Festzeitung* 1899. Reprinted in Achten, *Süddeutscher Postillon*, 90–91.
Fig 6.1   "Lassalle, der Kämpfer gegen die Kapitalmacht/Lassalle, Fighter against the Power of Capital," c. 1870, color lithograph. With permission of Deutsches Historisches Museum, Berlin/A. Spille.
Fig 6.2   "1863–1913. Zur Erinnerung an das 50-jährige Gründungsjahr der deutschen Sozialdemokratie/In Celebration of the 50th Anniversary of the Founding of German Social Democracy," postcard. With permission of Archiv der Sozialen Demokratie Bonn.

Fig 6.3   Frontispiece in Heinrich Büttner, *Ferdinand Lassalle, der Held des Volkes* (1892), frontispiece. With permission of Deutsches Literaturarchiv Marbach, Kosch Collection.
Fig 9.1   Karl Grünberg, *Brennende Ruhr* (Berlin: Neues Leben, 1953), dust jacket.
Fig 9.2   Karl Grünberg, *Brennende Ruhr* (Essen: RuhrEcho, 1999), cover design.
Fig 10.1 Franz Jung, Die *Eroberung der Maschinen* (Berlin: Malik, 1929), cover design by John Heartfield. Copyright 2017 The Heartfield Community of Heirs/Artists Rights Society (ARS), New York.
Fig 11.1 Franz Wilhelm Seiwert, *Sozialistische Republik*, 30 April 1925, front page.
Fig 11.2 Franz Wilhelm Seiwert, *Demonstration* (1925), oil on canvas. With permission of Merrill C. Berman Collection.
Fig 11.3 Franz Wilhelm Seiwert, *Die Arbeitsmänner/The Working Men* (1925), oil on canvas, Museum Kunstpalast Düsseldorf.
Fig 11.4 Franz Wilhelm Seiwert, "Klassenkampf/Class Struggle," linocut, *Die Aktion* 12.43/44 (1922), front page. With permission of Merrill C. Berman Collection.
Fig 11.5 Gerd Arntz, "Arbeitslose/Unemployed" (1931), woodcut, Neuer Berliner Kunstverein. Copyright 2017 Artists Rights Society (ARS), New York/o Pictoright Amsterdam.
Fig 11.6 Gerd Arntz, "Arbeitslose/Unemployed," Isotype, in Otto Neurath, *Gesellschaft und Wirtschaft* (Leipzig: Bibliographisches Institut, 1930), 87.
Fig 12.1 Bruno Schönlank, *Der gespaltene Mensch, Spiel für bewegten Sprechchor*, Sprech- und Bewegungschor der Volksbühne Berlin, 1928. With permission of Archiv der deutschen Jugendbewegung, Witzenhausen, AdJb, F 1 Nr. Seriennr. 289/Bildnr. 09.
Fig 12.2 Erno Peiser, *Wir Masse*, Sprech- und Bewegungschor der Volksbühne Berlin, 1928. With permission of Archiv der deutschen Jugendbewegung, Witzenhausen, AdJb, F1 Seriennr. 269/Bildnr. 04.
Fig 13.1 Conrad Felixmüller, *Der Agitator. Otto Rühle spricht/The Agitator. Otto Rühle Speaks* (1920), oil on canvas, Nationalgalerie Berlin, 1946 reproduction. Copyright 2017 Artists Rights Society (ARS), New York/VG Bild-Kunst Bonn.
Fig 13.2 Curt Querner, *Agitator* (1930), oil on canvas, Nationalgalerie Berlin. Copyright 2017 Artists Rights Society (ARS), New York/VG Bild-Kunst Bonn.
Fig 13.3 Magnus Zeller, *Volksredner/Agitator* (1920), oil on canvas, Los Angeles County Museum of Art (LACMA). Copyright 2017 Artists Rights Society (ARS), New York/VG Bild-Kunst Bonn.
Fig 13.4 Käthe Kollwitz, *Der Agitationsredner/The Agitator* (1926), lithograph, Käthe-Kollwitz Museum Berlin. Copyright 2017 Artists Rights Society (ARS), New York/VG Bild-Kunst Bonn.
Fig 13.5 Jean Weidt, "Der Arbeiter/The Worker" (1925), Sammlung Weidt. With permission of Universitätsbibliothek Leipzig, Tanzarchiv, Slg. Weidt.
Fig 13.6 Jo Mihaly, "Arbeiter/Worker" from "Feierliche Tänze," c. 1926, Photo: Atelier Stone. With permission of Deutsches Tanzarchiv Köln.
Fig 13.7 Das rote Sprachrohr, *Kuhle Wampe*, DVD capture.
Fig 15.1 Kinderrepublik Seekamp 1927, photograph. With permission of Schilksee-Archiv Pieper-Wöhlk.
Fig 15.2 Kinderfest der Sozialistischen Arbeiterjugend (SAJ) 1928, photograph. With permission of Archiv der deutschen Jugendbewegung, Witzenhausen, AdJb, F 1 Nr. Seriennr. 297/Bildnr. 02.

Fig 17.1 John Heartfield, *5 Finger hat die Hand/Five Fingers Has the Hand* (1928), KPD election poster, Bundesarchiv-Bildarchiv. Copyright 2017 The Heartfield Community of Heirs/Artists Rights Society (ARS), New York/VG Bild-Kunst Bonn.
Fig 17.2 Heartfield's KPD election poster on the streets of Berlin, photograph. With permission of Bundesarchiv-Bildarchiv.
Fig 17.3 John Heartfield, *Die Rote Fahne*, 20 May 1928, cover, Deutsches Historisches Museum. Copyright 2017 The Heartfield Community of Heirs/Artists Rights Society (ARS), New York/VG Bild-Kunst Bonn.
Fig 17.4 John Heartfield, 1920 self-portrait, photograph, Akademie der Künste Archiv, Berlin. Copyright 2017 The Heartfield Community of Heirs/Artists Rights Society (ARS), New York/VG Bild-Kunst Bonn.
Fig 17.5 1929 *Film und Foto* Exhibition in Stuttgart, John Heartfield exhibit "Benütze Foto als Waffe!/Use Photography as a Weapon!" *AIZ* 29.37 (1929): 17. This includes his 1929 self-portrait with Police Commissioner Zörgiebel. Akademie der Künste Archiv, Berlin.
Fig 17.6 John Heartfield, Rotfront logo, cover of *Der rote Stern* 11 (May 1928), Deutsche Nationalbibliothek Leipzig. Copyright 2017 The Heartfield Community of Heirs/Artists Rights Society (ARS), New York/VG Bild-Kunst Bonn.
Fig 17.7 John Heartfield, "Alle Fäuste zu einer geballt/All Fists Clenched into One," *AIZ* 13.49 (1934), photomontage, cover image. Copyright 2017 The Heartfield Community of Heirs/Artists Rights Society (ARS), New York/VG Bild-Kunst Bonn.
Fig 17.8 Gustav Klutsis, "Workers! Everyone Must Vote in the Election of Soviets" (1930), photomontage, The Art Institute of Chicago. Copyright 2017 Estate of Gustav Klutsis Artists Rights Society (ARS), New York.
Fig 17.9 John Heartfield, cover of *Freie Deutsche Kultur* 3 (March 1942), Deutsche Nationalbibliothek, Deutsche Exilarchiv 1933–1945. Copyright 2017 The Heartfield Community of Heirs/Artists Rights Society (ARS), New York/VG Bild-Kunst Bonn.
Fig 18.1 *Kuhle Wampe*, DVD capture. Male worker on the train: "And who will change the world?"
Fig 18.2 *Kuhle Wampe*, DVD capture. Female worker on the train: "Those who don't like it!"
Fig 18.3 *Kuhle Wampe*, DVD capture. The Bönike family: mother and son.
Fig 18.4 *Kuhle Wampe*, DVD capture. The Bönike family: father and son.
Fig 18.5 *Kuhle Wampe*, DVD capture. The Bönike family: father and daughter.
Fig 18.6 *Kuhle Wampe*, DVD capture. Anni and Fritz at the workers' sport festival.

Introduction

Social movements are based on, and sustained by, emotions – emotions that, simply by being evoked in the name of politics, become political emotions. Sometimes identified with "the soul of the people," "the spirit of the nation," "the collective unconscious," or "the will of the masses," these emotions function as sources of group unity and strength, as expressions of shared goals and beliefs, and sometimes even as political arguments themselves. Much of the power of emotions in social movements derives from their formative, if not transformative functions – namely, to provide identities, create communities, and sustain identifications and commitments. For these reasons, calls for revolutions, whether democratic, socialist, or nationalist, tend to be written in the language of emotions. Likewise, the appeals to emotion as a site of authenticity and truth are especially pronounced during political crises and social conflicts when expressions of anger and indignation provide legitimacy to oppressed and discriminated groups. This is also true for the symbolic politics of the working class during its historical alliance with Marxism, socialism, and communism. Understanding these kinds of political emotions, however, means turning attention to cultural practices in the widest sense and looking for expression of collective imaginaries in artistic forms and aesthetic styles.

The emotional communities dreamt up in the name of the proletariat, that elusive classed body examined in this book, depended fundamentally on images, stories, songs, performances, symbols, and rituals and their changing forms and functions during the late nineteenth and early twentieth century. Given the unique power of these cultural practices, especially as part of a movement with revolutionary aims, the politics of emotion that gives symbolic expression to needs, fears, and desires not always in line with Marxist theory cannot be explained away with reference to the primacy of economic conditions or dismissed as a manifestation of false consciousness. At the same time, there is no reason to assume that the aesthetic expressions of community and collectivity provided by what this study calls the proletarian dream translated directly into new mentalities and attitudes, whether through the cultivation and denunciation of specific emotions, their equation with specific social forms and public behaviors, or their enlistment in a larger class-based culture and politics of struggle. For that reason, the elusive connections between emotional and cultural practices must be reconstructed both through their class-specific articulations in late nineteenth and early twentieth century society, capitalism, and democracy and through their performative, anticipatory, and compensatory qualities in the larger narratives of class, nation, folk, and community. Concretely, this means treating political emotions also as aesthetic phenomena and, for instance, seeing resentment and rage as a public performance of antagonisms and as part of a highly mediated culture of grievances and complaints. Here the proletarian dream emerging out of late nineteenth and early twentieth century German culture, including its debts to bourgeois traditions, offers an important historical perspective on the powerful but little understood role of emotions in social movements and attests to the formative role of culture, defined here broadly as symbolic communication, as an integral part of political mobilizations.

To introduce the larger project through the metaphor of the book's title, what is the proletarian dream or, to use an alternative term, the dream of the proletariat? A daydream or a nightmare? An extension of communist ideology or an alternative to working-class reality? At once elusive and ubiquitous, the dream of the proletariat refers to the social imaginary that has survived in the countless texts produced in the name of the revolutionary working class. With other modern social imaginaries, the proletarian imaginaries share an unwavering belief in newspapers, books, and public debates as the building blocks of a functioning public sphere and in civil society as the foundation of modern democracy and the nation-state.[1] However, disagreements exist concerning the conditions of power and domination under which imaginaries serve legitimating functions and perform the purpose of what used to be called ideology as false consciousness. In the proletarian imaginary, democracy usually means the rejection of liberalism and individualism as enabling conditions of modern capitalism and the formulation of radical alternatives in the context of the workers' movement. A product of socialist and communist imaginaries, including their different genealogies, the proletarian dream is at once grounded in a Marxist analysis of class society and propelled forward by emotional energies that continuously destabilize these theoretical frameworks. Always exceeding the conditions of working-class life, the cultural texts and contexts created in the name of the proletariat function both as a laboratory for new commitments and attachments and as a repository for those needs and desires that are excluded from, or find no place in, official class-based narratives.

Drawing on the connection of dreams to the unconscious established in psychoanalytic thought, the book's title refers precisely to this unique ability of symbolic practices to make meanings, form identifications, and guide the emotional processes that, beyond political convictions, sustain the workers' belief in, and

---

[1] The discussion of social imaginary is informed by two very different conceptualizations, Cornelius Castoriadis, *The Imaginary Institution of Society*, trans. Kathleen Blamey (Cambridge: Polity, 1987) and Charles Taylor, *Modern Social Imaginaries* (Durham, NC: Duke University Press, 2004).

love of, socialism. As a collective fantasy, the proletarian dream promises the victory of class struggle and revolution and, for that reason, is inseparable from the work of the imagination and its representations and mediations. However, as an integral part of class-based politics, whether in the name of Social Democracy or Weimar-era Communism, the proletarian dream also has disciplining functions and normative effects, most obviously in the gendered hierarchies of labor and industry and in the communist habitus of discipline and self-control.

Speaking of dreams in combination with the proletariat means to apply aesthetic categories to the practice of collective dreaming, to highlight the utopian qualities usually reserved for works of art in the narrow sense, and to rethink working-class culture along the lines of what Siegfried Kracauer once concluded about another collective imaginary when he called films the daydreams of society. And evoking the proletarian dream resonates with reflections by Walter Benjamin on the phantasmagoria of commodity fetishism that allowed him in the Arcades Project to connect the nineteenth-century dreamworld of capitalism to a longer messianic history of catastrophe and redemption. Built around the promise of revolution, the dreamworld of socialism arises in conscious opposition to this dreamworld of capitalism. Nonetheless its emotional regimes, both through the dominant forms that are emphasized in William Reddy's definition of the term and the oppositional and alternative functions that are emphasized in this book, remain forever haunted by what might be called antagonism, contradiction, or Hegelian dialectics.[2] Today these forgotten archives of proletarian identifications can be accessed not by treating political emotions as a mere expression of class identity or a mere function of revolutionary praxis but by using them as a heuristic device in the reconstruction of socialist and communist imaginaries (rather than ideologies) and by reading them as a productive means in the making of working-class culture (rather than of the working class).

The conventional way of thinking about emotions in social movements has involved highlighting their destructive effect in the irrational behaviors of the uneducated masses and blaming the departure from reason for the mass appeal of nationalist, xenophobic, and populist ideologies. Liberal democracies, within this logic, are based on the rational pursuit of self-interest and its full articulation within the boundaries of civil society and the nation-state. The ongoing compromise between self-interest and the common good, which confirms the individual at the center of this elusive process, hinges on the characterization of

---

[2] The term "emotional regimes" is taken from William M. Reddy, *The Navigation of Feeling: A Framework for the History of Emotions* (Cambridge: Cambridge University Press, 2001). Historically, this argument about dreamworlds has been made by Susan Buck-Morss in *Dreamworld and Catastrophe: The Passing of Mass Utopia in East and West* (Cambridge, MA: MIT Press, 2002).

political emotion as dangerous irrationality, an argument first presented by conservative scholars in the context of nineteenth-century mass psychology and confirmed by the fascist mass movements of the twentieth century. In the German context, the argument for deliberative democracy has been made most forcefully in the 1960s by Jürgen Habermas in his influential theory of the bourgeois public sphere. The first doubts about the limits of communicative action and rational choice found expression in the concept of a proletarian public sphere developed by Oskar Negt and Alexander Kluge in evocative writings on public sphere, experience, history, and obstinacy since the 1970s.[3] The degree to which modern democracies, too, depend on cultures of emotion in both achieving social cohesion and organizing public dissent has become the subject of urgent concern across a range of scholarly fields. Until recently, the deep-seated suspicion toward emotions in politics has focused on the way shared convictions are articulated in the form of propaganda, demagoguery, or mass contagion. Given the continuing preference for measuring the politics of emotion against the allegedly superior qualities of critical reasoning and deliberative argument, there is an urgent need for historical studies that treat political emotions as distinct cultural practices with their own formal registers and symbolic functions.

The reclamation of emotion as a legitimate part of political debate is inseparable from the discourses of recognition associated in the United States with contemporary identity politics, new social movements, and the so-called culture wars. There is increasing awareness – at the intersection of cultural studies with gender and sexuality studies and critical race and ethnic studies – of the powerful role of emotions in the struggles of marginalized social and ethnic groups and the self-fashioning of countercultures and subcultures. Meanwhile, the social sciences have drawn attention to very different emotional economies established by the neoliberal world order and thematized in book titles such as *The Entrepreneurial Self* and *The Emotional Logic of Capitalism*.[4] Here more historically grounded perspectives on class, culture, and the politics of emotion can offer a much-needed corrective to the identity discourses that offer compelling in-

---

[3] The two key texts are Jürgen Habermas, *The Structural Transformation of the Public Sphere: An Inquiry into a Category of Bourgeois Society*, trans. Thomas Bürger (Cambridge, MA: MIT Press, 1989) and Oskar Negt and Alexander Kluge, *Public Sphere and Experience: Towards an Analysis of the Bourgeois and Proletarian Public Sphere*, foreword Miriam Hansen, trans. Peter Labanyi, Jamie Owen Daniel, and Assenka Oksiloff (London: Verso, 2016). For a further discussion of the significance of Negt and Kluge, see the Afterword.

[4] See Ulrich Bröckling, *Das unternehmerische Selbst. Soziologie einer Subjektivierungsform* (Frankfurt am Main: Suhrkamp, 2007) and Martijn Konings, *The Emotional Logic of Capitalism: What Progressives Have Missed* (Stanford: Stanford University Press, 2015).

sights into the intersectionality of race and gender but remain silent on the question of class. With their culturalist presumptions, these discourses have so far failed to adequately address the widespread anger, anxiety, and despair produced by growing social and economic inequality and, furthermore, been surprisingly uninterested in the culture of resentment fueling various populist, nativist, and fundamentalist movements worldwide.

The burgeoning interdisciplinary field known as the history of emotions has drawn attention to the transformative role of culture in establishing what scholars have called emotional communities, emotional regimes, and emotional practices – terms that will be clarified in the third section of the introduction. Historians have shown how legal, medical, educational, literary, and philosophical discourses are inseparable from theories of emotion; how definitions of public and private sphere and constructions of group identity are dependent on (gendered) hierarchies of emotions; and how both the minor rituals of belonging and the grand narratives of nation are contingent upon the symbolic politics of public emotions. Focusing on ideas about emotions, intellectual historians have shed light on how theories of the passions, sentiments, affects, and drives have profoundly influenced modern definitions of subjectivity, individuality, and identity. More recently, literary scholars have shown that aesthetic emotions must be treated as an integral part of the historical constellation of Enlightenment thought, idealist aesthetics, and bourgeois emancipation. All of these connections are important not only to dominant culture (whether feudal or capitalist, aristocratic or bourgeois) but also to social movements that rely on the literary, visual, and performing arts in their struggles for representation in the literal and figurative sense.

Political emotions – how they are defined, evaluated, interpreted, and represented – open up new perspectives on German working-class culture and help to rediscover the main works, genres, forms, styles, and debates – but without the underlying assumptions informing much of the scholarship produced during the 1970s and 1980s. These include the equation of working-class culture with socialist culture, the privileging of political categories over competing models of explanation, and the treatment of symbolic practices as extensions of working-class reality and Marxist theory. Resisting the search (then and now) for models of political committed art usable in the present, the symbolic forms and aesthetic registers chosen to generate emotions in line with the goals of the workers' movement in fact bear witness to the considerable debt owed to bourgeois culture and the culture of religion and bring out the strong continuities between the culture of class and the culture of community. Historicizing political emotions invariably means to emphasize the otherness of proletarian identifications and guard against the underlying assumptions that, in contemporary identity discourse, recast emancipatory movements in individual and, ultimately, affirmative terms. Here treating emotions as a heuristic device rather than the site of authenticity and truth protects against the pitfalls of social constructivism and its secret double, essentialism, and directs critical attention to the social imaginaries shared by socialist, populist, and nationalist movements, beginning with their almost ritualistic evocation of community, folk, and the people.

Studying the discourses of emotion emerging at the intersection of workers' movement, working class, and socialism means being cognizant of the methodological challenges intrinsic to the study of collective subjectivities and imaginaries. Mass revolts, populist uprisings, and socialist revolutions remain inaccessible to conventional forms of inquiry that assume the autonomous bourgeois individual as the normative model for political convictions and behaviors. The politics of class cannot be explained through the traditional tools of mass psychology either, given its origins in decidedly bourgeois fears about the modern masses. New ways of reading must move beyond the false alternatives of either denouncing the volatility of the masses or celebrating the authenticity of the people and focus instead on historically and culturally specific ways in which social movements give rise to collective imaginaries. These collective imaginaries, even if understood in the most materialist terms, always exceed the determinations of class, labor, and capital and sometimes reach their most powerful manifestations in marked opposition to Marxist theory and praxis. Here two methodological solutions offer themselves, to examine the formative role of emotions in social movements for their compensatory, anticipatory, liberatory, and compulsory functions and, based on the remarkable textual productivity that sustains such movements, to treat political emotions as cultural practices, in the sense that they are always already part of images, stories, traditions, conventions, and performances. This book proposes that one way of uncovering these intangible but powerful connections is through the historical example of German working-class culture and the culture of socialism and communism.[5]

I

Conceived as the first of a two-volume work (Vol. I: *The Proletarian Dream, 1863– 1933*, Vol. II: *The Workers' States, 1933–1989*), the larger project can be described

---

[5] A note on capitalization: Throughout this book, "socialist" and "communist" will be the preferred spelling; "Social Democratic" and "Communist" will be capitalized whenever they refer to specific political parties (SPD, KPD).

as part cultural history, part cultural theory, and part a series of case studies. The eighteen chapters in this book have been selected and arranged to perform symptomatic readings – not as part of a hermeneutics of suspicion but in a critical project of reconstruction: the main goal, after all, is to regain access to a forgotten (and vanquished) collective imaginary through its rich and diverse symbolic expressions. Given the dearth of comprehensive overviews on German working-class culture and critical studies on class as a category of cultural history, a related and equally important goal is to make these materials available in their sheer abundance and remarkable variety – either for the first time or with new questions and in new contexts.

This process of rediscovery and reassessment must start with the recognition of the utter foreignness of the voices and visions from the proletarian dream: their surprising distance from the world of the factory and the tenement, their effusive paeans to the beauty of nature and the power of love, and their impossible quest for harmony, unity, and community. These proletarian voices find their tone and rhythm in conscious opposition to dominant culture and society but, not infrequently, also connect to other expressions of opposition and subversion. They represent marginal sensibilities and ephemeral phenomena and are part of a poetics and politics of emotion that, across the historical divides, sometimes require special skills at deciphering. They are inseparable from the detours, dead ends, and sidelines of a larger history from below and, for that reason, so important to a different genealogy of working-class culture based on political emotions. In other words, these collective imaginaries open up a new perspective on the history of class struggles, social movements, and counterpublic spheres precisely through that which exists because, despite, and beyond social reality and political ideology.

All of these perspectives are brought to bear on the cultural and emotional practices that produced proletarian identifications during a formative period in the history of the workers' movement – specifically, from the founding of the precursor of the Social Democratic Party to the banning of SPD and KPD during the first months of the Third Reich. The conceptual slippages between social and political formations – working class, workers' movement, and socialist and communist parties – have been an integral part of their respective histories and historiographies but cannot be resolved through critical readings informed exclusively by Marxist terminologies. As distinct but interrelated analytical categories, class, movement, and ideology resonate in the competing definitions of working-class culture, proletarian culture, and socialist culture available at the time and include the subproletarian, plebeian, and subaltern perspectives that shed light on the nonsynchronicities through which culture – always overdetermined, always contradictory, always ambiguous – was expected to reconcile these differences through the making of proletarian identifications.

Offering access to these complicated processes, the selection of historical material is limited to members of the working class and those identifying with its struggles, including worker poets and dramatists, socialist novelists and polemicists, communist painters and dancers – and members of the labor aristocracy and worker intelligentsia. A few well-known figures such as Franz Jung, Franz Wilhelm Seiwert, John Heartfield, and Bertolt Brecht are included because of their contribution to what this study calls proletarian modernism, a formally innovative, collectively based, and politically committed art. However, the vast majority of the writers and critics are entirely unknown or familiar only to a few specialists. They published their novels, pamphlets, poems, and tracts in publishing houses founded by the major leftist parties and had their plays performed during the major anniversaries and celebrations of the workers' movement. Likewise, the artists mentioned showed their work primarily in socialist venues while maintaining a precarious relationship to bourgeois institutions. Their contributions are rescued from oblivion here not in order to give a more complete account of late-nineteenth and early-twentieth century German culture or add them to an expanded canon of great and minor works, but to shed light on the emotional practices that radicalized the working class in the name of the proletariat.

All research projects are defined through their inclusions and exclusions. The choice of a time framework roughly concurrent with Imperial and Weimar Germany was made in recognition of the power of the nation-state in defining the conditions under, and against, which the proletariat could be imagined as an emotional community – even as it never became one in the sociological or anthropological sense. The transnational networks of early socialism, the internationalist organizations of later communism, and socialists' individual routes of exile within Europe and to the United States will be referenced to the degree possible and desirable. Occasional detours through the Austro-Hungarian Empire serve to acknowledge the connections within a distinctly Germanophone workers' movement and culture of Social Democracy with a strong Jewish presence. For the same reasons, in the second part, the productive exchange of ideas between Berlin and Moscow and the Soviet domination of the Comintern are mentioned to establish the conditions under which the ethos of international solidarity reached its limits in confrontation with the new constellations of socialism and nationalism.

Regrettably, what cannot be considered here are the comparative perspectives that could follow the proletarian dream to other countries and cultures and trace the affinities between counterhegemonic and anticolonial movements, on one side, and the alliances between communist internationalism and cultural nationalism, on the other. These would have included the forms of cultural contact that gave rise to a brief proletarian moment in the United States and Latin America (e. g., in Mexico) after the October Revolution and set off proletarian waves throughout East Asia (e. g., in Korea, Japan, China).[6] In the United States, the flourishing of proletarian art and literature during the Great Depression and the Popular Front contributed to what Michael Denning has called a cultural front and examined as part of a broader progressive, democratic mass culture.[7] In Mexico, the designation "proletarian" played a key role in the desired convergence of folk and class culture that, among other things, aligned the project of revolution with the fight for national independence and indigenous autonomy. In several Asian countries, the proletarian moment brought together socialist, nationalist, and anticolonial movements that, from a European perspective, complicate the convenient binaries of national vs. international, socialist vs. populist, leftwing vs. rightwing, modern vs. traditional, and so forth. Comparative perspectives would go a long way in identifying the unique qualities of proletarian modernism, including such peculiar phenomena as the proletarian pastoral or the proletarian grotesque. The global configurations of cultural leftism could also provide points of comparison for how and why the relationship of Social Democracy to the bourgeois heritage constituted the greatest strength as well as the greatest weakness of the German workers' movement.

Keeping these larger questions and wider connections in mind, *The Proletarian Dream* opens with early sociological studies that set out to explain the presumed threats emanating from the modern masses and continues with the Marx-

---

[6] The references are to James F. Murphy, *The Proletarian Moment: The Controversy over Leftism in Literature* (Urbana: University of Illinois Press, 1991); Barbara C. Foley, *Radical Representations: Politics and Form in U.S. Proletarian Fiction, 1929–1941* (Durham, NC: Duke University Press, 1993); Elizabeth J. Perry and Li Xun, *Proletarian Power: Shanghai in the Cultural Revolution* (Boulder, CO: Westview, 1997); Mark Steinberg, *Proletarian Imagination: Self, Modernity, and the Sacred in Russia, 1910–1925* (Ithaca, NY: Cornell University Press, 2002); Samuel Perry, *Recasting Red Culture in Proletarian Japan: Childhood, Korea, and the Historical Avant-garde* (Honolulu: University of Hawaii Press, 2014); Heather Bowen-Struyk & Norma Field, eds., *For Dignity, Justice, and Revolution: An Anthology of Japanese Proletarian Literature* (Chicago: University of Chicago Press, 2015); Sunyoung Park, *The Proletarian Wave: Literature and Leftist Culture in Colonial Korea, 1910–1945* (Cambridge: Harvard University Press, 2015); and John Lear, *Picturing the Proletariat, Artists and Labor in Revolutionary Mexico, 1908–1940* (Austin: University of Texas Press, 2017).

[7] See Michael Denning, *The Cultural Front: The Laboring of American Culture in the Twentieth Century* (London: Verso, 1998). The continuities between socialist and populist imaginaries and their shared recourse to the discourse of the people will be examined in greater detail in the second volume on *The Workers' States*.

ist writings that established the world historical mission of the working class (chapters 1 and 2). Subsequent chapters follow the performance of proletarian identifications from the first workers' choral societies (chapter 4) to the Weimar-era speaking choruses (chapter 12) to the communist approaches to agitprop (chapter 13). The discourses of emotion are addressed explicitly through an examination of emotional socialism (chapter 3) and its resonances in the socialist celebrity phenomenon (chapter 6) and in the brief popularity of workers' life writings (chapter 7). Emotions also stand at the center of the socialist appropriation of classical allegory and mythology (chapter 5) and of bourgeois discourses of culture and education (chapter 8). The proletarian novels about failed revolutionary situations after World War I are particularly revealing because they provide therapeutic solutions through revisionist fantasies and experiment with formal and emotional alternatives to conventional modes of character identification (chapters 9 and 10). The ways in which the culture of emotions extends to pedagogical and psychological categories can be seen in the didactic function of proletarian children's literature and the sexual liberation promised by the Sex-Pol movement (chapters 15 and 16). Finally, the communist turn to socialist realism in the literary debates about tendency and partiality (chapter 14) and the experiments with modernist techniques in the context of photography and film (chapters 17 and 18) point to intensely emotional struggles over the meaning of the proletarian dream and its changing significance under the influence of Stalinism and in confrontation with National Socialism.

The individual chapters cover the historical period that saw the transformation of an estates-based society into a class-based society, that continued through the parallel processes of industrialization, modernization, massification, and urbanization, and that culminated in the double defeat in 1933 of the first German democracy and the largest organized working class worldwide. Just as the fight against social and economic inequality and for democratic forms of government during the Wilhelmine years is inconceivable without Social Democracy, the collapse of empire and monarchy after World War I is inseparable from the profound impact of the October Revolution on Weimar culture and society. Under these conditions, working-class culture developed into an alternative or oppositional public sphere between two historical moments, the struggle for national unification and democratization from 1848 to 1871 and the nationalization of labor and racialization of community after 1933. The rise of the Social Democratic Party as the first modern mass political party in Imperial Germany, the proliferation of working-class cultural associations and socialist, communist, and anarcho-syndicalist groups around the turn of the century, and the divisions between, and within, SPD and KPD during the Weimar Republic established the proletarian dream as both an essential part of Marxist critiques of capitalism and class society and a repository and laboratory for all the emotions involved in the process of political mobilization.

As a cultural history, *The Proletarian Dream* uses cultural practices, their definitions, institutions, forms, and practices, to gain a better understanding of the central role of emotions in proletarian identifications. To establish the lines of argumentation *ex negativo*, the book does *not* offer an overview of German socialist art and literature or introduce a new catalogue of proletarian classics; it also should not be mistaken for a contribution to the social history of the working class or the cultural history of the workers' movement. The struggles of Social Democracy during the Wilhelmine era and the divisions between SPD and KDP during the Weimar years are taken into account only in so far as they impact the institutions that made proletarian culture possible. If mentioned at all, the conditions of the working class – that is, questions of labor, industry, housing, family life, public health, social reform, and so forth – function only as absent signifiers against which the fantasies of revolution and community are meant to perform their intended emotional functions. With much of what characterized the life of a typical worker missing from the texts, the worst choice under these conditions would be to rely on a simplistic base-superstructure model to either highlight the artistic shortcomings of much socialist art and literature or diagnose the detrimental impact of false consciousness on working-class writers and thinkers. At the same time, the limitation to perspectives from the working class and those in solidarity with its struggles should not give license to exercises in leftist nostalgia or uncritical celebrations of forgotten voices from below. In line with the distinction made throughout the book between the historical working class(es) and the imaginary proletariat, few efforts will be made to locate collective imaginaries in the realities of working-class life, whether through individual practices of solidarity in the factory and neighborhood or through the top-down enforcement of strike action and party discipline. As a result, perusing the books in workers' lending libraries and the songs in worker's choral collections will not provide evidence of increased class consciousness; reading workers' letters and life writings will not a yield a formula for how socialist texts "produced" socialist workers. The only solutions available in the archives of proletarian identifications are therefore to focus on cultural practices as laboratories and repositories of political emotions and to limit critical analysis to the discourses of possibility – not factuality – that made culture a privileged site for imagining a future society and a community beyond class.

With eighteen chapters plus an afterword that doubles as a survey of the scholarship, *The Proletarian Dream* does not follow the standard choices for presenting previously neglected materials: a few close readings of important or typical works or a comprehensive overview of prevailing themes and motifs. Instead the book's relatively short chapters can be likened to fragments, snapshots, and excerpts – that is, building blocks in an ongoing process of critical reconstruction. This construction principle allows each chapter also to function as a test site for various approaches to the difficulties of writing about collective emotions and emotions in history and, in doing so, to establish a dialogue between the disciplines also on the level of methodological questions and conceptual solutions. On the one hand, the range of literary forms, theoretical arguments, visual styles, and theatrical experiments brings out surprising continuities and patterns of influence made possible largely by the socialist practice of cultural appropriation. On the other, the book's division into two parts separated by World War I and the German Revolution of 1918/19 points to a fundamental paradigm shift – on the level of emotional, aesthetic, and discursive modalities – between the nineteenth and twentieth century. Although the examples from literature, music, theater, dance, painting, photography, and film are presented in a roughly chronological fashion, they do not amount to a coherent history with distinct causes and effects. In fact, most chapters conclude either by noting later developments of their respective themes, forms, or styles or by following the critical reception of important theories and debates to the years after 1933 and, again, after 1945. Considerations of space prevented the inclusion of several cultural practices with strong links to the workers' movement, including workers' poetry and workers' sport; both will be discussed in the second volume.

Some chapters focus on an important socialist leader such as Ferdinand Lassalle or an influential literary genre such as the proletarian novel; others organize their arguments around a particular communist habitus (e. g., in agitprop) or visual motif (e. g., hands and fists); yet others use one particular text (e. g., *We!* or *Kuhle Wampe*) or aesthetic strategy (e. g., allegory or montage) to tease out the connections between political and aesthetic emotions. A conscious effort has been made to include a wide range of mass media, art forms, literary genres, and critical discourses and to make their sheer abundance, including in the form of multimediality and media convergence, an integral part of the overarching argument. The multiperspectivism inherent in such a transdisciplinary approach serves at once to highlight the expansive and integrative quality of proletarian culture and draw attention to the processes of exclusion applied to anything that does not fit into the Marxist master narrative. Within these parameters, literature nonetheless continues to occupy a privileged space given its elevated status in German culture, including its socialist appropriations, and the unique ability of fictional and discursive writing to provide access to collective imaginaries as mediated by, and in, language.

Using emotions as both a thematic focus and a heuristic device in the writing of cultural history means that individual chapters might start with questions such as the following: How did the emotional energies of choral singing promote identification with the political demands of the worker, laborer, or working man? How were workers' emotions written and revised for the needs of bourgeois readers? How did socialist leaders and ordinary workers experience socialism as an emotional community? How could proletarian children overcome feelings of inferiority? How did communist agitprop model a new physical and, by extension, political stance? And how were the promises of sexual liberation as political liberation enlisted in the cause of class struggle? Focusing on the emotional quality of specific artistic forms and styles might generate yet another set of questions: What was the role of pathos, melodrama, and sentimentality in the conception of the workers' movement as an emotional community? What were the contributions of allegory, montage, and mass spectacle to the emotional regimes of class struggle? And in what ways did specific modernist techniques cultivate a distinctly proletarian gestus and habitus? Channeled through the focus on individual emotions, these questions could also be redirected in the following way: How did cultural practices transform individual experiences of hopelessness and despair into collective expressions of anger and pride? How did love for the socialist leader sustain the dream of revolution and redemption? And how could rage or fear be turned into tools of political agitation and emotional conditioning in support of communism?

II

Critical attention to political emotions and the politics of emotion may be particularly relevant to the present conjuncture, but it is equally important to a historical reassessment of the largest and most organized socialist party of the late nineteenth century. From the early years of Social Democracy to the later divisions between SPD and KPD, the designation "working class" not only gave rise to an entire lifeworld made up of associations, festivities, rituals, and symbols; held together by distinct sensibilities, dispositions, and mentalities; and propelled forward by often heated debates about culture, politics, and society. Later described as alternative or oppositional, this "other" culture provided a metalanguage, including a language of emotions, through which to join together the identities of "worker" and "socialist" and conjure up their shared dreams of sociability, community, and collectivity – reason enough in the next section to clarify key terms such as proletarian, culture, and emotion and situate them within the larger debates in cultural studies.

No concept seems better suited to draw attention to the surprising similarities between new populist and early socialist movements than that of political emotion. At the same time, no term captures better the profound difference between current concerns about the rise in inequality and the future of democracy, on the one hand, and the Marxist belief in history's inevitable progression toward communism, on the other, than that of the proletariat – that strangely obsolete and radically other word that, from its first appearance in key Marxist texts, including *The Communist Manifesto*, to its obligatory mention in Social Democratic and Communist Party programs, came to embody the social, cultural, and political habitus of the revolutionary working class. As the particular and the universal class, the working class as defined by Karl Marx and Friedrich Engels united the critique of capitalism with a theory of revolutionary praxis. Entering the stage of history as the most radicalized part of the industrial working class, the proletariat promised to overcome the divisions in class society and realize the utopian promise of a classless society. At the same time, it was through this non-identity of proletariat and working class that the proletarian dream proved so important to the parties, groups, associations, and initiatives started to at once unleash and control the emotional regimes established in its name.

Today the proletarian dream is available only in the form of texts: poems, novels, songs, plays, paintings, photographs, films, and the countless essays, treatises, and polemics written in the name of the revolutionary working class. Inseparable from the parallel histories of mass media, literary genres, public rituals, and folk customs, the proletarian imaginary came to function as a site of class formation, an agent of revolutionary change, and a tool of party discipline, but, with special relevance to the study of political emotions, it also established working-class culture as a semiautonomous public sphere with its own forms, traditions, and conventions. The productive tension between politics, culture, and emotion – that is, between social and symbolic practices – offers ample evidence for what Critical Theory calls the utopian quality of the work of art and its anticipatory power of illumination. Retrieving these qualities from the social imaginaries of the past, however, requires an acknowledgement of the double historicity of culture and emotion and a return to actual archives and libraries; above all, it means to resist the kind of presentist readings that can easily reduce working-class culture to an object of sentimental longing or utter contempt.

To summarize the study's main conceptual difficulty and main critical intervention once more in the interest of clarity: The proletariat as conjured in countless images and stories from the past never existed, but its collective imaginaries had a profound influence on political ideologies, socialist parties, and workers' associations. Its constitutive elements were established in Marxist theory but invariably exceeded its conceptual frameworks – which also means that new approaches will have to move beyond economic determinist and social reflectionist readings but nonetheless accept the primacy of class to conceptions of culture.

More specifically, the sheer productivity of the proletarian imaginary can be evaluated only by recognizing proletarian culture as a semiautonomous sphere and by interpreting the socialist appropriation of the bourgeois heritage as a first step in the realization of the utopian function of art and literature. The connection to the Marxist critique of capitalism and class society and the adherence to universalist propositions about the emancipation of all of humanity only comes into clearer view through a corresponding critical terminology that focuses on proletarian identifications rather than identities.[8] Here the choice of identifications as the study's preferred term is intended to highlight the fundamental difference of the proletarian dream from the constructivist and essential categories of contemporary cultural studies that define identities primarily in relation to gender, race, and ethnicity. Like identities, proletarian identifications are fluid, contested, and subject to continuous revisions and negotiations; they do not require a working-class biography but a commitment to the socialist or communist cause. However, unlike identitarian claims, whose constructivist arguments often conceal essentialist assumptions, proletarian identifications are predicated on the analysis of class as a structural category and aim at the elimination of class differences. Their visions of community, sociability, and collectivity are developed precisely against the ideology of bourgeois individualism and western liberalism that, in modified terms, continues in contemporary identity discourse.

As the most powerful expression of the dream of community and collectivity, proletarian culture functioned at once as an extension of Marxist theory and socialist praxis, a vessel for older traditions and conventions, and a laboratory for new attitudes and mentalities. Emotions – their definition, evaluation, and cultivation – played a key role in the anticipated transition from economic oppression to political empowerment and functioned as a repository of all that had been left out of the official analyses of capitalist domination and exploitation. The conception of the working class as an imaginary community and the equation of socialism and communism with specific emotional regimes, however, cannot be analyzed apart from the historical struggles over the discourses of culture, its forms and functions, and its institutions and traditions. Especially the implicit and explicit assumptions about political and aesthetic emotions shared by Marxist theorists and socialist writers and artists draw long overdue attention to the centrality of aesthetic experiences to class mobilizations and the continuous transformation of the category of the aesthetic from its elevation in eighteenth-century idealist philosophy to its politicization in the historical avant-

---

[8] The distinction between identity and identification is based on Roger Brubaker and Frederick Cooper, "Beyond 'Identity,'" *Theory and Society* 29 (2000): 1–47.

gardes to its continuing diminishment in the anti-aesthetic of much cultural theory today.

Culture – defined, in the narrow sense, as symbolic practices and their interpretations and, in the wider sense, as what Raymond Williams calls a whole way of life – has been integral to the proletarian dream from its utopian beginnings to its dystopian endings. For that reason, it should not come as a surprise that scholars and intellectuals during the 1960s and 1970s first turned to working-class culture as a model for new alternative or oppositional public spheres. In the same way that socialists since the nineteenth century have sought to extend the Kantian notion of the aesthetic as disinterested pleasure toward the instructional functions that had always been part of folk culture, a new generation of scholars and activists from the 1960s and 1970s returned to the idealist philosophers and their Marxist interpreters to unite aesthetics and politics in the name of a democratic and progressive mass culture and a politically engaged art. During the Wilhelmine and Weimar years, and again during the heydays of Critical Theory and the New Left, the attendant processes of rereading were sustained by arguments that, in the traditions of Enlightenment thought, idealist aesthetics, and Weimar classicism, accorded heightened significance to culture as a system of meaning-making and tradition-building, that emphasized the emancipatory function of literature and the arts, and that invested the aesthetic with utopian qualities and critical faculties.

The proletarian dream emerged from the humanism and universalism of the Enlightenment and the Marxist analysis of capitalism and class society. As the main protagonist in the symbolic politics that came to distinguish working-class culture, the proletariat assumed its discursive function both as the self-appointed heir of bourgeois culture (*Kultur*) and as the defender of earlier traditions of folk (*Volk*) and community (*Gemeinschaft*). On the one hand, the indebtedness of the proletarian dream to nineteenth-century discourses of community confirmed the culturally mediated nature of emotions and the utopian function of the aesthetic as established during the Enlightenment. On the other hand, the socialist appropriation of the bourgeois heritage initiated an opening of the aesthetic (in the conventional sense) toward didactic and agitational modes that continues in twentieth-century forms of mass mobilization. Like the nation-states of the nineteenth century, the workers' movement depended on the invention of a tradition, to use Eric Hobsbawm's often cited phrase, in forging proletarian identifications and strengthening socialist commitments. And like the imagined communities studied by Benedict Anderson, the workers' movement relied on narratives, myths, and symbols in defining its internal structures and external boundaries. Of course, this includes the invention of a past and future for what this study calls imagined (and imagining) communities, two variations on Hobsbawm and Anderson that not only emphasize the workers' active contribution to this process but also give a first indication of the structural tensions within the proletariat as an imagined class and an imagining community in the making.

Since the rediscovery of working-class culture in the 1970s and 1980s, historians and literary scholars have produced numerous studies on the institutions and practices that made up the socialist and communist lifeworlds of Imperial Germany and the Weimar Republic. Their findings (to be summarized in the afterword) have contributed to a more nuanced understanding of working-class culture as an oppositional or alternative culture and introduced new critical perspectives on issues of labor, gender, leisure and everyday life. Scholars of German literature, theater, art, and music continue to study certain aspects of socialist culture but usually do so within the disciplinary logics of their fields – that is, of enlarging the existing corpus of works, discovering new authors and texts, questioning prevailing interpretations, and introducing new theoretical models. Throughout, the emphasis has been on the institutions of working-class culture, the debates on socialist literature, and the definitions of Marxist aesthetics. Very few scholars have examined individual works beyond their status as historical documents. In part, the widespread preference for thematic readings has to do with the derivative or conventional style of many of the works in question – and the implicit assumptions that close readings should be reserved for works of artistic quality. As a consequence, many interpretations tend to privilege approaches that treat working-class culture as little more than an extension of social reality or an expression of party politics. The study of socialist literature and art furthermore remains inordinately concerned with the question of reception or, more generally, political impact – thereby denying what the workers hoped to gain through their appropriation of the bourgeois heritage and their belief in the power of symbolic politics. By focusing on the emotional function of cultural practices, this book consciously brackets questions of originality or quality, deliberately avoids aesthetic evaluations, and instead organizes its readings around how writing workers dreamt about revolution, how they felt about the movement, and how they came to terms with political defeat. Accordingly, any questions of historical reception and political significance are bound to remain unanswerable beyond the circumstantial evidence provided by the sheer quantity of books, journals, treatises, performances, celebrations, spectacles, and exhibitions.

Few scholars have studied the culture of emotions in social movements, and even fewer have considered the role of the aesthetic in the discourses of socialism and communism. *The Proletarian Dream* argues that closer attention to the relationship between political emotions and aesthetic emotions offers new perspectives on these complicated dynamics and restores the aesthetic to its rightful place as a key category of cultural history and, by extension, cultural studies. Over the past decades, the concept of culture has been invested with almost magical powers – especially as regards the contest over meaning within the existing structures of power and domination and the available strategies of resistance to hegemony. The analysis of culture has become a privileged site for studying the negotiation of identities and assessing their ongoing re-articulation in the language of intersectionality, positionality, and performativity. In the process, symbolic practices have become the primary site for explaining – indeed, for establishing – social and political contests. Meanwhile, aesthetic questions have been increasingly marginalized, prompting Isobel Armstrong to speak polemically of an anti-aesthetic in cultural studies. The reduction of the aesthetic to a mere function of bourgeois ideology, in her view, has resulted in the abandonment of the critical potential of the aesthetic, of beauty and the sublime, to traditional sensibilities and conservative readings.[9] For that reason, the questions posed by Michael Bérubé, "Can politically motivated criticism have anything interesting to say about the *form* of cultural forms? What is the role of aesthetic evaluation in such criticism? [...] Can an understanding of the aesthetic augment an understanding of social movements, or is one necessarily a distraction from the others?," are answered here with an emphatic "yes."[10]

In fact, only serious engagement with aesthetic questions in the form of symptomatic readings provides critical access to the collective imaginaries produced at the intersection of socialism, class society, and the workers' movement. The eminent German historian George Mosse was one of the first to use symbolic practices to examine the parallel discourses of communitarianism and nationalism and highlight their emotional communalities even in the case of opposing political ideologies.[11] Continuing these lines of inquiry, aesthetic categories

---

[9] See Isobel Armstrong, *The Radical Aesthetic* (Malden: Blackwell, 2000), 1–23, plus her very critical response to Terry Eagleton's *The Ideology of the Aesthetic* in chapter 1. On the interlocking modalities of the aesthetic, the political, and the popular, see Irene Kacandes, "German Cultural Studies: What Is at Stake?" *A User's Guide to German Cultural Studies*, ed. Irene Kacandes, Scott D. Denham, and Jonathan Petropoulos (Ann Arbor: University of Michigan Press, 1997), 3–28. For a very different argument (from a sociologist's perspective) about the aesthetic politics of social movements, see Kenneth H. Tucker, *Workers of the World Enjoy! Aesthetic Politics from Revolutionary Syndicalism to the Global Justice Movement* (Philadelphia: Temple University Press, 2010).
[10] Michael Bérubé, Introduction, *The Aesthetics of Cultural Studies* (London: Blackwell, 2005), 9. In the same anthology, see Rita Felski, "The Role of Aesthetics in Cultural Studies," 28–43.
[11] See George L. Mosse, *The Nationalization of the Masses: Political Symbolism and Mass Movements in Germany from the Napoleonic Wars to the Third Reich* (New York: Howard Ferting, 2001).

can play an important role in reconstructing the historical configurations of socialism and nationalism in the context of cultural nationalism and its progressive and reactionary manifestations; the same holds true for the hidden affinities between socialism and populism that are evident in the overdetermined function of terms such as "folk" and "community" and their mass cultural appropriations in public rituals and spectacles. Last but not least, greater attention to the aesthetic in the study of symbolic politics can even open up a conceptual space for revisiting the Benjaminian distinction between the fascist aestheticization of politics and the communist politicization of art that is so central to another critical cliché in cultural studies, the automatic identification of the politicization of art with leftist, progressive causes and the implicit denunciation of aestheticization as mass manipulation and propaganda.[12] The case studies of this book give a first indication (to be developed further in the second volume on *The Workers' States*) in what ways the aestheticization of class struggle, whether in the registers of the pathetic or the sentimental, functioned as an integral part of the politicization of emotion since the early socialist movement. It can in fact be traced back to the legacies of German romanticism and the enormous influence on proletarian culture of Friedrich Schiller and his concept of aesthetic education and his belief in theater as a moral institution.

Socialist claims to idealist aesthetics departed from the Kantian definition (from *The Critique of Judgment*) of the aesthetic as disinterested pleasure and affirmed its designation as a precondition of subjectivity. At the same time, the meaning of the aesthetic was expanded toward older notions that included didactic and agitational modalities and newer combinations of the useful and the beautiful. In both cases, *Einbildungskraft*, translated as imagination and fantasy, was reclaimed as a productive force in the imagination of other worlds, including socialist utopias. Aesthetic emotions assumed new functions as a technique of intensification and transformation, with the true, the beautiful, and the good made available to the workers through socialist versions of the heroic, pathetic, and melodramatic, and with the class-based distinctions reproduced in the high-low culture divide being overcome through the translation of bourgeois traditions into socialist forms and registers.

These processes of cultural appropriation are particularly relevant for analyzing the continuous reconfigurations of folk, community, nation, and society and require at least a brief mention of two other eighteenth-century thinkers,

---

[12] See Walter Benjamin, *The Work of Art in the Age of Mechanical Reproducibility and Other Writings on Media*, eds. Michael W. Jennings, Brigid Doherty, and Thomas Y. Levin (Cambridge, MA: Harvard University Press, 2008).

Christoph Martin Wieland and Johann Gottfried Herder, who may be even more important to the socialist claims on culture and education than the venerated Schiller. Wieland was one of the first to emphasize the formative role of the aesthetic in the making of good citizens, especially in the fight for freedom and democracy. Similarly, Herder's characterization of the poet as a creator of the nation, his belief in language as the basis of national identity, and his validation of collective individuality as the foundation of society resonated deeply in socialist discourses of community that often treat class and folk as synonymous terms. Their shared belief in the unique contribution of poets and philosophers to the project of aesthetic education and the establishment of a republic of letters, based on either a classicist dream of Hellas or a vision of authentic folk, established the foundation for the hoped-for convergence of national literature, national identity, and the nation-state and found its socialist equivalent in the Marxist master narrative of class struggle as the only path to true humanity.

The resonances of idealist philosophy in nineteenth and early twentieth-century debates on culture and politics have been analyzed in two books that illustrate well the genealogy of the anti-aesthetic in cultural studies: Terry Eagleton's work on the ideology of the aesthetic and Josef Chytry's work on the aesthetic state. Practicing ideology critique as the hermeneutics of suspicion, both theorists acknowledge the significance of the Hellenic world as a model of democracy and public life and emphasize the heavy debt of German classicism and romanticism to the aesthetic humanism henceforth identified with ancient Greece. Locating the aesthetic in the larger traditions of European thought since the Enlightenment, Eagleton delineates how aesthetic practices and debates became inseparable from the political struggles of the bourgeoisie. The aesthetic not only played a key role in creating "the dominant ideological forms of modern class society," he argues, but also provided "an unusually powerful challenge and alternative to these dominant ideological forms."[13] Making a similar point concerning the politics of the aesthetic, Chytry characterizes the aesthetic state as "a social and political community that accords primacy, although not exclusiveness, to the aesthetic dimension in human consciousness and activity."[14] These shared convictions established the practices of aesthetic education, public sphere, and political life and defined the broader meaning of polis, state, and community – but did so in the context of oppositional and alternative public spheres. And if idealist aesthetics and bourgeois culture

---

13 Terry Eagleton, *The Ideology of the Aesthetic* (Malden, MA: Blackwell, 1990), 3.
14 Josef Chytry, *The Aesthetic State: A Quest in Modern German Thought* (Berkeley: University of California Press, 1989), xii.

proved so important to the making of the proletarian dream, the same can be concluded about the discourses of emotion, including their historical definitions, cultural expressions, and gendered divides.

III

Emotions in history and historical emotions are inseparable from representations. They exist only in the form of textual and discursive practices and are available to critical interpretation only through an ongoing reflection on their own historicity. These connections can be reconstructed in a number of ways: through writings about emotions and emotionality; through representations of specific emotions, such as hope, fear, hatred, and pride; and, most importantly, through the emotional discourses embedded in cultural practices, beginning with the recognition of pain and suffering in melodramatic genres and the celebration of solidarity in performances of community. Treating political emotions as a transformational force in social movements, however, means to acknowledge their contribution to, and place in, a longer history of emotions. Moreover, using aesthetic emotions in reconstructing the proletarian dream requires recognition of their shared dependence on cultural traditions, including theories of emotion, that originate in hegemonic practices but sometimes continue in counterhegemonic contexts.

Emotions have emerged as an exciting new subject of inquiry in what, following the various linguistic, visual, spatial, and performative turns, is sometimes called the emotional turn.[15] Intellectual historians, social historians, literary scholars, cultural anthropologists, and cultural theorists have produced numerous studies on the history of emotions and the place of emotions in history

---

[15] For discussions of the emotional turn in history, see Peter N. Stearns and Carol Z. Stearns, "Emotionology: Clarifying the History of Emotions and Emotional Standards," *American Historical Review* 90.4 (1985): 813–836; Barbara H. Rosenwein, "Worrying about Emotions in History," *American Historical Review* 107.3 (2002): 821–845. A useful summary can be found in Ute Frevert, "Defining Emotions: Concepts and Debates over Three Centuries," in *Emotional Lexicons: Continuity and Change in the Vocabulary of Feeling 1700–2000*, ed. Ute Frevert (Oxford: Oxford University Press, 2014), 1–30. For a comprehensive overview, see Jan Plamper, *The History of Emotions: An Introduction*, trans. Keith Tribe (Oxford: Oxford University Press, 2015). For a more theoretical discussion of emotional practices, see Monique Scheer, "Are Emotions a Kind of Practice (and Is That What Makes Them Have a History)? A Bourdieuian Approach to Understanding Emotion," *History and Theory* 51.2 (2012), 193–220. For a similar approach, see Benno Gammerl, "Emotional Styles—Concepts and Challenges," *Rethinking History* 16.2 (2012): 161–175.

that continue to expand the boundaries of the humanities – sometimes in dialogue with the life sciences. As part of the critical terrain marked by poststructuralism and postcommunism, the emotional turn can in part be interpreted as a response to the inherent limitations of textualism and the overdetermined status of language in cultural critique. With special relevance to this study, the growing interest in emotions furthermore reflects a fundamental shift from the universalist claims buttressing most class analyses to the particularist categories that have made identity a key site of social mobilizations – with all the problematic implications. To *homo laborans* and *homo economicus*, two figures that heretofore defined the human condition in relation to labor and capital, can now be added the neologism *homo emotionalis*. As a critical tool, emotions have allowed scholars to rethink key categories of historical inquiry and use the differences among passions, sentiments, feelings, and affects to study the complicated relationship between cultural practices and social formations.[16] The growing interest in the role of emotions in social movements, just like the scholarly discovery of working-class culture almost fifty years ago, is closely connected to the theoretical debates on culture as ideology that started during the 1970s and today continue in contemporary discourses of class, race, ethnicity, gender, and sexuality.

Within the evolving field called history of emotions, a shared consensus has formed around three main points: that emotions have a history and are part of history; that emotions are socially and culturally constructed; and that emotions in history are available to analysis only in the form of symbolic practices – that is, as texts in the broadest sense. Applied to the subject of this book, this means that the historical workers' shared sense of injustice and refusal of suffering, to reference an early study by Barrington Moore, cannot be examined without recognition of the social constructions and aesthetic manifestations that defined such emotions as political ones in the first place.[17] By the same token, under-

---

[16] Recent monographs on emotions in literary studies and intellectual history include Philip Fisher, *The Vehement Passions* (Princeton, NJ: Princeton University Press, 2002); Charles Altieri, *The Particulars of Rapture: An Aesthetics of the Affects* (Ithaca, NY: Cornell University Press, 2003); and Thomas Dixon, *From Passions to Emotions: The Creation of a Secular Psychological Category* (Cambridge: Cambridge University Press, 2006). For two contributions from the German perspective, see Katrin Pahl, *Tropes of Transport: Hegel and Emotion* (Evanston, IL: Northwestern University Press, 2011) and Rüdiger Campe and Julia Weber, eds., *Rethinking Emotion: Interiority and Exteriority in Premodern, Modern, and Contemporary Thought* (Berlin: De Gruyter, 2014). For two anthologies that deal with specific emotions, see Jan Plamper and Benjamin Lazier, eds., *Fear: Across the Disciplines* (Pittsburgh: University of Pittsburgh Press, 2012) and Michael Ure and Mervyn Frost, eds., *The Politics of Compassion* (London: Routledge, 2014).
[17] See Barrington Moore Jr., *Injustice: The Social Bases of Obedience and Revolt* (White Plains, NY: M.E. Sharpe, 1978), especially Part II.

standing emotional practices as cultural practices does not mean that they can be studied only through, and in, language, as implied by historian Gareth Stedman Jones in one of the first books to apply the insights of the linguistic turn to British labor history.[18] In fact, the visual, dramatic, literary, and musical practices examined in the following chapters open up new perspectives beyond emotional essentialism, constructivism, and textualism and, by adding the perspective of the aesthetic, expand the definition of culture toward its unique functions in symbolic politics and what Fredric Jameson calls socially symbolic acts.[19]

The emotional turn has brought critical attention to the formative role of emotions in the struggle for social and political changes, the definition of national and ethnic identities, and the invention of group rituals and traditions. Reading emotions as social and cultural practices always involves awareness of the choice of terminology – in the registers of theory as well as fiction. Here the insight that emotions are discursively and historically constructed has allowed scholars to move beyond the universalizing of emotions that, whether in literary history or intellectual history, tends to reproduce gender- and class-based hierarchies. Emotions, after all, are historical not only in relation to the social practices that sustain family, community, and society, define groups in religious, ethnic, and national terms, and legitimate class divisions and gendered hierarchies. Since the eighteenth century, theories of the sentiments, passions, feelings, and affects have been enlisted to distinguish mind from body, and body from soul, and to establish the boundaries between public and private, personal and political, and individual and collective emotions that are so crucial to the culture of class societies and the study of social movements.

Not surprisingly, the emotional turn has inspired new ways of writing history in dialogue with social anthropology and cognitive psychology and with special emphasis on periods of historical crisis and change. To mention a few important figures, Barbara Rosenwein has introduced the notion of emotional communities – that is, the particular emotional norms, values, and forms of expression shared by distinct social groups – to map the transition from the medieval to the modern period. In his work on the French Revolution, William Reddy has used the term emotional regimes, which refers to the dominant norms of emotional life, to examine their connection to political regimes and assess their availability to various forms of resistance, including (in his case) sentimentalism. Finally, Peter N. and Carol Z. Stearns have identified a distinctly American

---

18 See Gareth Stedman Jones, *Languages of Class: Studies in English Working-Class History, 1832–1982* (Cambridge: Cambridge University Press, 1984).
19 The term is taken from Fredric Jameson, *The Political Unconscious: Narrative as a Socially Symbolic Act* (Ithaca, NY: Cornell University Press, 1981).

genealogy of anger in the struggle for political control and measured the growing significance of public emotions in modern mass societies.[20] More detailed studies on the nineteenth and early twentieth century have used the critical lens of emotions to explain the sudden appearance of moral panics, ethnic resentments, and mass delusions. Literary studies on the culture of public sentiment, the phenomenon of nervousness, and the aesthetics of shock have extended these lines of inquiry to modern and modernist sensibilities.

The study of the history of emotions and of emotions in history has proven particularly useful in arguing for the decisive role of sentiments in the making of new collectivities – in totalitarian regimes as well as liberal democracies. From Adam Smith, whose theory of moral sentiments establishes sympathy as the basis of all community, to Jean Jacques Rousseau, whose reflection on inequality introduces compassion as a quintessential democratic sentiment, to Karl Marx, whose theory of class struggle calls for solidarity as the first step toward a future classless society, clear connections between public and private emotions and the cultures of democracy and capitalism can be identified. Recent book titles such as *Passionate Politics*, *Emotions in Politics*, *Moving Politics*, and *Feeling Politics* attest to the sense of possibility as well as anxiety with which the convergence of politics and emotion has been examined for its positive and negative effects on modern democracy, civil society, and public life. By the same token, evocative terms such as emotional labor, emotional capital, and emotional investment have been introduced to describe the emotional economies of capitalism in the postindustrial age, especially in low-wage service jobs.[21] Critical theorists, social philosophers as well as sociologists and political scientists have noted the

---

20 For references in chronological order, see Peter N. and Carol Z. Stearns, *Anger: The Struggle for Emotional Control in America's History* (Chicago: University of Chicago Press, 1986); William M. Reddy, *The Navigation of Feeling: A Framework for the History of Emotions* (Cambridge: Cambridge University Press, 2001); and Barbara H. Rosenwein, *Emotional Communities in the Early Middle Ages* (Ithaca, NY: Cornell University Press, 2007) and *Generations of Feeling: A History of Emotions, 600–1700* (Cambridge: Cambridge University Press, 2015).
21 The bibliographical references (in chronological order) are to Jeff Goodwin, James M. Jasper, and Francesca Polletta, eds., *Passionate Politics: Emotions and Social Movements* (Chicago: University of Chicago Press, 2001); Nicolas Demertzis, ed., *Emotions in Politics: The Affect Dimension in Political Tension* (New York: Palgrave Macmillan, 2013); and Michael Ure and Mervyn Frost, eds., *The Politics of Compassion* (London: Routledge, 2014). The two terms mentioned are taken from Arlie Russell Hochschild in *The Outsourced Self: Intimate Life in Market Times* (New York: Metropolitan, 2012) and *Strangers in their Own Land: Anger and Mourning on the American Right* (New York: The New Press, 2016). In the German context, terms such as the neologism *Wutbürger* (enraged citizen) and Bernhard Pörksen's concept of *Empörungsdemokratie* (democracy of indignation) point to similar developments and debates.

profound changes brought about by digital technologies and information architectures and the highly mediated spectacles of public emotion in advanced capitalist societies. In sociology, to give one example, these developments have revealed the shortcomings of traditional studies on social movements that rely on the rational choice paradigm to explain political convictions and affiliations and inspired more popular scientific inquiries about contemporary phenomena such as the making of emotional capitalism.[22]

The growing awareness of the role of emotions in politics has partly to do with the explanatory vacuum left by the disappearance of political ideologies in the postcommunist world and, closely related, the failure of educated elites in North America, Europe, and elsewhere to imagine valid alternatives to global capitalism and the neoliberal world order. There are many reasons to insist on the importance of emotional faculties to modern democracies, as shown by George E. Marcus's concept of the sentimental citizen, Andrew Burstein's notion of sentimental democracy, and Martha Nussbaum's argument for the power of love in the fight for justice.[23] These scholars all share a strong desire to move beyond the earlier juxtaposition of reason and emotion and to counter the assumption that emotion in politics is inevitably a destructive force. Compelling arguments have been made for studying the politics of fear and compassion and recognizing the unifying effect of passions and enthusiasms. However, there is no evidence to conclude that empathy is always beneficial for social cohesion and that emotion, or affect, to use the term preferred by affect theorists, is somehow "always already sutured into a progressive or liberatory politics."[24]

As the history of modern mass movements has shown, nothing could be further from the truth. The political emotions that were claimed as part of the proletarian dream can be described as anticipatory as well as restorative, generative as well as prescriptive, and aspirational as well as compensatory. However, they cannot be forced into the familiar binaries of progressive versus reactionary and subversive versus affirmative that have become an almost meaningless critical

---

[22] The reference is to Eva Illouz, *Cold Intimacies: The Making of Emotional Capitalism* (London: Polity, 2007).
[23] See Andrew Burstein, *Sentimental Democracy: The Evolution of America's Self Image* (New York: Hill & Wang, 1999); George E. Marcus, *The Sentimental Citizen: Emotion in Democratic Politics* (University Park, PA: Pennsylvania State University Press, 2002); and Martha Nussbaum, *Political Emotions: Why Love Matters for Justice* (Cambridge, MA: The Belknap Press of Harvard University Press, 2015).
[24] Gregory J. Seigworth and Melissa Gregg, "An Inventory of Shimmers," in *The Affect Theory Reader*, ed. Melissa Gregg and Gregory J. Seigworth (Durham, NC: Duke University Press, 2010), 10. In fact, Paul Bloom makes a polemical argument against empathy in *Against Empathy: The Case for Rational Compassion* (New York: Ecco, 2016).

cliché of cultural studies and identity politics. Even more important, recent diagnoses of the decline of civil society have coincided with rising concerns over the divisive impact of emotions in the context of new mass mobilizations. With the resurgence of nativism, populism, and xenophobia, critics now warn, fear and anger have not simply taken over public debate but actually taken the place of political arguments. Confirming this point, formulaic expressions of empathy (with victims), hollow phrases about tolerance (of others), and public performances of what Germans call *Betroffenheit* (i.e., of being moved, concerned, and involved) have further ritualized the culture of political emotions and profoundly altered the traditional public sphere as a place of reasoned and rational debate.

IV

"A specter is haunting Europe – the specter of socialism." Thus begins the most influential German-language text of the nineteenth century, *The Communist Manifesto*. In a variation of the theme of haunting, the point of departure for this book can be identified by a similar sentence: A specter has been haunting socialism – the specter of the proletariat. For about one hundred and fifty years, the proletarian dream embodied the hopes, needs, and desires of the revolutionary working class, but it also troubled the project of socialism through its compensatory and disciplining effects. In *Proletarian Nights*, Jacques Rancière recalls sitting in the Bibliothèque nationale in Paris during the 1970s and searching for authentic voices from the French proletariat:

> I set out looking for wild expressions of revolt, but I came across politely written texts requesting that workers be treated as equals. [...] I went to consult the archives of a carpenter to find information about working conditions, and I came across letters from the 1830s in which this worker told a friend about a Sunday in May when he set out with two companions to enjoy the sunrise on the river. [...] It became apparent that workers had never needed the secrets of domination explained to them, as their problem was quite a different one. It was to withdraw themselves, intellectually and materially, from the forms by which this domination imprinted on their bodies, and imposed on their actions, modes of perception, attitudes, and a language.[25]

---

25 Jacques Rancière, *Proletarian Nights: The Workers' Dream in Nineteenth-Century France*, trans. John Drury (London: Verso, 2012), ix. First published in French in 1981 and previously published in English as *The Nights of Labor* (1991). On the return of the proletariat as a political and theoretical concept, also see Jacques Rancière, Preface, *Staging the People: The Proletarian and His Double*, trans. David Fernbach (London: Verso, 2011), 7–19.

Rancière's polemical intervention was directed against the dreams of class struggle that prompted leftist intellectuals during the 1960s to "rediscover" the proletariat – guided by the assumption that the workers' lives were, and still are, reducible to the problem of wage labor and the promise of revolution. His conclusion that "What he [i.e., the worker] lacks and needs is a knowledge of self that reveals to him a being dedicated to something else besides exploitation"[26] redirects attention to the legacies of humanism as an emancipatory project and recognizes the importance of bourgeois notions of subjectivity for the workers' movement. However, the historical and theoretical relevance of what Rancière calls the workers' dream cannot be reduced to the recognition, across the class divide, of a shared humanity asserted against the regimes of wage labor and expressed in amateur poems about love, nature, and beauty. Covering a much later and much longer time period, *The Proletarian Dream* presents a closely related but ultimately very different story: that German workers also did not write many plays about the factory and the tenement; that the conditions of labor and labor struggles played a surprisingly small part even in their autobiographical writing; but that poems about nature and love coexisted with poems about revolution and class struggle; and that their novels treated the male camaraderie of radicalized workers as more important than marriage and family life. Rancière is right that only recognition of the radical otherness of the proletarian dream – that is, its incommensurability with working-class reality and Marxist theory – can produce a deeper understanding of the nineteenth-century culture of class and socialism. However, for the German case, that radical otherness includes the belief in social utopias and the yearning for collective imaginaries that not only go a long way explaining the emotional culture of the workers' movement but also shed new light on the functioning of cultural practices as emotional practices in social movements more generally.

Recognition of the seemingly unbridgeable divide that separates the contemporary conjuncture from the proletarian dream must include the acknowledgment of exclusion, discrimination, and persecution as an integral part of working-class culture and the difficult conditions of its emergence. Covering about seventy years of German history, *The Proletarian Dream* develops this argument through the contributions of a large group of radicalized workers and socialist activists both famous and unknown. Although the focus will be on collective imaginaries, it cannot remain unmentioned that the proletarian dream was invented, revised, disseminated, promoted, and defended with considerable costs to individual lives. Across generations, most of these activists mentioned

---

26 Rancière, *Proletarian Nights*, 20.

made great personal sacrifices because of their political commitments; these included experiences of censorship and vilification, exile and inner emigration, incarceration and persecution, and sometimes even death in prisons, gulags, and concentration camps. In other words, the fate of the texts and contexts created under such conditions is inseparable from the history of authoritarianism, antisemitism, racism, anticommunism, and totalitarianism. Several of the nineteenth-century radicals fled the German states for neighboring countries in the aftermath of the 1848 Revolutions; others immigrated to the United States because of the Anti-Socialist Laws. After 1933, almost all SPD and KPD politicians and politically committed writers and artists went into exile to the United States or the Soviet Union. Many Communists returned to the GDR to less than welcoming conditions; a few became anticommunists in US-American exile. As their published autobiographies, memoirs, diaries, and correspondences acknowledge, a life committed to the proletarian dream often meant a life under conditions of precarity – including for members of the workers' intelligentsia and for the vaunted organic intellectuals in Gramsci's sense.

Despite deliberate efforts at silencing and more pervasive modes of forgetting, the proletarian dream – written in the German language, but always reaching beyond German borders – has been preserved in books, libraries, collections, and archives. Printed on cheap paper, published in small editions, and distributed by underfunded publishers, the numerous books, magazines, and newspapers circulating within the socialist and communist lifeworlds have survived as a tribute and a testament to the remarkable productivity of the proletarian imaginary. There is no doubt that the ban of socialist authors during the period of the Anti-Socialist Laws, the Nazi book burnings of 1933, the conflagration of German cities in 1944/45, and the German-German contest over working-class culture during the Cold War have contributed to the ongoing marginalization of working-class perspectives in public memory, national history, and academic research. For the cultural historian today, this long history of suppression and indifference can be a belated blessing. Precisely because the proletarian archives have been forgotten and ignored, a surprising number of books have survived, some of them unopened and unread for almost one hundred and fifty years. In the United States, the centrifugal forces of exile and migration, but also the internationalism of the workers' movement, have left traces in the provenance of rare titles and their location in research libraries far away from their places of publication. Hidden away in storage facilities, more and more works are now being made available through digital repositories; the project of the digital humanities has given them a second life. Already a cursory look at *ex libris*, marginalia, and other ephemera indicates in what ways the books' difficult journeys from Europe to North America function as an integral part of the proletarian dream and its forms of cultural contact and symbolic communication. The names of first readers on the flyleaves and their extensive notes on the margins give a first indication of the powerful identifications formed in the act of writing and reading, of publishing and collecting and continued in the waves of scholarship on working-class culture and the culture of socialism and communism since the 1970s.[27]

Two very contemporary developments have provided the original impetus for the larger project, the renewed urgency surrounding questions of social and economic inequality and related questions about the nature of new populist movements and the future of liberal democracies. The growing historical distance, marked by the prefix "post," from the formative period of modern capitalism and class society that gave rise to the workers' movement has made a critical reassessment of German working-class culture both possible and necessary. As this introduction has argued, it is precisely through the profound otherness un-

---

[27] To give a few examples, the socialist pulp novels housed in public libraries in Texas and the Midwest follow the waves of post-1848 immigration of German socialists but also lay the ground for the contribution of German working-class communities in New York, Chicago, and elsewhere to the struggles of American organized labor. Meanwhile the uncut pages in a socialist utopian novel from the 1880s and the Vienna tram ticket used as a bookmark in a 1920s treatise on socialist education point to more troubling histories of reading and non-reading. A book from the library of the Touristenverein Naturfreunde in Philadelphia appears like a missive from an almost forgotten American labor movement that provided a new home for recent European immigrants. By contrast, the survival of a book from the Israelitische Kultusgemeinde in Vienna or the City Library in Schwerin in an American university research library draws attention to the routes of flight that made possible the survival of ideas far removed from their original sites of articulation and circulation. Similarly, the library stamp from a small college library in the Midwest pasted over that of the Jewish community in Breslau, the *ex libris* from the personal archives of exiled sociologist Paul Honigsheim now housed at Michigan State University, and the imprint of the Central Committee of the Communist Party of Czechoslovakia next to the barcode of the research library of Brigham Young University bear witness to the brutal suppression of SPD, KPD, and labor unions after the Nazi ascent to power. On the other side of the Atlantic, the personal archives of leading Weimar-era leftist activists and scholars held in the International Institute of Social History (IISH) in Amsterdam attest to the endurance of internationalist commitments even under the difficult conditions of exile after 1933. The former German Library in Leipzig (now part of the German National Library) still has extensive holdings that reflect the city's historical role as a center of the workers' culture movement and its postwar enlistment in the reclamation of the socialist heritage through the public rituals of legitimacy in the German Democratic Republic (GDR). Impressive collections can be found in large research libraries such as the Berlin State Library and more specialized archives such as the Fritz Hüser Institute in Dortmund; both highlight the regional character of the workers' movement, concentrated in the German capital and the Ruhr region, and attest to the significance of Social Democracy to the self-understanding of the Federal Republic of Germany (FRG).

covered by this distance that the proletarian dream can shed light on the contemporary politics of emotion – in what prematurely has been called the posthistorical, postideological, and postdemocratic age. The end of master narratives and the disappearance of universals have created an opening for a resurgence of political emotions in the context of right wing, nationalist, and populist movements in Europe and the United States. Meanwhile, new forms of publicity and public life made possible through social media and the internet have blurred the boundaries between politics and entertainment and further expanded the role of culture – in this case, media culture – in defining social imaginaries and organizing political emotions. Written under the influence of such developments, a book on the proletarian dream offers a much-needed historical perspective on the long history of emotions in social movements and the close connection between emotional practices and cultural practices.

Part One: **Imperial Germany**

Chapter 1
The Threat of the Proletariat and the Discourse of the Masses

> I call him a proletarian whose parents neglected him, did not bathe him, did not groom him, and neither raised him to be a good person nor encouraged him to attend church and school. He never masters his trade, marries without money and raises his brood in his image, ready to damage the property of other people and be a cancer sore on the community. Furthermore, I call proletarians the drunks and lechers who do not fit into the social order and keep Blue Monday more sacred than Sunday.
>
> Friedrich Harkort

In the midnineteenth century, the specter of the working class gave rise to new academic disciplines deeply concerned with crowd behavior and mass action. The emerging mass discourse in psychology and sociology relied heavily on emotional categories to describe the social and psychological processes of mass formation and, consciously or unconsciously, to define the relationship of the bourgeois elites to the modern masses – which invariably meant the working classes. Taking advantage of the resulting surfeit of projections and displacements, the first chapter consequently introduces the subject of this study not through a Marxist definition of the proletariat, but from the outside, that is, the nineteenth-century writings that introduced mass discourse in the social sciences and established the antagonistic terms that revealed its historical origins in class discourse.

In the quotation above, the railroad magnate and liberal politician Friedrich Harkort (1793–1880), a key figure in the early industrialization of the Ruhr region, defines proletarians first and foremost through their shared condition of lack: of resources, skills, morals, and so forth.[1] Where others might have responded with compassion and joined the fight for social justice, Harkort's palpable sense of disgust expresses his belief in the natural order of inequality, but it also reveals his fear of the wrath of the oppressed. About half a century later,

---

[1] Friedrich Harkort, quoted in Isolde Dietrich, "Überlegungen zur Rolle der Literatur in der Lebensweise großstädtischer Industriearbeiter in Deutschland um 1900," in *Literatur und proletarische Kultur. Beiträge zur Kulturgeschichte der deutschen Arbeiterklasse im 19. Jahrhundert*, ed. Dietrich Mühlberg and Rainer Rosenberg (Berlin: Akademie, 1983), 297–298. All translations are my own unless noted otherwise.

Julius Werner describes the same phenomenon with a strong sense of foreboding that implies acceptance of the inevitability of dramatic social and political changes. "It seems that the spiritual birthmark of inner resentment will not disappear from the forehead of the modern wage-earning class," the Lutheran pastor concedes, concluding that, "Even as the manifestations of their wild, eruptive hatred have changed, the original sting (*Stachel*) is bound to remain."[2]

Meaning "sting" or "prick," the ambiguity of the German word captures perfectly the tension between guilt (about having injured the other) and fear (of being injured by the other) that informs most middle-class conceptions of the working class during the late nineteenth and early twentieth century. It would be easy to dismiss all of mass discourse as elitist and conservative by quoting the nationalist historian Heinrich Treitschke who insisted that, "the masses must forever remain the masses. There would be no culture without kitchenmaids."[3] In fact, the writings of scholars who opposed the socialist movement offer privileged access to the personification of what has to remain unnamed, namely the destructive forces released by capitalist modernity. In other words, they bring forth the other – that is, the elusive, ubiquitous masses – against which the proletarian dream announces its emancipatory functions and prefigurative effects. Moreover, contempt for the new social underclass should not automatically be equated with antimodern, antiurban, and antidemocratic positions. As the second verse of the "Workers' Marseillaise" confirms, contempt for the masses was alive and well in the socialist movement: "The enemy that we hate the most,/ That surrounds us thick and black,/ It is the foolishness of the masses,/ That can only be broken with the sword of the spirit."[4]

Nineteenth-century mass discourse is inseparable from the rise of the working class and the socialist movement. Nowhere is this connection clearer than in the work of Gustave Le Bon, the influential French anthropologist and sociologist. While his *La psychologie des foules* (1895, in English as *The Crowd: A Study of the Popular Mind*) became a founding text of mass psychology, his follow-up book *Psychologie du socialisme* (1899, translated as *The Psychology of Socialism*) has been largely forgotten. Yet it is in the latter work that the general observations on crowd behavior find their clearest application in relation to the

---

[2] Julius Werner, *Das moderne Proletariat und die deutsche Nation* (Stuttgart: Chr. Belsersche Verlagsbuchhandlung, 1907), 13. The book was published in a series on "Zeitfragen des christlichen Volkslebens."
[3] Heinrich von Treitschke, *Politics*, trans. Blanche Dugdale and Torben de Bille, foreword A. Lawrence Lowell (New York: Macmillan, 1916), 42.
[4] Jacob Audorf, "Arbeitermarseillaise," in *Proletarier singe! Kampf- und Volkslieder*, ed. Carl Hoym (Hamburg: A. Willaschek, 1919), 104–105.

urgent social problems of his time. In fact, Le Bon's description of socialism as a mass movement contains *in nuce* the main elements of mass discourse and, as an introduction to the topic, deserves to be quoted in full:

> Socialism, whose dream is to substitute itself for the ancient faiths, proposes but a very low ideal, and to establish it appeals but to sentiments lower still. What, in effect, does it promise, more than merely our daily bread, and that at the price of hard labour? With what lever does it seek to raise the soul? With the sentiments of envy and hatred which it creates in the hearts of multitudes? To the crowd, no longer satisfied with political and civic equality, it proposes equality of condition, without dreaming that social inequalities are born of those natural inequalities that man has always been powerless to change.[5]

Outside the socialist movement, two distinct ways of thinking about the proletariat can be distinguished: mass psychological studies that treat the masses as a new social phenomenon beyond class distinctions and sociological studies that see the proletariat as a new social formation within the class structure. While the former draw on the language of emotions in describing and evaluating mass phenomena, the latter aspire to scientific objectivity in offering structural analyses of modern society. In their relationship to the subject matter, both lines of inquiry are sometimes difficult to distinguish, with the masses treated as the origins of the working class and the proletariat seen as the vanguard of socialism. But given the ubiquity of the specter of socialism as the hidden reference point, the methodological differences separating mass psychology and modern sociology become ultimately less relevant than their shared preoccupations, if not obsessions.

The earliest empirical studies on radicalized workers played a key role in establishing sociology and anthropology as new academic disciplines during the mid-nineteenth century; mass psychology, to be discussed in the chapter's second part, did the same for the more elusive connection between social sciences and cultural criticism. In the German context, the first scholarly excursions into what was often described as unknown territory took place during the 1860s, well before the publication of Le Bon's book, and continued as an integral part of larger German (and Austrian) discussions about empire, nation, capitalism, and modernity. As will be shown, Lorenz von Stein's study of social movements in France established a model for the social sciences that included comparative transnational perspectives and offered concrete recommendations for social re-

---

5 Gustave Le Bon, *The Psychology of Socialism* (Kitchener: Batoche, 2001), 8. A note on the translation of non-English book titles: when the books have been translated into English, the titles are given in italics; in all other cases, only the standard rules of capitalization are applied.

form. By contrast, Wilhelm Heinrich Riehl advanced a uniquely German view of society as community that, based on ethnography (*Volkskunde*) as the study of peoples and nations, incorporated the proletariat into older narratives of belonging. Both lines of argumentation continued in the sociological studies by Werner Sombart and Theodor Geiger that sought to account for such elusive mass phenomena as the urban crowd in the context of early twentieth-century understandings of capitalism and modernity.

Der Sozialismus und Communismus des heutigen Frankreich (1842, in English as *The History of the Social Movement in France, 1789–1850*) by Lorenz von Stein (1815–1890) is the first scholarly account of the dangerous forces unleashed by the French Revolution and the July Revolution that introduces the proletariat as the herald of a different social order. A professor of political science, von Stein was forced to leave Germany during the restoration period and taught at the University of Vienna for almost thirty years. His book proved very influential at the time, not least through its focus on the emotional appeal of the socialist movement; scholars remain unsure about his influence on Marx. In the book, von Stein starts out by defining the proletariat as "the entire class of those who can claim neither education nor property as the basis of their standing in society and who nonetheless feel called upon not to remain without all the properties that constitute the worth of the individual in the first place."[6] Like Marx and Engels, he insists that workers and proletarians should not be used as synonymous, as only the latter possess critical awareness of their situation. He also shares their diagnosis of the withholding of recognition as a major source of working-class discontent.

Notwithstanding occasional references to the triumph of capital over labor in the age of industrialization that recall socialist treatises, von Stein's basic approach to the proletariat remains grounded in a combination of empirical observation and sociopsychological analysis and derives its critical thrust from his urgent demand for social reform. Significantly, he identifies fluidity and ubiquity as the most unsettling qualities of this new social class or formation, qualities that for him reveal the limits of economic determinism and point to the importance of emotional factors in social(ist) identifications. There was widespread disappointment after the French Revolution that the First Republic's commitment to equality had remained an abstract idea and that the realities of inequal-

---

[6] Lorenz von Stein, *Proletariat und Gesellschaft*, ed. and intr. Manfred Hahn (Munich: Wilhelm Fink, 1971), 11; the reprint is based on the second edition of *Der Sozialismus und Kommunismus des heutigen Frankreichs*. An abbreviated English translation of the three-volume work appeared as *The History of the Social Movement in France, 1789–1850*, trans. and intr. Kaethe Mengelberg (Totowa, NJ: Bedminster, 1964).

ity had been preserved in the country's social, economic, and legal structures. Under these circumstances, the workers' deep sense of betrayal, combined with growing awareness of their numerical strength, had created a revolutionary situation. This is how von Stein describes the process:

> The class of the propertyless has unified; they have gained awareness of their situation; they recognize that it is based on laws that exist outside the individual; they feel controlled through a power that they have fought in vain; they are excluded from participation in state government; they confront the impossibility for the majority of their members to ascend to a higher class. In response, they have become an estate (*Stand*), and this estate, literally the embodiment of all the demands originating in the principle of equality without satisfying them, is the *French proletariat*.[7]

A number of propositions and assumptions give rise to what can be called a paradigmatic scene of proletarian identification. For von Stein, class mobilization begins with an experience of exclusion from representation in the political sense. The cognitive and emotional processes associated with verbs such as "recognize" and "feel" set into a motion a learning process that provides the disempowered with the appropriate skills to "fight" and "confront." Aware of the false promises made in the name of "equality," the propertyless eventually come to understand their condition of lack. Without access to the rewards of individualism, they choose to join the "unified" many that embody the abstract principles of emancipation but, as the particular and universal class, also possess the political tools to make those principles a historical reality.

While von Stein used the postrevolutionary situation in France to predict similar developments in neighboring European countries, other authors responded to the threat of revolution with specialized treatises that offered practical solutions in the name of economic progress and political stability. Thus, in a work with the lengthy title *Ueber das dermalige Missverhältniss der Vermögenslosen oder Proletairs zu den Vermögen besitzenden Klassen der Societät in Betreff ihres Auskommens, sowohl in materieller, als intellektueller Hinsicht, aus dem Standpunkt des Rechts betrachtet* (1835, About the Current Disparity between the Propertyless or Proletarians and the Propertied Classes ...), Franz von Baader (1761–1841), a mining engineer turned social reformer, proposed to solve the problem of proletarianization through greater legal reforms and public policies that increased social mobility. In *Unsere Gegenwart und Zukunft* (1846, Our Present and Future), the National Liberal politician Friedrich Karl Biedermann (1812–1891) located the origins of the proletariat in the phenomenon of pauperism and

---

7 von Stein, *Proletariat und Gesellschaft*, 203–204.

argued for extensive reforms as the best defense against what he termed theoretical and applied socialism. Along similar lines, the Prussian reformer Herrmann Graf zu Dohna (1802–1872), in *Die freien Arbeiter im preußischen Staat* (1847, The Free Workers in the Prussian State), called on the state to mitigate the suffering of the workers, whereas the Austrian jurist Johann von Perthaler (1816–1862), in *Ein Standpunkt zur Vermittlung socialer Mißstände im Fabriksbetriebe* (1843, A Proposal for the Mitigation of the Deplorable State of Affairs in the Factories) suggested improvements in the factory system.

Indicative of the permeable boundaries separating the social imaginary in political theory from its appearance in literary fiction, their arguments would soon be reproduced in countless nineteenth-century social novels and social dramas about the modern factory as the source of human misery and class strife. By the same token, the descriptions of the infamous masses in city novels and social dramas attest to the wide familiarity of literary writers and critics with the prevailing tropes of mass discourse in the scholarship. These easily reconstructible patterns of influence confirm the mutual dependency of scholarly and literary practices on the emotional regimes organized through the specter of the proletariat in mass discourse. Of course, the same can be concluded about von Stein's comments, and those of many other bourgeois scholars, on the sheer energy of the revolutionary working class and its resonances in artistic and literary representations of the Paris Commune.

The importance of von Stein's description of the proletariat as a new social formation becomes even clearer through a comparison to the backward-looking approach taken by his contemporary Wilhelm Heinrich Riehl (1823–1897), one of the founders of German ethnography. His belief in the *Volk* as a political, social, and cultural defense against modern society played a key role in the establishment of *Volkskunde* as an academic discipline and prepared the ground for the proliferation of *völkisch* thought throughout the early twentieth century. In his multivolume *Die Naturgeschichte des Volkes als Grundlage einer deutschen Social-Politik* (1851–1869, The National History of the People as the Basis of a German Social Policy), Riehl explains what he calls the essence of a people through the natural and cultural landscape and its manifestation in national character.[8] Not surprisingly, in *Die bürgerliche Gesellschaft* (1861, Bourgeois Society), the fourth estate is introduced through its opposition to this established order, namely as those "who have moved away, or been expelled, from society's existing systems of groups and estates, who consider it an outrage to talk about mas-

---

[8] See Wilhelm Heinrich Riehl, *Die Naturgeschichte des Volkes als Grundlage einer deutschen Social-Politik* (Stuttgart: Cotta, 1894).

ters, burghers, and peasants, who declare themselves to be the 'true' people, and who want to dissolve all naturally developed estates into the big primordial mush of the 'true' folk."[9]

Much of Riehl's writing is concerned with eliminating the category of *Arbeiter* from German public discourse and integrating it into older traditions of social thought and the body politic. Throughout the threat posed by the socialist movement remains a hidden reference point, from his conclusion that the proletariat, lacking property, fatherland, and community, "incessantly uses theoretical reflection to agonize about its position in society"[10] to his own preoccupation with creating stable critical categories to contain this dangerous threat. First, he rejects the term *Arbeiter* as a Germanized version of the *ouvrier* that, linguistically as well as politically, ends up importing French conditions to the German states. Then he distinguishes the ideal worker with his roots in the traditional guild system from the modern proletarian as a figure of abjection and destruction. Finally, he separates the manual laborer from the industrial worker, with the latter defined through his experiences of deracination. However, by equating socialists with workers and workers with proletarians, he ends up describing a rather disjointed group comprised of workers, loafers, journeymen, and beggars distinguished above all through their corrosive effect on traditional estate-based society. The main problems caused by their shared *Fessellosigkeit* (i.e., the lack of social and religious ties) are analyzed as moral rather than economic in nature. The curse of the working class subsequently comes from being uprooted and stranded between the simple peasantry and the educated middle class.[11] Riehl acknowledges the problems of the fourth estate but insists on the integration of the workers into the estate system as the best defense against the antagonisms unleashed by class struggle. His distinction between a rising class that aims to take the place of the people and a traditional folk that confirms the eternal laws of heredity recasts contemporary struggles in the biologistic terms of natural history. In what ways such ethnographic categories continued to dominate scholarly engagement with the proletariat can be seen in a much later study by Will-Erich Peuckert (1895–1969) titled *Volkskunde des Proletariats* (1931, Ethnography of the Proletariat) that starts out by asking: "Does the prole-

---

9 Wilhelm Heinrich Riehl, *Die bürgerliche Gesellschaft* (Stuttgart: Cotta, 1861), 347.
10 Riehl, *Die bürgerliche Gesellschaft*, 470. His greatest scorn is reserved for the *Geistesproletariat* (i.e., intellectuals) who incite social tensions and arouse class hatred in order "create" the German worker based on the historical model of the revolutionary French *ouvrier*.
11 Wilhelm Heinrich Riehl, "Die Arbeiter. Eine Volksrede aus dem Jahre 1848," reprinted in *Die Eigentumslosen. Der deutsche Pauperismus und die Emanzipationskrise in Darstellungen und Deutungen der zeitgenössischen Literatur* (Freiburg im Breisgau: Alber, 1965), 394–405.

tarian originate in peasant culture that has been the focus of ethnography or is he an entirely new type? Is his life completely changed on that day he first walks into a factory?"[12]

Von Stein, Riehl, and several others contributed to the scientific and pseudoscientific discourses that constituted the proletariat and its discursive double, the masses, as subjects of scholarly inquiry and objects of emotionally charged projections. This emerging mass discourse typically imagines the proletariat as a negating force, the absolute other of existing culture and society whose presumed formlessness at once threatens and confirms society's need for structure. In identifying the proletariat as a transformative force through which (in the famous formulation by Marx) "all that is solid melts into air," mass discourse brings into relief the destructive forces unleashed by modern capitalism. These intended effects and the underlying processes of displacement account for the conflation of revolutionary proletariat and socialist movement in the specter of the modern masses. The rhetorical figures developed as a result of mass discourse had a profound influence on political thought, academic scholarship, and cultural criticism; this is most evident in the frequent equation of the urban masses with criminality and pathology. At the same time, it is entirely possible that the impact of mass discourse on antisocialist laws and antilabor policies strengthened the spirit of opposition that made the SPD "the first true mass political party in modern history."[13]

The historiography on mass discourse has taken advantage of the theoretical perspectives opened up by poststructuralism and drawn close attention to the overdetermined function of the modern masses as a marker of difference. From their respective disciplinary backgrounds, Susanne Lüdemann, Michael Gamper, and Stefan Jonsson have shown how mass discourse functions above all as a mode of distinction and a strategy of exclusion that proceeds from the juxtaposition of individuals and masses and that, given its precarious nature, relentlessly works to fortify its discursive boundaries.[14] Defined by the historical

---

12 Will-Erich Peuckert, *Volkskunde des Proletariats: Aufgang der proletarischen Kultur* (Frankfurt am Main: Neuer Frankfurter Verlag, 1931), 4. For the continuities in ethnographic approaches to proletarian culture, see Wolfgang Jacobeit and Ute Mohrmann, eds., *Kultur und Lebensweise des Proletariats: Kulturhist. -volkskundl. Studien u. Materialien* (Berlin: Akademie, 1973).

13 Andrew Bonnell, *The People's Stage in Imperial Germany: Social Democracy and Culture 1890–1914* (London: Tauris Academic, 2005), 1.

14 The references are Susanne Lüdemann, *Metaphern der Gesellschaft. Studien zum soziologischen und politischen Imaginären* (Munich: Wilhelm Fink, 2004); Michael Gamper, *Masse lesen, Masse schreiben: Eine Diskurs- und Imaginationsgeschichte der Menschenmenge 1765–1930* (Munich: Wilhelm Fink, 2007); and Stefan Jonsson, *Crowds and Democracy: The Idea and Image of the Masses from Revolution to Fascism* (New York: Columbia University Press,

conditions of its emergence, mass discourse invariably constitutes the masses as the abject other of an ideal society alternately called estates system, class society, or folk community. This discursive function of otherness in mass discourse is reinscribed through an almost obsessive preoccupation with distinctions: between masses, groups, and crowds; between mass, people, folk, and class; between active and passive masses; between spontaneous, violent eruptions and more stable social formations; and between the masses as spectacle, event, and state of being. Needless to say, neither the masses nor the people exist as social facts. Lüdemann and Gamper insist that they are discursive constructions. But as Jonsson rightly argues, although the masses may not be a historical reality, they are also not just a historical construction; they are "an effect of representation."[15]

All historical contributions to mass discourse (and later scholarly assessments of these debates) can be traced back to Le Bon's *The Crowd* and, more specifically, his belief in a soul of the masses (*l'ame des foules*). In this influential work, Le Bon presents a psychologically based model of the masses that identifies suggestion and contagion as its constitutive principles. Le Bon's motivation is obvious: to prevent mass rule – that is, the socialist movement – through the affirmation of conservative values. The same can be said about his critical method: to reduce complex social phenomena to the alternatives of individualism versus collectivism. References to "the threatening invasion of socialism" and "an army of proletarians" make clear that the so-called popular classes emerging in "the era of crowds" must be regarded as a serious threat to the (bourgeois) individual as the embodiment of reason, liberty, and civilization.[16]

Le Bon's mass psychology emerged as part of a larger scholarly project that began with his affirmation of the primacy of national and ethnic identity in *Lois psychologiques de l'évolution des peuples* (1894, translated as *The Psychology of Peoples*) and culminated in his analysis of contemporary political problems in the above-mentioned *The Psychology of Socialism*. These books, in turn, must

---

2013). For a useful comparison of French mass psychology and German sociology of the masses, also see Susanne Lüdemann, "'Zusammenhanglose Bevölkerungshaufen, aller inneren Gliederung bar.' Die Masse als das Andere der Ordnung im Diskurs der Soziologie," *Behemoth. A Journal on Civilization* 7.1 (2014): 103–117.
15 Jonsson, *Crowds and Democracy*, 27.
16 Gustave Le Bon, *The Crowd: A Study of the Popular Mind* (Kitchener: Batoche, 2001), 41. To what degree the ideological work performed by mass discourse and its suppressed historical referent, class, involved an affirmation of traditional notions of (bourgeois) subjectivity was first made clear by Sigmund Freud in his critical rereading of Le Bon in *Massenpsychologie und Ich-Analyse* (1921), translated into English as "Group Psychology and the Analysis of the Ego."

be read in dialogue with similar attempts across Europe to theorize the modern masses in the age of revolutions, from Gabriel Tarde's writings on crowd mentality and the power of suggestion to Scipio Sighele's work on collective psychology and the criminal mind. Much of what became the dominant conservative view on massification is based on Le Bon: the presentation of modernization and urbanization as a history of loss (i.e., of community and tradition), the explanation of mass phenomena in terms of contagion and suggestion, the characterization of the mass soul through its irrational, unconscious tendencies, and the portrayal of the masses in highly gendered terms, that is, as impulsive, instinctual, and irrational – in short, as feminine and feminizing. Rather surprisingly, *The Crowd* includes a lesser-known line of argument that complicates this almost clichéd view of massification as a denunciation of socialism. Repeatedly, Le Bon concedes that the crowd can also be heroic and selfless. Not always reducible to base instincts, it is sometimes guided by lofty ideas. In *The Psychology of Socialism*, he describes that the appeal of socialism was strongest not among Parisian workmen, artisans, and small proprietors but among intellectuals, bohemians, and discontents of all kinds – adding a further complication to the standard explanations of class politics. Today it might be tempting to draw a clear line between (the history of) mass psychology and modern sociology and their different perspectives on class society and mass society, but when it comes to emotions, the conceptual differences between mass and class sometimes disappear and draw attention to shared defensive strategies. To give one example, a version of Le Bon's soul of the masses, namely in the form of the proletarian soul, reappears in the writings of Werner Sombart (1863–1941) and other social and cultural conservatives. For Sombart, whose later studies on modern capitalism established him as one of the leading sociologists of his time, the proletariat was not only a direct result of the forces of modern industrialization and capitalist development; it also embodied all of its social and cultural problems. In *Das Proletariat* (1906, The Proletariat), a slim volume written for a series on contemporary life edited by Martin Buber, Sombart starts with a familiar definition: "Proletariat is what we call the social class in our modern society that is composed of penniless wage workers, who [...] are obliged to temporarily hand over their labor power to a capitalist entrepreneur for a wage."[17] However, this initial focus on economic relations of exchange (i.e., "temporarily hand over") remains at odds with his cultural conservative quest for the essence of the proletariat, especially those

---

[17] Werner Sombart, *Das Proletariat. Bilder und Studien* (Frankfurt am Main: Rütten & Loening, 1906), 3. A reprint with commentary by Friedhelm Hengsbach SJ was published in 2008 by Metropolis.

he calls full-blooded proletarians (*Vollblutproletarier*). References to their separation from nature, home, family, and fatherland rehearse standard conservative arguments against modernity. The same holds true of his diagnosis of the loss of community found in villages and small towns that ends with the triumph of the big city as the home of the modern masses. Sombart's somber view of massification finds expression in his repeated use of the prefix "Ver-" as he denounces the *Verrohung* (brutalization) of public morals, the *Verödung und Verkümmerung* (devastation and impoverishment) of the soul, and the *Vernichtung* (destruction) of all existing social structures, forms, and conventions. Crudeness of feelings and baseness of drives are the inevitable consequences. Under these conditions, the proletarian soul finds emotional release only in politics, especially (though not exclusively) in socialism.

Sombart further elaborates on the close connection between the workers' rootlessness and their political radicalism in *Sozialismus und soziale Bewegung* (1905, Socialism and Social Movement), a comprehensive overview of the international socialist movement, its national organizations and political factions. Like many of his predecessors, he recognizes the social problems that gave rise to the socialist movement and proposes a return to the shared values rooted in the narratives of nation. Aware of the attractiveness of the socialist ethos of unity and solidarity, he describes its transformation of true feelings of community (*Gemeinschaftsempfinden*) into a divisive and destructive class consciousness as follows:

> They [i.e., the members of this new class] find support only among comrades with the same fate who are also not treated as individuals but who no longer belong to any traditional community. He joins them, he becomes a comrade, and that is how a crowd of comrades is born that values one thing above all others: not the uniqueness of the individual but of the crowd, the belonging to the masses. [...] Translated into psychological terms, this results in a powerful strengthening of mass consciousness in each individual, and a promotion of mass-specific emotions that grow in the fight for mass-specific demands. In the end, belonging to his class for the proletarian means the same as belonging to a noble family, clan, city, and state once meant for others; with pride the proletarian identifies with his class: *proletarius sum*."[18]

Sombart's writings must be read within the larger debates that made sociology the academic discipline best suited for addressing the culture and politics of class in the early twentieth century. There was wide agreement already then on the profound influence of Max Weber's conceptual distinction between es-

---

[18] Werner Sombart, *Sozialismus und soziale Bewegung* (Jena: Gustav Fischer, 1908), 11–12. Republished in 1924 as the two-volume *Der proletarische Sozialismus* by Gustav Fischer in Jena.

tate, class, and stratum as different historical manifestations of a longer process thereafter known as social differentiation.[19] Most scholars welcomed the opening of the emerging field toward sociopsychological perspectives, and some even experimented with literary formats (e.g., in the workers' life writings discussed in chapter 7) to gain insights into the so-called mass soul and better understand the actual problems of real workers. Intellectual historians disagree to what extent the historical preoccupation with the masses was nothing more than a displaced reaction to the threat of class struggle and in what ways mass discourse also represented a productive response to profound changes in modern industrial societies. Helmuth Berking has argued that the tension between the abstract quality of mass discourse and the concrete demands by new social groups and movements attests above all to the fear of cultural elites about their loss of influence in a culture where massification invariably meant democratization.[20] The disappearance around 1930 of mass discourse as a subject of scholarly inquiry confirms its dependence on the initial provocations of class society and Marxist critique – but it also marks the beginning of very different configurations of socialism, populism, and nationalism that continue to hallucinate the masses as their abject others.

To summarize the various positions presented thus far, the modern masses cast a powerful spell over the social imaginary of the nineteenth and early twentieth century and retained their heightened status as a subject of scholarly inquiry until the end of the Weimar Republic. Once safely contained within the registers of mass discourse, the masses became a convenient way of talking about the working class without mentioning its name. But mass discourse never acquired the status of a stable set of scholarly methods and practices. On the one hand, the theoretical armature of mass psychology remained haunted by the threat of revolution embodied by the proletariat since that utopian moment known as the Paris Commune. On the other, modern sociology expanded the economically based definitions of class to make sense of the unique nature of mass mobilizations with the help of psychological categories. This emerging typology and icon-

---

19 See Max Weber, *Essays in Sociology*, trans. and ed. Hans H. Gerth and C. Wright Mills (New York: Oxford University Press, 1946), especially Section II on power. For an introduction, see Wolfgang Mommsen, *The Political and Social Theory of Max Weber: Collected Essays* (Chicago: University of Chicago Press, 1989). On the change in social categories, see Jürgen Kocka, "Stand–Klasse–Organisation. Strukturen sozialer Ungleichheit in Deutschland vom späten 18. bis zum frühen 20. Jahrhundert im Aufriß," in *Klassen in der europäischen Sozialgeschichte*, ed. Hans-Ulrich Wehler (Göttingen: Vandenhoeck & Ruprecht, 1979), 137–165.
20 Helmuth Berking, *Masse und Geist. Studien zur Soziologie in der Weimarer Republik* (Berlin: Wissenschaftlicher Autorenverlag, 1984), 67.

ography of the modern masses continued to reproduce the conceptual slippage between "mass" and "class" even in the more methodical studies written after the war. Later readers of mass psychology from Sigmund Freud to Theodor Geiger repeatedly used Le Bon to make sense of the ruptures caused by World War I and the German Revolution of 1918/19. Many used a decidedly prewar sense of fear and awe of mass society in order to work through their own ambivalences about social and political change. Yet when conceptualized as part of the configurations of mass culture and modernity, mass discourse also facilitated new ways of thinking about the disappearance of cultural hierarchies and the process of democratization spearheaded by the culture industry. Siegfried Kracauer's notion of the mass ornament represents but one model for a reading of surface phenomena that acknowledges as legitimate the demands of the modern masses for representation in the artistic and political sense.

From a Marxist perspective, it would be easy to deconstruct nineteenth- and early twentieth-century descriptions of the singular mass (*die Masse*) and the plural masses (*die Massen*) by referring to the antithesis of spirit and mass in idealist philosophy. Marx identified the problem early on when he called this antithesis "nothing but the *speculative* expression of the *Christian-Germanic* dogma of the antithesis between *Spirit* and *Matter*, between God and the world. This antithesis finds expression in history, in the human world itself in such a way that a few chosen *individuals* as the *active Spirit* are counterposed to the rest of mankind, as the *spiritless Mass*, as *Matter*."[21] The semiotic slippage between inanimate mass in the material sense and animated mass in the sense of multitudes functions as an important generative principle in standard mass discourse, with the marked preference among conservative thinkers for the singular mass (with its connotations of uniformity and conformity) the clearest example of language functioning as ideology. As evidence of the term's persuasive powers throughout the Weimar years, this juxtaposition of "mass" and "spirit" continues in the tropes of massification used by Oswald Spengler, Paul Tillich, and Karl Jaspers when diagnosing the tragedy of culture and lamenting the decline of the west. Likewise, the conservative reaction against the so-called revolt of the masses, to cite the influential 1929 book by José Ortega y Gasset, confirms to what degree mass discourse channels the cultural elites' fears of losing influence. Behind the categories of taste and distinction that equate the mass with mediocrity, there always lurks a deep distrust or hatred of democracy. The fact that left-wing writers sometimes employ the same tropes to discursively separate organized workers

---

21 Marx and Engels, "The Holy Family," *Marx/Engels Collected Works*, trans. Richard Dixon et al. (London: Lawrence and Wishart, 1975–2004), 4: 85. Henceforth abbreviated as *MECW*.

from unorganized masses does not invalidate the hidden affinity of mass discourse with antidemocratic positions. For similar reasons, the depiction of the mass as lacking (e.g., in character, intelligence, and influence) cannot be evaluated apart from a countervailing imaginary that (usually with equally negative connotations) presents the masses as expansive, excessive, and explosive, propelled forward by too much spirit, attitude, and, ultimately, revolutionary will.

During the Weimar Republic, sociologists continued to analyze the changing structures of class society and did so increasingly in direct response to the rise of white-collar workers. After the historical rupture of war and revolution, mass discourse thus briefly gained new relevance through its ability to combine morphological and empirical approaches to social stratification – a development closely identified with the names of Leopold von Wiese and Alfred Vierkandt. However, even the most exacting scientific methodologies could not prevent these scholars from reproducing the polemical equation of workers and masses with dangerous irrationality and turning to emotional registers to diagnose their destructive effect on the body politic. In a lengthy treatise on "Das gewerbliche Proletariat" (1926, usually translated as *The Proletariat: A Challenge to Western Civilization*), Catholic social philosopher Goetz Briefs (1889–1974) presented massification as an emotional and spiritual problem, including through its detrimental impact on public morality. And in *Die Masse. Ein Beitrag zur Lehre von den sozialen Gebilden* (1930, The Mass: A Contribution to the Study of Social Formations), sociologist Wilhelm Vleugels (1893–1942) proposed new approaches to the study of mass movements by focusing on what he described as their elusive powers as a *Gefühlsgemeinschaft* (emotional community).

The most ambitious study on new social formations as emotional communities, *Die Masse und ihre Aktion* (1926, The Mass and its Action) was contributed by Theodor Geiger (1891–1952), a scholar sympathetic to Social Democratic positions but highly critical of Marxism. For Geiger, *die Masse* – like many contemporaries, he preferred the singular – represented an entirely new formation without the structures and traditions found in comparable social forms – a social gestalt in its own right. Two propositions buttressed his argument: that the mass is brought forth by revolutionary situations – specifically the Revolution of 1918/19 – and that the mass has a largely destabilizing effect. His initial description of "an unstructured complex of uncountable or at least uncounted uniform parts"[22] speaks to widespread fears about the undifferentiated and fluid na-

---

[22] Theodor Geiger, *Die Masse und ihre Aktion. Ein Beitrag zur Soziologie der Revolution* (Stuttgart: Ferdinand Enke, 1926), 1. The implications of these developments are exampled further in *Die soziale Schichtung des deutschen Volkes* (1932).

ture of this mysterious mass. His later references to formless multitudes more specifically present the mass as a phenomenon of disintegration and decline. To what degree the masses always serve as a stand-in for the proletariat is confirmed by definitions of the proletariat as both the *"human material of the social entity of the mass"* and "the multitude unified, the quantity transformed into a subject."[23] Later distinctions introduced by Geiger between the proletariat as such (i.e., as an oppressed, excluded class), the organized working class (i.e., in the form of unions and parties), and the insurrectionist, terroristic, proletarian masses (i.e., the communists) do not substantially change the overwhelming association of the masses with the destructive (rather than constructive) forces of social change.

The function of the modern masses as a stand-in for the revolutionary working class resonates even in Geiger's description of mass phenomena that involve different social classes. He pays close attention to various kinds of multitudes, from the spatial accumulation of large numbers of people as audiences, crowds, swarms, and mobs to their long-term organization in voluntary associations and political parties. And he is acutely aware of the close bonds forged through what he calls I-you and we-you relationships. At the same time, his conceptualization of the masses remains haunted by a politics of public anger and resentment always threatening to explode in violence. His preoccupation with classifying masses based on composition, duration, and behavior only highlights his unwillingness to address the underlying structural causes and effects. In trying to reconcile these two sides in his argument, Geiger repeatedly refers to the centrality of emotions in the making of proletarian identifications. Like von Stein and Sombart, he describes formative experiences that fuel the desire of the masses to put an end to their suffering. This transformative potential not only establishes resistance and opposition as the organizing principles of mass formation, but also indirectly confirms destruction as the only legitimate position of negation through which the proletarian masses, placing themselves outside existing social forms, can imagine a new kind of community for themselves.

To conclude, the masses in the nineteenth century emerged as a central preoccupation of the social sciences in response to the rise of modern democracies and nation-states. From Le Bon's sociological reflections on the soul of the masses to Freud's psychoanalytic theories of group identification to Peuckert's ethnographic studies on the emotional life of the proletariat, we can identify a number of recurring themes: the characterization of the masses as dangerous and irrational, their description as feminine and feminizing, and their denunciation as

---

23 Geiger, *Die Masse und ihre Aktion*, 40 and 41.

the absolute other of bourgeois society and folk community. Later chapters will show in what ways mass discourse – that is, the fear of, and fascination with, the masses – continued in socialist visions of organic community and communist models of collective militancy. Socialist and communist writings on political strategy, too, remained beholden to the emotionally charged distinctions introduced by mass discourse and reproduced in the distinction between revolutionary and reformist groups. In fact, mass discourse – together with the competing discourses of folk and nation – can be described as one of the enduring patterns of explanation that connect the nineteenth to the twentieth century: at times in very explicit tones, at others in more hidden ways: but always present as a point of reference, and often a reference to that which cannot be named. As a result, just as the first scholarly studies on socialism attest to the long shadow cast by the *Vormärz* years, later contributions to the sociology and psychology of the masses never break free of the experience of war and revolution in 1918/19. Moreover, just as conservative mass discourse draws heavily on explicit and implicit assumptions about the politics of emotion, the proletarian dream establishes its own imaginaries through a similar dynamic of either celebrating or denouncing emotions in politics and of either cultivating or controlling their elusive powers. The various ways in which emotions came to occupy a central, if contested, position in Marxist definitions of the proletariat will be examined in the next chapter.

Chapter 2
Proletarian Dreams: From Marx to Marxism

> In direct contrast to German philosophy, which descends from heaven to earth, here we ascend from earth to heaven. That is to say, we do not set out from what men say, imagine, conceive, nor from men as narrated, thought of, imagined, conceived, in order to arrive at men in the flesh. [...] Life is not determined by consciousness, but consciousness by life.
>
> Karl Marx and Friedrich Engels, "The German Ideology"

In the introduction, the term "proletarian" has been defined as part of a strategy of political radicalization that gave the working class historical agency. It has also been likened to a number of identifications – mostly related to class, but also to community and humanity – grounded in the socialist and communist lifeworlds but not reducible to them. Most significant for this context, "proletarian" has been described as an imaginary construct brought to life through symbolic politics and sustained through emotional and aesthetic practices. In Marxist theory, the proletariat enters the world historical stage as an agent of historical necessity but not of inevitability. It remains inseparable from a history and theory of class struggles that translate the critique of class society into class consciousness and identify the social conditions conducive for revolution. The political demands made in the name of the proletariat eventually developed into an elaborate theory alternatively known as scientific socialism or historical materialism. Yet as this chapter argues, the concept of emotional community remained an integral part of the theorizing of the proletarian dream.

In the famous Marx quote above, German idealist philosophy functions as the influential model against which Marxism establishes its critical method and radical potential.[1] Unlike the bourgeois scholars presented in chapter 1, the socialist politicians, writers, and thinkers quoted on the pages that follow firmly believed that "life is not determined by consciousness, but consciousness by life." However, this does not mean that their "corresponding forms of consciousness" did not continuously exceed and confound these determinations. Similarly, although Marxist theory and socialist praxis provided clear instructions for "the ascent from earth to heaven," the proletarian dream, nonetheless, retained many of the qualities associated dismissively with this religious image of heaven. In recognition of these contradictions, the reconstruction of the larger discursive field demarcated by the proletarian dream in this chapter will focus

---

[1] Karl Marx and Friedrich Engels, "The German Ideology," *MECW* 5: 36–37.

exclusively on proletarians "as narrated, thought of, imagined, conceived" and establish in what ways the "proletariat" functioned as an imaginary construct from the beginning.

Few of the key terms identified with Marxist theory are as distinctive and divisive as the terms "proletarian" and "proletariat." An initial brief survey of their etymology helps to untangle the "proletarian" (whether as noun or adjective) from both the theoretical claims made in the history of Marxism and the political claims made in the history of German socialism, communism, and the workers' movement. To begin with, the structural tension between universalist claims to human emancipation and particular claims to social revolution must be considered central to any analysis of the proletariat as the focus of intense emotional attachments. This tension organizes the ways the proletariat acquires its discursive function in relation to the working class – namely as its logical conclusion and affective supplement. In the process, the more descriptive "working class" and the more agitational "proletariat" establish a clear division of labor as complementary terms in theories of capitalism and class society. They become crucial to the conceptualization of the relationship between class and party and the later debates between the proponents of revolution and reform. The unique status of the proletarian as an affective supplement already in Marxist thought can subsequently be used to make sense of the strong emotions projected onto the working class or, to use the terminology examined in the previous chapter, the modern masses, and to follow their reinsertion into the languages of class through the aesthetic forms and conventions available at the time.

To make one point clear: this is not a chapter about Marxist theories of class. The changing definitions of the proletariat from Karl Marx and Friedrich Engels to Georg Lukács and Karl Korsch are important to party programs and theoretical debates, and not to forget the larger history of Marxism, but they cannot explain the enduring power of proletarian identifications throughout the early twentieth century. Here the conceptual realignment implied through the focus on political emotions requires that Marxist theory be treated not as a superior form of knowledge but a coequal contribution to the kind of social imaginaries that are accessible only through images, narratives, symbols, and rituals. The fact that Marx's early writings were not even published before the 1930s or that many socialist leaders never read his works is immaterial to their significance as templates for collective narratives of class struggle. Therefore, calls by historians for more differentiated approaches to the culture of the working class or more detailed attention to the existing social cleavages and regional differences do not invalidate the heuristic value of the proletariat as an imagined emotional community. Even the lack of any consideration for the similarities with the rural underclass and the petty bourgeoisie, the gendered division of labor, the influence of organized religion, and the continuities with the guild system do not diminish the overdetermined emotional function of the proletariat in Marxist theory and related symbolic practices. Accordingly, the purpose of this chapter cannot be to establish the usefulness of "working class" or "proletariat" as critical categories in cultural history but to identify the points of contact where such categories presuppose and prefigure important emotional regimes.

Nineteenth-century sociologists and mass psychologists modeled the power of naming in establishing the threatening otherness of the proletariat – or, in their preferred terminology, the modern masses. As the previous chapter has argued, most definitions by conservative scholars aim to identify the most radicalized members of the working class with both a position of negation and a process of intensification. On the structural level, we find a surprisingly similar use of "proletarian" as a marker of difference in *The Communist Manifesto*'s rousing conclusion, "The proletarians have nothing to lose but their chains. They have a world to win. Working Men of All Countries, Unite!"[2] Originally written in German and first published in London in 1848 (and, in 1872, in Leipzig), the manifesto's famous summons "Proletarier aller Länder, vereinigt euch!" has been translated into English as both "Workers (or: working men) of the world (or: all countries), unite!," a first indication of the discursive slippages that would henceforth characterize the relationship between "workers" and "proletarians." The question remains unresolved whether Marx and Engels are referring to a distinct social class or a heterogeneous group of people. Their assertion "that the proletariat is recruited from all classes of the population"[3] at least opens up the possibility toward a broader appeal to practices of solidarity beyond classes in the orthodox Marxist sense.

Whether in mass psychological studies or foundational Marxist texts, "proletarian" since the mid-nineteenth century tends to demarcate a position of difference, of abjection; but it also refers to an act of exclusion and disruption. First recognized in Louis-Auguste Blanqui's description of the proletarian as remaining "on the outside,"[4] the underlying process of othering is typically set into motion through a shared sense of revulsion and contempt that serves to shore up bourgeois sensibilities. On the other side of the class divide, among the workers themselves, the same process finds expression in an equally strong sense of outrage and resentment that propels them to claim their alleged deficiencies as a mark of distinction. This transformation of an original term of exclusion into

---

[2] Karl Marx and Friedrich Engels, "Manifesto of the Communist Party," *MECW* 6: 519.
[3] Marx and Engels, "Manifesto of the Communist Party," *MECW* 6: 519.
[4] Louis-Auguste Blanqui, "The Trial of the Fifteen," 12 January 1832. https://www.marxists.org/reference/archive/blanqui/1832/defence-speech.htm, 1 March 2017.

one of exclusivity can be traced back to the names chosen by the first socialist groups during their years in exile. When the Bund der Geächteten (League of the Abject), a conspiratorial group founded in 1834 by German socialists in Paris, became the Bund der Gerechten (League of the Just), one of the London-based splinter groups founded by Wilhelm Weitling (1808–1871) in 1836, the original experience of disrespect was thus magically transformed into an attitude of moral superiority. In the 1848 *Manifesto of the Communist Party*, to use the original title, the role of the communists in uniting the perspectives of class and party is spelled out in clear terms, but the precarious status of the "proletarian" as a figure defined by deficiencies – that is, of being ignorant and irrational – leaves behind many conceptual ambiguities, including those related to mass discourse:

> The Communists, therefore, are on the one hand, practically, the most advanced and resolute section of the working-class parties of every country, that section which pushes forward all others; on the other hand, theoretically, they have over the great mass of the proletariat the advantage of clearly understanding the line of march, the conditions, and the ultimate general results of the proletarian movement.[5]

Etymology offers a useful way of accessing the emotional quality of proletarian identifications, for it clarifies the constitutive elements that can turn a category of abjection into one of empowerment. In Latin, *proletarii* (from *proles*, meaning offspring or progeny) refers to those citizens who, in the Roman census, were listed as being without property. In other words, they were classified through their condition of lack and exclusion. Their only wealth? Their labor and their offspring, the workers of the future. In nineteenth century discourses, this structural definition continues in descriptions of the workers as a new social group brought forth by two connected, but opposing forces, the industrial revolution and the socialist movement. Taking inspiration from the French *proletariat*, the revolutionary workers first appeared in the German language as *Proletarier* and *Proletariat* in the 1846 poem "Von unten auf!" ("Up from below!") by Friedrich Freiligrath (1810–1876). Henceforth two cognate nouns, similar to that of "bourgeois" and "bourgeoisie," can be distinguished, with the more descriptive "proletarian" usually referring to individual agents and the more abstract "proletariat" typically describing social processes. Within the time period covered by this book, "proletariat" seems the preferred term in studies that focus on the structures of domination in class society, whereas "proletarian" prevails in crit-

---

5 Marx and Engels, "Manifesto of the Communist Party," *MECW* 6: 497.

ical and fictional texts that focus on social practices and emphasize human agency.

A first indication of underlying conceptual tensions, "proletarian" and "proletariat" in Marxist discourse may be primarily identified with processes of empowerment, but both terms also appear frequently in relation to the phenomena of downward mobility known as proletarization. As diagnosed since the late nineteenth century, the experience of proletarization can refer to the artisan who becomes a factory worker and the rural laborer who is forced to join the urban underclass. Related to the older concept of pauperization and often described in the language of feminization, this neologism acknowledges the impoverishment of large parts of the population but does no longer come with the attendant demands for charity by the churches or protection through poverty laws that reduce the pauper to an almost natural state of destitution. The pervasive sense of disrespect, displacement, and disorientation associated with proletarization is even more pronounced in another term, namely *Plebs* (plebeian), which likewise denotes a condition of abjection. The ways in which the language of contempt reproduces existing social hierarchies and often translates them into moral and aesthetic registers is also evident in the less class-specific and more situation-based *Pöbel* (mob) that hallucinates all crowds, masses, and multitudes as uncontrolled, uneducated, and uncivilized – that is, as fundamentally different from proper middle-class culture and society. In 1903, Georg Hirth, publisher of the turn-of-the-century journal *Jugend*, captures the prevailing sentiment when he describes the typical prole as a churlish man, "an ordinary man, crude, not capable of any noble sentiments, a repulsive intruder into decent society whose background, attire, and money play no role at all."[6] However, when the same *Prolet* (prole) is appropriated as a figure of self-identification by the workers and used as a gesture of defiance in agitational speeches, songs, and poems, he overcomes his identification with a position of abjection and challenges the very hierarchies, including linguistic ones, that relegated him to a position on the outside of bourgeois society.

The discursive function of "proletarian" in nineteenth-century socialist writings can be further clarified through a brief comparison to the more general term *Arbeiter* (worker, laborer), which usually refers to skilled craftsmen as well unskilled workers, factory workers as well as farm laborers.[7] Historically, "worker"

---

6 Georg Wirth, "Prolet und Proletarier," *Jugend: Münchner Illustrierte Wochenschrift für Kunst und Leben* 8 (1903): 774. In current German slang, adjectives such as *prollig*, *prol*, or *prolo* perpetuate such patterns of exclusion in the registers of bad taste.
7 For a good summary of the discursive formations that gave rise to the concept of the worker, see Manfred Scharrer, *Arbeiter und die Idee von den Arbeitern 1848 bis 1869* (Cologne: Bund,

and related categories such as *arbeitende Klasse* and *Arbeiterklasse* (working class) made a first appearance in the early 1800s in order to announce the fundamental difference of the capitalist mode of production and its social organization of labor from the medieval *Zunft* (guild) system. In the paternalistic structures of the guild system, *Handwerker* (artisans, craftsmen) were distinguished through their particular craft (e. g., cobbler, locksmith, carpenter) rather than their membership in a social group made up of equal (i.e., equally oppressed) members. The reference to *Lohnarbeiter* (wage laborer) acknowledged the dependent nature of labor under capitalism and the centrality of work to the organization of modern life. Later compound nouns such as *Geistesproletarier* (intellectual proletarians) included intellectual work in these new structures of dependency and exploitation, a point picked up by Weimar-era studies about the so-called *akademische Proletariat* (academic proletariat). Meanwhile, the distinction between *Handarbeiter* (manual worker) und *Kopfarbeiter* (mental worker) reintroduced old hierarchies based primarily on social status and prestige and superimposed them on analyses of modern class society. A similar system of differentiation was at work in relation to the infamous *Lumpenproletarier*, or subproletarian, who subsequently came to function as the ultimate category of otherness against which the class-conscious proletarian could assert his power and knowledge.

Located at the intersection of the particular and the universal, the concept of the proletariat allowed Marx and Engels to establish the theoretical foundations for a socialist movement no longer beholden, like the utopian socialists, to visions of a future community living in perfect harmony. Instead their thought was propelled forward by the inevitability of tension and struggle. In the "Economic and Philosophic Manuscripts of 1844" (first published in 1932), Marx early on defined the proletarian as "the man who, being without capital and rent, lives purely by labor and by one-sided, abstract labor, is considered by political economy only as a *worker*. Political economy can therefore advance the proposition that the proletarian, the same as any horse, must get as much as will enable him to work. It does not consider him when he is not working, as a human being."[8] Marx's continuing clarification of the term had a pronounced literary dimension, as evidenced by his quotes from Heinrich Heine's poem *The Silesian Weavers* when reflecting on the conditions for revolution and his references to Eugène Sue's *The Mysteries of Paris* (1842/43) when distinguishing a proletarian

---

1990). My discussion is indebted to Karl Erich Heidolph, "Arbeiter, Arbeiterklasse, Revolution, Ausbeutung." *Untersuchungen zur Herausbildung gesellschaftswissenschaftlicher Termini bei K. Marx und F. Engels* (Berlin: Akademie der Wissenschaften, 1975).

8 Karl Marx, "Economic and Philosophic Manuscripts of 1844," *MECW* 3: 241.

ethics from the hypocrisies of bourgeois morality. As Elfriede Adelberg has documented in great detail, Marx and Engels used the terms "worker" and "proletarian" in line with a particular text's theoretical or political function but did so inconsistently and inconclusively.[9] In the transition from early to late Marx, "proletarian" lost some of its original charge, with Adelberg noting a higher frequency in the political commentaries and agitational treatises compared to the scholarly economic writings that favor the more neutral "working class." Under these conditions, the proletariat resisted full determination by the social and economic conditions of capitalism and ended up being roused by its own fluid condition, in Lenin's dismissive word, as an amalgamation of German philosophy, English political economy, and French socialism.[10]

As a social type and critical concept, the proletarian in Marxist thought made an early appearance in Friedrich Engels's influential report on *Die Lage der arbeitenden Klasse in England* (1845, *The Condition of the Working Class in England*). His extensive studies in Manchester, the center of the industrial revolution, had allowed Engels to recognize the proletarian as a new kind of worker who turns the experience of suffering into an attitude of struggling. The workers' hatred of the rich and mighty and their sense of powerlessness in front of the machines appear as recurring themes in his harrowing descriptions of working-class lives. Yet even more demoralizing than hunger or poverty, Engels concludes, is the daily experience of living hand to mouth, which puts the proletarian "in the most revolting inhumane position conceivable for a human being." Unlike the slave in the plantation economy or the serf in tenant farming, "the proletarian must depend upon himself alone, and is yet prevented from so applying his abilities as to be able to rely upon them [...] He is the passive subject of all possible combinations and circumstances, [...] and his character and way of living are naturally shaped by these conditions."[11] In Engels's words, since "no single field for the exercise of his manhood is left him, save his opposition to the

---

9 See the useful summary in Elfriede Adelberg, "Arbeiter," in *Zum Einfluß von Marx und Engels auf die deutsche Literatursprache. Studien zum Wortschatz der Arbeiterklasse im 19. Jahrhundert*, ed. Joachim Schildt et al. (Berlin: Akademie, 1978), 113–172. We can probably trace a similar shift during the *Vormärz* period from "socialist" to "communist" as the preferred term of self-identification.
10 See Vladimir Ilyich Lenin, "The Three Sources and Three Component Parts of Marxism," *Collected Works* 19: 21–28.
11 Friedrich Engels, "The Condition of the Working-Class in England," *MECW* 4: 413. For a compelling analysis of the Engels text through the concept of the proletariat, see Stathis Kouvelakis, *Philosophy and Revolution: From Kant to Marx*, preface Fredric Jameson, trans. G. M. Goshgarian (London: Verso, 2003), 167–231.

whole conditions of his life, it is natural that exactly in this opposition he should be most manly, noblest, most worthy of sympathy."[12] Thus empowered, the (male) proletarians join the project of class struggle, convinced that "they, as human beings, shall not be made to bow to social conditions, but social conditions ought to yield to them as human beings."[13]

As a social group, the proletariat could be first studied in the factories and tenements of Manchester, yet as a social imaginary, it arrived on the world historical stage largely through the unique combination of idealist philosophy and political backwardness that, in truly dialectical fashion, created the conditions for a revolutionary situation. As Marx insists in his *Contribution to the Critique of Hegel's Philosophy of Law* (1844) the proletariat is "not the naturally arising poor but the artificially impoverished." It is a product not of industrial development but of the exploitative nature of capitalism. Precisely through its status as the particular class, the proletariat is able to take on the emancipatory project of all of humankind: for "by proclaiming the *dissolution of the hitherto world order* the proletariat merely states the *secret of its own existence* for it is *in fact* the dissolution of that world order." Identifying the proletarian as the designated mediator between matter and spirit and establishing his proper place on the world historical stage, Marx concludes that, "As philosophy finds its *material* weapons in the proletariat, so the proletariat finds its *spiritual* weapons in philosophy." Significantly, Marx achieves the materialist appropriation of idealist philosophy through the clichéd language of emotion, namely the opposition between mind and heart, with the proletariat cast in the role of all-powerful mediator: "The *emancipation of the German* is the *emancipation of man*. The *head* of this emancipation is *philosophy*, its *heart* the *proletariat*."[14]

The discursive field established by the terms "worker" and "proletarian" and the emotional investments organized through their complicated relationship can be traced back to one of the core contradictions haunting Marxist theory – namely its status as both an analysis of capitalism and an alternative to capitalism. Whereas the figure of the worker is evoked to draw attention to the conditions of labor and the laws of capital, the figure of the proletarian allows the social imagination to anticipate a different future in the present. Given this prefigurative quality, it should not surprise that the enlistment of the "heart" in the proj-

---

12 Engels, "The Condition of the Working-Class," 502.
13 Engels, "The Condition of the Working-Class," 506.
14 Karl Marx, Introduction, "Contribution to the Critique of Hegel's Philosophy of Law," *MECW* 3: 186–187. The passage is crucial for understanding Marx's argument that the conditions for a true revolution in Germany originated in the backwardness of its political institutions—in other words, that the lack of particularity allowed for the realization of universality.

ect of emancipation requires a heavy dependence on literary models and aesthetic modalities and involves extensive references to collective emotions. Marxist theory affirms labor as an essential part of being/becoming human (i.e., in the notion of *homo laborans*) but also identifies it as the main cause of dehumanization in the context of capitalist exploitation. The introduction of *homo emotionalis* represents an attempt, located in the realms of critical reflection as well as literary fiction, to move beyond these contradictions and take full advantage of their complementary qualities.

Later Marxist distinctions in the name of scientific socialism, historical materialism, and socialist humanism continuously reenact this underlying tension between humanist universalism and class struggle in the figure of the proletarian as an instrument of conception, imagination, and agitation. These competing functions are brought together in a highly gendered rhetoric of class that serves to reconcile the universal and the specific through the symbolic equation of revolution with masculinity. Together the universalism of humanism, which assumes the male position as the normative position, and the class analysis of Marxism, which posits the working class as the universal one, establish the enabling conditions under which the proletarian dream acquires its distinct masculinist qualities. As illustrated by the Engels quotes above, the exploitation of the workers is invariably described as a feminizing experience, against which the process of radicalization promises remasculinization. Based on an understanding of labor that privileges wage labor over the reproduction of labor power, the resultant conflation of man, mankind, and human being, in turn, validates the male position as the universal one. The proletariat is confirmed as the universal class because it embodies human suffering and, through its revolt against the inhuman conditions of the class system, puts an end to all inhuman conditions. Communism, according to this argument, must be understood as a theory and praxis of human emancipation. In his impassioned response to Hegel, Marx is very clear on this point and deserves to be quoted at length:

> Where, then, is the *positive* possibility of a German emancipation? *Answer:* In the formulation of a class with *radical chains*, a class of civil society which is not a class of civil society, an estate which is the dissolution of all estates, a sphere which has a universal character by its universal suffering and claims no *particular right* because no *particular wrong* but *wrong generally* is perpetuated against it; which can invoke no *historical* but only *human* title; which does not stand in any one-sided antithesis to the consequences but in all-round antithesis to the premises of the German state; a sphere, finally, which cannot emancipate itself without emancipating itself from all other spheres of society and thereby emancipating all other spheres of society, which, in a word, is the *complete loss* of man and hence can win

itself only through the *complete rewinning of man*. This dissolution of society as a particular estate is the *proletariat*.[15]

Marx and Engels introduced the notion of the proletariat to make sense of the historical conditions that produced both the industrial worker in capitalist class society and the revolutionary program outlined in *The Communist Manifesto*. Some scholars have used the differences between the utopian humanism of the young Marx and the scientific materialism of the mature Marx to diagnose, in the words of Louis Althusser, an epistemological rupture, a rupture that reverberates through many later schisms in the socialist and communist parties. Other scholars have pointed to Marx and Engels's considerable debts to earlier philosophical, religious, and aesthetic traditions to explain the underlying contradictions as productive tensions. Emphasizing the mythic structure of the proletariat in Marx, political scientist David Lovell has noted the simultaneously abstract and expressive nature of his definitions. The main discursive function of the proletariat, according to Lovell, was to embody the proclaimed unity of theory and praxis. Accordingly, Marx developed the term not through direct involvement with working-class struggles but in critical dialogue with the Young Hegelians and their proposals for using philosophy as the basis of social transformations. From then on, Marx continuously refined his basic argument in response to new socialist groups and workers' movements and their various reformist and revolutionary agendas. The widespread phenomenon of pauperism prompted him to respond to the rising numbers of working poor living below subsistence levels and to challenge prevailing assumptions about poverty as either predetermined (i.e., part of the eternal order) or a result of low intelligence, moral degeneracy, and personal laziness. Through the theoretical apparatus built around the concept of the proletariat Marx was able to mobilize the deep reservoirs of myth, ritual, and symbolism that could infuse such analyses with political meaning. For Lowell, recognizing the mythic nature of the proletariat ultimately means jettisoning the idea "that socialism was a product of the working class, that it was formulated solely in the interests of the working class, and that it was founded on the notion of class struggle."[16] Furthermore, it means embracing the hetero-

---

[15] Marx, Introduction, "Contribution to the Critique of Hegel's Philosophy of Law," *MECW* 3: 186.

[16] David W. Lovell, *Marx's Proletariat: The Making of a Myth* (London: Routledge, 1988), 1. His main critique of Marx comes in the conclusion: "Marx believed that the philosophical, political and economic models of the proletariat were simply aspects of one whole" (216) but failed to properly integrate these aspects; instead he tried to resolve the problems through the dialectics

geneity of a movement that also included anarchists and labor unions and that, on the level of discourse, required continuous adjustments in response to the repeated failures of the historical working class as a revolutionary agent.

If, in Marx's words, "the working class is revolutionary or it is nothing" and if revolutions are indeed locomotives of history, then the proletariat assumed its historical role as the most radicalized part of the working class with considerable theoretical baggage and emotional weight.[17] This constitutive tension between critique and imagination can be clarified through the often-misunderstood distinction between class in itself (*an sich*), a social class defined through its relation to the means of production, and class for itself (*für sich*), a class united in its active pursuit of shared human interests and goals. The distinction lays outs how the economic and social conditions in capitalism can transform the infamous masses of mass psychology into the revolutionary working class of Marxist theory. This is how Marx describes the process: "This mass is thus already a class against capital [i.e., *an sich* or in itself], but not yet for itself. In the struggle [...] this mass becomes united, and constitutes itself as a class for itself."[18] Yet in order for this transformation to take place, the workers have to experience themselves as an oppressed and exploited class; they develop class consciousness only in, and through, class struggle. To phrase it differently, class in itself refers to an external necessity, whereas class for itself describes a human necessity, with only the proletariat able to complete the transition from the one to the other. Confirming the importance of symbolic politics to this long and complicated process, the conditions of being "for itself" were established with the creation of a proletarian counterpublic at once separate from bourgeois society and linked to its culture through acts of appropriation – including of the notion of *Bildung* (education) as both cultivation and formation examined in chapter 8.

Mapping the discursive field established by the proletarian imaginary must extend to one of the most misunderstood terms in Marxist theory, the dictatorship of the proletariat. In introducing the concept, Marx concludes "that the class struggle necessarily leads to the *dictatorship of the proletariat* [and] that this dictatorship itself only constitutes the transition to the *abolition of all classes*

---

of the particular and universal. For a similar but less developed argument, also see Timothy McCarthy, *Marx and the Proletariat: A Study in Social Theory* (Westport, CT: Greenwood Press, 1978).
17 See Karl Marx, Letter to Engels, 18 February 1865, *MECW* 42: 96. Lenin's insistence on the vanguard function of the Bolsheviks (rather than the working class) simply reverses this logic in accordance with the new power dynamics in the Soviet Union.
18 Karl Marx, "The Poverty of Philosophy," *MECW* 6: 211. On this point, also see Edward Andrew, "Class in Itself and Class Against Capital: Karl Marx and His Classifiers," *Canadian Journal of Political Science* 16.3 (1983): 577–584.

and to a *classless society*."[19] In his 1875 critique of the Gotha Program, the founding document of the SPD, Marx insists that dictatorship of the proletariat refers only to the temporary suspension of democratic rule during the initial transformation from a capitalist to a communist (i. e., classless) society. Against contemporary misreadings of the term as despotism of the people, which for many conservatives was simply another name for the tyranny of democracy, Marx emphatically insists on its original meaning as a kind of popular sovereignty based on the long overdue conquest of political power – a point of particular relevance for understanding later configurations of socialism, nationalism, and totalitarianism developed around the overdetermined figure of the worker.

The adaptable meaning of the proletariat as a theoretical concept can be measured by its continuing revisions since the Wilhelmine years. As the main protagonist in the narratives of progress promoted in the name of scientific socialism, the proletariat appeared across the entire range of socialist literary, musical, and visual practices and played a key role in the imagination of the working class as an emotional community. Yet in socialist theory and political debate, references to the proletariat often amounted to little more than empty formulas and clichés. Responding to these developments, Eduard Bernstein (1850–1932), the main proponent of what became known as revisionism, questioned the historical inevitability of revolution and the status of the proletariat as the revolutionary class. The frequent descriptions of the proletariat as the largest and most unified social class, in his view, attested above all to the self-delusions of Social Democracy, with the so-called dictatorship of the proletariat amounting to little more than "the dictatorship of lecturers and literati."[20] Along similar lines, in *Die Diktatur des Proletariats* (1918, *The Dictatorship of the Proletariat*), Karl Kautsky (1854–1938), the most influential Marxist thinker after Engels's death, used the comparison of dictatorship and democracy as forms of governance to formulate a critique of the Leninist model of revolution and to argue for a democratic road to socialism in western democracies and advanced industrial societies; this pro-

---

19 Karl Marx, Letter to Joseph Weydemeyer in New York, 5 March 1852, *MECW* 39: 58. For a critical assessment, see Mehmet Tabak, "Marx's Theory of Proletarian Dictatorship Revisited," *Science and Society* 64.3 (Fall 2000): 333–356. An overview of the concept in the writings of Marx, Kautsky, Lenin, and others can be found in Hal Draper, *The "Dictatorship of the Proletariat" from Marx to Lenin* (London: Monthly Review, 1987).
20 Eduard Bernstein, *Die Voraussetzungen des Sozialismus und die Aufgaben der Sozialdemokratie* (Stuttgart: J. H. W. Dietz, 1899), 183.

posal prompted Lenin to denounce him as the "renegade Kautsky."[21] After the October Revolution, it was left to Georg Lukács (1885–1971), in *Geschichte und Klassenbewußtsein* (1923, *History and Class Consciousness*), to reaffirm the proletariat as the true subject of history and the sole producer of the totality of society. In fact, he developed his theory of alienation and reification precisely to account for the dialectics within proletarian class consciousness.[22] Lesser-known but equally influential, Karl Korsch (1886–1961), in *Marxismus und Philosophie* (1923, Marxism and Philosophy), used the notion of a proletarian dialectic, "the transformation of the 'natural' class viewpoint of the proletariat into theoretical concepts and propositions,"[23] to propose new models for political action.

The writings of Marx and Engels established the structure of meanings, and of feelings, in which the proletariat came to occupy a unique place between the critique of capitalism and the theory of revolution. The proletariat's non-identity with the working class gave rise to a surfeit of utopian fantasies, which were as grounded in Marxist theory as they were influenced by philosophy and aesthetics. This fundamental tension between two different kinds of imagination, a theoretical and an aesthetic one, provided a seemingly inexhaustible source of inspiration and resonated throughout the socialist lifeworld. It also established a force field in which both sides could preserve the revolutionary potential embodied by the proletariat. The different function of political theories and symbolic practices (and their respective disciplines and institutions) may account for the fact that the proletarian dream as conjured by novels, poems, memoirs, songs, and plays remained largely unaffected by the theoretical controversies that followed in the wake of Bernstein's initial revisionist intervention. In fact, this can be read as further evidence that the proletarian imaginary was reducible neither to Marxist theory nor to social reality.

The further revisions of the proletarian dream from the Wilhelmine to the Weimar years can be tracked with the help of SPD party programs and their changing voice, mood, and tone. These party programs not only attest to the remarkable productivity of the proletariat as a theoretical concept forever suspended between the particular and the universal. They also confirm its overdetermined status in the competing narratives of revolution and reform, including

---

21 Karl Kautsky, *The Dictatorship of the Proletariat*, trans. H. J. Stenning (Ann Arbor: University of Michigan Press, 1964). For Lenin's response, see "The Proletarian Revolution and the Renegade Kautsky" (1918), https://www.marxists.org/archive/lenin/works/1918/prrk/, 1 March 2017.
22 Georg Lukács, *History and Class Consciousness: Studies in Marxist Dialectics* (Cambridge, MA: MIT Press, 1971).
23 Karl Korsch, "The Marxist Dialectic (1923)," https://www.marxists.org/archive/korsch/1923/marxist-dialectic.htm, 1 March 2017.

through the alternating use of "proletariat" or "working class" as the preferred term. Thus the SPD's founding document, the Eisenach Program of 1869, defines the struggle for the liberation of the working class as the abolishment of wage labor and class rule in the name of democracy. The Gotha Program of 1875 upholds the leadership role of the working class and concludes that, "the liberation of labor must be the work of the working class." Meanwhile, the Erfurt Program of 1891 expands the party's historical mission by calling for "the liberation not just of the proletarian but of the entire human race." Convinced of the imminent demise of capitalism, it proposes to achieve these goals through reformist rather than revolutionary means.

After the October Revolution, however, and as part of the growing divisions within the European left after World War I, the status and function of the proletariat becomes increasingly precarious, as evidenced by the vacillation between *Arbeiterklasse* (working class) and *arbeitendes Volk* (working people) in the three Weimar-era programs. The 1919 founding program of the USPD (Independent Social Democratic Party of Germany) still calls for "the creation of a revolutionary international of workers of all countries ready for action" and determined to defeat the divisive forces of nationalism. The Görlitz Program of 1921 already draws on older notions of folk and community when describing the SPD as "the party of working people in city and country." And the Heidelberg Program of 1925 affirms the party's commitment to the Weimar Republic, concluding, "the democratic republic is the best foundation for the liberation struggle of the working class and thus for the realization of socialism."[24] The SPD's gradual abandonment of the revolutionary project in favor of active participation in government comes into even clearer view through a comparison to the 1918 founding document of the KPD that ends on a militant note: "Onward, proletarians! To battle! You are called to conquer a world and fight against a world. In this final class struggle in world history, for the loftiest goals of mankind, the word to the enemy must be: thumb on the eye and knee on the chest."[25]

To conclude: Marxist definitions of worker and proletarian may have served as the basis of Social Democratic party programs and undergone continuous revisions during the Second and Third Internationals. However, from the 1870s to the 1930s, the discursive field marked by the term "proletarian" remained fluid

---

[24] See Daniela Münkel, ed., *"Freiheit, Gerechtigkeit und Solidarität". Die Programmgeschichte der Sozialdemokratischen Partei Deutschlands* (Berlin: Vorwärts, 2007), 388, 379, 372, 363, and 343. For a history of the party that makes the disappearance of the proletariat its telos, see Franz Walter, *Die SPD. Vom Proletariat zur neuen Mitte* (Berlin: Alexander Fest, 2002).
[25] *Protokoll des Gründungsparteitags der Kommunistischen Partei Deutschlands 1918*, https://www.marxists.org/deutsch/geschichte/deutsch/kpd/1918/programm.htm, 1 March 2017.

and elusive enough to operate on multiple and contradictory levels: as a political program, a social myth, a cultural construction, and an ideological fantasy; it remained an object of intense emotional attachments and investments. The conventional description of Marxist thought as a rupture of the veil of illusions (i.e., ideology) was achieved precisely through the creation of a new set of illusions called the proletarian dream. On the level of Marxist theories and SPD and KPD party programs, its remarkable productivity throughout the late nineteenth and early twentieth century can be explained through its overdetermined status within the collective imaginaries that sustained working-class culture in Imperial Germany and that distinguished the Social Democratic and Communist lifeworld in the Weimar Republic. As the next chapter on emotional socialism shows, emotions in politics played a key role in defining the proletarian dream and sustaining the individual commitment to socialism.

Chapter 3
Emotional Socialism and Sentimental Masculinity

> Back then I was in the most awful emotional state imaginable. That they had expelled us, as if we were vagrants or criminals, and separated us from our wives and children, without due legal process, I experienced as a deathly insult that I would have avenged if I had had the power to do so. No trial or verdict has ever aroused such feelings of hate, bitterness, and resentment as the annual expulsions, until the rescinding of the untenable law brought this cruel game with human lives to an end.
>
> August Bebel, *Aus meinem Leben*

Referring to deadly insults and fantasies of revenge, August Bebel, one of the founders of the SPD, draws on the confessional tones familiar from autobiographical writing. Yet here, his references to being overwhelmed by emotion appear in a 1910 memoir about the early years of socialism.[1] For labor historians, the memoirs of socialist leaders offer intimate perspectives on the difficult conditions under which the SPD emerged as a political party and mass movement. These confessional moments shed a light not only on the required individual sacrifices but, for the cultural historian, also provide access to the conflicting (and conflicted) views of Social Democrats on the proper place of emotions in the growing mass movement. The official term used by early socialists to describe this phenomenon was *Gefühlssozialismus* (emotional socialism), a term that, on the following pages, will function as a guide through the interior landscape of the proletarian dream in late nineteenth-century Social Democracy.

The conceptual challenges of describing the proletariat as an emotional community are considerable, even if the analysis remains limited to collective imaginaries rather than social practices or lived experiences. The same can be concluded about the equation of the socialist movement with specific emotional regimes (e.g., harmony, fraternity, solidarity) and the overdetermined status of the proletariat as the discursive figure through which two social bodies, the working class and the workers' movement, were meant to become one. There is no way to distinguish between feelings felt and thoughts remembered, or feelings and thoughts imagined, affirmed, and evaluated. The agitational, communicative, and performative nature of emotions in social movements adds an additional layer of mediation that can only be acknowledged through close attention to the respective modes of representation, that is, the accessibility of these emo-

---

[1] August Bebel, *Aus meinem Leben*, 3 vols. (Stuttgart: Dietz, 1910), 3: 183.

tions only in the form of texts. In writing, emotions are endowed with political relevance through a system of differences: by distinguishing one emotion from another (e.g., resentment versus resignation), by differentiating private from public emotion (e.g., suffering versus indignation), and by comparing emotion to cognition (e.g., class hatred versus class consciousness). Similarly, emotional styles are modeled on existing literary genres – with the sentimental and the melodramatic offering the greatest political rewards for the workers' movement. Understanding emotions as a thus defined medium of transformation (i.e., from feeling to thinking to feeling, from aesthetics to politics to aesthetics) is especially important for understanding the formative contribution of emotions in the making of the proletarian dream.

The cultural practices that imagined the proletariat as an emotional community and distinguished Social Democracy through its emotional regimes point to the powerful influence of the Enlightenment and its reverberations in the making of the bourgeois public sphere. Nineteenth-century understandings of collective emotion (e.g., Le Bon's mass soul) developed between eighteenth-century Enlightenment discourses of emotion, which emphasize the fluid relations between bodily sensation and aesthetic emotion, and twentieth-century psychoanalytic theories of the drives, which insist on the necessity of repression and sublimation. Both paradigms confirmed the individual as the starting point of all critical inquiry, with the perspective of class recognized through the preoccupation with mass contagion and subsequently managed by mass psychology and related disciplines. Between these temporal markers, the nineteenth century made emotions available through the scientific disciplines of psychology and sociology and the critique of mass society and modernity that emerged under the influence of Nietzscheanism, including the will to power, and that continued in the context of *Lebensphilosophie* (vitalism) and, much later, the Frankfurt School's Critical Theory. New perspectives on the significance of emotions for aesthetics and hermeneutics opened up through Wilhelm Wundt's system of internal perception with its fluid distinctions between feelings and ideas and Wilhelm Dilthey's hermeneutic method with its emphasis on *Einfühlung* (empathy) as a critical faculty. This growing interest in emotion as a heuristic device continued with Georg Simmel's reflections on the mentality of modern life and Siegfried Kracauer's essays on the cult of distraction. The attendant refinement of critical methods, often at the intersection of art and science or in the contact zone between high and low culture, must be seen as recognition of the remarkable ability of emotion across the cultural and social divides at once to produce aesthetic experiences, organize social relations, and sustain political commitments.²

A complication to be considered in this context is the influence of bourgeois notions of *Innerlichkeit* (interiority or inwardness) and their formative role in the invention of German national character. This discursive construction of an interior and exterior world is inseparable from the politicized distinctions between public and private sphere that resonated throughout the nineteenth century and contributed to the transformation of inwardness into a site of resistance and a form of recognition. In fact, if there is one recurring theme in the memoirs of August Bebel (1840–1913), Wilhelm Liebknecht (1826–1900), Karl Kautsky (1854–1938), and several others, it is their feeling of powerlessness and, closely related, their raging against injustice. All three men cite lack of recognition in the legal, political, and social spheres as formative moments in their personal radicalization, and all point to painful experiences of disrespect and discrimination as powerful motivation for their commitment to the cause. Their revelations indicate to what degree the project of socialism was founded on, and sustained by, specific emotional regimes, scripts, and lexicons. This language of emotions is closely modeled on bourgeois notions of subjectivity and the public sphere. Yet in their almost exclusive focus on political emotions, the refunctionalization of these traditions in the socialist movement shifts the site of feeling from individual to collective modalities. Against the bourgeois cult of inwardness, which justifies the retreat from public life by cultivating mind and soul, the socialists took core liberal values – personal responsibility, individual initiative, and freedom of speech and assembly – and reconfigured them to promote values and behaviors emphasizing community. This refunctionalization was helped by their references to a decidedly Prussian ethos of discipline, order, duty, and sacrifice for the common good that may have remained undeveloped in the socialist culture of male sentimentality but that took center stage in the later culture of communist militancy and Nazi community. Highlighting these continuities, Oswald Spengler later extolled the Prussian roots of German socialism in his influential book on *Preußentum und Sozialismus* (1919, *Prussianism and Socialism*).

Moral questions and ethical concerns were of central relevance to the imagining of the proletariat as the universal class – that is, the class whose particular interests coincided with the needs of humanity as a whole. The recourse to moral

---

2 A useful overview of emotional cultures in the nineteenth century can be found in Ute Frevert et al., eds., *Emotional Lexicons: Continuity and Change in the Vocabulary of Feeling 1700–2000* (Oxford: Oxford University Press, 2014). For a case study from the history of social movements, see Christian Koller, "Es ist zum Heulen. Emotionshistorische Zugänge zur Kulturgeschichte des Streikens," *Geschichte und Gesellschaft* 36.1 (2010): 66–92.

categories (e. g., virtues and vices) and the belief in a moral order (e. g., justice vs. injustice) indicate that the phenomenon of emotional socialism was firmly situated within nineteenth-century forms of religiosity – or, to be more precise, the social conventions that made Christian tropes and figures an integral part of the socialist public sphere. The many religious references especially in the writings of Bebel and Liebknecht attest to the enduring influence of faith, though less in the form of church doctrine than in the morals and values that translate ethical principles into everyday life. This includes the close connection to Protestantism and its emphasis on personal behavior, the influence of eighteenth-century discourses of the sentiments, and the religious roots of the culture of sentimentality more generally. To give one example, the literature of *Empfindsamkeit* (sentimentalism) celebrated authentic feeling as a conduit to the truth of human nature and an essential tool in the cultivation of "a good heart." In this context, suffering and self-sacrifice appeared less as a sign of weakness than as an expression of authenticity and, ultimately, of empowerment – with obvious implications for the mutual articulation of aesthetic and emotional registers in socialist utopias and modern mass societies.

Further complicating the issue, the emotional confessions about personal sacrifices by well-known Social Democrats as well as their public debates about the pitfalls of emotional socialism are inseparable from the problem of working-class masculinity. The gendered divisions in the proletarian imaginary not only opened up a space for expressions of male sentimentality but also used the identification of masculinity with cognition and of femininity with emotion to eventually replace the vestiges of utopian socialism with the certainties of scientific socialism. By translating private emotion into political emotion, Social Democracy ended up creating a space wherein masculinity and emotionality became not only compatible terms but also mutually reinforcing ones, as long as emotions could be defined in political terms.[3] For these reasons, the contested status of political emotions cannot be explained solely with regards to the historical transition from utopian socialism to scientific socialism. As a cultural phenomenon, emotional socialism remained inseparable from the aesthetic registers of the sentimental and the melodramatic, which in the so-called socialist

---

[3] It would be interesting to consider the emotional approach to socialism in the autobiographies by women socialists such as Lily Braun's two-volume *Memoiren einer Sozialistin* (1909–11) and Ottilie Baader's *Ein steiniger Weg. Lebenserinnerungen einer Sozialistin* (1921). For a comparative perspective, see Mary Chapman and Glenn Hendler, eds., *Sentimental Men: Masculinity and the Politics of Affect in American Culture* (Berkeley: University of California Press, 1999) and Glenn Hendler, *Public Sentiments: Structures of Feeling in Nineteenth-Century American Literature* (Chapel Hill: University of North Carolina Press, 2001).

tendentious novels (*Tendenzromane*) opened up an imaginary space where public and private feelings could become one, and which in the political memoirs relied on empathetic identification to draw readers into the utopian worlds of socialism. The result was a distinctly Social Democratic version of working-class masculinity: marked by suffering, motivated by indignation, and united in the demand for recognition. It will be the main purpose of this chapter based on these preliminary remarks to identify some of the constitutive elements of a socialist discourse of male sentimentality that has been forgotten in favor of the equation of proletarian identifications with militant masculinity since World War I.

The opening quotation from Bebel illustrates well how his deeply felt sense of injustice became a political emotion through highly gendered scenarios – in this case, the separation from his wife and children and his inability to provide for the family. Described as an experience of emasculation, his imprisonment exposes the abyss between his sense of self and his understanding of the world, ultimately drawing attention to the conditions that produce social and economic inequalities. Read in more optimistic terms, his reminiscences also attest to the growing strength of civil society – and, of course, of Social Democracy both of which made possible the publication of his thoughts. More specifically, Bebel's personal perspectives on felt injustices, large and small, would have been seen as both a measure of, and a tool in, the workers' long fight for equality. His presentation of suffering as a sign of moral authority and a source of political strength attested to the growing confidence of the workers' movement and its ability to appropriate existing definitions of right and wrong for an emerging socialist morality. Articulated in opposition to dominant society and mainstream culture, "hatred, bitterness, and resentment" and its political alternatives of hope, unity, and solidarity thus became part of what, from the perspective of hindsight, can be called the emotional archives of an emerging proletarian public sphere.

In *Aus meinem Leben* (1910–1914, *My Life*), Bebel for the most part recounts the internal and external struggles of the SPD with little attention to his private life. Nonetheless, the apparent bracketing of the personal does not mean that emotions were not essential to the promotion of socialism as a new way of life, namely as a solution to the psychological wounds caused by oppression and exploitation in capitalist society. As the author of the widely read *Die Frau und der Sozialismus* (1878, *Women and Socialism*), Bebel was well aware of the problems of working-class women, marriage, and family life and, closely related, the party's insufficient attention to what, in Marxist terminology, is sometimes referred to as the subjective factor. On the one hand, he acknowledged the power of political emotions when he described the ideal socialist leader as someone who earns the trust of the masses by responding to their innermost feelings and acting as "the chosen advocate of their demands, the translator of their longings, their hopes, and their wishes."⁴ On the other hand, he questioned the long-term prospects of social movements committed only to the individual pursuit of happiness and denounced support for such positions by fellow socialists as surrender to the cult of bourgeois individualism. "I think very little of the saying that men are the masters of their own happiness," he explained, "Only 'happy circumstances' give individuals their 'proper' place in life. For the great many who are not given that proper place, the table of life is not set."⁵

The emotional culture of nineteenth-century Social Democracy can be reconstructed best through the voices of its most fervent defenders and doubtful observers. Capturing the mood of the early socialist movement, the utopian socialist Wilhelm Weitling was one of the first to declare in 1842, "that cold reason alone has never produced a revolution."⁶ The anarchist Rudolf Rocker recalled, "in the small circles of scholars, pure theories may have played a certain role; they had no influence whatsoever on the actual development of the movement. The broad mass of Social Democratic supporters did not even understand the political jargon that was spoken in those circles."⁷ Many party leaders openly admitted that proletarian identifications were not formed on the basis of any party programs or theoretical treatises but resulted primarily from the sentiments, moods, and sensibilities that developed in the social and cultural rituals of associational life. Unsurprisingly, the power of emotions haunted the socialist movement from the very beginning. Already in *The Communist Manifesto*, Marx and Engels took issue with early socialists' preoccupation with working-class suffering. The founding fathers of Marxism accused their lesser-known rivals "of caring chiefly for the interests of the working class as being the most suffering class" and concluded that, "Only from the point of view of being the most suffering class does the proletariat exist for them."⁸ Determined to establish the scientific foundations of Marxism, Marx and Engels had no patience for the "communism of starry-eyed love, based on 'love' and overflowing with

---

4 Bebel, *Aus meinem Leben*, 2: 122.
5 Bebel, *Aus meinem Leben*, 1: 42.
6 Wilhelm Weitling, quoted by Frank Trommler, *Sozialistische Literatur in Deutschland: Ein historischer Überblick* (Stuttgart: Kröner, 1976), 187.
7 Rudolf Rocker, *Aus den Memoiren eines deutschen Anarchisten* (Frankfurt am Main: Suhrkamp, 1974), 46.
8 Karl Marx and Friedrich Engels, "Manifesto of the Communist Party," *MECW* 6: 515.

love"⁹ promoted by the London-based Bund der Kommunisten (Communist League) and similar groups. In a circular distributed around the same time, they mocked socialist agitators like Hermann Kriege (1820–1850) of the New York-based *Volks-Tribun* for having succumbed to "fantastic emotionalism" while presenting himself as an "apostle of love" and turning communism into a form of lovesickness.¹⁰ Concerned about the long-term political implications, Marx accused a faction in the Communist League headed by Karl Schapper (1812–1870) of advertising the revolution with the same false promises found in conservative appeals to some mystical version of folk. "Just as the word 'people' (*Volk*) has been given an aura of sanctity by the democrats, so you have done the same for the word 'proletariat,'"¹¹ he wrote to Schapper, displaying uncanny foresight about the corruption of the proletarian dream by twentieth-century forms of state socialism. In speaking out against strong emotions, however, Marx also tried to come to terms with his own personal attachments to socialism. This includes a short poem written at the age of eighteen and filled with romantic longing and rebellious spirit. Called "Empfindungen" (1836, Feelings), it contains the following lines:

> I am caught in endless strife,
> endless ferment, endless dream.
> I cannot conform to life,
> will not travel with the stream.
> Heaven I would comprehend,
> I would draw the world to me.
> Loving, hating, I intend
> that my star shine brilliantly.¹²

Adding a gendered dimension to the early attacks on emotional socialism, Engels used his contributions to the discussion on socialist literature to chastise two socialist women writers for their heavy reliance on emotionality as a conduit to character identification. His letters to Minna Kautsky, the author of *Die Alten und die Neuen* (1884, The Old and the New), and to the English socialist novelist and critic Margaret Harkness are on the surface concerned solely with the all-important question of tendency and intentionality. Yet as a contribution to the de-

---

9 Friedrich Engels, "On the History of the Communist League," *MECW* 26: 319.
10 Karl Marx and Friedrich Engels, "Circular against Kriege (1846)," *MECW* 6: 34–51.
11 Karl Marx, "Revelations Concerning the Communist Trial in Cologne," *MECW* 11: 403.
12 Karl Marx, "Feelings," https://www.marxists.org/archive/marx/works/download/Marx_Young_Marx.pdf. On the beginnings of Marxism and literature, see Peter Demetz, *Marx, Engels, and the Poets: Origins of Marxist Literary Criticism* (Chicago: University of Chicago Press, 1967).

bate on emotional socialism, they can also be read as a recommendation specifically to women to hold back and practice restraint. Accordingly, Engels's advice to Miss Harkness, "the more the opinions of the author remains hidden, the better for the work of art,"[13] draws on the familiar idealist aesthetic argument in favor of disinterested pleasure. And his instruction to Kautsky that she "does not have to serve to the reader on a platter the future historical resolution of the social conflicts he [i.e., the novel's author] describes"[14] hinges on a revealing slippage in the gendering of authorship that assumes all authors to be male yet describes any literary shortcomings in housewifely terms.

Emboldened by growing mass support and eager to solidify political alliances, some Social Democrats around the turn of the century began to voice long-standing concerns about the large role of emotions in proletarian identifications. The language used to describe this "problem" invariably presupposed a female or feminizing subject position. Adjectives such as "soft" and "vague" were frequently enlisted, with the words' implied sense of indeterminacy intended to highlight the clarity and truth provided instead by scientific socialism. Eduard Bernstein's description of the "fuzzy emotional communism" prevalent among the lower classes not only established a clear gendered hierarchy between the uneducated masses, the worker intelligentsia, and the labor aristocracy, but also used the language of emotions to separate the scientific claims of historical materialism from the romantic utopianism of the early socialists.[15] Karl Kautsky in fact coined the term *Gefühlssozialismus* in order to marginalize the irrational tendencies still found in the effusive rhetoric of Kurt Eisner, the editor of *Vorwärts*, and to underscore the need of a more mature, restrained, and manly approach to socialism.[16] In his commentary on the Erfurt Program, Kautsky singled out the workers' desire to desire – that is, their dreams of a better life – for its potentially destabilizing effects. In his view, their discovery of personal needs and their expression of individual demands ahead of any real improvements in the economic conditions were bound to create problems for the socialist

---

13 Friedrich Engels, Letter to Minna Kautsky, 26 November 1885, http://www.marxists.org/archive/marx/works/1885/letters/85_11_26.htm, 1 March 2017.
14 Friedrich Engels, Letter to Margaret Harkness, c. 1 April 1888, http://www.marxists.org/archive/marx/works/1888/letters/88_04_15.htm, 1 March 2017.
15 Eduard Bernstein, *Die Geschichte des Sozialismus in Einzeldarstellungen* (Stuttgart: Dietz, 1895), 39.
16 Karl Kautsky, "Die Fortsetzung einer unmöglichen Diskussion. Gefühlssozialismus und wissenschaftlicher Sozialismus," *Die Neue Zeit* 2.23 (1905): 717–727. For a very different view of the role of enthusiasm in the cultivation of class instinct, see Kurt Eisner, "Wenn und aber," *Vorwärts*, 9 September 1905.

movement; hence his conclusion: "The consequence of class struggle can therefore only ever be an increase in the dissatisfaction of the proletariat with its fate,"[17] that is, the moment when the ethos of collective solidarity comes up against the boundlessness and unpredictability of individual desire.

In his own proposal for reconciling emotional socialism and scientific socialism, Kautsky repeatedly called for spiritual elevation through cultivation of the ethical dimension of socialism. Noble ideals, he insisted, are important for they ensure that the original "idealism is not taken over by the banalities of everyday life and that the proletariat does not lose awareness of its great historical tasks."[18] However, in his own memoirs, Kautsky (like Bebel before him) highlighted the importance of enthusiasm to explain his conversion to socialism as a young Czech-German who had experienced ethnic discrimination firsthand. Remembering the inner feelings of an impressionable young boy, he writes:

> Over and over again I was tormented by the thought: how can an idea [i.e., the idea of socialism] be rational if only an uneducated boy like myself thinks of it that way, whereas all thinking, well-educated people around me dismiss it as ludicrous? And yet, I could not decide to jettison this idea. I held on to it, but not because of any deep insight. I clung to it with all fibers of my being; it satisfied a desire that had arisen in me since the Commune and had completely taken hold of me, the desire for the elevation and liberation of all those in misery and bondage.[19]

The Social Democrats' anxieties over any surfeit of emotions in the workers' movement and their efforts at managing the consequences in the medium of literature can be illustrated through a series of literary debates, beginning with the so-called naturalism debate of the 1890s. At party conventions and in party publications, speaking about socialist (or proletarian) literature invariably meant speaking about attachments and identifications. Historically, the naturalism debate represented a first attempt to clarify the relationship of Social Democracy to modern literature and, by extension, modernity.[20] In the scholarship, this debate

---

17 Karl Kautsky, *Das Erfurter Programm in seinem grundsätzlichen Teil* (Stuttgart: Dietz, 1908), 232.
18 Karl Kautsky, *Bernstein und das sozialdemokratische Programm. Eine Antikritik* (Stuttgart: Dietz, 1899), 195.
19 Karl Kautsky, *Erinnerungen und Erörterungen*, ed. Benedikt Kautsky (The Hague: Mouton, 1960), 187. For Kautsky and his views on enthusiasm, also see "Ein sozialdemokratischer Katechismus," *Die Neue Zeit* 12.13 (1893–94): 402–410.
20 The contributions to the naturalism debate have been reprinted in Norbert Rothe, ed., *Naturalismus-Debatte 1891–1896. Dokumente zur Literaturtheorie und Literaturkritik der revolutionären deutschen Sozialdemokratie* (Berlin: Akademie, 1986). For a good summary of the positions, see Georg Fülberth, *Proletarische Partei und bürgerliche Literatur: Auseinandersetzungen*

has been interpreted as evidence of the conservative tastes of SPD party leaders and their enduring belief in the classics, positions that will be considered in greater detail through the bourgeois discourses of culture and education analyzed in chapter 8. Yet as an integral part of the campaign against emotional socialism, the naturalism debate and the later Schiller debate can also be read as referendums on pessimism and optimism as very different approaches to the role of literary criticism in managing political emotions.

Responding to the serialization of two popular novels in the SPD's popular weekly *Die Neue Welt*, several speakers at the 1896 Gotha party convention had attacked their depiction of contemporary social problems as too pessimistic, too depressing, and too insulting to Social Democrats, given the official emphasis on moral and spiritual uplift. The naturalist preoccupation with social milieu, the influential thinker Franz Mehring (1846–1919) argued, was conclusive evidence, "that modern art has a deeply pessimistic attitude whereas the modern proletariat has a deeply optimistic attitude."[21] Ignoring the enormous significance of Gerhart Hauptmann's *Die Weber* (1892, *The Weavers*), about the revolt of the Silesian Weavers, Karl Kautsky, too, lamented that the representatives of the Youngest Germany "prefer to find the proletariat in the neighborhood pub and the brothel and pay no attention to the revolutionary proletariat."[22] Socialism, both Mehring and Kautsky concluded, required an unyielding optimistic worldview. Its emotional regimes demanded that the workers be protected from the corrosive qualities of modern literature and be exposed to the great humanist traditions that alone could provide emotional guidance and support.

The formative and controversial role of emotions in the self-understanding of early Social Democracy confirms class as a relational (rather than structural) category. And far from settling the underlying conceptual issues, the historical scholarship on working-class culture reveals the continued emotional investment in questions of class and class politics. This is because, as Eric Hobsbawm conceded in 2011, even intellectuals "were linked to the politics of the left not so much through theoretical reflection as an emotional commitment of their practi-

---

in der deutschen Sozialdemokratie der II. Internationale über Möglichkeiten und Grenzen einer sozialistischen Literaturpolitik (Neuwied: Luchterhand, 1972), 84–105.
21 Franz Mehring, "Kunst und Proletariat" (1896), rpt. in two parts in *Werkauswahl*, 3 vols., ed. Fritz Raddatz (Darmstadt: Luchterhand, 1975), 3: 17. The novels in question were Hans Land's *Der neue Gott* (1891) and Wilhelm Hegeler's *Mutter Bertha* (1893). The novels of Emile Zola and the dramas by Henrik Ibsen served as main exhibits in the arguments against naturalism.
22 Karl Kautzky, "Der Alkoholismus und seine Bekämpfung," *Die Neue Zeit* 9.2 (1890), 86. The reference is to Gerhart Hauptmann's *Vor Sonnenaufgang* (1889).

tioners and admirers to the struggles of the period."²³ Given the strong utopian tendencies in the history of the British working class, it is not surprising that the first arguments for emotions as a productive category in cultural analysis were presented by Marxist scholars E. P. Thompson and Raymond Williams during the 1950s, in the early years of what would eventually become British cultural studies. Against communist orthodoxy and its insistence on the correct interpretation of canonical texts, Thompson stressed the importance of common experiences in the making of working-class consciousness. His often quoted insistence on saving the ephemeral and the forgotten "from the enormous condescension of posterity" can easily be extended to the emotional attachments usually ignored or dismissed by early labor historians and scholars of socialist literature.²⁴ Since then, the emergence of cultural studies as an academic discipline and the various linguistic, material, and emotional turns have allowed researchers across the disciplines to acknowledge the importance of popular culture and everyday life and to recognize the close connection between representational practices and discourses of identity. This has included critical self-reflection on the ways humanist conceptions of selfhood and authenticity have helped to perpetuate the leftist romance with the working class. The intellectuals' infatuation with this modern version of the folk, or the people, has sometimes distracted from the constitutive power of language and the historical nature of the discourses of class. With these larger questions in mind, Gareth Stedman Jones in the 1980s became one of the first to examine the languages of class, recognizing that "consciousness cannot be related to experience except through the interpretation of a particular language which organizes the understanding of experience."²⁵

Williams's writings on working-class culture and what he calls structures of feelings have played a key role in the emergence of cultural studies. His contribution appeared in the tradition of socialist humanism against which Stedman Jones enlisted insights from the linguistic turn to shift the larger debates about class to questions of language and signification. But precisely through this embeddedness in an older tradition of socialism, Williams's notion of "struc-

---

23 Eric Hobsbawm, *How to Change the World: Reflections on Marx and Marxism* (New Haven, CT: Yale University Press, 2011), 265.
24 Edward Palmer Thompson, *The Making of the English Working Class* (New York: Vintage Books, 1966), 12.
25 Gareth Stedman Jones, *Languages of Class: Studies in English Working-Class History 1832– 1982* (Cambridge: Cambridge University Press, 1984), 101. On the discourse of class, also see Patrick Joyce, *Visions of the People: Industrial England and the Question of Class 1848–1914* (Cambridge: Cambridge University Press, 1991).

tures of feelings" can be used here to make sense of the growing opposition to emotional socialism during a crucial period in the history of German Social Democracy. Williams introduced the often-cited term as part of a fundamental reconsideration of the role of culture in forging identifications and attachments. Culture, he argues, must be seen as an expression of social relations. Not only are its forms and practices multiple and dialogic, they also belong to different social and historical formations that he calls residual, emergent, and dominant. Residual culture, in this context, refers to cultural traditions formed in the past, closely linked to older social formations, whereas emergent culture includes new forms and practices and the relationships established through them. Against a static conception that treats culture only in hegemonic and epochal terms, Williams's close attention to residual and emergent cultures (in the plural) brings out the dynamic, contested, and nonsynchronous qualities that, in the case of nineteenth-century working-class culture, are most evident in its heavy debts to older folk traditions and its close alliances with other emergent forms. The same relational qualities characterize dominant culture as an ongoing institutional and ideological project that, for the time period under consideration, must be located at the intersection of (bourgeois) high culture, national culture, and imperial culture.

It is as part of this ongoing struggle among residual, emergent, and dominant cultures that structures of feelings according to Williams acquire their all-important communicative functions as "meanings and values as they are actively lived and felt." These structures, he explains, establish internal relations and fluid processes in ways that defy existing conceptual binaries, namely as "not feeling against thought, but thought as felt and feeling as thought."[26] For Williams, the usefulness of this formulation as a cultural hypothesis lies in identifying social experiences in the state of becoming. In the context of this chapter, "structures of feeling" describes perfectly the individual experiences of political radicalization shared by many Social Democratic leaders, beginning with that transformative moment when the personal turns into the political. The discursive divisions enlisted to narrate this process of formation, including its own mechanisms of exclusion, are most apparent in the forms of gendering that imagine a socialist public sphere by converting feelings of weakness into feelings of strength and, in the process, purge all residues of emotional socialism. Sustained by the collective imaginaries and their theoretical foundations offered by the term "proletariat" analyzed in Chapter 2, socialist mobilization around the

---

[26] Williams, "Structures of Feeling," *Marxism and Literature* (Oxford: Oxford University Press, 1977) 132–133.

turn of the century can therefore be described as a process of masculinization, with pathos and sentiment increasingly seen as a threat to the proper balancing of "thought as felt and feeling as thought."

To summarize the points made thus far, political emotions perform their historically specific functions through culturally mediated processes of translation and transformation. One example, the conversion of individual suffering into collective indignation, can be used on the remaining pages to delineate how this process finds expression in a particular heroic narrative, namely that of Social Democratic self-sacrifice. A self-conscious emotion rather than a primary or even secondary one, self-sacrifice (just like self-discipline and self-restraint) can be described as the product of a continuous feedback loop between cognition and emotion along the lines of Williams's "feelings thought and thoughts felt." The willingness to sacrifice individual happiness for a larger cause and the steadfast belief in the rightness of this decision are only conceivable inside oppositional groups or milieus that offer a strong collective identity and provide emotional scripts that validate such sacrifices. The emotional scripts evoked by Bebel and others illustrate how Protestant notions of suffering and redemption and Prussian virtues such as duty, honor, and hard work could be claimed for socialist narratives. Allusions to a Protestant work ethic or to a Christian eschatology, for that matter, should not be read as proof that socialism functioned as little more than secular religion. On the contrary, the rewriting of the scripts of self-sacrifice in the languages of class, which invariably meant a process of masculinization, involved a profound change in the authorship, and hence ownership, of dominant discourse and implied dramatic challenges and changes to the power dynamics within Wilhelmine culture and society.

Read in this light, the confessions by party leaders about their very personal relationship to the party reveal a uniquely Social Democratic structure of feeling that revolves around the above-mentioned conversion of suffering into indignation and the transfiguration, to stay with Christian tropes, of indignation into sacrifice for the cause. In these new class-based narratives of sacrifice, moral righteousness joins forces with belief in certain victory, and a collective habitus of smugness sometimes finds cover under the Marxist rhetoric of historical inevitability. Not surprisingly, in the culture of Social Democracy, selflessness was highly valued and admired – in sharp contrast to any public expressions of envy and resentment. Even worse, hatred and rage, sometimes described as eruptive emotions, were strongly censored within the cultural traditions from which the workers' movement emerged, namely Protestantism and bourgeois humanism. Both subscribed to an ethos of civility and moderation and attributed special value to the cultivation of interiority. Meanwhile, political challenges to this Social Democratic culture of sacrifice, which usually included the demand for radical change, indirectly gave credence to the other workers' movements, especially anarcho-syndicalism, from which the SPD separated officially in the Second International, and cast doubt on the determinist view of history promoted in the name of scientific socialism.

The following examples serve to illustrate this close connection between the nineteenth-century habitus of self-sacrifice and moral judgment established in the name of Marxism and Social Democracy. During his 1872 trial for high treason, Wilhelm Liebknecht proudly declared: "I have never sought my own political advantage; whenever there was a choice between my interests and principles, I never hesitated to sacrifice my interests. If I am impoverished after outrageous harassments, there is no shame in it – no, I am proud of it, because it is the most telling testimony to my political honor."[27] At the 1890 party convention in Halle, he went on to formulate a general theory of socialism based on this practice of selflessness:

> Do we not have what accounts for the power of religion, namely belief in the highest ideals? Does socialism not represent the highest morality: selflessness, sacrifice, and love of humanity? [...] During the years of the Anti-Socialist Laws we happily made the greatest sacrifice [...] simply to serve the cause. In that sense it was religion, [...] the religion of humankind. It was the belief in the victory of everything good and of the idea: the unshakeable conviction and the steadfast belief that justice must triumph and injustice disappear. We will never lose this religion because it is one with socialism.[28]

Liebknecht invokes the ethos of individual sacrifice to present socialism as the legitimate heir of religion, an argument that confirms his intellectual and emotional formation in the nineteenth century. In so doing, he also showcases the virtue of humility and the ethos of suffering, including their transformative effects. How this religious language sometimes acquired a more ecstatic tone can be seen in a contribution by Emil Barth (1879–1941), a metalworker turned council member, who was inspired by the revolutionary months in 1918/19 to call for an authentically Christian solidarity

> not only anchored in the minds, but also in the hearts, the kind of solidarity that alone entitles a man to call himself a socialist, that with awareness and joy propels him to move

---

27 Quoted in Wilhelm Liebknecht, *Sein Leben und Wirken*, ed. Kurt Eisner, second enlarged edition (Berlin: Vorwärts, 1906), 75.
28 Wilhelm Liebknecht, "Protokoll über die Verhandlungen des Parteitages des Sozialdemokratischen Partei Deutschlands, Halle an der Saale, 12–18 October 1890," quoted in Brigitte Emig, *Die Veredelung des Arbeiters: Sozialdemokratie als Kulturbewegung* (Frankfurt am Main: Campus, 1980), 94.

beyond the fundamental truth of Christianity, "Love your neighbor as yourself," and allows him to adopt the maxim "Love your neighbor more than yourself." An organization filled with this spirit, but only this spirit, is the ultimate goal of the proletariat.[29]

There is plenty of evidence that Social Democrats recognized emotions as a powerful source of proletarian identifications and socialist commitments. Nonetheless, they often did so with great ambivalence, aware that emotions could never be separated from representations and, by extension, the ideological formations that gave rise to them in the first place. During the Weimar Republic, this meant simultaneously drawing on and downplaying the Christian language of suffering and redemption. It meant distinguishing socialist models of collective organization and class solidarity from the hallucination of the modern masses as the absolute other of bourgeois society – in other words, as uncontrollable and unpredictable. Above all, after the cataclysms of war and revolution, dealing with the legacies of emotional socialism meant drawing a clear line between the prewar Social Democrats – creatures entirely of the nineteenth century – and the younger generations of activists politicized through the October Revolution. On the one hand, the desire for emotional renewal continued to find expression in calls for a socialist morality that anticipated a classless society through its spiritual values. It was with that goal that journalist Georg Ledebour (1850–1947) at the 1922 USPD party convention implored fellow socialists that, "we cannot limit ourselves to the economic and political struggle but must carry out a revolution within ourselves that allows the people to leave behind the age of exploitation, whose final phase we are now experiencing, and turn themselves into the ideal people of the future."[30] On the other hand, the need to develop more effective strategies of mass mobilization, whether through the community building activities favored by the cultural socialists or the agitprop methods promoted by the Communists, injected a decidedly pragmatic tone into the continuing debates about proletarian identifications. KPD chief ideologue Clara Zetkin (1857–1933) acknowledged the depth of suffering among the workers, conceding that, "they are not just intent on filling their bellies; no, the best among them are searching for release from deepest spiritual torment." But above all, she was eager to instrumentalize these emotional needs in the larger fight against capitalism and fascism; her recommendation: "We must compel every proletarian

---

[29] Emil Barth, *Aus der Werkstatt der deutschen Revolution* (Berlin: A. Hoffmann, 1919), 6.
[30] Georg Ledebour, Speech during USPD party congress in Leipzig, 1922, quoted by Emig, *Veredelung*, 12.

to believe: I make a difference. Without me things don't work out. I have to be part of this. Victory is mine."[31]

Notwithstanding the existence of a uniquely German culture of sentimentality and self-sacrifice, the actual transformation of the working class into an emotional community rarely followed the proposals laid out by SPD politicians or leftwing intellectuals and encountered its most stubborn obstacles in the form of private life and individual desire. One of the first to acknowledge this nonidentity of collective and individual subjectivity was Karl Renner (1870–1950), the father of Austrian Social Democracy and first chancellor of the Republic of Austria after World War I. "The worker is above all a social being, a man of his class," he agreed, "Nonetheless, he never ceases to be a private being. Too often, it is overlooked that a crowd cannot constantly and without pause be held under the pressure of class ideology. Every worker demands the right and the possibility to feel, at least occasionally, as if he is a private being."[32]

Unwilling to address the unresolved question of the individual in modern societies, whether capitalist or socialist, Weimar-era Social Democrats eventually jettisoned the emotional and aesthetic baggage of nineteenth-century socialism, including its cult of male sentimentality, and either focused on organizational, tactical questions related to party politics or retreated to the very different emotional world created by the cultural socialists through their cult of community. In unexpected ways, even the leftwing intellectuals associated with the newly founded Frankfurt-based Institute for Social Research remained highly ambivalent about the role of political emotions, and that despite their short-lived theoretical romance with messianism and insurrectionism. Demonstrating the usefulness of emotions as a category of distinction, the philosopher Ernst Bloch perceptively identified two variants within Marxism, a cold and a warm stream, and made a compelling argument for a successful socialist praxis based on revolutionary passions and sustained by a Marxist metaphysics not hostile to religious traditions.[33] But even those arguing in favor of emotions as a productive force in emancipatory politics could be quite dismissive when it came to the wrong emotions. Thus in his evocative reflections on the concept of history, Walter Benjamin used his palpable contempt for Social Democrats and brief infatuation with the Communists to conclude that, "Social Democracy sought to assign

---

31 Clara Zetkin, "Der Kampf gegen den Faschismus" (1923), reprinted in *Ausgewählte Reden und Schriften*, 2 vols. (Berlin: Dietz, 1960), 2: 724 and 728.
32 Karl Renner, *Was ist Klassenkampf?* (Berlin: Vorwärts, 1919), 9.
33 Ernst Bloch, *The Principle of Hope*, trans. Neville Plaice, Stephen Plaice, and Paul Knight, 2 vols. (Cambridge, MA: MIT Press, 1995), 1: 205.

to the working class the role of redeemer of future generations. [...] This training made the working class forget both its hatred and its spirit of sacrifice, for both are nourished by the image of enslaved ancestors rather than of liberated grandchildren."[34] In rather predictable ways, his endorsement during the 1930s of an empowering, liberating hatred ends up projecting the failures of the Weimar left back onto the contradictions of bourgeois humanism and German Protestantism and finds emotional release only in the desperate actionism and decisionism shared at the time by leftwing and rightwing groups.

Histories of modern Germany describe the SPD as the "first true mass political party in modern history."[35] As this chapter has shown, it also was the first social movement to recognize the role of emotion in politics and use associational structures to at once organize emotional attachments and work through the inevitable contradictions. Much of this emotional labor was focused on the production of (the image of) a unified working class out of its actual differences and divisions. Here it warrants repeating that the socialist lifeworld was not the same as the working class, given the continued influence of the Catholic and Protestant Churches, the significance of local and regional networks and traditions, and the enduring influence of the guild system. The focus on the industrial proletariat in party programs and initiatives meant that the perspectives represented by artisans, craftsmen, and skilled laborers, as well as members of the rural proletariat were neglected, if not ignored. Despite inroads made by the proletarian women's movement, the culture of Social Democracy showed little interest in the woman's question and problems of family life. And despite growing numbers of female workers, the workers' movement remained male-dominated and male-

---

[34] Walter Benjamin, "On the Concept of History," *Selected Writings, Vol. 4: 1938–1940*, ed. Howard Eiland and Michael W. Jennings (Cambridge: Harvard University Press, 2006), 389–400.
[35] Andrew Bonnell, *The People's Stage in Imperial Germany: Social Democracy and Culture 1890–1914* (London: Tauris, 2005), 1. For historical overviews of Social Democracy and German communism, see Gary Steenson, *"Not One Man! Not One Penny!" German Social Democracy, 1863–1914* (Pittsburgh: University of Pittsburgh Press, 1981); Wilhelm L. Guttsman, *The German Social Democratic Party, 1875–1933* (London: Allen & Unwin, 1981); and Richard Saage, ed., *Solidargemeinschaft und Klassenkampf. Politische Konzeptionen der Sozialdemokratie zwischen den Weltkriegen* (Frankfurt am Main: Suhrkamp, 1986). For more recent studies, Eric D. Weitz, *Creating German Communism, 1890–1990: From Popular Protests to Socialist State* (Princeton: Princeton University Press, 1997) and, with David E. Barclay, eds., *Between Reform and Revolution: German Socialism and Communism from 1840 to 1990* (New York: Berghahn, 1998); Thomas Welskopp, *Das Banner der Brüderlichkeit: Die deutsche Sozialdemokratie vom Vormärz bis zum Sozialistengesetz* (Bonn: Dietz, 2000); Stefan Berger, *Social Democracy and the Working Class in Nineteenth and Twentieth Century Germany* (New York: Longman, 2000); and Ralf Hoffrogge, *Sozialismus und Arbeiterbewegung in Deutschland: Von den Anfängen bis 1914* (Stuttgart: Schmetterling, 2011).

oriented. To the Anti-Socialist Laws, as well as other laws limiting the right of free assembly and association, Social Democrats responded with the founding of seemingly apolitical clubs and associations where socialist ideas could continue to thrive. These external pressures may have been a factor in the emergence of the party's bureaucratic structure, institutional hierarchies, and what is sometimes dismissively called *Vereinsmeierei* (clubbishness); but they do not fully explain its locally based and socially validated culture of homosociality. The lifeworld of associations, clubs, anniversaries, festivities, rituals, and symbols continued to thrive after the oppressive Anti-Socialist Laws were allowed to lapse in 1890, and the workers' emotional attachment to party and movement inspired ever more examples of socialist kitsch, from plaques, banners, steins, to proletarian pictures of the saints (see figures 3.1 and 3.2).

Fig 3.1. Wilhelm Liebknecht, August Bebel, Ferdinand Lassalle, et al., "Die Befreier des Proletariats/The Liberators of the Proletariat, 1863–1913," 50-Year Celebration of the Founding of the SPD 1913, postcard. With permission of Archiv der sozialen Demokratie der Friedrich-Ebert-Stiftung.

Fig 3.2. August Bebel, "'Ich hämmre jung das alte morsche Ding den Staat./I Am Hammering that Old Decrepit Thing Called the State,' Gruß zur Maifeier!/May Day Greetings," postcard, c. 1905. With permission of Archiv der sozialen Demokratie der Friedrich-Ebert-Stiftung.

The proletarian lifeworld consisted of three distinct but related milieus, the political party, the labor unions, and the various *Genossenschaften* (associations, cooperatives), with the relationships among these "three pillars" of socialism subject to ongoing negotiations and competing critical assessments. As expected, these assessments include the contested role of emotions and can be used on the remaining pages to establish political emotions as an integral part even of the history of Social Democratic organizations and institutions. Historical accounts especially from the post-World War II period tend to reproduce the disparagement of emotional socialism that, since the 1890s, had been closely tied to the question of masculinity – first by defining a space for the expression of male suffering and indignation and, later, as a liability in the pursuit of more heroic and militant scenarios of class struggle. Here the recollections by Austrian-American Joseph Buttinger (1906–1992) offer a good summary of the prevailing patterns of interpretation emerging during the Cold War. Implying that political emotions are inseparable from totalitarian tendencies, the former SPÖ politician in exile assumed a sentimental and slightly condescending tone as he recalled his own political past in 1951:

> For tens of thousands [i.e., of socialists], party work was a self-evident duty, gladly performed. The very annoyance attached to all social activities seemed to tie them to it. Often – in choir singing, at giant rallies of the party, in admiring their leaders, and under the magic spell of the great incantations of their world struggle for freedom – they had lost their own sense of insignificance. A wonderful, self-surrendering mood seized them and lent them a greater dignity, more self-assurance, more courage, and a stronger socialist faith. Those were the hours of their ultimate bliss – and of the knowledge that all beauty in their lives came from the better sentiments that had brought them to the socialist movement. There, by their unselfish, satisfying endeavors, they were tied up with greater ends – with the harmony the party preached between their daily political activities and a higher destination of man. To lose the party was nothing less to them than to lose home, fatherland, and religion.[36]

According to Buttinger's description, associational life provided a social context, a lifeworld, and above all, an emotional community held together by a "wonderful, self-surrendering mood." Promising "a whole way of life,"[37] to use Williams's famous formulation, culture functioned as an important building block in the

---

36 Joseph Buttinger, *In the Twilight of Socialism: A History of the Revolutionary Socialists of Austria*, trans. E. B. Ashton (New York: Praeger, 1953), 67. Some of these characterizations may be more typical of Austrian than German Social Democracy, a point that cannot be pursued any further in this context.
37 Raymond Williams, "Culture," in *Keywords: A Vocabulary of Culture and Society*, rev. ed. (New York: Oxford University Press, 1983), 87–93.

imagination of the revolutionary working class. Notwithstanding his own emotional ambivalence, Buttinger's descriptions bear witness to the "structures of feeling" that constituted working-class culture as a social experience at a particular historical conjuncture. His ironic references to "self-evident duty" and "ultimate bliss" suggest that strong emotions in mass movements should always be seen as problematic – a conclusion that may reflect his personal response to the averted threat of National Socialism and the new danger of world communism and that would not have been shared by Williams writing about working class and emotions around the same time. Furthermore, Buttinger's allusion to the workers' emotional dependency on the Social Democratic lifeworld, with the destruction of its institutions by the Nazis likened to a complete loss of self, serves to validate liberal democracy as a superior form of government based on rational self-interest and to downplay the historical continuities between socialism and National Socialism. Last but not least, the comparisons with "faith" and "religion" may recall the language of the early socialists but are added here to diagnose the failure of all collectivist ideologies – except, of course, for the ideology of Americanism. Buttinger's conclusion that nothing poses a greater threat to the wellbeing of mankind than "the magic spell" of ideology, and nothing is more important to the future of democracy than the protection of individual and society from political emotions of any kind can be read as a final and conclusive break with the legacies of emotional socialism. However, the overdetermined status of emotions in his descriptions of Wilhelmine Social Democracy suggests that emotions, especially in the context of collective identifications, remain an unsettling presence even in the most insistent arguments for individualism. With these historical continuities in mind, including in assessments that have become historical themselves, the next chapter on choral singing returns to one of the founding sites of emotional socialism and offers the first of several case studies that examine how symbolic (here: musical) practices at once relied on, and contributed to, the imagination of the proletariat as an emotional community.

Chapter 4
On Workers Singing in One Voice

> Nothing brings the hearts and minds of a large group of people together more deeply and strongly [than when] they, filled by one and the same feeling and thinking, give voice to their overflowing hearts in univocal songs.
>
> Manfred Wittich

There are few cultural practices that attest to the emotional basis of proletarian identifications as powerfully as the act of singing in unison and, in the process, finding a voice and claiming a name – whether as worker, working man, or proletarian. And there few traditions that show the close connection between political and musical practices as clearly as the workers' choral societies that formed during the second half of the nineteenth century and became an integral part of German working-class life, including on the long routes of exile and immigration that often ended in the Americas.

In the following chapter, the crucial role of workers' songs in the making of proletarian identifications will be reconstructed through the relationship to older folk and bourgeois musical traditions. Especially the workers' choice of songs and ways of singing, including the univocal plainsong hailed by the socialist writer Manfred Wittich (1851–1902) as an expression of class unity, can be used productively as both an entry point into the musical culture of the working class and a first indication of the conceptual difficulties in gaining access to its underlying emotional energies.[1] Any critical reconstruction of the musical articulation of political and aesthetic emotions, after all, needs to take into account two complicating factors, the connection between choral singing and working-class masculinity and, closely related, the competition between two models of sociability, the workers' choral movement and the Social Democratic Party. The very different assessments in the scholarship of choral societies as either a powerful tool of class formation or an apolitical form of social recreation suggests that the derogatory comments already by contemporaries about "a new sacrament of social communality (*Gottesdienst socialer Gemütlichkeit*)"[2] cannot

---

1 Manfred Wittich, quoted in Inge Lammel, ed., *Arbeiterlied—Arbeitergesang. Hundert Jahre Arbeitermusikkultur in Deutschland* (Berlin: Hentrich & Hentrich, 2002), 119–120.
2 Ferdinand Gregorovius, quoted in James Garratt, *Music, Culture and Social Reform in the Age of Wagner* (Cambridge: Cambridge University Press, 2010), 200. Gregorovius was a nineteenth-century German historian.

be dismissed as mere antisocialist prejudice. Closely related, the workers' choral societies bring into sharp relief the historical affinities of socialism with what this book calls cultural nationalism – that is, the cultivation (or invention) of national traditions by diverse social groups specifically during periods of emergence and the central role of writers, artists, and composers in inventing nation-based models of community, often prior to national unification or liberation.[3] Through the notion of *Volkssele* (folk soul), Herder laid the foundation for the equation of nation with folk, including in ethnic and linguistic terms. He also established the philological practices that made collecting and cataloging the myths, tales, legends, and songs of a thus defined people a key component in the narrativization of a nation's mythical past and heroic future. The nineteenth-century workers' movement shows that oppositional cultures and social movements could be fully compatible with emerging discourses of cultural nationalism, especially through their selective appropriation of folk traditions and bourgeois forms for the larger project of political emancipation. The dependency of cultural nationalism on gendered constructions of national identity must be treated as an integral part in this complicated process; the same can be said about the centrality of emotions in negotiating the meaning of tradition and modernity in the making of the proletarian dream.

The musical contributions to the discourses of folk, nation, and class have complicated historical assessments of the workers' choral movement and, more generally, working-class culture, around the following problematics: First, no cultures are authentic in the sense claimed by their proponents, although many rely on myths of authenticity to assert their legitimacy. Second, all cultures develop by appropriating existing traditions and conventions and by making them their own; this includes the moments of cultural contact and exchange across national borders. Third, cultural practices exist within hierarchies of power and under conditions of cultural hegemony. The resultant strategies of emulation, affirmation, denunciation, and exclusion are always socially defined, politically mediated, and historically situated. For all these reasons, workers' choral singing cannot be reduced to its aspirational, agitational, com-

---

[3] For studies on cultural nationalism, see F. M. Barnard, *Herder on Nationality, Humanity, and History* (Montreal: McGills-Queen's University Press, 2003), and, beyond the German context, Anthony D. Smith, *The Cultural Foundations of Nations: Hierarchy, Covenant, and Republic* (London: Wiley-Blackwell, 2008) and John Hutchinson, *The Dynamics of Cultural Nationalism: The Gaelic Revival and the Creation of the Irish Nation-State* (London: Routledge, 1987). On the connection between cultural nationalism and mass movements, see George L. Mosse, *The Nationalization of the Masses: Political Symbolism and Mass Movements in Germany from the Napoleonic Wars through the Third Reich* (New York: H. Fertig, 1975).

municative, or compensatory functions and, without further qualification, be praised for its radicalizing impact on the working class or dismissed as a substitute for political radicalism. Performative and associational practices shed light not only on the strong connection between musical culture and political emancipation but also on the normative definitions that, time and again, equate working-class identity with traditional masculinity. The same can be concluded about the ways in which choral singing, through its heavy debt to folk and regional culture, reproduces traditional forms of sociability, community, and public life in dialogue with decidedly modern forms of populism and popularity.

Conceived as an alternative to bourgeois musical culture and its class-based institutions, workers' choral societies were founded, quite literally, to give a voice to the working class and advance the goals of the socialist movement. They exerted their greatest influence during the years of the Anti-Socialist Laws and reached their highest numbers during the Weimar Republic. Performing during the annual May Day celebrations, appearing at party events and public parades, and belonging to the local networks of voluntary associations and civic organizations, these choral societies played a key role in the establishment of what has been described as an oppositional or alternative public sphere. With names such as "Hope," "Dawn," "Unity," "Freedom," and "Fraternity," the choral societies during the 1870s provided a safe space for the expression of socialist ideas outside the traditional channels of labor activism and party politics. They fulfilled all these various social, cultural, and political functions by drawing on the rich nineteenth century traditions that established music as a driving force in the making of German national identity in the context of high culture and reproduced these connections in the practices of popular culture.[4]

Combining old tunes with new texts, workers' songs openly attacked the institutions of class society, railed against exploitative labor conditions, and expressed the depths of working-class suffering. In their fight against class oppression, they emphasized the importance of freedom, justice, and equality and promoted the values of unity and solidarity. Their lyrics acknowledged the workers' hopelessness and despair but, through appeals to historical precursors, also modeled new forms of emotional resilience. Essential to the imagination of the proletariat as an emotional community, choral singing offered a performative solution to individual experiences of defeat and promised musical relief in moments of doubt and resignation. By displacing present struggles into precapitalist times and by conjuring blissful, idyllic socialist futures, workers' songs also

---

[4] On this point, see Celia Applegate and Pamela Potter, eds., *Music and German National Identity* (Chicago: University of Chicago Press, 2002).

performed more problematic compensatory functions. Choral leaders frequently argued over the competing demands of artistic quality and political aspiration and tried to resist the corruption of the proletarian dream by reactionary discourses of nation and people (or folk). What some socialist leaders saw as self-affirmation, others criticized as self-segregation. The frequent accusation that workers' choral societies existed in competition with the socialist movement can be traced through the most recent scholarly debates over their (a)political nature – reason enough to take a closer look at the collective emotions and imaginaries produced through choral singing.[5]

Musically, workers' song developed as a hybrid form, with the typical repertoire consisting of revolutionary anthems, traditional folk songs, church hymns, and bourgeois *Kunstlieder* (art songs). Religion remained an important reference point in the language of suffering and salvation that allowed worker poets to imagine the proletariat as a Christ-like figure distinguished, in the words of one song, by "your crown of thorns." Choral singing drew rich inspiration from oral traditions and local customs, prompting SPD politician Emanuel Wurm (1857–1920) to declare, "the folksong of our times is the workers' song."[6] While *Vormärz* writers and worker poets provided the revolutionary messages, the tunes usually came from folkloric, patriotic, and religious songs. The substitution of one text by another, known as *contrafactum* in vocal music and examined here as an example of the widespread socialist practice of appropriation and refunctionalization, often involved dramatic shifts in the discursive field: from sacred to profane, or from reactionary to progressive.

Bourgeois conventions of public sentimentality are most noticeable in the songs' abundant nature metaphors: the ubiquitous rays of sun, dawns of day, and storms of revolution. Meanwhile middle-class forms of sociability, including the conviviality of student fraternities, influenced the singing and drinking rituals perfected in the corner pubs of working-class neighborhoods. Workers' choral societies drew heavily on the traditions established by various trades and crafts and identified with specific regions and ethnic groups. The discovery during the romantic movement of the "authentic" voice of the folk and the emphasis

---

[5] See Severin Caspari, "'Wann wir schreiten Seit an Seit'. Zur mythenbildenden Kraft des Arbeiterliedes für die SPD," in *Mythen, Ikonen, Märtyrer. Sozialdemokratische Geschichten*, ed. Franz Walter and Felix Butzlaff (Berlin: Vorwärts, 2013), 223–238.
[6] Emanuel Wurm, quoted in Lammel, *Arbeiterlied—Arbeitergesang*, 133. The continuities between folk song and workers' song are evident in the collection put together by Wolfgang Steinitz and republished in *Der große Steinitz. Deutsche Volkslieder demokratischen Charakters aus sechs Jahrhunderten* (Frankfurt am Main: Zweitausendeins, 1983).

on musical education in the bourgeois public sphere profoundly influenced the conception of the workers' chorus as a model of community and class. Significantly, this collective body was imaginable only in all-male terms and required the equation of the male voice with the universal position. Historians have documented the contribution of women's choruses and mixed choruses to the workers' choral movement and argued for the importance of amateur choral singing.[7] However, the existence of songs that thematize the exclusion of women suggests that workers' choral societies may have continued to thrive in the twentieth century partly because of their affirmation of the workers' movement as a homosocial milieu.

Songs and anthems accompanied the socialist movement from the beginning and contributed greatly to its internationalist orientation and transnational reach. "The Workers' Marseillaise" (1864, lyrics Jacob Audorf) and "The Internationale" (1871, lyrics Eugène Pottier) established the French revolutionary tradition, including the *chant des ouvriers* (workers' song), as an important influence.[8] Workers' choral societies thrived in Austria and Switzerland and played a long-recognized role in German immigrant communities in the United States, especially in Chicago.[9] Proudly local in their musical commitments, individual societies celebrated the differences between, say, miners in the Ruhr region, textile workers in Saxony, and dockworkers in Hamburg.[10] In accordance with the

---

[7] See Karen Ahlquist, "Men and Women of the Chorus: Music, Governance, and Social Models in Nineteenth-Century German-Speaking Europe," in *Chorus and Community*, ed. Karen Ahlquist (Urbana: University of Illinois Press, 2006), 265–292.

[8] For comparative studies, see William Koehler, *The Politics of Singing: The German Workers' Choral Association in Comparative Perspective* (Saarbrücken: Lambert, 2011) and Axel Körner, *Das Lied von einer anderen Welt. Kulturelle Praxis im französischen und deutschen Arbeitermilieu 1840–1890* (Frankfurt am Main: Campus, 1997). On the connection between musical culture and working-class masculinity in Britain, also see Denise Odello, "Musical Athleticism: Victorian Brass Band Contests and the Shaping of Working-Class Men," *Nineteenth Century Contexts: An Interdisciplinary Journal* 38.2 (2016): 141–154.

[9] See the songs reprinted in Hartmut Keil and John B. Jentz, eds., *German Workers in Chicago: A Documentary History of Working-Class Culture from 1850 to World War I* (Chicago: University Illinois Press, 1988), 331–336.

[10] On the role of workers' choral societies in regional culture, see Antoinette Hellkuhl, *Empor zum Licht. Arbeitergesangvereine im westfälischen Ruhrgebiet, 1878–1914* (Stuttgart: Bertold Marohl, 1983); Margret Tewes, *Bochumer Arbeitersänger vor 1933* (Bochum: Arbeitskreis Arbeitende Jugend, 1985); and Paul Pach, *Arbeitergesangvereine in der Provinz: "Vorwärts" Pirkensee und "Volkschor" Maxhütte* (Berlin: Tesdorpf, 1987). On the early period, see Bettina Hitzer, *Schlüssel zweier Welten. Politisches Lied und Gedicht von Arbeitern und Bürgern 1848–1875* (Bonn: Friedrich-Ebert-Stiftung, 2001), online at http://library.fes.de/fulltext/historiker/01141toc.htm, 1 March 2017.

competing perspectives on the socialist heritage during the Cold War, GDR musicologists have claimed the history of workers' choral societies for a German socialist master narrative, while West German scholars have favored (nostalgic) regionalist perspectives, especially after the demise of the Ruhr steel and coal industries.[11] However, most scholars today agree that poetry, considered the literary form most conducive to expressions of (national) identity in the so-called *Vormärz* period, the years leading up to the 1848 March Revolution, provided the worker's choral societies with a medium of enunciation ideally suited for shifting the very terms of articulation from bourgeois to proletarian identifications.

After the nationalistic Wars of Liberation against Napoleon and the German Revolution of 1848, poetry had emerged as the preferred genre for giving voice to long-simmering feelings of injustice and growing demands for recognition. Quickly memorized, easily recited, and widely distributed, poems forged meaningful connections between collective emotions and social movements. Establishing the workers as the main subject of political poetry was considered instrumental to a transformative process that required the reinscription of private feeling into collective expressions of class, folk, and community. Some contemporaries described this process through the image of an overflowing heart. In the words of one observer, the socialist poets wanted only "to give voice to all the sadness, all the joy that accompanied the proletarian struggle for liberation throughout its various phases and to relieve the heart of the surfeit of emotions threatening to burst open the chest."[12]

The poetry of the *Vormärz*, especially the songs inspired by the 1844 Silesian Weavers Uprisings, provided an influential emotional and agitational model for the early worker's movement. Eventually, the demands for freedom and justice by a broadly defined *Kampfdichtung* (agitational poetry) gave way to a more explicit emphasis on the working class as a historical subject and subject of history.[13] In "Hunger Song" (1844), one of the earliest instantiations of such an antag-

---

11 For an early GDR study, see Arno Kapp, *Vom Gesang der Handwerksgesellen zum ersten deutschen Arbeitergesangverein unter Bebel* (Halle: Mitteldeutscher Verlag, 1950). On the reception of workers' musical culture in the socialist press, see Werner Kaden, *Signale des Aufbruchs. Musik im Spiegel der "Roten Fahne"* (Berlin: Verlag Neue Musik, 1988). For a historiography of this important part of the socialist heritage, see Inge Lammel and Ilse Schütte, eds., *Hundert proletarische Balladen, 1842–1945* (Berlin: Verlag Tribüne, 1985).
12 Anon., quoted in Peter Kiefer, *Bildungserlebnis und ökonomische Bürde. Franz Mehrings historische Strategie einer Kultur des Proletariats* (Frankfurt am Main: Peter Lang, 1986), 124.
13 The most extensive collection is *Deutsche Arbeiter-Dichtung. Eine Auswahl Lieder und Gedichte deutscher Proletarier*, 5 vols. (Stuttgart: Dietz, 1893). The five volumes feature works by 1: Walter Hasenclever, K. E. Frohme und Adolph Lepp; 2: Jacob Audorf; 3: In Reih und Glied. Gedichte von einem Namenlosen; 4: Max Kegel; and 5: Andreas Scheu.

onistic "we," Georg Weerth (1822–1856) recounts shared experiences of starvation before he ends with an open political threat: "Otherwise we pack up on Sundays,/ and devour you, oh king."[14] Heinrich Heine (1797–1856), in "The Poor Weavers" (1844), uses the pronoun "we" in a similarly confrontational way: first by declaring, with growing intensity that, "We're weaving! We're weaving!" and then, instead of resorting to tears or pleas, placing a curse on God, king, and fatherland: "Old Germany, we are weaving your funeral shroud./ We're weaving, we're weaving!"[15] The "we" took an even more class-specific turn in the figure of the "proletarian machinist" who, in "Up from Below!" (1846) by Ferdinand Freiligrath (1810–1876), threatens to overthrow the existing order.[16] Two models of history, with the one implying eternal, immutable laws and with the other emphasizing individual agency, henceforth informed the appeal to the revolutionary working class. Johann Christian Lüchow in "The Proletariat" of 1848 describes the rise of the working class as part of a natural history, a spring awakening: "Swelling and sprouting from below/ like an early seeded crop./ It grows well out of the soil,/ the proletariat!"[17] By contrast, Georg Herwegh (1817–1875) in the 1863 "Bundeslied for the ADAV," the precursor of the SPD, presents the struggle between labor and capital in explicitly socialist terms and concludes with an empowering message to the workers: "Man of labor, awaken!/ And recognize your power!/ All the wheels will stand still,/ if this is the will of your strong arm."[18]

The proliferation of workers' choral societies can be measured by the countless songbooks published in the years that followed, from Adolf Strodtmann's *Die Arbeiterdichtung in Frankreich* (1863, Workers' Poetry in France) to Johann Most's *Proletarier-Liederbuch* (1873, Proletarian Songbook) to Carl Hoym's *Proletarier singe! Kampf- und Volkslieder* (1919, Proletarian, Sing!) to Edwin Hoernle's *Rote Lieder* (1924, Red Songs). These collections not only attest to the changing composition of the working class and its political organizations from *Vormärz* craftsmen's associations to Weimar-era communist groups. The songbooks' re-

---

[14] Georg Weerth, "Hungerlied," online at https://de.wikisource.org/wiki/Das_Hungerlied, 1 March 2017. Weerth wrote for Marx's *Neue Rheinische Zeitung*.
[15] Heinrich Heine, "Die armen Weber," online at https://de.wikisource.org/wiki/Die_armen_Weber, 1 March 2017.
[16] Ferdinand Freiligrath, "Von unten auf," online at http://gutenberg.spiegel.de/buch/ferdinand-freiligrath-gedichte-5009/33, 1 March 2017.
[17] Johann Christian Lüchow, "Das Proletariat," reprinted in Lammel and Schütt, *Hundert proletarische Balladen 1842–1945*, 22.
[18] "Arbeiterlied" (lyrics: Georg Herwegh), in *Most's Proletarier-Liederbuch*, ed. Gustav Geilhof, 5th ed. (Chemnitz: G. Rübner und Co., 1875), 4. Different versions (here: from the third edition of 1873) are added in parentheses.

vised and expanded editions also register changing views of the proletariat's role in the competing political projects of revolution and reform, a point illustrated best by Most's immensely popular *Proletarian Songbook*. Most (1846–1906), a journeyman bookbinder turned socialist author/activist, served as a SPD member of the Reichstag during the 1870s and died as an anarchist in American exile. He contributed several of his own songs to the collection, with the best-known "Arbeitsmänner" (Workingmen) written during his imprisonment for high treason.

Of special relevance to this discussion on cultural appropriation, Most's *Proletarian Songbook* contains several typical examples of *contrafactum* – parodies of militaristic and patriotic songs. The choice of names and the process of naming produce the intended liberating effects and involve declarative, imperative, as well as appellative modes of speaking. There are numerous references to proletarians, workers, working men, men of labor, comrades, and brothers, with some songs changing titles in later editions (e.g., from "Worker Song" to "Proletarian Song"). A few examples may suffice to show the liberating effect of *contrafactum* on the emerging proletarian voice. Set to the Prussian patriotic hymn "Hail to Thee in Victor's Crown," "Appeal to the Workers" starts out with the demand "Workers, awaken all!" and ends with a call for class unity: "Go, you, oh fourth estate,/ true and strong,/ hand in hand,/ steadfast surge forward,/ to liberate yourself!"[19] "Proletarian Song," which turns the patriotic anthem "Watch on the Rhine" into a socialist battle song, calls on the workers to fight against tyranny. Its refrain offers only two available options for the future: "The red flag flies high:/ To live working or to die fighting!"[20] "Worker Choral," a parody of the eponymous choral by Martin Luther, starts out with the familiar "A mighty fortress is our God:/ the 'free spirit of truth!'" and, in the mocking spirit of the added scare quotes, ends with a clear warning to the ruling class that, "Your world of lies is collapsing!/ Finally, with confidence/ the people raise their voices/ for freedom, equality, and love!"[21]

Meanwhile, "The Song of the Shirt" about "the most magnificent, most beautiful attire" uses the fraternity song "Gaudeamus Igitur" to introduce the working-class subject through a distinctive piece of clothing, the collarless shirt worn by most industrial workers. In this socialist invitation to joyous conviviality, the all-important question of the *Kragenlinie* (collar line) allows one worker

---

19 "Aufruf an die Arbeiter" (tune: "Heil dir im Siegerkranz"), in *Most's Proletarier-Liederbuch*, 5–6. On Most, see Werner Hinze, *Johann Most und sein Liederbuch. Warum der Philosoph der Bombe Lieder schrieb und ein Liederbuch herausgab* (Hamburg: Tonsplitter, 2005).
20 "Proletarier-Lied" (tune: "Die Wacht am Rhein"), in *Most's Proletarier-Liederbuch*, 21.
21 "Arbeiter-Choral" (tune: "Ein feste Burg ist unser Gott"), in *Most's Proletarier-Liederbuch*, 45.

to declare his love to the simple shirt and, by extension, his class and conclude: "Thus, whether torn or mended,/ whether oily or sooty,/ with love my eyes always look/ upon my trusted blouse."[22] Pointing to more problematic patterns of cultural appropriation, "Come Join Us" bases its equation of mass mobilization with masculinization on Theodor Körner's patriotic poem "Arise People" from the Wars of Liberation. The opening lines "Ready for manly action and battle,/ we are seized by the vortex of time!" enthusiastically present class struggle in militaristic terms and thus establish a pattern that would continue in the musical soundtracks of two world wars: "Come join us, man for man,/ whoever can join the struggle for truth!"[23]

Two well-known songs from the Most collection shed further light on the empowering effects attributed to the very act of naming the working-class subject. "Die Arbeitsmänner" ("The Working Men"), originally called "Proletarian Song" and based on the Tyrolean patriotic hymn "At Mantua Bound," became the official hymn of the so-called Eisenacher, one of the two precursor parties of the SPD. The 1875 version opens with a set of probing questions:

> Who makes the gold?
> Who hammers ore and stone?
> Who weaves fabric and silk?
> Who plants corn and wine?
> Who gives the rich all their bread
> and at home lives in abject poverty?
> It is the working men,
> the proletariat ...

The ending offers the singers hope and confidence, with the differences in the earlier 1873 version shown in parenthesis:

> You have power in your hands
> if only you were united!
> Therefore, hold on to one another,
> and then you will soon be free!
> Do not tire in spiritual battle! (1873: Charge, on the double, into battle!)
> Even if the enemy libels you, (1873: Even if the enemy spews canister shots,)
> in the end, you working men will be victorious! The proletariat![24]

---

22 "Das Lied von der Blouse," in *Most's Proletarier-Liederbuch*, 37.
23 "Schließt Euch an" (tune: "Das Volk steht auf"), in *Most's Proletarier-Liederbuch*, 52.
24 "Die Arbeitsmänner" (tune: "Zu Mantua in Banden"), in *Most's Proletarier-Liederbuch*, 24–25. Andreas Hofer was the leader of the 1809 populist insurgency against the French occupation.

The even more famous "Arbeiter-Marseillaise" ("Workers' Marseillaise"), with lyrics by Jacob Audorf (1834–1898), was originally written for the ADAV and regularly performed at SPD party conventions; the author added a stanza to be sung at Lassalle's funeral in the same year. The 1864 version cited below is the original version inspired by Freiligrath's 1848 revolutionary song *Reveille*, with the later changes again given in parentheses. The second stanza is cited here because it includes a rare reference to the difficulties of proletarian mobilization. Perhaps to compensate for this, the revisions come with a more militant tone:

> The enemy that we hate the most,
> that surrounds us thick and black,
> it is the foolishness of the masses
> that can only be broken with the sword of the spirit.
> If we can overcome this obstacle,
> who would dare to resist us?
> Soon on all heights
> the banner of freedom will fly.
> In unity and strength, (1873: The new rebellion,)
> you free fraternity, (1873: The full rebellion,)
> stay firm! (1873: March! march!)
> say firm! (1873: March, march!)
> and do not sway! (1873: March, if need be, till death,)
> the slave shackle is breaking! (1873: for our flag is red!)[25]

As expressed openly in the lyrics, the main psychological function of choral singing was to promote unity, solidarity, and class pride, and to advance the cause of socialism. Through the rhetorical questions at the beginning ("Who makes/ hammers/ weaves?") the collective subject is invited to recognize the conditions of oppression and, at the same time, believe in the certainty of victory. Addressed to the audience and the chorus itself, admonitions such as "Stay firm!" or, in the later version, "March! March!" serve to strengthen commitment to the cause. Meanwhile, familiar symbols of oppression such as shackles and swords allow the workers to see their local battles as part of world historical struggles.

All of these encouragements required the careful management of emotions and attachments. If "the singing of authentic songs stimulate[d] and revive[d] the comrades' spirits and allowed them to contribute more actively to the task of political agitation,"[26] closer attention needs to be paid to the performative na-

---

[25] "Arbeiter-Marseillaise," in *Most's Proletarier-Liederbuch*, 41–42. A new verse was added after the death of Lassalle but not included in the various Most editions.
[26] Anon, cited by Hellkuhl, *Empor zum Licht*, 51.

ture of singing and its prefigurative function in the making of class identifications. In the context of nineteenth-century German culture, this means considering the role of aesthetic experience and aesthetic education in the sense defined by Friedrich Schiller. His reflections, in *Letters on the Aesthetic Education of Man* (1794), address most explicitly the inherent potential of aesthetic experiences to advance the process of social change and have been discussed extensively in relation to theater and literature. In fact, workers' choral singing offers an equally compelling model for the interrelatedness of aesthetic education and political mobilization. For Schiller, the demands of aesthetic autonomy and individual self-realization are inseparable, and in the form of moral cultivation, aesthetic cultivation becomes inextricably linked to social transformation – that is, the realization of shared human ideals. Schiller's original conception of the theater as a moral institution may have been developed with a view toward the enlightened elites, but it also draws on a retrospective conception of folk, producing contradictions that find foremost expression in the complicated status of aesthetic autonomy in the workers' movement. In the Social Democratic approach to culture and education discussed in chapter 8, the aesthetic is confirmed as a social category that, beyond individual works and authors, reinscribes the public nature of culture and foregrounds its potential as an agent of change. Through its communal and communicative qualities, the aesthetic continuously combines forms, genres, and styles, bringing together images and texts, originals and adaptations, and theories and fictions. In the process, aesthetic practices are turned into an experiential category that, instead of organizing the retreat from politics, facilitates their realignment in accordance with the interests of the working class. For the aesthetic, at least for Schiller, aims at engagement rather than detachment – a point recognized by several scholars who have studied workers' choral societies and their contribution to the historical alliance of German musical culture with oppositional politics.

In the most important work on the subject, musicologist James Garrett has examined the remarkable continuities of nineteenth-century musical culture from the fight for national unity and liberal democracy to the modern project of social reform and artistic innovation.[27] Bourgeois institutions, such as the musical societies known as *Singakademie* and various singing clubs called *Liederkranz*, provided important models for workers' choral societies through their use of associational life as a model of community or public sphere and their belief in the translatability of musical emotions into political emotions. For Garrett,

---

[27] For a good discussion of the workers' choral movement in the context of bourgeois musical culture, see Garratt, *Music, Culture and Social Reform in the Age of Wagner*, 197–215.

the productive reception of Schiller's ideas about aesthetic education is most evident in the politicization of music performance, strongly criticized from liberal and conservative perspectives, and in the democratization of musical culture and education in schools and communities. At the same time, the cult of the classics that inspired the 1927 Erfurt performance of Beethoven's "Ode to Joy," with one thousand workers singing on the occasion of the one hundredth anniversary of the composer's death, furthered a cult of musical genius that, according to Garrett, left little room for the cultivation of popular music as an egalitarian practice and contributed to later conflicts in the workers' choral movement.

Fig. 4.1 Bundesfest of the Arbeitersängerbund "Rheinland," Düsseldorf, 13–14 July 1908, postcard. With permission of Archiv der sozialen Demokratie der Friedrich-Ebert-Stiftung.

Fig. 4.2 Erstes Deutsches Arbeitersängerbundfest, Hannover, 16–18 June 1928, postcard. With permission of Historische Bildpostkarten, Universität Osnabrück Sammlung Prof. Dr. Sabine Giesbrecht.

Once again, the resulting musical and political conflicts and their impact on the proclamation of a proletarian "we" can be traced to the ideological divisions of the late Weimar Republic, with the development of competing emotional regimes easily equated with the cultural organizations of SPD and KPD. Conceived as an alternative to the bourgeois Deutsche Sängerbund (DSB, German Choral Society), the workers' choral societies had first joined forces in 1877 in the loosely structured Erste Allgemeine deutsche Arbeiter-Sängerbund (First General German Workers' Choral Society) and greatly expanded their numbers after the 1908 founding of the Deutsche Arbeiter-Sängerbund (DAS, German Workers' Choral Society). The DAS grew to more than two hundred thousand members during the 1920s and, after 1926, supported the professionalization of choral singing and musical education through the publication of the *Deutsche Arbeiter-Sänger Zeitung*. During that time, DAS conductor Alfred Guttmann (1891–1945) put together a vast collection of workers' songs and published widely available sheet music for men's, women's, and mixed choruses.²⁸ Through the inclusion of mass choruses in theatrical performances, choral singing became an integral part of various Weimar-era experiments with choral drama and mass cultural forms, including the *Sprechchor* movement discussed in chapter 12.²⁹ Meanwhile the DAS's 1928 Bundesfest in Hannover, which celebrated the workers' choral movement with posters, calendars, postcards, newsreels, and sound recordings, saw the first public eruptions of long-simmering tensions over the proper role of choral singing between political militancy and apolitical recreation (see figures 4.1 and 4.2).

The motto of the worker singers during the Weimar Republic may have been that "workers' song means class struggle."³⁰ Yet in many cases, this musical commitment to struggle amounted to little more than hollow phrases and clichés. The clubby atmosphere and quaint rituals cultivated by workers' choral societies and disparaged by many critics as provincial *Liedertafelei* (singsong joviality) proved increasingly unattractive to younger workers raised on new mass cultural diversions and interested in more forceful expressions of class pride. According to an article published in the KPD's *Rote Fahne*, the main goal of a new workers' choral movement spearheaded by the Communists was therefore to offer "proof of the cultural strength of the working class" and, in response to residual nationalist and *völkisch* influences, to liberate workers' songs "from the spirit of the people's community."³¹ Siegfried Günther, an influential music critic associated with DAS, promoted a closer alignment of choral singing with agitational efforts by calling for the development of a more combative, confrontational *Tendenzlied* (tendentious song). Based on the proper definitions of tendency and partiality that had preoccupied socialist critics since the prewar years, Günther described the tendentious song as "the manifestation of the emotional opposites found in the juxtaposition of matter and idea, of master and

---

28 Alfred Guttmann, *Chorsammlung des Deutschen Arbeiter-Sängerbundes* (Berlin: Verlag des DAS, 1926). Also see his *Gemischte Chöre ohne Begleitung* (Berlin: Verlag des DAS, 1926), with special volumes for tenor, bass, soprano, and alto voice. On the history of DAS, see Dietmar Klenke and Franz Walter, "Der Deutsche Arbeiter-Sängerbund bis 1933," in *Illustrierte Geschichte der Arbeiterchöre*, ed. Rainer Noltenius (Essen: Klartext, 1992), 54–64 and Dietmar Klenke, *Nationale oder proletarische Solidargemeinschaft? Geschichte der deutschen Arbeitersänger* (Heidelberg: Stiftung Reichspräsident-Friedrich-Ebert Gedenkstätte, 1995).
29 On the close connection between workers' music and theater, also see Dietmar Klenke et al., ed., *Arbeitersänger und Volksbühnen in der Weimarer Republik* (Bonn: Dietz, 1998).
30 Quoted by Rainer Stübling, *Kultur und Massen in Frankfurt: Das Kulturkartell der modernen Arbeiterbewegung in Frankfurt am Main von 1925 bis 1933* (Offenbach am Main: Saalbau, 1983), 28. The reference is to a 1929 article in *Volksstimme*.
31 Quoted in Kaden, *Signale des Aufbruchs*, 14.

slave, of individual and society, and hence of egoism [i.e., capitalism] and socialism. In this sense *bourgeois* means an emphasis on the *individual* personality and hence on class distinctions, against the *proletarian* accentuation of the *communal* elements." All aspects of choral singing were to reflect these ideological positions, with choral techniques "in the bourgeois context insisting on the individual personality, and hence the estate system, and with the proletarian context emphasizing the communal elements."[32] The decision by some choral directors to place less emphasis on vocal technique and instead focus on emotional expressivity can be interpreted as a logical extension of their primary goal of *Gemeinschaftsbildung* (community building).

Even if there existed wide agreement that the workers' chorus, in the words of Gustav William Meyer, gave voice to the spirit of class solidarity, the musical expression of this spirit could take classical or modernist forms and draw on pastoral or militant tones.[33] Gustav Adolf Uthmann (1867–1920), the conductor who wrote more than four hundred workers' songs, including the popular "Upward, to the Light," long dominated the repertoire with his classic-romantic melodies. Through the initiatives of the conductor Hermann Scherchen (1891–1966) and others, the workers' song movement during the 1920s slowly opened up to avant-garde and American influences, including jazz. Not surprisingly, discussions over the form and function of properly agitational workers' songs reflected growing musical schisms and emotional divides. The experiments with atonality by socialist composers associated with New Music and the agitational use of musical performances inspired by Proletkult only added to these difficulties of translating Marxist ideas into musical forms. The confrontational approach chosen by the KPD in close coordination with the Comintern eventually led to a series of splits within workers' theater and workers' sport associations, including in 1932 in the German Workers' Choral Society.

The Kampfgemeinschaft der Arbeitersänger (KdAS), the main product of that split, was founded as part of various initiatives for proletarian-revolutionary literature, theater, art, and film coordinated by the KPD and took the lead in articulating a more militant approach to choral music in its short-lived journal, appropriately called *Kampfmusik*; the close connections to agitprop will be discussed in greater detail in chapters 13 and 14. Presenting the official arguments for the "agitpropization" of workers' choruses, Alfréd Kemény (aka Durus) asked polemically: "Are our times of intensifying class conflicts to be rep-

---

[32] Siegfried Günther, *Kunst und Weltanschauung* (Berlin: Deutscher Arbeiter-Sängerbund, 1925), 10.
[33] Gustav William Meyer, "Gemeinschaftsfördernde Musik" and "Chorgesang und Klassenkampf," both in *Arbeiter-Sänger-Zeitung* 2 (1931): 26–30.

resented musically through harmony or disharmony, in simple unison folksong, or do they call for polyphonic composition principles?" Confronted with the false alternatives of reform and revolution, the class-conscious worker could find an answer only in the return to militant masculinity promised by the Communists; thus the motto had to be: "Down with tame-lame men's choruses! Down with that gossip hub and marriage bureau called mixed chorus!"[34]

One of the most influential voices in the project of agitpropization was the Austrian-born composer Hanns Eisler (1898–1962), who studied under Arnold Schönberg and worked closely with Bertolt Brecht. Eisler sought to break, once and for all, with the legacies of the bourgeois *Kunstlied*, including its conventional forms of sociability and offer an alternative to the pathos-laden, bombastic styles perfected by Uthmann. The workers' choruses, he argued, had been reduced to "a musical (performance) movement that cultivated a very backward, petty-bourgeois musical style, a sedate chumminess that actually made its members more apolitical and went hand in hand with a dreadful clubbiness."[35] According to Eisler, the typical *Tendenzlied*, the kind that relied heavily on *contrafactum*, combined revolutionary content with traditional musical styles and promoted passive listening rather than active engagement.[36] By contrast, the communist *Kampflied* (battle song or militant song), just like the *Kampfdichtung* promoted by KPD literary critics, was to mobilize the workers through what he called its "great comprehensibility, easy accessibility, and energetic, precise habitus"[37] and, in combination with short skits, profoundly change proletarian musical culture. Eisler's "Solidarity Song" from the 1932 *Kuhle Wampe* film, which will be examined in chapter 18, may not fit the definition of singing in one voice given at the beginning, but it certainly attests to the revolutionary energy behind any musical expression of "the same feeling and thinking." Despite considerable changes in the organizational structures and performance practices of

---

34 Durus, "Arbeitergesang und Agitprop," *Arbeiterbühne und Film* 3 (1931): 12 and 13.
35 Hanns Eisler, "Geschichte der deutschen Arbeitermusikbewegung von 1848," in *Musik und Politik. Schriften 1924–1948*, ed. Günter Mayer (Munich: Rogner & Bernard, 1973), 215. The importance of choral societies to the socialist movement is confirmed by a short article by Vladimir Ilyich Lenin, "The Development of Workers' Choirs in Germany," https://www.marxists.org/archive/lenin/works/1913/jan/03.htm, 1 March 2017.
36 Hanns Eisler, "Die Kunst als Lehrmeisterin im Klassenkampf," in *Musik und Politik. Schriften 1924–1948*, 120–129.
37 Hanns Eisler, "Unsere Kampfmusik" (1932), reprinted in Lammel, *Arbeiterlied—Arbeitergesang*, 130. The continuities between communist *Kampfmusik* in the late Weimar Republic and cultural leftism in the United States can be seen in Robbie Lieberman, *My Song Is My Weapon: People's Songs, American Communism, and the Politics of Culture, 1930–50* (Urbana: University of Illinois Press, 1989).

workers' choral societies, and despite sharp political divisions over their relationship to earlier discourses of folk and nation, working-class masculinity remained the ultimate reference point in all musical expressions of a collective "we," from the performances of sentimental masculinity in Wilhelmine Social Democracy to the habitus of militant masculinity in Weimar-era Communist agitprop. Even a cursory survey of existing choral societies (i.e., *Sängerrunden*) today, including in the centers of German immigration in the United States, would confirm that the historical connection between worker's movement and choral singing may have entirely disappeared from view; but the gendered nature of the chorus as a model of emotional community has survived even the end of traditional class society and the death of communism. This is definitely not the case for socialist allegory, which likewise involves processes of appropriation and refunctionalization but, as will be argued in the next chapter, remains entirely caught within the aesthetic sensibilities of the nineteenth century.

Chapter 5
The Proletarian Prometheus and Socialist Allegory

> Only through the death of the old
> have new lineages achieved victory.
> He [i.e., Prometheus] confronts violence
> with the sharp arrow of knowledge.
> With the weighty hammer of logic
> he drives a wedge into everything.
> Following eternal laws,
> he must be victorious in this fight,
> and thus he will liberate himself,
> the Prometheus of our time.
>
> Eduard Fuchs, "Der Prometheus unserer Zeit"

One of the more puzzling aspects of late nineteenth-century socialist culture is the infatuation with classical antiquity as mediated by Weimar classicism and German romanticism. In the making of proletarian identifications, the gods and demigods rediscovered during that era came to perform a unique role that speaks to enduring influences as well as transformative potentials. Emboldened by these discursive possibilities, in Eduard Fuchs's version of the Prometheus myth, the famous rebel against the gods returns as the personification of key socialist beliefs: that building a better future requires a radical break with the past; that the working class possesses the means and skills to liberate itself; and that History follows an inherent logic toward the emancipation of all of humankind.[1] First published in 1892 in the *Süddeutsche Postillon*, the Fuchs poem was later reprinted in an anthology, programmatically titled *Aus dem Klassenkampf* (1894, From the Class Struggle), whose title attests to the unique status of Prometheus in the socialist imaginary as "the patron saint of the proletariat."[2] The

---

[1] Eduard Fuchs, "Der Prometheus unserer Zeit," *Süddeutscher Postillon* 9 (1892). The poem was reprinted in 1894 in *Aus dem Klassenkampf. Soziale Gedichte* 4, ed. Karl Kaiser, Ernst Klaar, and Klaus Völkerling (Berlin: Akademie, 1978) and is quoted from that edition.

[2] George Derwent Thomson, *Aeschylus and Athens: A Study in the Social Origins of Drama* (London: Lawrence & Wishart, 1941), 317. The British utopian socialist John Goodwyn Barmby, who claimed to have introduced the term "communism" into the English language, founded a journal titled *The Promethean, or Communitarian* (later: *Communist*) *Apostle*. The enduring appeal of the

Prometheus figure made possible the appropriation of the bourgeois narrative of the self-liberation of man through labor by, and for, the historical struggles of the working class. As this chapter argues, this process involved not only the refunctionalization of established aesthetic modalities – in this case, allegory and mythology – for explicitly socialist purposes. It also depended on the kind of emotional labor that, through aesthetic means, could transform pain and suffering into feelings of class pride and thus put aesthetic emotions in the service of political emotions.

Numerous works inspired by the Prometheus figure circulated throughout the socialist lifeworld, announcing the seemingly inevitable return of the rebel Titan in the revolutionary working class. In all cases, the rewriting of the Greek myth as a performance of socialist praxis relied on image-text combinations closely dependent on allegory, which involved specific reading strategies that treated images as representations of ideas. Most importantly, this process of transformation required the alignment of old and new aesthetic modalities through which the proletariat could be imagined as an emotional community and, ultimately, a revolutionary class. In the case of Prometheus, this realignment concerned the expression of pain and suffering in established formal registers – rather predictably, pathos – and the explanation of Prometheus's rebellion against authority (i.e., Zeus) in explicitly Marxist terms. Notwithstanding the fact that Prometheus's rebellion was the very reason for his wretched state, his original act of defiance in the name of humankind now served as a compelling reminder of the continued existence of oppression and inequality and the need for a very different revolution against power structures.

Whereas poetry, through its temporal structure, can replicate the conversion of suffering into struggling, images require additional formal elements in order to capture the underlying causes and effects (see figure 5.1). The resultant need for textual anchoring can be seen in a satirical drawing titled "Prometheus Bound" from *Der Wahre Jacob* 136 (1891) that looks very much like an illustration of the Fuchs poem (rather than the modified Goethe lines accompanying it). Naked save for a red cloth draped around his loins, Prometheus appears pinned against a rock, with his muscular masculinity on full display. According to the captions, the chained Titan personifies the proletariat, with his expressive gaze conveying both terror and rage. The vulture (instead of the eagle) drawing blood represents the forces of capitalism, and the small civil servant applying a bandage to his wounds embodies the futility of social reform.

Prometheus figure during the Comintern has been discussed at some length in John Lehmann, *Prometheus and the Bolsheviks* (New York: A. Knopf, 1938).

Fig. 5.1 "Der gefesselte Prometheus/Prometheus Bound," *Der Wahre Jacob* 136 (1891): 1104. With permission of Universitätsbibliothek Heidelberg.

The elevated status of Prometheus as the patron saint of the proletariat raises a number of basic questions that are relevant to most cultural practices developed in the name of socialism: How can the thematic and formal choices made to visualize rebellion against authority in "Prometheus Bound" be explained? Or, to rephrase the question in more general terms, what accounts for the proliferation of mythological figures and the preference for allegorical readings in the socialist lifeworld of Imperial Germany? If myths are stories about gods and demigods, and if the proletariat takes the place of Prometheus, is this a socialist form of deification, or the substitution of a socialist cosmology for a classical one? How did the Prometheus myth inspire the very different visions of progress, labor, and industry promoted in the name of capitalism and socialism? Is socialist allegory merely a refunctionalizing of existing forms and conventions? Or must its conventionality be read as a convenient vehicle for imagining brief moments of discursive mastery, of allegoresis as omnipotence, that hinge on the erasure of the gap between socialist utopian thought and the harsh realities of working-class life?

Along similar lines, what accounts for the enduring popularity of allegory and mythology among socialist workers who believed in economic determinism and, during the heydays of scientific socialism, saw world history as an objective process? How is the self-presentation of the SPD as the party of science and progress to be reconciled with allegory's propensity for idealization, sentimentality, and kitsch? Are the references to antiquity, as channeled through the lens of German classicism, yet another example of the SPD's complicated relationship to the bourgeois heritage? Or do they represent a long overdue recognition of the abundance of allegories, emblems, and symbols in folk culture and religious life? The related functions of Prometheus as an emotional template for proletarian identifications and a highly gendered embodiment of rebellion shed light on some of these interrelated questions.

The degree to which gender played a formative role in the rewriting of a rebellious body politic is confirmed by two other Prometheus poems written by Fuchs after the rescinding of the Anti-Socialist Laws. His "Socialism-Prometheus" builds on the equation of masculinity and productivity through a male birth fantasy that has the Titan promise the workers that "I, the enlightened son/ born in the depth of misery/ rise above and bring to mankind/ joy-making/ blessing-giving/ divine life [...] that is how I turn you into gods!"[3] Meanwhile, Fuchs's "The Young Titan" identifies woman as the greatest threat to the heroic narrative of class struggle. Her most powerful weapons are the comforts of domesticity that she advertises with the following instructions: "Remember Prometheus./ He thought like you. [...] Chose instead to follow me./ Fetch fire from the Aetna./ [...] and heat my stove/ and cook my gruel."[4] In what ways the gendered juxtaposition between male rebellion and female contentment becomes a recurring theme in the proletarian imaginary is confirmed by a polemical poem on "Bourgeois and Proletarian Art" that presents the latter in the body of a strong and decidedly male "young art of labor [...] born of the people, pure and true" who, unlike a tired, worn-out bourgeois art, requires no "prostitute's makeup."[5]

The gendered nature of the Prometheus myth – that is, its depiction of class struggle as a process of masculinization – is complicated by the fact that ideal-

---

[3] Eduard Fuchs, "Sozialismus-Prometheus," in *Stimmen der Freiheit. Blüthenlese der hervorragendsten Schöpfungen unserer Arbeiter- und Volksdichter*, ed. Konrad Beißwanger, third ed. (Nuremberg: Litterarisches Bureau, 1902), 275.
[4] Eduard Fuchs, "Der junge Titan," *Süddeutscher Postillon* 24 (1893). Reprinted in Thomas Huonker, *Revolution, Moral & Kunst. Eduard Fuchs, Leben und Werk* (Zurich: Limmat, 1985), 280.
[5] Eduard Fuchs, "Bourgeoisie- und Proletarierkunst," *Süddeutscher Postillon* 15 (1893), reprinted in Norbert Rothe, ed., *Frühe sozialistische satirische Lyrik aus den Zeitschriften "Der wahre Jacob" und "Süddeutscher Postillon"* (Berlin: Akademie, 1977). 47–48. Some editions use the hyphenated spelling *Süd-Deutscher Postillon*. A number of complete issues have been reprinted in *Süddeutscher Postillon. Ein Querschnitt in Faksimiles*, ed. and intr. Udo Achten (Bonn: Dietz, 1979).

ized versions of the arts and, by extension, of socialist utopias often take a female form, including in allegorical representations of Social Democracy. The proletarian Prometheus restages the class struggle through his physical body's double presence as god and man. By contrast, a decidedly ethereal Libertas comes to embody the SPD through her association with universal values such as truth, beauty, and happiness. This identification with abstract ideas precludes any direct contact with social reality, including the dynamics of suffering and empathy. The most powerful emotions remain reserved for the spectacle of masculinity – evidence that emotional socialism should not automatically be interpreted as female and feminizing. In fact, the emotional confessions by party leaders (in chapter 3) and the cult of celebrity surrounding Lassalle (in chapter 6) suggest that the popular fascination with the Prometheus myth draws on deep reservoirs of male emotion.

Today Eduard Fuchs (1870–1940) is remembered best as the Weimar-era author who wrote a successful illustrated cultural history, a six-volume *Sittengeschichte*, and the art collector who inspired Walter Benjamin's evocative reflections on the affinities between the collector, allegorist, and historical materialist.[6] Correcting widespread claims that socialist culture was primarily literature-based, Ulrich Weitz has highlighted Fuchs's contribution to the development of "the visual language of the German workers' movement" and his promotion of caricature as a form of political agitation and, with implications beyond the socialist movement, a visual aesthetic of dissent.[7] During the Wilhelmine years, Fuchs played a key role in the creation of a distinctly socialist visual culture, most prominently as the editor – after 1892 – of *Süddeutscher Postillon*, a satirical journal that introduced itself as the proletarian among Munich-based journals in its 1887 inaugural issue.[8] *Süddeutscher Postillon* openly announced its political commitments in a fake advertisement from 1892 (perhaps written by Fuchs himself) that singled out satire for "having a very refreshing and invigorating effect on proletarian souls."[9] Unlike the serious tomes written by Engels

---

[6] See Walter Benjamin, "Eduard Fuchs, Collector and Historian," in *Selected Writings, Volume 3 1935–1938* (Cambridge, MA: Harvard University Press, 2002), 260–302. For a reading of Fuchs along these lines, see Michael P. Steinberg, "The Collector as Allegorist: Goods, Gods, and the Objects of History," in *Walter Benjamin and the Demands of History*, ed. Michael P. Steinberg (Ithaca, NY: Cornell University Press, 1996), 88–118.
[7] Ulrich Weitz, *Salonkultur und Proletariat. Eduard Fuchs, Sammler, Sittengeschichtler, Sozialist* (Stuttgart: Stöffler & Schütz, 1991), 7.
[8] "Abonniert den Süddeutschen Postillon," *Süddeutscher Postillon* 1 (1887).
[9] Quoted in Huonker, *Revolution, Moral & Kunst*, 234–235. On political satire in the journal, see Ursula E. Koch, "Eduard Fuchs und das politische Arbeiter-Witzblatt *Süddeutscher Postillon*," *Ridiculosa* 2 (1995), online at http://www.eiris.eu/index.php?option=com_content&view=arti

and Kautsky, illustrated journals such as *Süddeutscher Postillon* and *Der Wahre Jacob* used irreverent humor and sharp wit to reach large numbers of workers in the local pub and factory hall. Taking advantage of new color-print technologies, both journals built on long-established traditions that, from the emblems in religious tracts to the symbols on political fliers, relied heavily on image-text relationships to convey their view of the world. With more than a quarter of a million subscribers during the 1890s, *Der Wahre Jacob* at one point was even more successful than the bourgeois satirical weekly *Simplicissimus*. The combination of political caricatures, socialist allegories, agitational poems, and polemical essays in the more confrontational *Süddeutscher Postillon* played an important role in modeling an attitude of contrariness toward the institutions of dominant culture, especially the Prussian military and bureaucracy.

Whereas social types became the most effective way of satirizing the class enemy, allegories prevailed in the representation of the socialist movement and the working class. These idealized representations of Social Democracy would fit any definition of socialist kitsch, but in the larger context of allegory as a didactic form and prebourgeois tradition, the continuities between folk culture and proletarian culture are ultimately more important. These new formal registers became available because the diminishment of allegory in the age of the romantic symbol. The resultant reconfigurations of folk and class through the allegorical method can be seen in two examples from *Süddeutscher Postillon*. The first, "Capital and Labor" (in *SP* 9/1895), depicts the struggle between capital and labor as a fight between two medieval horsemen, a fat knight wielding an old-fashioned morning star and a romantic hero (with open collared shirt) armed with a shiny new sword. Retreating even more into fantasy, "I Am a Proletarian" (on the cover of *SP* 6/1902) introduces the *Proletar* as a stout wrestler who strangles the steely serpent of capitalism draped decoratively around his lower calf (see figures 5.2 and 5.3). The allusion to Siegfried slaying the dragon could easily have been presented with nationalist slogans – evidence of the close connections within the allegorical mode between seemingly contradictory political traditions.

As an instrument of socialist agitation, *Süddeutscher Postillon* had to deal with frequent bans by the state censors and charges of *lèse majesté* against its editors. It would be shortsighted, however, to interpret the widespread prefer-

---

cle&id=505:eduard-fuchs-und-das-politische-arbeiter-witzblatt-sddeutscher-postillon&catid=70&Itemid=124, 1 March 2017. For a comparative study, also see Klaus Völkerling, "Die politisch-satirischen Zeitschriften *Süddeutscher Postillon* (München) und *Der Wahre Jacob* (Stuttgart). Ihr Beitrag zur Herausbildung der frühen sozialistischen Literatur in Deutschland und zur marxistischen Literaturtheorie" (PhD diss., Pedagogical College of Potsdam, 1969).

Fig. 5.2 "Kapital und Arbeit/Capital and Labor," *Süddeutscher Postillon* 9 (1895): n. p. With permission of Deutsches Historisches Museum, Berlin.

Fig 5.3. "Ich bin ein Proletar!/I Am a Proletarian!," *Süddeutscher Postillon* 21.6 (1902), title page. With permission of Deutsches Historisches Museum, Berlin.

ence for allegory as a mere strategy of concealment in response to political censorship. In visualizations of the future of socialism, positive emotions – mostly involving happiness and joy – are expressed with little formal restraint. This is especially true for the colorful journal covers and popular annual *Mai-Festzeitungen* published by the SPD's Vorwärts publishing house. Responding to what Fuchs called the workers' insatiable hunger for images, well-known illustrators, including Bruno Paul, Max Slevogt, and Hugo Höppener (Fidus), set out to establish the thematic and formal conventions of socialist allegory. They developed a class-based visual sensibility in close dialogue with mainstream Wilhelmine culture and new developments in the graphic arts. Their allegories of socialism, in particular, attest to the strong influence of historicism, including an enduring fascination with the medieval period, and an affinity for the organic modernism of Jugendstil. The availability of allegory to mass cultural applications and socialist appropriations was undoubtedly helped by its widespread denunciation as an ossified form since the romantic movement, compared to the rich semiotic complexities of the symbol. The same can be said about the promotion of realism as a more appropriate form of engaging with social reality. The inclusion in *Süddeutscher Postillon* of illustrations by the British arts-and-crafts illustrator Walter Crane suggests that the socialist configurations of modernity and myth, including the staging of a socialist posthistory through its feudalist prehistory, must be regarded as a widespread European phenomenon. Confirming this point, the conditions under which outmoded modalities such as allegory became available to proletarian perspectives continued throughout the next decades and can be traced all the way across the Atlantic to the Mexican *Revista CROM*, an illustrated magazine for radicalized workers and peasants, and to the US-American *New Masses*, the most influential organ of leftwing politics and popular visual culture during the years of the New Deal.[10]

Increasingly marginalized within high culture, allegory in the late nineteenth century was eagerly adopted in the context of industrial culture, commodity culture, and socialist culture. Allegorical representations became an integral part of everyday life during the second half of the nineteenth century, with personifications of nation, folk, and community adorning buildings, machines, and pieces of furniture and appearing in everything from historical pageants to nationalist festivals. Allegorical plays in the style of *tableaux vivants* proved especially popular in the workers' movement. Offering relief from the social problems addressed in naturalist dramas and poems, mythical figures and allegorical modes continued to flourish in the languages of turn-of-the-century symbolism where they took on a more stylized form. The restaging of modernity as myth found perfect expression in countless allegories of electricity and steam that celebrated technological innovation and economic growth.[11] In these visualizations of class society, the most heterogeneous discourses could be reconciled: the promotion of science and technology, the veneration of classical antiquity and humanism, the cult of labor and industry, and the mythification of Prussia and the Reich.

---

10 On the Mexican connection, see John Lear, *Picturing the Proletariat: Artists and Labor in Revolutionary Mexico, 1908–1940* (Austin: University of Texas Press, 2017), chapter 4. In addition to Libertas, the dragon-slaying proletarian of "I Am a Proletarian" makes an almost uncanny return (though in reverse) in Santos Balmori's cover for *Revista Lux* (March 1936); but now the enemy is not just capitalism but capitalism and fascism (229–231).
11 For a discussion of this phenomenon, see Dirk Schaal, "Bild und Ikonographie der Elektrizität. Über den Wahrnehmungs- und Bedeutungswandel einer Energieform seit dem Industriellen Zeitalter—Überlegungen für eine Ikonographie der Wirtschaft," in *Energie in der modernen Gesellschaft*, ed. Thomas Kroll (Göttingen: Vandenhoeck & Ruprecht, 2012), 33–55. For a comparative perspective, see Cindy Weinstein, *The Literature of Labor and the Labors of Literature: Allegory in Nineteenth-Century American Fiction* (Cambridge: Cambridge University Press, 1995).

In his monumental history of caricature published in 1903, Fuchs brings together two key terms, pathos and allegory, to identify a particular shortcoming of socialist visual culture, namely the marked preference for pathetic allegories that feature mythological figures over satirical caricatures that deal with urgent contemporary problems (*Wirklichkeitssatiren*). While never clearly defined, pathos for him represents the continuing influences of utopian socialism and (messianic) Christianity and their shared promises of deliverance from suffering. Speaking to the emotional qualities of allegory and satire, Fuchs uses highly evocative adjectives such "disdained, ridiculed, ignored, attacked, [and] singled out" to describe the derogatory treatment of the socialist movement in mainstream political caricature and to explain the workers' general preference for allegory and their deep suspicion of satire within this unequal dynamic of bourgeois contempt and socialist defiance. "The worker, he explains, "has little appreciation for humor. He lacks the latter because the struggle forced upon him is very hard, and his life in most cases is too serious, if not perhaps too tragic. This kind of mentality is not conducive to the development of caricature."[12]

As part of these patterns of reading and rereading, socialist allegory may be understood best through its alternately anticipatory and compensatory functions, especially in relation to fantasies of rebellion. As a personification of abstract ideas, allegory in the most basic sense establishes a direct connection between representation and interpretation. It models constellations of knowledge and power based on implicit assumptions about the full readability of the world. In making visible the invisible, allegory blurs the lines between image and text and uses specific reading strategies to establish its highly codified system of signs and significations. As the distinctions between images and texts disappear, everything becomes readable – and part of an imagined sense of mastery over present and future. In the process, the constitutive tension between meanings concealed and revealed offers an interpretative template for the heroic struggles of the proletarian Prometheus. Of course, the correct reading of the mythological body, both bound and unbound, depends on the transformation of emotions into a radicalizing force, here through the depiction of physical pain and its aestheticization in pathos. Upon closer inspection, socialist allegory always seems to rely on such divided emotional regimes: of suffering and bliss, dejection and elation, and, in explicitly political terms, of tyranny and liberty. Located either in a mythological past or a utopian future, its personifications rarely make contact with social reality and the world of contemporary politics. This ap-

---

[12] Eduard Fuchs, *Die Karikatur der europäischen Völker vom Jahre 1848 bis zur Gegenwart* (Berlin: Hofmann, 1903), 470 and 483.

parent shortcoming indirectly confirms that socialist allegory resists conventional definitions that – based on the distinction in Hegel's aesthetics between good metaphor and bad allegory – invariably dismiss the latter as too formalistic and mechanistic.

Given Fuchs's humanistic education, it can be safely assumed that his description of pathetic allegory draws on key insights from Friedrich Schiller's influential essay on "The Pathetic" (1793). The representation of suffering in art, Schiller argues, functions as a means, not an end, in facilitating man's rise as a reasonable being (*Vernunftswesen*) over his existence as a sensuous being (*Sinnenwesen*). Just as the tragic hero must pass through the crucible of emotion, all actions and decisions in life are prefigured in, and facilitated by, aesthetic experiences. "The first law of the tragic art was to represent suffering nature. The second law is to represent the resistance of morality opposed to suffering,"[13] writes Schiller. With the aesthetic conceived as a means of self-liberation, his definition of pathos reads very much like a description of the proletarian Prometheus:

> Pathos is a sort of artificial misfortune, and brings us to the spiritual law that commands our soul. Real misfortune does not always choose its time opportunely, while pathos finds us armed at all points. By frequently renewing this exercise of its own activity, the mind controls the sensuous, so that when real misfortune comes, it can treat it as an artificial suffering and make it a sublime emotion. [...] Thus pathos takes away some of the malignity of destiny and wards off its blows.[14]

In the European tradition, the Prometheus figure has long embodied the dialectics of suffering and rebellion and allowed artists to reflect on the contradictions of human self-emancipation. Part of a group of demigods that includes Icarus, Sisyphus, and Tantalus, the most famous of the Titans has often been cast as a personification of the struggle between freedom and tyranny. This tension has found telling expression in his association with fire as a tool of innovation. And since Prometheus is also known as a trickster, the figure has inspired countless versions and competing interpretations, beginning with Hesiod and Aeschylus and continuing with Horace, Ovid, and many others. Prometheus stole fire from the gods and gave it to humans, thus making possible their liberation through labor, technology, and, in the most general terms, creativity. As punishment, Zeus ordered Prometheus chained to the mountains and condemned to a life of eternal suffering, with an eagle every night eating his liver. In early ver-

---

13 Friedrich Schiller, "The Pathetic," in *Aesthetical and Philosophical Essays*, online at http://www.gutenberg.org/files/6798/6798-h/6798-h.htm#link2H_4_0034, 1 March 2017.
14 Friedrich Schiller, "On the Sublime," in *Aesthetical and Philosophical Essays*, online at http://www.gutenberg.org/files/6798/6798-h/6798-h.htm#link2H_4_0033, 1 March 2017.

sions, Zeus at one point sends Pandora, the first woman, to bring unhappiness to humans by releasing all the evils of the world from her "box" (except, of course, for hope); in later versions, he eventually allows Hercules to unchain Prometheus.[15]

The meanings attributed to the myth are just as varied and contradictory. As many interpreters have pointed out, the long-fought struggle of human beings for a life of self-determination in the Golden Age simultaneously condemned them to a life of toil in the Iron Age. During the nineteenth century, Prometheus was claimed for the competing narratives of bourgeois emancipation, modern capitalism, as well as proletarian revolution. Writers Johann Wolfgang von Goethe, Lord Byron, and Percy Bysshe Shelley, composers Ludwig van Beethoven, Franz Liszt, and Alexander Scriabin, and painters Gustave Moreau, Arnold Böcklin, and Max Klinger all turned to the famous Titan as the embodiment of the modern individual, his heroic struggles, failures, and triumphs. Socialist appropriations translated the underlying cult of bourgeois individualism into collectivist terms, but retained the original equation of individual agency with masculinity.

Evoking Prometheus in the German context, of course, meant citing Johann Wolfgang von Goethe – that is, the drama fragment written during the 1770s under the influence of the French Revolution. Goethe's Prometheus famously rails against the ancient gods and, in the name of bourgeois emancipation and humanistic thought, asserts his free will. "I should honor you? For what?/ Have you softened the sufferings,/ ever, of the burdened?/ Have you stilled the tears,/ ever, of the anguished?," he asks defiantly, incensed about the existence of suffering in the world. Significantly, it is men's ability to feel strongly and deeply, "to suffer, to weep, to enjoy and to delight themselves, and to mock you – as I do!", that create the conditions for their resistance to authority.[16] Modeling an emotional praxis of dissent, the drama fragment was repeatedly reprinted in socialist publications and contributed to a veritable cult of Goethe and Schiller in socialist circles.[17] Goethe's *Prometheus* fragment was included in

---

[15] For an introduction to the history of the mythological figure, see Carol Dougherty, *Prometheus* (London: Routledge, 2006). With a special focus on the nineteenth century, see Caroline Corbeau-Parsons, *Prometheus in the Nineteenth Century: From Myth to Symbol* (London: Legenda, 2013). For a philosophical reading of Prometheus in the Goethean tradition, also see Hans Blumenberg, *Work on Myth*, trans. Robert M. Wallace (Cambridge, MA: MIT Press, 1985).

[16] Johann Wolfgang von Goethe, "Prometheus," in *Johann Wolfgang von Goethe: Selected Poetry*, trans. David Luke (London: Penguin, 2005), 11.

[17] A typical example can be found in *Arbeiter-Jugend. Monatsschrift der sozialistischen Arbeiter-Jugend Deutschlands* 1.4 (1909): 48.

Karl Henckell's *Buch der Freiheit* (1893, Book of Freedom), a collection of poems commissioned by the SPD's Vorwärts publishing house. The introduction expresses support for the struggle for freedom "as it has been understood and advanced primarily by the organized proletariat as both the heir of unrealized bourgeois ideals and the creator and bearer of a new consciousness of mankind."[18] Yet by including only classical and naturalist authors, the editor ends up settling on an abstract notion of freedom that has little in common with the confrontational stance taken by Fuchs's Prometheus of *From the Class Struggle* published only one year later.

Endowed with a distinct *Sturm and Drang* sensibility, the Goethean Prometheus became available to proletarian identifications through the same processes of critical appropriation that had facilitated the productive encounter between Hegelianism and Marxism. Inspired by Prometheus's defiant declaration (taken from Aeschylus's *Prometheus Bound*) that "I hate the pack of gods," Marx recognized the famous bringer of fire "as the most eminent saint and martyr in the philosophical calendar."[19] He occasionally used the myth to make his analysis of class society more accessible, for just as Prometheus was chained to the mountain by Zeus, the proletariat was "chained by a law of nature to the naked rock of capitalist production."[20] In fact, the editor of the *Rheinische Zeitung* himself appeared as *Prometheus Bound* in a humorous cartoon published in response to the newspaper's first ban in 1843. Marx is depicted chained to a printing press as the Prussian eagle pecks at his liver and a tiny squirrel, a reference to Prussian Minister of Culture Friedrich Eichhorn, tightens his chain. The five bare-breasted Rhine Maidens swimming at his feet bemoan the loss of the free press (see figure 5.4).

---

18 Karl Henckell, ed., *Buch der Freiheit* (Berlin: Vorwärts, 1893), v. Henckell's book was a reworking of the first semiofficial anthology of socialist poems edited by Rudolf Lavant under the programmatic title *Vorwärts!* (1886, Forward!).
19 Karl Marx, "The Difference between the Democritean and Epicurean Philosophy of Nature," *MECW* 1: 31.
20 Karl Marx, "Capital. A Critique of Political Economy. Volume One," *MECW* 6: 584. The Marxist appropriation of Prometheus has prompted Leonard P. Wessell to insist on the mythico-religious and mytho-poetic nature of Marxist thought; see his *Karl Marx, Romantic Irony and the Proletariat: The Mythopoetic Origins of Marxism* (Baton Rouge: Louisiana State University Press, 1979) and *Prometheus Bound: The Mythic Structure of Karl Marx's Scientific Thinking* (Baton Rouge: Louisiana State University Press, 1984).

Fig. 5.4 Karl Marx as "Der gefesselte Prometheus/Prometheus Bound," 1843. With permission of Heinrich-Heine Institut, Düsseldorf.

Just like the countless personifications in official Wilhelmine culture, socialist allegories aimed to convey a sense of unity and power, but in contrast to allegories of nation, their emotional rewards only addressed one particular class: the working class. Like mainstream allegorical practices, socialist versions operated on three interrelated levels: through their ritualistic function in festival culture and associational life, their agitational function in promoting socialist concepts and ideas, and their emotional function in conveying an attitude of optimism and faith in the future. Most relevant to the making of proletarian identifications, socialist allegories promised a fully decipherable world, if viewed from a properly socialist perspective. These qualities set socialist allegory apart from the material culture of the nineteenth century as examined by Walter Benjamin in his famous Arcades Project. Approaching the culture of mass consumption and reading the signs of historical change through his earlier study on the baroque mourning play allows Benjamin to draw on the affinities of allegory to mourning, which in his view makes it ideally suited as a hermeneutics and a method of historical materialism. Although his reading of "allegory as the armature of modernity"[21] is part of an analysis of capitalism and commodity fetish-

---

21 Walter Benjamin, "Central Park," in *Selected Writings, Vol. 4, 1938–1940*, ed. Howard Eiland

ism, it proves surprisingly ill-suited in making sense of socialist allegory. For instead of revealing the signs of decline, allegory's very conventionality and obsolescence set a different history into motion once the capitalist dream world yields to the socialist utopia of the nineteenth century.

To ensure their correct interpretation, socialist allegories sometimes came with detailed instructions on reading images as texts. The presentation of a work by Max Slevogt (1868–1932) in the 1903 *Mai-Festzeitung* is based on the assumption that interpretive stability requires a surfeit of textuality, both as part of the image and in the form of additional commentary. Titled "We Are the Power!," the image features a young, muscular blacksmith with a hammer tucked into his apron and two eagles perched on his extended arms. The caption reads: "We are the power! We hammer the state, that old, decrepit thing, into new shape!/ Born of the wrath of God, we are today the proletariat!" Lest that figure be seen as a typical worker standing in front of smoking factory chimneys, the accompanying text describes the image's "painted Marxism" as a much-needed antidote to the "painted socialism of emotion" and elaborates: "There he stands, 'all muscle, nerve, and tendon' and surely [he] does not say: 'My life is so bad! Dear people, please feed me!' He also does not say: 'Look, how virtuous I am, my virtue is bound to win!' No, if there is one word written on his pressed lips, it reads short and simple: 'I will!'"[22] (see figure 5.5). Allegory's dependence on highly formalized reading practices is confirmed by Walter Crane's earlier representation of "The Capitalist Vampire" (1885) in the SPD's 1901 *Mai-Festzeitung* (see figure 5.6). Depicted as an angel with a torch, this Arts and Crafts personification of Socialism aggressively confronts the capitalist vampire as he is about to attack sleeping "Labor," shown here as a kind of anti-Prometheus. The accompanying interpretation calls the image "a clarion call to the ears of indifferent workers. With the torch of knowledge and enlightenment in hand and the trumpet of socialism at the lips, the genius of freedom approaches to awaken the last worker from the leaden sleep of indifference and ignorance that allows the vampire of capitalism to suck his heart's blood in the form of religious hypocrisy and political stultification."

---

and Michael W. Jennings (Cambridge, MA: Belknap Press, 2003), 183. For such a reading, see Heinz Dieter Kittsteiner, "The Allegory of the Philosophy of History in the Nineteenth Century," in *Walter Benjamin and the Demands of History*, ed. Michael P. Steinberg (Ithaca, NY: Cornell University Press, 1996).

22 Reprinted in Udo Achten, ed., *Zum Lichte empor! Mai-Festzeitungen der Sozialdemokratie 1891–1914* (Berlin: Dietz, 1980), 125 and 126.

Fig. 5.5 Max Slevogt, "Wir sind die Kraft/We Are the Power," *Mai-Festzeitung* 1903, back cover. Reprinted in Udo Achten, ed. and intr., *Süddeutscher Postillon. Ein Querschnitt in Faksimiles* (Bonn: Dietz, 1979), 126.

Fig. 5.6 Walter Crane, "The Capitalist Vampire," *Mai-Festzeitung* 1901, back cover. Granger, New York. All rights preserved.

The emotional intensities of pathetic allegory and the overdetermined function of its mythological references come into closer view once its gendered divisions are considered in greater detail. As a personification of the proletariat, Prometheus brings together three moments in the heroic narrative of working-class emancipation, rebellion against authority, punishment for insubordination, and eventual self-liberation. Literary and visual treatments of the myth translate the Greek ideal of physical beauty into a muscular, classed body. Sometimes the spectacle of industrial labor gives expression to a rarely acknowledged male eroticism. By contrast, Libertas, the female allegory of Social Democracy, offers an almost serene picture of beauty, virtue, and happiness, an impossible ideal only achievable in utopian settings – hence her frequent placement on flowering meadows in front of open skies and shining suns. Whereas the proletarian Prometheus is introduced to illustrate key Marxist concepts, including the necessity of class struggle, the socialist Libertas serves to celebrate the idea of freedom as a universal value. The inevitable tension between history and myth is evident already in their respective costumes, with Prometheus's loincloth referencing the professional attire of the quintessential proletarian, the blacksmith. Meanwhile, the draped tunics worn by the Roman Libertas mark her as profoundly different from actual working-class women, rendering her – the female figure – into a conventional symbol.

Inspired by the gendered iconography of the July Revolution, a fully harnessed and armed Germania was promoted since the Revolutions of 1848 as a personification of national unity. But unlike the French original with the Phrygian cap who, in the famous rendition by Delacroix, is animated by a passion for liberty that exceeds traditional notions of female beauty and propriety, Germania exudes a well-fortified sense of calm and stability. Similarly, her socialist sister Libertas remains strangely constrained in her emotions. Her modesty not only attests to socialists' traditional views on gender roles but also raises questions about the party's commitment to the woman's question. Given her close association with Social Democracy, Libertas repeatedly inspired mocking treatments in the mainstream press that, among other things, resulted in her transformation into an ugly shrew. For instance, a caricature with the title "Hasselmann's Revelations" from the satirical mainstream journal *Ulk* 43 (1878) portrays her as a disheveled, bare-breasted woman who emerges from behind a theater curtain labeled "Fraternity and Other Ideals," held open by an SPD member of the Reichstag named Wilhelm Hasselmann. Leading a group of armed revolutionaries, the frightful apparition clutches a dagger in her right hand and a banner in the left – with the "true" reasons for the mass appeal of socialism "revealed" in the banner's mottos "Envy" and "Covetousness" (see figures 5.7 and 5.8). The gendering of socialist allegory becomes even more explicit in mixed allegorical representations that involve the proletariat and the party. Published in the 1899 *Mai-Festzeitung*, "The Union of Art and Labor" by the popular illustrator Ephraim Moses Lilien (1874–1925) stages a highly symbolic scene through a literal reframing of Arnold Böcklin's *Libertas/Helvetia* (1891).

Fig. 5.7 Hermann Scherenberg, "Hasselmanns Enthüllungen/Hasselmann's Revelations," *Ulk* 42 (1878). With permission of Bayerische Staatsbibliothek München, Signatur 2Z 2008.79–7.

Fig. 5.8 Ephraim Moses Lilien, "Die Einheit von Kunst und Arbeit/The Union of Art and Labor," *Mai-Festzeitung* 1899. Reprinted in Achten, *Süddeutscher Postillon*, 90–91.

Under the approving gaze of a Böcklin-like figure hovering far above the clouds, a barrel-chested locksmith (representing the workers) and a Greek goddess with laurel wreath (representing the arts) are depicted shaking hands, a gesture that expresses the party's equal commitment to labor and culture. For unknown reasons, the Böcklin painting is reproduced as a mirror image. Similar representations of Prometheus and Libertas appear regularly in the party press until the early years of the twentieth century, evidence of the surprising longevity of pathetic allegory as a didactic device and emotional modality. Throughout, Prometheus maintains his strong connection to the actual working class – quite literally, by appearing side by side with German workers and fully integrated into German landscapes. A postcard commemorating the 1908 Bundesfest of the Arbeitersängerbund "Rheinland" introduces the familiar Titan together with an Orpheus-type figure with lyre. Prometheus's left hand holds up a torch while his right rests on a hammer. Vignettes of Düsseldorf landmarks and the official festivities surround the mythological figures representing labor and music and corroborate their full integration into working-class culture (see figure 4.1).

Scholars have grappled with the nonsynchronicities that sustained socialist allegory and its ongoing transformation of obsolescence into futurity. Their contributions started as part of the highly politicized debates of the 1970s on proletarian culture and may be used here to summarize the chapter's findings. Predictably, a major point of contention at the time involved the socialist appropriation of the bourgeois heritage. In an important historical survey of early attempts at an "authentic proletarian visual language," Knut Hickethier acknowledges the heavy reliance on bourgeois graphic arts and the difficulty of negotiating artistic sensibilities and political expectations.[23] Studies by Klaus-Dieter Pohl and Ursula Zeller on the agitational uses of visual allegory highlight its origins in the productive tension between bourgeois convention and socialist appropriation. They note a gradual shift during the 1890s from the universal themes represented by female allegories to the more confrontational and decidedly male iconographies of the prewar years.[24] Offering a more critical perspective, Klaus-Michael Bogdal interprets the widespread preference for clothing social conflicts in historical costumes as compensation for the scientism of historical materialism – an aesthetic choice borne of the desire to preserve a place where ideas and ideals still prevail and where history can still be imagined in embodied terms.[25] Diagnosing a clear break between the symbolic politics of Social Democracy and its very different Weimar-era successors, Gottfried Korff explains the eventual demise of socialist allegory as a result of what at the time was seen as an irreversible process of secularization: "The wine leaves in

---

23 Knut Hickethier, "Karikatur, Allegorie und Bilderfolge—Zur Bildpublizistik im Dienste der Arbeiterbewegung," in *Beiträge zur Kulturgeschichte der deutschen Arbeiterbewegung, 1848–1918*, ed. Peter von Rüden (Frankfurt am Main: Büchergilde Gutenberg, 1979), 79–165.
24 Klaus-Dieter Pohl, "Allegorie und Arbeiter. Bildagitatorische Didaktik und Repräsentation der SPD 1890–1914. Studien zum politischen Umgang mit bildender Kunst in den politisch-satirischen Zeitschriften 'Der Wahre Jacob' und 'Süddeutscher Postillon' sowie in den Maifestzeitungen" (PhD diss., University of Osnabrück, 1986). On nineteenth-century political posters and the preference for female allegories, also see Ursula Zeller, *Die Frühzeit des politischen Bildplakats in Deutschland (1848–1918)* (Stuttgart: Ed. Cordeliers, 1988), 59–93. On the larger context, see Günter Hess, "Allegorie und Historismus. Zum 'Bildgedächtnis' des späten 19. Jahrhunderts," *Verbum et Signum. Beiträge zur mediävistischen Bedeutungsforschung*, ed. Hans Fromm, Uwe Ruberg, and Wolfgang Harms (Munich: Fink, 1975), 555–591. For an overview of socialist visual culture in general, see Michael Klant, ed., *Der rote Ballon: Die deutsche Sozialdemokratie in der Karikatur* (Hanover: Fackelträger, 1988). And on the iconography of the proletariat in bourgeois and socialist publication, see Helmut Hartwig and Karl Riha, *Politische Ästhetik und Öffentlichkeit. 1848 im Spaltungsprozeß des historischen Bewußtseins* (Fernwald: Anabas, 1974), 89–138.
25 Klaus-Michael Bogdal, *Zwischen Alltag und Utopie. Arbeiterliteratur als Diskurs des 19. Jahrhunderts* (Opladen: Westdeutscher Verlag, 1991), 153–159.

the hair, the Phrygian cap on the head, and the goddesses of freedom disappeared as visual and symbolic motifs – reason to conclude that the symbolism of the workers' movement in the Weimar Republic is brought into being by a loss of utopia – or better, by secularization."[26]

In a compelling analysis of nineteenth-century workers' literature that is also applicable to socialist allegories, Klaus-Michael Bogdal speaks of an aesthetic discourse whose constitutive elements were located entirely in the nineteenth century and whose formal conventions were already considered obsolete before the war. The anachronistic nature of these traditions, he argues, cannot be adequately analyzed through formal criteria but instead requires close attention to the intended subject effects, i.e., what Bogdal analyzes as discourse and what this study describes as the interface of emotional and cultural practices. Accordingly, the discursive functions of workers' literature, its double temporality as a trace of everyday life and a movement toward the not yet, are realized not in aesthetic registers that, in hindsight, seem derivative and obsolete but only through the historical subjects interpellated in the process, the proletariat.

Thus defined, socialist allegory and, more generally, proletarian culture around the turn of the century remain caught between two discourses, Marxism and bourgeois humanism. However, precisely because the scenarios of class struggle are displaced into some mythological past, the adaptation of bourgeois aesthetic traditions to socialist contexts acquires new emotional qualities. For Bogdal, the aesthetic modalities of pathos, satire, and sentimentality are of particular relevance here: "Pathos is the strategy for representing and establishing the still frail *proletarian self-image*. It serves a class-forming function. Satire imagines *the image of the other*. Sentimentalism imagines a space of *class synthesis* on the basis of the 'all too human' and the personal."[27] All three modalities are not only rooted in idealist aesthetics, including Schiller's validation of pathos as a form of resistance, but they also confirm the ability of emotions to escape the confinements of aesthetic form and survive in more contemporary versions – a definition that applies perfectly to the power of socialist allegory in images as well as texts. Last but not least, Bodgal's definition draws attention to the less obvious similarities between the sentimental masculinity of emotional socialism and the heroic masculinity of socialist allegory. With special relevance for the next chapter on the socialist celebrity phenomenon, the political symbolism of sentiment and pathos points to the dependency of the proletarian dream

---

26 Gottfried Korff, "Rote Fahnen und geballte Faust. Zur Symbolik der Arbeiterbewegung in der Weimarer Republik," in *Fahnen, Fäuste, Körper. Symbolik und Kultur der Arbeiterbewegung*, ed. Dietmar Petzina (Essen: Klartext, 1986), 60.
27 Bogdal, *Zwischen Alltag und Utopie*, 152.

on an imaginary folk culture and mythic antiquity as channeled through German classicism and, increasingly, nationalism. As later case studies on socialist mass culture will corroborate, these examples of cultural appropriation can only be understood as an integral part of the socialist culture industry and its heavy reliance on new mass media, from illustrated journals to pulp novels, in forging proletarian imaginations through emotional attachments.

Chapter 6
Ferdinand Lassalle, the First Socialist Celebrity

> I believe in Ferdinand Lassalle,
> the messiah of the nineteenth century,
> and in the social and political resurrection
> of my people languishing in misery,
> in the irrefutable dogmas of the working class
> as taught by Ferdinand Lassalle,
> who was born with a reviled name,
> lived in the heart of the people,
> suffered under bourgeoisie and political reaction,
> died through treacherous hands,
> rose again in the bosom of faithful disciples,
> and ascended in the spirit of the working people
> through whom he will one day return
> to sit in judgment over all enemies of his creed.
>
> Karl Freundschuh

Who was the "I" speaking with such religious fervor? Why did the "working people" choose Ferdinand Lassalle as their messiah? And how did they become his "faithful disciples"?[1] These questions are essential to understanding the emotional attachments that sustained proletarian identifications within the workers' movement, often in blissful ignorance of Marxist theories. Making sense of such declarations of faith means to take a closer look at Lassalle's unique status as the first socialist celebrity – that is, as an object of intense admiration, infatuation, and fantasy production especially after his death. Unlike fame and renown, which require some measurable talent or accomplishment, celebrity is primarily media-driven and inseparable from the rise of the modern culture industry in the mid-nineteenth century.[2] And unlike charisma, which according to Max Weber

---

[1] Karl Freundschuh, quoted in Heiner Grote, *Sozialdemokratie und Religion. Eine Dokumentation für die Jahre 1863 bis 1875* (Tübingen: J.C.B. Mohr, 1968), 17. The reference is to The Apostles' Creed. The prevalence of messianic thought in the early socialist movement can also be seen in the writings of Wilhelm Weitling, including his notion of messianic dictatorship.

[2] For a helpful introduction to the notion of celebrity, see P. David Marshall, *Celebrity and Power: Fame in Contemporary Culture* (Minneapolis: University of Minnesota Press, 1997). On posthumous celebrity, see Steve Jones and Joli Jensen, eds., *Afterlife as Afterimage: Understanding Posthumous Fame* (New York: Peter Lang, 2005). Max Weber famously defines charisma (in the secular sense) in "Charismatic Authority," in *Economy and Society*, ed. Guenther Roth and Claus Wittich (Berkeley: University of California Press, 1978), 241–254. On the changing config-

describes individuals with exceptional qualities, the celebrity phenomenon depends to a large degree on public fantasies about private lives and is sustained by the active contribution of devotees, followers, and enthusiasts.

The notion of celebrity – and, more specifically, of posthumous celebrity – sheds new light on the emotional functions of the Lassalle cult and its presumed incompatibility with the collective narratives of class. The widespread preoccupation with his personal life long after his death falls outside standard definitions of charisma but should not be reduced to the psychological mechanisms of mass contagion (examined in chapter 1). Moreover, belief in his individual greatness seems entirely at odds with the realities of working-class life and the collective virtues promoted in socialist party programs. Instead the Lassalle cult bears witness to the growing influence of mass cultural diversions on the workers' movement and the enduring appeal of emotional socialism (discussed in chapter 3), and that despite repeated socialist campaigns against both phenomena and their continued devaluation in the historiography of working-class culture. In this chapter, these continuities will be reconstructed through a forgotten *Kolportageroman* (pulp novel) by Heinrich Büttner with the lengthy title *Ferdinand Lassalle, Der Held des Volkes oder: Um Liebe getödtet! Socialer Roman* (1892, The Hero of the People, or: Killed for Love! Social Novel) and the sensationalist literary treatments of Lassalle's life and work published before and after his death.

---

urations of charisma in nineteenth-century Europe, see Edward E. Berenson and Eva Giloi, eds., *Constructing Charisma: Celebrity, Fame, and Power in Nineteenth-Century Europe* (New York: Berghahn, 2010).

Fig. 6.1 "Lassalle, der Kämpfer gegen die Kapitalmacht/Lassalle, Fighter against the Power of Capital," c. 1870, color lithograph. With permission of Deutsches Historisches Museum, Berlin/A. Spille.

Fig. 6.2 "1863–1913. Zur Erinnerung an das 50-jährige Gründungsjahr der deutschen Sozialdemokratie/In Celebration of the 50th Anniversary of the Founding of German Social Democracy," postcard. With permission of Archiv der Sozialen Demokratie Bonn.

Today Ferdinand Lassalle (1825–1864) is remembered best as one of the founding fathers of Social Democracy (see figures 6.1 and 6.2). Having been approached by a group of socialists who felt that his reputation as an inspiring public speaker would attract more followers to the movement, he became the first president of the first German workers' party, the ADAV (General German Workers' Association).[3] His early death at age thirty-nine only a few months after the party's founding congress on 23 May 1864 made Lassalle, rather than Marx or Engels, the perfect embodiment of the romance of socialism that united radicalized workers with middle-class intellectuals in their fight for a better society. According to the historian Heiner Grote, the fascination with Lassalle was most pronounced in small provincial towns and widespread among petty bour-

---

[3] The reformist Lassallians and the more militant Eisenacher eventually joined forces at the 1875 Unity Congress in Gotha to form the Sozialistische Arbeiterpartei Deutschlands (SAP, Socialist Workers' Party of Germany); after the lapse of the Anti-Socialist Laws in 1890, that party was renamed Sozialdemokratische Partei Deutschlands (SPD, Social Democratic Party of Germany).

geois elements of the working class.⁴ Women, who were largely excluded from workers' associations, played an important role in preserving his legacy after his death, and in the many biographies, novels, and dramas inspired by his life, often appeared in the place of the working class as his designated love interest. Extending far beyond German borders and making use of various literary genres and styles, the Lassalle cult reached a high point during the 1880s and continued until the 1920s when very different heroes, martyrs, and cults of personality took hold of the communist imagination.

Lassalle's biography proved to be well suited for posthumous appropriations. Born in Breslau as the son of a Jewish silk merchant, he studied philosophy in Berlin and quickly came under the influence of Hegelian thought. A strong believer in the republic as the best form of government, he became involved in radical democratic causes during the Revolutions of 1848. Charged with inciting armed rebellion, he spent six months in prison – a good time to concentrate on writing. Hefty tomes on the philosophy of Heraclitus and the theory of retroactive rights established his credentials as a scholar. Meanwhile, he devoted much time to Countess Sophie von Hatzfeldt who was seeking a divorce from an abusive husband. Taking her on as a human rights case, Lassalle represented the older woman's claims in an almost decade-long lawsuit that was settled in her favor in 1854. An annual stipend from the countess, by then also his closest confidante, allowed him to live as a public intellectual equally at home in the literary salons of the Prussian capital and the meeting halls of disgruntled workers. Soon he spoke out in favor of universal suffrage, commented on the constitutional struggle in Prussia, and wrote about current political and economic topics, including the so-called iron law of wages. Lassalle's dreams of a great political future came to an unexpected end when he died in Geneva on 31 August 1864 from a fatal shot in the groin sustained during a duel with the fiancé of the woman he wanted to make his wife, twenty-one-year old Helene von Dönniges (1843–1911).

This melodramatic ending straight out of a pulp novel brings together the seemingly irreconcilable elements – great romance, high society, and radical politics – that characterized the Lassalle cult as a whole. The unusual circumstances of his death and the romantic fantasies that kept his legacy alive validated the utopian project of socialism precisely by blurring the boundaries between

---

4 See Grote, *Sozialdemokratie und Religion*, 8–25. For a voluminous psychobiography that also discusses Lassalle's Jewishness, see Shlomo Na'aman, *Lassalle* (Hanover: Verlag für Literatur und Zeitgeschehen, 1970). For a brief English-language summary of the Lassalle cult, see Andrew G. Bonnell, "The Lassalle Cult in German Social Democracy," *Australian Journal of Politics & History* 35.1 (1989): 50–60.

the personal and the political. Even the salacious gossip about his private life, by validating the power of emotions, helped to strengthen the workers' emotional ties to socialism as the ultimate object of desire. Similarly, the endless speculation about Lassalle's psychological problems became a measure of the depth of his own commitment – a connection that appealed especially to middle-class readers whose interest in socialist causes was often driven by pity for the lower classes.

Lassalle's self-fashioning played a crucial role in his celebrity status even if it cannot account for its adaptability to changing political and cultural contexts. From the beginning, he conceived of his relationship to socialism in the highly personal terms that included a deep need to be loved and admired. Already in "Confessions of a Twenty-Year Old," he draws on his own experiences of discrimination when he describes the denial of the workers' humanity rather than their lack of property as the real curse of the times – a curse to be broken by the modern gods of vengeance, the proletarians, and their future leader, Lassalle.[5] His often-cited characterization of the workers in the 1862 Workers' Program as "the rock on which the Church of the present is to be built"[6] establishes his self-chosen role as the messiah to their St. Peter in unmistakably religious terms. Doing away with any pretense of class analysis, Lassalle describes the workers as all of us "in so far as we have even the *will* to make ourselves useful in any way to the community."[7] Offering them a dream of themselves, he praises the members of the fourth estate as born democrats, exemplars of community, and heralds of a flowering of culture and science. The proletariat, he declares, is "synonymous with the *whole human race*. Its interest is in truth the interest of the *whole of humanity*, its freedom is the freedom of humanity itself, and its domination is the domination of *all*."[8]

According to Franz Mehring, the SPD's most influential cultural theorist, it was Lassalle's "burning passion" that held together all these disparate influences and ideas.[9] In a 14 October 1863 address to the workers of Berlin, the party leader had famously declared, "Without passion in history no stone is ever lifted

---

[5] Ferdinand Lassalle, "Der Bekenntnisbrief des Zwanzigjährigen," (1864), in letter to Baron Hubert von Stücker, reprinted in Konrad Haenisch, *Ferdinand Lassalle. Der Mensch und Politiker in Selbstzeugnissen* (Leipzig: Kröner, 1925), 48. The original reference is to the Eumenides.
[6] Ferdinand Lassalle, *The Working Man's Programme (Arbeiterprogramm)*, trans. Edward Peters (London: The Modern Press, 1884), 59.
[7] Lassalle, *The Working Man's Programme*, 46.
[8] Lassalle, *The Working Man's Programme*, 44.
[9] Franz Mehring, Introduction to Ferdinand Lassalle, *Arbeiter-Programm* (Berlin: Vereinigung Internationaler Verlagsanstalten, 1923), 8.

off the other!" and announced that only four months after the founding of the ADAV, "passion already takes up residence in the heart of the people!"[10] However, if the workers chose not to follow through with actions, Lassalle confessed in private, they only had themselves to blame. As he explained to a friend, "if they [i.e., my words] fail to incite agitation in the workers, then that is the clearest proof that nothing more can be accomplished with them."[11] Later commentators have read such passages as evidence of serious character flaws or, as psychoanalyst Erwin Kohn argues in *Lassalle, der Führer* (1926, Lassalle, the Leader), a narcissistic personality disorder; of course, this diagnosis does not contradict the psychological dynamics of the celebrity phenomenon.[12] In fact, Lassalle's wavering in his own writings between dependence on the love of the masses and contempt for their weakness finds its corresponding psychological disposition in the emotional volatility – from deep despair to uncontrolled rage to exuberant hope – attributed to the workers in the fictional encounters included in almost all literary treatments of his life.

These mutual projections were established and solidified through Lassalle's various public personas: the ladies' man with a strong attachment to a maternal figure, the Countess Hatzfeldt; the socialist activist who repeatedly met with Chancellor Bismarck to discuss aspects of German nationalism; the champion of the working class who worshipped the Prussian state; and the luxury-loving dandy who turned into an advocate of the voiceless and dispossessed.[13] Contemporaries called him brilliant, charming, and fascinating but also arrogant, impervious, and self-righteous. Even political allies described him as a complicated, volatile character ill-suited for the responsibilities of party leadership. Dönniges's remark in her later tell-all book that Lassalle liked to imagine his glorious future as a plebeian-tribune-turned-absolute-ruler known as "Ferdinand *der*

---

10 Ferdinand Lassalle, *An die Arbeiter Berlins. Eine Ansprache im Namen der Arbeiter des Allgemeinen Deutschen Arbeiterverbandes* (Berlin: Schlingmann, 1863), 9. Many of these texts have been reprinted in *Arbeiterlesebuch und andere Studientexte*, ed. Wolfgang Schäfer (Reinbek: Rowohlt, 1972).
11 Lassalle, quoted in Eckard Colberg, *Die Erlösung der Welt durch Ferdinand Lassalle* (Munich: List, 1969), 90. The reference is to the "Offenes Antwortschreiben" of 3 March 1863 to the men with whom he would soon found the ADAV.
12 Erwin Kohn, *Lassalle, der Führer* (Vienna: Internationaler Psychoanalytischer Verlag, 1926), 70.
13 On literary treatments of the Bismarck connection, see Martin Kane, "'Er spielt so ein verwickeltes Spiel' (Wilhelm Liebknecht). Literary Representations of the Association between Ferdinand Lassalle and Otto von Bismarck," in *The Text and Its Context: Studies in Modern German Literature and Society*, ed. Nigel Harris and Joanne Sayner (Berne: Peter Lang, 2008), 109–120.

Volkserwählte"[14] adds some credence to such unflattering portrayals. Indeed, the epithet "chosen by the people" openly recognizes his active pursuit of, and deep need for, the mass adoration associated with the celebrity phenomenon. In light of such surfeit of images and imaginations, his posthumous persona as a socialist martyr can and must be considered his greatest political achievement.

The elaborate commemorative events after Lassalle's death not only confirm the dependency of the workers' movement on the emotional regimes shared by established religious traditions and other social movements. They also attest to the latter's acute awareness of the performative nature of public emotion in the age of massification and medialization. Thus for the funeral, ADAV functionary Jacob Audorf rewrote the final verse of the Workers' Marseillaise, the unofficial anthem of the workers' movement, to declare Lassalle their true spiritual leader: "We are not counting the enemy,/ and not the dangers all!/ March, march, march, march./We follow the bold course,/ shown to us by Lassalle!"[15] Georg Herwegh, in a poem titled "At the Grave of Lassalle," captured the general mood when he openly admitted, "for once, tears are allowed to flow even on men's cheeks."[16] Meanwhile Countess Hatzfeldt, who had initially planned to display his embalmed body as part of somber obsequies all over Germany, declared herself the sole executor of his political will. Conspiracy theories about Lassalle's death and succession battles in the ADAV added to frequently voiced feelings of loss and defeat among radicalized workers.[17] Pilgrimages to his final resting place in Breslau and annual celebrations on the day of his death established his political martyrdom, complete with Christian tropes of sacrifice and resurrection. After the passing of the Anti-Socialist Laws, commemorative practices and objects ranging from hymns and elegies to busts and beer steins further confirmed Lassalle's status as a repository for the illegitimate needs and desires henceforth identified with the emotional culture of early socialism.[18]

The enduring fascination with Lassalle prompted several of his contemporaries to consider its libidinal sources and gauge its political consequences. Bernhard Becker, another founding member of the ADAV, conceded that Lassalle's ideas may not have been particularly original or coherent, but their unique pre-

---

14 Helene von Racowitza (née von Dönniges), *Meine Beziehungen zu Ferdinand Lassalle* (Breslau: Schottländer, 1879), 109.
15 See http://de.wikipedia.org/wiki/Deutsche_Arbeiter-Marseillaise, 1 March 2017.
16 Georg Herwegh, "Am Grabe Ferdinand Lassalles," *Die Neue Zeit* 1.15 (1896): 438.
17 For an early example of such conspiracy theories, see Bernhard Becker, *Enthüllungen über das tragische Lebensende Ferdinand Lassalle's* (Schleitz: Hübscher, 1868).
18 For an example of this commemorative discourse, see Max Kegel, *Ferdinand Lassalle. Gedenkschrift zu seinem 25jährigen Todestag* (Stuttgart: J. H.W. Dietz, 1889).

sentation greatly benefited Social Democracy and the workers' movement. This did not stop Becker from expressing his intense distaste for this "messiah of the nineteenth century" and describing Lassalle's self-serving reenactment of the life of Christ in derisive terms: "His Mary Magdalene was called Helene, he died from a pistol shot rather than on the cross, and Countess Hatfield had the right personality to play Mother of God."[19]

Lassalle became an object of cult-like veneration through the fantasies of intimacy that made him an effective spokesperson for socialism in his early thirties and, long after his death, continued to fuel an intense interest in his love life. Many party members saw the quasi-religious nature of the Lassalle cult as detrimental to the socialist endorsement of atheism, scientism, and materialism. Nonetheless, even his most outspoken critics acknowledged that the phenomenon's underlying psychological mechanisms sustained the movement especially during the 1880s. Lassalle's presence in the everyday life of party members was apparent, among other things, in their choice of wall decorations, the kind advertised in *Süddeutscher Postillon* as "tasteful showpieces for proletarian apartments. Marx and Lassalle portraits in high quality chromolithographs."[20] Confirming the full compatibility of socialism, nationalism, and Catholicism, factory worker-turned-SPD senator Moritz Bromme (1873–1926) remembered that a portrait of Lassalle was displayed prominently in his parents' living room together with Marx, Bebel, Bismarck, Wilhelm I, and several popular saints.[21] KPD politician Paul Frölich described a family home filled with pictures of Lassalle, Marx, and Bebel on the wall and a book of Lassalle's speeches on the table, right next to the *Brockhaus Conversations-Lexicon*, the SPD journal *Die Neue Zeit*, and a few popular scientific books. About his father, a typical worker, he concluded: "Did he ever study Marxism in a serious way? I don't think so. His socialism was based on Lassalle whose views he fully accepted even as he continued to evolve within the milieu of Leipzig radicalism."[22]

The remarkable textual productivity inspired by Lassalle attests to the enduring appeal of older forms of romantic infatuation and sentimental feeling that,

---

[19] Bernhard Becker, *Geschichte der Arbeiter-Agitation Ferdinand Lassalle's. Nach authentischen Aktenstücken* (Braunschweig: W. Bracke, 1875), 307. Another disillusioned assessment of Lassalle by another ADAV founding member can be found in Julius Vahlteich, *Ferdinand Lassalle und die Anfänge der deutschen Arbeiterbewegung* (Munich: Birk, 1904).
[20] Advertisement in *Süddeutscher Postillon* 16.10 (1897).
[21] Moritz William Theodor Bromme, *Lebensgeschichte eines modernen Fabrikarbeiters* (Leipzig: Diederichs, 1905), 71.
[22] Paul Frölich, *Im radikalen Lager. Politische Autobiographie 1890–1921*, ed. and with afterword by Reiner Tosstorff (Berlin: Basis, 2013), 21.

especially in their political manifestations, resisted easy integration into the heroic narratives of working-class mobilization. Contemporaries were particularly troubled by the deep longing shared by fictional and actual workers for a leader who would be worthy of their love and adulation – and who, in fact, lived in a world far removed from the poor and the oppressed. Equally disconcerting, in light of the socialist belief in knowledge and reason as the most powerful tools of self-emancipation, was the preoccupation with love, passion, beauty, sensuality, wealth, and luxury in the sensationalist treatments of his life. In all of the recognition scenes to be discussed next, the desiring gaze of the working class constitutes Lassalle as someone both far removed and intimately known – in short, a celebrity. Through these dynamics of looking and being looked-at, the workers become part of a model performance of political mobilization. These scenes build on the concept of *anagnorisis* in the Aristotelian *Poetics*, where it denotes a character's move from ignorance to knowledge; only here, the cognitive process is redefined as an emotional one. For the workers, the intended subject effects organized through the first-person plural involve the following cognitive steps: By desiring you (i.e., Lassalle), we desire socialism. By recognizing you, we understand our historical role as the revolutionary proletariat. By choosing you as the leader, we acknowledge our responsibilities as the universal class and the embodiment of true humanity. Faced with such imaginary scenarios, one might ask (in a variation on Freud's famous question): What does a worker want? Or, in an awareness of the central role of fantasy: What do socialist intellectuals want the workers to want? Can scholars reclaim these stories and images for a forgotten, suppressed and, for that reason, all the more important archive of socialist feelings? Or must these five decades of heightened textual productivity be seen as a gradual process of elimination – of religiosity, emotionality, and sexuality – from a revolutionary project that, after the carnage of World War I, would become much more narrowly defined along party lines?

Ferdinand Lassalle, The Hero of the People, the historical novel that sheds light on some of these questions, was written by a certain Heinrich Büttner (or a writing team working under that name) and allegedly based on personal letters, official documents, and interviews with close relatives. Published in serial form, it appeared in seventy-seven installments of twenty-four pages each. A popular genre distinguished by its mode of distribution, *Kolportageromane* were sold door to door by so-called colporteurs on a subscription basis.[23] Written

---

[23] On the *Kolportageroman* and the culture industry, see Andreas Graf, "Kolportageromane. Produktion, Distribution und Rezeption eines Massenmediums," *Leipziger Jahrbuch zur Buchge-*

for working-class and lower-middle-class readers, these novels addressed urgent social problems but did so in a highly sensationalist, derivative style. Feedback by subscribers often led to changes in the interwoven storylines and large cast of characters, confirmation to what degree serialization drew on a wide range of literary genres and styles to hold readers' attention. Colportage novels played an important role in mediating between two very different forms of engagement, the world of political activism and associational life and the world of fantasy, illusion, and escapism. Like the Lassalle cult in general, these products of an emerging socialist culture industry – two better-known examples are August Otto-Walster's *Am Webstuhl der Zeit* (1873, At the Loom of Time) and Minna Kautsky's *Die Alten und die Neuen* (1884, The Old and the New) – dissolved the public/private (and male/female) oppositions that, in official pronouncements on working-class culture, required the denunciation of excessive emotionality as a symptom of false consciousness. The novels' sentimental and melodramatic modalities provided pleasures not always available in the socialist lending libraries with their insistence on moral uplift and cultural refinement. Scrambling literary genres and styles, they introduced contemporary problems into fantastic settings and incorporated socialist messages into illusionist scenarios and, in this particular case, promised the magical reconciliation of the proletarian imaginary with social reality. Musing about this hidden dream world of colportage, Ernst Bloch was one of few Weimar intellectuals who early on recognized its utopian qualities. "The proletarian revolution," he noted at one point, "is mostly hostile to 'fantastic' literature; yet in fairytale and colportage tension and colorfulness have their serviceable refuge, from here they can become troops."[24]

The frontispiece in Büttner's *Ferdinand Lassalle* illustrates perfectly how the personal and the political converge in the socialist celebrity, how class divides are articulated in gendered terms, and how the medium of colportage brings together all these disparate elements (see figure 6.3). A young girl has been sexually assaulted by the feudal lord whose castle looms high above in the back-

---

*schichte*16 (2007): 29–63; for a general overview, see Werner Faulstich, *Medienwandel im Industrie- und Massenzeitalter (1830–1900)* (Göttingen: Vandenhoeck & Ruprecht, 2004). On media convergence and the colportage novel, also see Jessica Plummer, "Selling Fiction: The German Colportage Novel 1871–1914" (PhD diss., University of Texas at Austin, 2016). For an early discussion of popular and socialist literature, see Tanja Bürgel, "Das Problem der Unterhaltungsliteratur in der deutschen Arbeiterpresse vor dem Sozialistengesetz," in *Literatur und proletarische Kultur. Beiträge zur Kulturgeschichte der deutschen Arbeiterklasse im 19. Jahrhundert* (Berlin: Akademie-Verlag, 1983), 163–182.

24 Ernst Bloch, *The Heritage of Our Times*, trans. Stephen and Neville Plaice (Cambridge: Polity, 1991), 168.

Fig. 6.3 Frontispiece in Heinrich Büttner, *Ferdinand Lassalle, der Held des Volkes* (1892), frontispiece. With permission of Deutsches Literaturarchiv Marbach, Kosch Collection.

ground. She now rests (dead? unconscious?) in the arms of her aggrieved father; both are surrounded by a group of workers. This typical scene from the melodramatic imagination reenacts the conditions of working-class abjection from two perspectives, the trauma of violation and the rage of powerlessness. The arrival of Lassalle rewrites this tragic moment by shifting the center of attention and, ultimately, of power from the old ruling classes to the new advocate of the people. This process involves the above-mentioned experiences of recognition and revelation that, in the Bible, establish the conditions for the possibility of resurrection known in Marxist theory as revolution. Confirming this political dimension, the visual presentation alludes to the rape of Lucretia, which in Roman mythology functions as a catalyst in the transition from tyranny to republicanism. Additionally, it references the Swiss Rütli oath and, by implication, Schiller's *Wilhelm Tell*, as a foundational myth for populist and nationalist liberation movements. As soon as he announces (in the caption), "I am Ferdinand Lassalle," the workers undergo a profound transformation, with the repeated evocation of his name taking on an almost ritualistic quality. This moment of interpellation, in turn, allows him to claim his role as their designated savior:

> Like a burst of magic, the expressions of those standing around him changed. The name Ferdinand Lassalle affected them as if they had suddenly heard the sound of liberating

bells, as if someone had announced that a rescuer, a helper, a true friend was near. "Ferdinand Lassalle," they shouted and pressed closer to the young man, "is it true then, Ferdinand Lassalle is among us, he whom the people in Berlin idolize, in whose chest a heart beats for us, Ferdinand Lassalle is with us?" "He is with you!" answered the young man straightening up with pride, "Oh, if you only knew how much your trust honors me, how it fortifies me with powers of steel. Yes, I am Ferdinand Lassalle, and here upon the body of this dying girl [...] I take this solemn oath. Listen to me, all of you who stand around me, and remind me of my vow should I ever falter, I swear, from this day forward, to stand unwaveringly with the people and their cause."[25]

After this dramatic moment of personal and political radicalization, the novel recounts several unrelated adventure and romance stories. Time and again Lassalle returns and repeats this transformative moment in various unexpected settings. In accordance with the conventions of the historical novel, his political significance is established through meetings with Heinrich Heine, Ferdinand Freiligrath, and Otto von Bismarck. Meanwhile his inner struggles are recognized through the women in his life, Countess von Hatzfeldt, Helene von Dönniges, and, in a cameo appearance, Sophie von Sontzeff. The *Vormärz* years place him in Berlin at the center of political life, admired by influential women and courted by powerful men. "But even in this wealthy, magnificent environment," the narrator assures his readers, "Lassalle had not forgotten for a moment that he belonged to the people and that it was his mission to challenge and reduce the rights of those with whom he now associated." (*FL*, 164) A little later, Lassalle and the countess are riding through town in a carriage when they suddenly find themselves surrounded by an angry mob. Once again, he announces himself to the people, and once again, "the flinging of Lassalle's words into the excited masses" produces a state of collective frenzy:

> First it was completely still. But then it flew from mouth to mouth. "Have you heard, it is Lassalle, Ferdinand Lassalle, our Lassalle." And "our Lassalle" thundered through the air, "our Lassalle" shouted from every mouth, and those who just before had faced the countess with hostility now pressed toward him and wanted to shake his hand. "Long live Lassalle," they cried, "long live our protector and our savior." (*FL*, 220–221).

---

25 Heinrich Büttner, *Ferdinand Lassalle, der Held des Volkes oder: Um Liebe getödtet! Socialer Roman. Nach Briefen, Acten und Angaben naher Verwandter Lassalle's*, 3 vols (Berlin: Friedrichs, 1892), 14–15. Hereafter quoted in parentheses in the text as *FL*. Only a few copies of this novel have survived in the archives, including one in the Günter Kosch collection of colportage novels housed in the Deutsche Literaturarchiv in Marbach; I am grateful to Jessica Plummer for drawing my attention to this rare find.

Another three hundred pages later, Lassalle resurfaces once more during a masked ball in Paris where he barely escapes an attempt on his life. "Only through a miracle, I know it now, did I escape certain death yesterday," he announces: "But that should not hold me back from staying true to my cause, the cause of the people. Because even if after several years only a few thousand workers are freed from the conditions that oppress them now, I will have been amply compensated!" Proof of his world historical mission arrives in the form of an attractive young lady who approaches him in Notre Dame and offers to sacrifice her life for him. "Do not misunderstand me, Mr. Lassalle," she explains:

> "When your facial features were engraved on my soul, it happened out of reverence for the man who bears the weight of the hopes of millions of people living under oppressive conditions, it happened so that your face, at least spiritually, could always be with me, the face of the man who, as someone once told me, renounced status and honor to be a champion of the oppressed." (*FL*, 1087)

Almost all literary representations of Lassalle from the period are structured around his double identity as public figure and private person. Given the frequent identification of narrative point-of-view with supporting characters that know of him but are not known to him, the recognition scenes cited so far may legitimately be compared to the semipublic encounters known as celebrity sightings. Their main function at the time was to produce an illusion of intimacy that, because of its voyeuristic/ exhibitionist structure, resisted easy integration into the prevailing forms of sociability available within Social Democracy. Moreover, the identifications from below (or afar) facilitated by the socialist celebrity set up a convenient emotional structure for translating social problems into romantic scenarios. The promised reconciliation of the personal and the political may have been beyond reach, but the fantasies produced in its name were nonetheless legitimate expressions, in the commodified forms of socialist mass culture, of the workers' demand for recognition in the political and psychological sense.

The adaptable and transferable nature of emotional intensity is particularly relevant to understanding the religious language of the Lassalle cult, beginning with the reference to the Last Judgment in the socialist version of the Apostles' Creed cited in the epigraph. In explaining these connections, several historians have pointed to the continuing influence of Christian faith, ritual, and doctrine. For Eckard Colberg, the apocalyptic structure of Lassalle's revolutionary history attests to the inevitable failure of all secular forms of redemption. Sebastian Prüfer uses what he calls the deification of Lassalle to question whether early socialism functioned "as religion" or "instead of religion." And Franz Walter and Arno Herzig point to the commemorative practices after Lassalle's death and conclude that "cult and kitsch" were an integral part of socialist festivities and mythologies.²⁶ The comparison to idolatry in some of these studies, however, ignores not only the discursive function of religiosity in socialist mass culture but also perpetuates the denunciation of emotion started by August Bebel and others eager to leave behind the utopianism of the early socialist movement.

The characterization of socialism as secular religion indicates that religious traditions had indeed remained an important part of working-class life. Progressive Catholic and Lutheran groups in the Wilhelmine era became actively involved in social reform projects, and Catholic labor organizations in some areas of the country competed openly with Social Democratic initiatives. In understanding the connections on the level of symbolic practices, however, we must distinguish between religion and religiosity and consider the growing significance of the latter as a lingua franca for oppositional social movements and alternative visions of community. It is only as a shared emotional and cultural tradition that religious references survived in the similarities between messianic socialism and chiliastic Christianity and the reclamation of *Urchristentum* (Early Christianity) as a precursor of socialism.²⁷

Given the appropriation of the habitus of religiosity by the discourses of secular humanism and socialist mass culture, it would indeed be simplistic to interpret the religious elements of the Lassalle cult as evidence of the enduing influence of Christianity. Faith and community since the Enlightenment had emerged as important reference points in interrelated struggles for social, political, and cultural rights that, among other things, resulted in the parallel processes of democratization and secularization. The French Revolution and its aftereffects had released the emotional attachments, which until then had concentrated on the absolute ruler and, in the place of these stable identifications, introduced the more elusive attachments embodied by new types of popular politicians and

---

26 For references in chronological order, see Colberg, *Die Erlösung der Welt durch Ferdinand Lassalle* (see fn. 11); Arno Herzig, "Die Lassalle-Feiern in der politischen Festkultur der frühen deutschen Arbeiterbewegung," in *Öffentliche Festkultur. Politische Feste in Deutschland von der Aufklärung bis zum Ersten Weltkrieg*, ed. Dieter Düding, Peter Friedemann, and Paul Münch (Reinbek: Rowohlt, 1988), 321–333; Sebastian Prüfer, *Sozialismus statt Religion. Die deutsche Sozialdemokratie vor der religiösen Frage 1863–1890* (Göttingen: Vandenhoeck & Ruprecht, 2002), 287–294; and Franz Walter, "Ferdinand Lassalle. Zwischen Kult und Kitsch," in *Mythen, Ikonen, Märtyrer. Sozialdemokratische Geschichten*, ed. Franz Walter and Felix Butzlaff (Berlin: Vorwärts, 2013), 15–25.
27 For an early Catholic study on the so-called worker question, see Wilhelm Emmanuel Freiherr von Ketteler, *Die Arbeiterfrage und das Christentum* (Mainz: Franz Kirchheim, 1864). On the religious dimension of social movements in general, see Gottfried Korff, "Politischer Heiligenkult im 19. und 20. Jahrhundert," *Zeitschrift für Volkskunde* 71 (1975): 202–220.

public intellectuals (e.g., Napoleon Bonaparte as revolutionary-dictator, Friedrich Schiller as revolutionary-poet). In fact, the Schiller cult was equally pronounced among Social Democrats and members of the bourgeoisie, reached new height during the centennial of his death in 1905, and acquired even more frenzied qualities during the Third Reich as a cult of revolutionary genius.

Lassalle was one of the first to take advantage of the emotionalization of politics that fueled the parallel projects of nation and democracy when he visited the hero of the *risorgimento*, Giuseppe Garibaldi, and later wrote a book about the Italian War of Independence. However, Lassalle could not have known how Garibaldi's role as a charismatic leader in the fight for national unification and his own posthumous celebrity status would be used in the very different constellations of nationalism, socialism, and the culture industry emerging in the late nineteenth century. Seen in this light, the Lassalle cult had much in common with the frenzied fandom known as Lisztomania and the mass adoration showered on the "divine Sarah" (i.e., Bernhardt). All three celebrities promised to compensate for the privatization of religion in the age of secularization and profoundly changed the dynamics of aesthetic experience and public emotion, not least by making both available to the process of commodification. In the fictional worlds inhabited by Lassalle and his lovers and followers, sexuality henceforth provided a model of political attraction, and romance became a conduit to new social and socialist commitments. Not surprisingly, Wilhelmine-era Social Democrats, despite their attacks on the so-called trash and smut produced by the culture industry, depended heavily on mass cultural practices in imagining a simultaneously socialist and populist politics of identification.

Being a celebrity means being recognizable. For that reason, it makes sense to return to the recognition scenes discussed earlier and consider in greater detail the overdetermined function of Lassalle's face in the gendered and racialized scenarios of political mobilization. Most literary treatments contain one or more scenes in which he is recognized by the workers or, as their stand-in, a beautiful woman. All involve some form of personal introduction ("I am Lassalle") followed by external verification ("You are Lassalle"). Crossing literary genres and styles, this dialogic structure not only facilitates the semiotic slippage between romance and revolution that immortalizes Lassalle as a romantic revolutionary, it also keeps alive the dream of revolution, even if only in terms of religious faith and romantic love. Undoubtedly, the resultant subject positions depend on the repeated reenactment of the conditions that produce the need for the socialist redeemer in the first place. Narrative motivation and dramatic tension are sustained through individual stories of exploitation and oppression that can only be made right through the promise of salvation – that is, deliverance from the evils of capitalism. The choice of religious conversion and erotic seduction as templates for proletarian identifications might initially seem baffling – but only if content is privileged over form and the transferable nature of emotional intensities ignored. Responding to these established conventions, early contributors to the Lassalle cult drew extensively on the heightened modalities of the sentimental and the melodramatic associated at the time with the popular novel, drama, and film. Later treatments incorporated physiognomic categories and psychological theories in ways that must be considered as derivative as the religious language and imagery used by their predecessors.

Through these emotional and discursive constellations, and especially the substitution of one language of enchantment for another, the Lassalle cult came to function as a projection screen for more hidden resentments. These resentments often survived beneath the public expressions of love and admiration and involved very different patterns of recognition focused on his Jewishness as a source of empathic identification as well as antisemitic prejudice. Contemporaries such as Heinrich Heine had hailed Lassalle as the messiah of the nineteenth century and Richard Wagner (in a rare generous moment) described him as "that type of the future men of note I would like to call Germanic-Jewish."[28] By contrast, Karl Marx, in a letter to Friedrich Engels, had referred to their greatest competitor as "the Jewish nigger" and, in so doing, established a pattern that would henceforth allow others to channel their feelings of attraction and revulsion through the language of antisemitism. Recounting a recent visit by Lassalle, Marx in 1862 could barely control himself:

> Add to this, the incessant chatter in a high, falsetto voice, the unaesthetic, histrionic gestures, the dogmatic tone! [...] And on top of it all, the sheer gluttony and wanton lechery of this "idealist"! It is now quite plain to me – as the shape of his head and the way his hair grows also testify – that he is descended from the negroes [sic] who accompanied Moses' flight from Egypt (unless his mother or paternal grandmother interbred with a nigger). Now, this blend of Jewishness and Germanness, on the one hand, and basic Negroid stock, on the other, must inevitably give rise to a peculiar product. The fellow's importunity is also nigger-like.[29]

---

28 The Heine reference (from a letter to Varnhagen von Ense of January 3, 1846) is from Werner Telesko, *Erlösermythen in Kunst und Politik. Zwischen christlicher Tradition und Moderne* (Vienna: Böhlau, 2004), 108. The Wagner quote is from Hugo Dinger, *Richard Wagners geistige Entwicklung. Band 1. Die Weltanschauung Richard Wagners in den Grundzügen ihrer Entwicklung* (Leipzig: E. W. Fritzsch, 1892), 376.
29 Karl Marx, Letter to Engels, 30 July 1862, *MECW* 41: 388. Confirming the antisemitic elements in the public construction of the Lassalle persona, the novelist Friedrich Spielhagen used Lassalle as a model for the (identifiably Jewish) characters in two *Zeitromane* (novels with contemporary themes), Bernhard Münzer in *Die von Hohenstein* (1864, The Hohensteins) and Leo Gutmann in *In Reih' und Glied* (1866, Rank and File). For an early discussion of the Lassalle

Even if such remarks are read as a mocking reenactment of then-fashionable physiognomic ideas, as some Marx defenders have done, or dismissed as an obvious example of Jewish self-hatred, this does not address the troubling fact that many descriptions of Lassalle include references to physical features and character traits that identify him as a "typical" *Ostjude* (East European Jew). These instances of racial othering are inseparable from the political struggles within European Marxism and German Social Democracy but cannot be explained through personal rivalries alone. Literary authors, in the obligatory recognition scenes, acknowledge that Lassalle had features that could be read as Jewish (e.g., dark curly hair) but then spend a considerable time reinterpreting these features as classically and traditionally masculine – in other words, as attractive. Political rivals such as Marx, meanwhile, produce a surfeit of emotion to denounce Lassalle's version of socialism as feminized and feminizing. In all cases, it is through his racialized and sexualized body that identification with the workers' movement is articulated within the political imaginaries and mass cultural practices available at the time. The fact that later literary and historical treatments of Lassalle often reduce the rise of socialism to the individualized scenarios of erotic attraction confirms the perceived threat of emotional socialism both to Marxist orthodoxy and bourgeois society.

Two recognition scenes from two later historical novels suffice to highlight the growing distance from the religious tone in Büttner and are offered here as yet another perspective on the profound social, political, and emotional ruptures marked by 1918/19 and the reconfigurations of socialism in either nationalist or internationalist terms. In *Lassalle. Ein Leben für Freiheit und Liebe* (1902, Lassalle: A Life for Freedom and Love), the novelist and screenwriter Alfred Schirokauer still uses the encounter between Lassalle and the workers to reenact his elevation to an object of socialist desire. Once again, this process is witnessed by a woman, in this case one of his many working-class lovers. Significantly, her recognition of his true face as that of the socialist messiah requires that it be separated from any traces of Jewishness and claimed for a classical lineage:

> A new world of misery had just opened up to him. Ashen his Caesarian head (*Cäsarenkopf*) emerged from the darkness of the coach. Marie could not turn her eyes from him. Never before had he appeared so demanding of worship and yet so removed from all earthly affection. Her tender love sensed the world-toppling forces arising within him and unleashed

---

references in these novels, see Heinrich Georg Schumacher, *Ferdinand Lassalle as a Novelistic Subject of Friedrich Spielhagen* (Annapolis, MD: Advertiser-Republican, 1914).

by the exchange. He stared, stared outside, at the thousand-headed mass. And suddenly he knew who was waiting for the messiah.³⁰

Toward the end of the Weimar Republic, the literary scholar Arno Schirokauer, in the appropriately titled *Lassalle. Die Macht der Illusion, die Illusion der Macht* (1928, *The Power of Illusion and the Illusion of Power*), summons the mystery of Lassalle's face once more but only in order to make a mockery of the cult of romantic love and, by extension, the dream of socialism. In this example, the recognition scene features Helene von Dönniges and Lassalle, now again with "dark and frizzled locks," meeting for the last time at the Rigi thermal baths in Switzerland before the duel. Instead of the messiah, the readers find only the figure of Narcissus, a troubling commentary on the attachments that sustained proletarian identifications during the Wilhelmine years and increasingly haunted Social Democracy toward the end of the Weimar Republic.

> At the moment that he [i.e., Lassalle] says farewell to politics, buries ambition, and after aspiring to lead the masses, becomes a simple and straightforward wooer, at the moment when he drops the banner of the revolution and is concerned only with the conquest of one human heart, he is victorious! It is the sweetest, the happiest of victories. Both of them passionately in love, they give themselves up to a riot of the sentiments [...] They multiply their love by their self-love. Narcissus falls in love with Narcissus. [...] Beneath [her] crown of red-golden hair, a gentle, voluptuous forehead; beneath [his] dark and frizzled locks, a solid, rebellious cranium. Narcissus has fallen in love with Narcissus.³¹

The implicit diagnosis of a profound crisis in the emotional attachments organized through Social Democracy offers one explanation for the transition from the clichéd romance of socialism in the Alfred Schirokauer work from the prewar years to the almost cynical deconstruction of the Lassalle myth in the Arno Schirokauer work from the postwar years. As the next chapter documents, emotional confessions and attachments also feature prominently in turn-of-the-century workers' life writings and, in ways not yet addressed, draw attention to the important role of bourgeois mediators in the making of the proletarian dream.

---

30 Alfred Schirokauer, *Lassalle. Ein Leben für Freiheit und Liebe* (Berlin: Bong, 1912), 93. The book was adapted to the screen by Rudolf Meinert in 1918 under the title *Ferdinand Lassalle, Des Volkstribunen Glück und Ende*. For the larger context in which physiognomic categories were mobilized in modern discourses of charisma, see Claudia Schmölders, "Facial Narratives: The Physiognomics of Charisma, 1900–1945," *New German Critique* 38.3 (2011): 115–132.
31 Arno Schirokauer, *Lassalle: The Power of Illusion and the Illusion of Power*, trans. Eden and Cedar Paul (London: G. Allen & Unwin, 1932), 290–291. For a critical assessment and a selection of writings from the Weimar years, see Ferdinand Lassalle, *Nachgelassene Briefe und Schriften*, ed. Gustav Mayer, 6 vols. (Stuttgart: DVA, 1921–25).

Chapter 7
Re/Writing Workers' Emotions

> The modern worker does not live on bread alone; he cannot be reduced to his working life. He is, to a large percentage, a spiritual being, lives in an imaginary world, and because of that, also in a spiritual sphere.
>
> Adolf Levenstein, *Aus der Tiefe*

Adolf Levenstein (1870–1942) introduces his 1909 anthology of workers' letters by making a compelling case for the importance of psychological studies on the working class. Welcomed by social reformers, labor activists, and sociologists for its innovative approach, his book with the lengthy title *Aus der Tiefe. Arbeiterbriefe: Beiträge zur Seelen-Analyse moderner Arbeiter* (Out of the Depth. Letters from Workers: Contributions to the Psychology of Modern Workers) promised privileged access to workers' emotional lives, their anger, hopelessness, resentment, and above all, their need to be recognized as human beings.[1] Confirming the continuing influence of emotional socialism, Levenstein wanted to communicate the "spiritual being" of "the modern worker" to educated readers concerned about the social question and receptive to psychological explanations.

Three years after *Out of the Depth*, Levenstein published *Die Arbeiterfrage* (1912, The Worker Question), the result of a large-scale questionnaire about the sociopsychological effects of industrial labor on the working class. He was especially interested in workers' individual strategies of accommodation and resistance, including their emotions. In his solicitation letter, Levenstein wrote: "Dear friend, I want to ask you a big favor. I want to know more about your feeling and thinking, how work affects you, what kinds of hopes and desires you have. [...] Just write freely straight from your heart."[2] Questions such as "How

---

[1] Adolf Levenstein, ed., *Aus der Tiefe. Arbeiterbriefe: Beiträge zur Seelen-Analyse moderner Arbeiter* (Berlin: Morgen, 1909), 1–2. On Levenstein, see Klaus M. Beier, "'Individuum' und 'Gemeinschaft': Adolf Levenstein und die Anfänge der sozialpsychologischen Umfrage in der arbeiterpsychologischen Forschung," *Internationale wissenschaftliche Korrespondenz zur Geschichte der deutschen Arbeiterbewegung* 24.2 (1988): 157–171.

[2] Adolf Levenstein, *Die Arbeiterfrage, mit besonderer Berücksichtigung der sozialpsychologischen Seite des modernen Grossbetriebes und der psychophysischen Einwirkungen auf die Arbeiter* (Munich: E. Reinhardt, 1912), 5. Reprinted by Arno Press in 1975. On the Levenstein project, see Dennis Sweeney, "Cultural Practice and Utopian Desire in German Social Democracy: Reading Adolf Levenstein's *Arbeiterfrage* (1912)," *Social History* 28.2 (2003): 174–201. On the Levenstein and Göhre projects as contribution to the public demand for social justice and expression of

do political parties and labor unions influence you?" or "Do you have hopes that your situation will improve soon?" or "Are you without hope and, if so, why?" indicate that Levenstein was looking for answers that could validate his belief in the importance of emotions to the making of proletarian identifications.

The workers' answers confirmed that it was not the Marxist critique of capitalism but their personal need for recognition that gave them a sense of hope and belonging in the workers' movement. Several miners declared: "I have become one and the same with the movement." Another confessed that the movement "has turned me into a thinking person" and "filled me with hatred against the divine world order and the capitalist class." A metal worker spoke for many when he described the workers' movement as "life-giving, giving me relief, enjoyment, and a sense of belonging." Several textile workers acknowledged that the movement "has profoundly changed my entire thinking and feeling" and "is the spring of life that restores and renews me in my darker hours." And drawing on humanistic ideas about education as cultivation, a weaver concluded that through the movement "man is being refined and thus becomes a refined human being."[3]

Levenstein's anthology of workers' letters and his questionnaire on the worker question were part of a wave of workers' life writings published before World War I that suggests a brief opening in the management of the social question, made possible through the belief in a shared language of emotion. His speculations about "what nuances of feeling our day laborer, that helot, is capable of" confirm the surfeit both of expectations and projections that made this self-taught sociologist an important mediator between working-class writers and middle-class readers. Moreover, his conclusion that, "the proletarian of today demands more: cultivation of innate natural energies, satisfaction of his spiritual hunger (Seelenhunger),"[4] indicates to what degree the widespread interest in workers' life writings around the turn of the century originated in contemporaneous debates about the social question, bourgeois concepts of psychological interiority, and romantic ideas about the soul of a people.

These musings about workers' inner lives can be read as responses to the problems of modernization and massification, projected onto the social class that was finally being given a voice in the bourgeois public sphere. Confirming his own emotional investment in the process, Levenstein confessed in the intro-

---

moral outrage, see Barrington Moore, Jr., *Injustice: The Social Basis of Obedience and Revolt* (White Plains, NY: M. E. Sharpe, 1978), 191–216.

3 Levenstein, *Die Arbeiterfrage*, 287, 306, 308, and 316.

4 Adolf Levenstein, Introduction to Georg Meyer, *Lebenstragödie eines Tagelöhners* (Berlin: Frohwein, 1909), 11.

duction to another collection how much "editing books involves emotional suffering. Not being able to extend one's hand to all those human beings yearning 'at the bottom.'"[5] Usually known for their suspicion about any excess of "authentic, overflowing emotion," several sociologists even saw opportunities for future scientific inquiry and better public policy. One was Max Weber who reviewed Levenstein's book positively even as he cautioned against false attributions, concluding "that initially proletarian sensibilities [...] appear much more *similar* to bourgeois sensibilities than aprioristic class theoreticians are inclined to believe. [...] In fact, it is not easy at all to determine at *what* point exactly an authentic, independent proletarian sensibility developing along its own separate tracks and searching for *new* cultural values actually finds expression."[6]

Of course, this is one of the underlying questions in this book as well: In what ways did proletarian identifications depend on, and were in fact constituted through, representations, and how did the modes of describing, telling, and remembering one's life as a worker differ from the shared conventions of writing emotions at the time? There is no doubt that the tentative opening of modern sociology toward literary perspectives profoundly influenced Rudolf Broda and Julius Deutsch's *Das moderne Proletariat* (1910, The Modern Proletariat), the first sociopsychological study on the working class.[7] Guided by their "deepest sympathy for the suffering and loving, the aspiring and striving, of the proletariat," the two Austrian Social Democrats drew extensively on workers' writings to uncover what they described as distinct mental and spiritual characteristics. For Broda and Deutsch, scholarly inquiry was inseparable from political activism, with all methodological choices informed by their desire to intervene in public debate and influence public policy. As regards the symbolic politics of proletarian identifications, Weber's concerns in his review of Levenstein draw attention to the limits of scholarship as a form of activism. However, in this case, the underlying problems can be used productively to uncover how knowledge about the work-

---

[5] Adolf Levenstein, *Arbeiter-Philosophen und -Dichter, Vol 1: Blech-, Berg-, Metall- und Textilarbeiter, Sticker, Handschuhmacher, Bäcker, Buchdrucker, Weberinnen, Dienstmädchen* (Berlin: Eberhard Frowein, 1909), 7. An annotated reprint with an afterword by Uwe-K. Ketelsen was published in 2009 in Bielefeld by Aisthesis.
[6] Max Weber, "Zur Methodik sozialpsychologischer Enquêten und ihrer Bearbeitung," in *Zur Psychophysik der industriellen Arbeit. Schriften und Reden 1908–1912*, ed. Wolfgang Schluchter and Sabine Frommer (Tübingen: J. C. B. Mohr, 1998), 183. The influence of Levenstein's study can also be seen in Hendrik de Man's *Der Kampf um die Arbeitsfreude* (1927) and Erich Fromm's *Arbeiter und Angestellte am Vorabend des Dritten Reiches, Eine sozialpsychologische Untersuchung* conducted between 1929 and 1930.
[7] Rudolf Broda and Julius Deutsch, *Das moderne Proletariat. Eine sozialpsychologische Studie* (Berlin: Georg Reimer, 1910), iv.

er's soul is in fact produced – beginning with the extensive exchanges between the workers' writers and their bourgeois editors. For both participants in these very unequal exchanges, emotions function as a privileged marker of subjectivity, including a collective subjectivity in the making. Reconstructing the processes by which specific feelings are identified and interpreted as proletarian not only draws attention to the cultural conventions and traditions that enter into such decisions. It also offers a unique opportunity to reflect on the conditions under which speaking across class lines, and specifically speaking about the working class, almost always involves hierarchies of power and knowledge and complicated gestures of accommodation and resistance. For that reason, this chapter on workers' life writings will pay special attention to how editors such as the above-mentioned Levenstein and Paul Göhre, the Lutheran-pastor-turned-Social-Democrat who features prominently in the second part, presented the worker-writer as a sentient being, in full awareness of their own investment in the all-important process of communication and rapprochement.

The writing of workers' emotions always involved a collaborative process, but one with unequal participants, conflicting interests, and different language competencies. The emotional intensities unleashed through the "discovery" of the worker's soul are on full display in a long letter written by the miner Max Lotz in response to Levenstein's original request for a contribution to *Out of the Depth*. Lotz begins by confessing that, "rarely has anything moved me as much as the moment when my wife handed me your letter as I was coming home from my shift. An expression of recognition." But his gratefulness soon gives way to barely concealed anger about what he sees as the editor's preconceived notions about his inner life:

> Individuality smiles triumphantly! That's what you once wrote to me. Why did you write that? I am consumed by rage, an indescribable, untamable rage. My heart is filled with hatred and my soul devoured by its sick pleasures. You are challenging me? But wait, what a fool I am! No, you are not challenging *me*, this carnal lustful cadaver; you want to force the soul, the nature of the mind, that adversary and apostate of plain facts, to speak up and confess. I am furious, inhumanly enraged. Why have you done this? The *full* bosom should speak? The *awakened, troubled* personality? Oh, fury! Trampled dreams should speak to you? Go ahead and retrieve them from the great democratic swamp of egoism, the Orcus of envy. There, in its poisonous gases, the last shards of the shattered soul are roaring, screaming, craving, and raging – for redemption. For much, much too long have I suppressed aspects of my personality. Redemption? Brutally foolish philosophy! The world does not know this language. Reality, existence, and life are unrelenting in their natural tragedy. Even the embryo shivers in the diaper of downfall. Nothing is immortal, nothing

except profane matter. Matter is immortal in the process of *development*. And beyond matter? Nonsense. There you have your redemption.[8]

In this rambling, incoherent outburst, Lotz attacks Levenstein for expecting a re-enactment of working-class suffering. Yet in his response, this particular worker also experiments with a number of rhetorical personas, including the moralist and the cynic. Two competing impulses can be identified, his gratefulness for having been recognized as a fellow human being and his anger about being enlisted in a sociological experiment. His use of literary tropes, complete with appeals to the gods of antiquity, reveals his desire to partake in the bourgeois cultural habitus that, as will be shown in chapter 8, was an important part of the Social Democratic program of *Kultur* and *Bildung*. At the same time, his insistence on a materialist worldview suggests an unwillingness to share Levenstein's belief in open dialogue as a conduit to social peace and reconciliation. The depth of the worker's soul, Lotz seems to be saying, is a function of bourgeois individualism, in which the worker's "true" feelings exist outside discourse and are bound to remain unknowable. "The world does not know this language," he concludes; meanwhile Levenstein believes that this language can be learned and used to good ends.

For the most part, workers' life writings from the 1900s and 1910s offer unvarnished depictions of the difficult working and living conditions of manual and rural laborers, often far removed from the large factories, steelworks, and coal mines typically associated with the industrial proletariat. These books give harrowing accounts of poverty, hunger, sickness, vagrancy, and delinquency. They also include appalling examples of physical mistreatment, ethnic discrimination, and political persecution, as well as (for the times) shockingly casual accounts of premarital sex, sexual violence, and part-time prostitution. In sharing their stories, the worker-writers draw heavily on established literary genres and offer confessional narratives in the tradition of Augustine and Rousseau and coming-of-age stories modeled on the Goethean *Bildungsroman*, or novel of education. The activists among them offer up socialist versions of what Katharina Gerstenberger describes as the trajectory "from suffering to salvation,"[9] complete with the religious imaginary known from the cult surrounding Lassalle.

---

8 Max Lotz, Letter of 31 August 1908, in Levenstein, *Aus der Tiefe*, 73–74.
9 This is the title of Chapter 3 on Adelheid Popp in Katharina Gerstenberger, *Truth to Tell: German Women's Autobiographies and Turn-of-the-Century Culture* (Ann Arbor: University of Michigan Press, 2000).

Others undermine genre-related expectations by emulating the chronicle format with its primary focus on facts and events.

In all cases, writing functions as a form of self-assertion that includes performative elements, which Peter Sloterdijk, in his study of autobiography as a method of organizing social experiences, calls nonsubjective subjectivity.[10] Accordingly, the workers' refusal of intimacy neither proves that workers live only in, and for, the collective, nor does their preoccupation with daily survival suggest an undeveloped inner life. In fact, their unwillingness (or inability) to perform the roles of "typical" worker and "simple" human being and to grant access to their "true" thoughts and feelings provides a valuable entry point into the complicated dynamics between, to use anthropological terms, native informant and participant observer that must be considered an integral part of the proletarian dream. The same can be said about the heavy reliance on literary conventions. Generally speaking, workers' life writings can be grouped into stories of victimization by birth and circumstance, stories of upward mobility through determination and hard work, and stories of political mobilization in the context of the workers' movement. These narrative categories correspond with three basic emotional scripts, individual resignation, self-advancement, and class solidarity. The fact that similar scripts can be found in the socialist novels of Minna Kautsky, August Otto-Walster, and others points to the close affinities between autobiographical, fictional, and scholarly treatments of the provocation of class politics and its role in changing conceptions of public and private life.

The wide public interest in workers' life writings was the result of a number of interrelated factors: the growing political influence of Socialist Democracy after the lapsing of the Anti-Socialist Laws in 1890; the coordinated efforts by government agencies, philanthropic groups, and the Lutheran and Catholic Churches in addressing the so-called social question; and the role of new academic disciplines such as sociology, ethnography, and cultural anthropology in explaining the infamous modern masses to middle-class readers. On the one hand, the workers' stories of widespread and unrelenting misery confirmed bourgeois fears of revolutionary uprisings and provided compelling arguments in favor of social reforms. On the other, the workers' belief in the exemplary individual and his ability to overcome social and economic inequality validated the foundational scripts of self-discovery and self-advancement shared by liberal democracy, bourgeois subjectivity, and the project of life reform.

---

10 Peter Sloterdijk, *Literatur und Organisation von Lebenserfahrung. Autobiographien der Zwanziger Jahre* (Munich: Hanser, 1978), 8.

Just as the public fascination with workers' life writings lasted little more than a decade, the scholarly interest in workers' life writings remained short-lived. The discovery of this forgotten body of work during the 1970s and 1980s was closely linked to the reconceptualization of proletarian culture as an oppositional culture and the political investment in its continued possibilities by a critical *Germanistik* (i. e., the academic study of German literature).[11] These contributions, in turn, were part of a broader attempt to at once move beyond the high-culture model then still dominant in traditional literary studies and to develop an alternative to the economic determinism of orthodox Marxism. The findings from that period can be used here to further clarify the problems of reading workers' life writings at once as historical documents, literary texts, and archives of emotions. Published as part of an ambitious history of German socialist literature, GDR scholar Ursula Münchow's study on workers' life writings rather predictably focused on their contribution, however flawed, to a Marxist-Leninist interpretation of history.[12] In West Germany, scholars used these republished works to test some of the arguments developed in the context of Critical Theory and the New Left. Bernd Witte argued against the automatic equation of workers' life writings with socialist literature and pointed to the strong influence of the *Bil-*

---

[11] See the two dissertations on the topic, Petra Frerichs, *Bürgerliche Autobiographie und proletarische Selbstdarstellung. Eine vergleichende Darstellung unter besonderer Berücksichtigung persönlichkeitstheoretischer und literaturwissenschaftlich-didaktischer Fragestellungen* (Frankfurt am Main: Haag und Herchen, 1980) and Michael Vogtmeier, *Die proletarische Autobiographie 1903 – 1914. Studien zur Gattungs- und Funktionsgeschichte der Autobiographie* (Frankfurt am Main: Peter Lang, 1984). For the larger context, see Otfried Scholz, *Arbeiterselbstbild und Arbeiterfremdbild zur Zeit der industriellen Revolution. Ein Beitrag zur Sozialgeschichte des Arbeiters in der deutschen Erzähl- und Memoirenliteratur um die Mitte des 19. Jahrhunderts* (Berlin: Colloquium, 1980). On methodological questions, see Wolfgang Jacobeit, "Volkskunde und Arbeiterkultur," in *Die andere Kultur. Volkskunde, Sozialwissenschaften und Arbeiterkultur. Ein Tagungsbericht*, ed. Helmut Fielhauer and Olaf Bockhorn (Vienna: Europaverlag, 1982), 11 – 25. And for a critical assessment of the fascination with workers' life writings in the history/historiography of the working class, see Ralf Roth, "Tempi passati: Die kurze Konjunktur der Arbeiteralltagsgeschichte. Eine Reminiszenz," in *Historie und Leben. Der Historiker als Wissenschaftler und Zeitgenosse. Festschrift für Lothar Gall zum 70. Geburtstag*, ed. Dieter Hein, Klaus Hildebrand, and Andreas Schulz (Munich: R. Oldenbourg, 2006), 161 – 173.
[12] Ursula Münchow, *Frühe deutsche Arbeiterautobiographien* (Berlin: Akademie, 1973), 66 – 67. The earliest scholarly treatment of the topic appeared during the Third Reich, Cecilia A. Trunz, *Die Autobiographien von deutschen Industriearbeitern* (Freiburg im Breisgau: Buchdruckerei Herder, 1934), 110 – 135. A selection of workers' autobiographies has been translated into English in Alfred Kelly, *The German Worker: Working-Class Autobiographies from the Age of Industrialization* (Berkeley: University of California Press, 1987). For a comparative perspective, see Mary Jo Maynes, *Taking the Hard Road: Life Course in French and German Workers' Autobiographies in the Era of Industrialization* (Chapel Hill: University of North Carolina Press, 1995).

dungsroman, the novel of education so crucial to conceptions of bourgeois subjectivity.[13] By contrast, Wolfgang Emmerich emphasized the operative (i.e., didactic and agitational) function of what he called proletarian self-representations and interpreted the latter in line with Lenin's theory of two cultures – the theory that every national culture consists of two cultures, a hegemonic bourgeois culture and a proletarian culture that, by definition, is democratic and socialist.[14] Given the unresolvable tension between the pseudo-objectivism of the chronicle format and the subjectivism of the confessional mode, Georg Bollenbeck, in the most theoretically sophisticated contribution, proposed *Lebenserinnerung* (life memoir) as a more appropriate term in the context of working-class culture.[15] Unlike autobiography, he argued, the notion of life memoir acknowledges the difficulty of developing a personality under conditions of capitalist exploitation and recognizes class consciousness (or the lack thereof) as an often underestimated part of the problem. Similar arguments have over the last decades lead to a growing preference for the term "life writings" in Anglo-American scholarship on the genre of autobiography.

Situated within these larger histories of reading and rereading, the exchanges between Lotz and Levenstein in *Out of the Depth* raise important questions about how workers' life writings can be read today: as documents of working-class empowerment or of middle-class goodwill? Is their main purpose to promote social reform or socialist mobilization? Are they modeled on bourgeois narratives of individual advancement or directed toward a collectivist view of society? Can this kind of writing be likened to a therapeutic process through which a clear sense of self is acquired or restored? Or do the writers merely produce the performances of subjectivity considered necessary for admission to the bourgeois public sphere? Do the editors import bourgeois literary genres, including autobiography, into working-class contexts and for decidedly socialist purposes? Or do they use the distinction between literacy and orality to place folk culture outside of history and enlist the voice of the other in a critique of modernity?

---

[13] Bernd Witte, "Literatur der Opposition. Über Geschichte, Funktion und Wirkmittel der frühen Arbeiterliteratur," in *Handbuch zur deutschen Arbeiterliteratur*, 2 vols., ed. Heinz Ludwig Arnold (Munich: edition text + kritik, 1977), 1: 7–45.
[14] Wolfgang Emmerich, ed. and intro., *Proletarische Lebensläufe. Autobiographische Dokumente zur Entstehung der zweiten Kultur in Deutschland*, 2 vols. (Reinbek: Rowohlt, 1980), 1: 9–39. Lenin develops his theory of two cultures in "Critical Remarks on the National Question" (1913), *Collected Works* in (London: Lawrence & Wisehart, 1960), Vol. 20: 17–51.
[15] Georg Bollenbeck, *Zur Theorie und Geschichte der frühen Arbeiterlebenserinnerungen* (Kronberg: Scriptor, 1976), especially the introduction.

Chapter 3 draws on the memoirs of famous socialist leaders to argue for the central role of emotional attachments in the making of proletarian identifications. Chapter 5 examines socialist allegory as an example of cultural appropriation wherein a subordinate social group adopts (and adapts) artistic forms and styles from a dominant one, in this case through the detour of Greek mythology and Schiller's theory of the pathetic. Shifting the site of inquiry to that mysterious entity called the worker's soul, workers' life writings offer powerful templates and models for the kind of emotional work required of individual workers gaining class consciousness and joining the workers' movement. Psychological interiority is presented as an important enabling condition in class mobilization, not least because of its implicit claims on bourgeois subjectivity. As Rüdiger Campe and Julia Weber have recently argued, the distinction between interiority and exteriority and the cultivation of interiority as *Innerlichkeit* (inwardness) since the late eighteenth century must be traced back to its equation in German romanticism with both high culture and a high social position. Accordingly, Campe and Weber use the term "interiorization" to analyze the discursive strategies that established the distinctions between interiority and exteriority and made them an integral part of new political demands and promises of social mobility. Through their binary structure, exteriority and interiority defined the boundaries between public and private life and made the close connection between interiority, subjectivity, and political emancipation one of the enabling conditions of liberal democracy and the nation-state. In accordance with its elevated status in bourgeois culture, literature, including autobiography, was designated as the ideal medium for a thus defined process of interiorization and its related discourses of psychologization and individualization.[16]

If autobiographical writing played a key role in the making of bourgeois subjectivity, how can socialist claims to individual agency be enlisted in a critique of class society? More specifically, how did the editors of workers' life writings re-functionalize distinctly bourgeois modalities in their role as mediators across the class divide? A preliminary answer can be found in the extensive exchanges between worker-writers and their editors and the emotional nature of these exchanges. In most cases, the editors functioned as confidantes for first-time authors and as translators of the working-class experience to a largely middle-class readership. The first-person singular allowed the worker-writer to imagine his struggles as part of a distinct class biography and connect his individual tri-

---

[16] See Rüdiger Campe and Julia Weber, eds., *Rethinking Emotion: Interiority and Exteriority in Premodern, Modern, and Contemporary Thought* (Berlin: De Gruyter, 2014), especially the introduction.

umphs and defeats to the larger narrative of class struggle. The readers, in turn, were able to discover the individuals behind what the conservative scholars (introduced in chapter 1) imagined as the modern masses, and what the Marxist theorists (presented in chapter 2) conceptualized as the proletariat. Through empathetic identification, middle-class readers were invited to accept the workers as part of the people, the nation, or all of humanity. The role of the editor consisted in negotiating the competing perspectives of individualism and communitarianism and managing the languages of emotion that were being created at the intersection of the personal and the political. As all editors quickly found out, however, unmediated emotions rarely functioned as a conduit to better understanding. Instead, emotional irruptions only highlighted the mutual projections that caused Levenstein to muse about expressivity and authenticity and that prompted Lotz to experiment with various speaking positions. The (unequal) dialogic nature of this process becomes glaringly apparent whenever the worker-writers refuse to perform the role of the exploited and oppressed or perform it all too well; especially instructive are those moments when they assume the mask of bourgeois interiority, including its sentimental registers, and when they draw on Marxist theories to explain their personal choices.

Part of the hidden struggles over discursive authority that Levenstein avoided in *The Worker Question*, Lotz's emotional response to Levenstein in *Out of the Depth* draws attention to the non-identity of the worker as author and the worker as protagonist of his own life story, with any surfeit of emotion reserved for the former. This problematic has less to do with his difficulties of developing a strong sense of self than his acute awareness of a double consciousness, with the first explained through the actual deprivations and difficulties of working-class lives and the second related to the editor's demands for a public performance of working-class identity. The focus on autobiographical writing as a dialogic and performative process guarantees that the workers are not silenced again and their voices reduced to the two discursive modalities available at the time: that of social reform, with its innate tension between genuine empathy and moral superiority, and that of bourgeois slumming, with its exoticizing and pathologizing tendencies. An example of the latter can be found in the introductory comments by Hans Ostwald, a prolific chronicler of disenfranchised groups, who praised the recollections of his own worker-writer, a migrant worker, for the "shocking authenticity" of his "breathtaking accounts" from the "purgatory of working-class life."[17]

---

[17] Hans Ostwald, preface to Ernst Schuchart, *Sechs Monate Arbeitshaus. Erlebnisse eines wandernden Arbeiters* (Berlin: Hermann Seemann, 1907), n. p.

While Ostwald published "authentic" voices from the working class alongside volumes on prostitution, homosexuality, and the Berlin *bohème*, Paul Göhre (1864–1928) became interested in workers' life writings because of his deep commitment to the social question. The former Lutheran pastor had personally experienced the harsh working conditions in the modern factory during a social experiment recounted in *Drei Monate Fabrikarbeiter und Handwerksbursche* (1891, Three Months as a Factory Worker and Journeyman). This expedition to lifeworlds more foreign to middle-class readers than distant continents was received with great excitement. As Rudolf Lavant noted in a poem: "The book was a hit./ It was devoured/ And passed on from hand to hand."[18] In a later lecture published under the title *Wie ein Pfarrer Sozialdemokrat wurde* (1900, How a Parson Became a Social Democrat), Göhre described his eventual conversion to socialism as a logical evolution of his Christian faith. As several scholars have noted, however, his indiscriminate references to workers as a mass, a class, and a people betray an enduring conservatism. In fact, Göhre's initial goal as a social reformer had been "the education, the refinement, and the Christianization of a wild, heathen Social Democracy and the obliteration of its contrarian materialistic worldview."[19]

Göhre's ambitious editorial project started with Carl Fischer's *Denkwürdigkeiten und Erinnerungen eines Arbeiters* (1903, published in English as *Recollections of a Worker)*, which were inspired by Göhre's own excursions into working-class life and served as a model for many later contributions. Throughout, these literary debts do not necessarily imply shared socialist convictions, despite their focus on the special role of school, church, and police in preserving feudal and patriarchal structures in modern class society. In a letter to the publisher, written before learning of Göhre's conversion to Social Democracy, Fischer expresses his "full sympathy" for Göhre as an author and calls him "the man most suited" to become his interlocutor and editor.[20] Concerned that Fischer's unfamiliarity with

---

18 Rudolf Lavant, *Gedichte* (Berlin: Akademie, 1965), 52.
19 Paul Göhre, *Drei Monate Fabrikarbeiter und Handwerksbursche. Eine praktische Studie* (Leipzig, Grunow, 1891), 222. Alexander Graf von Stenbock-Fermor, who reported similar excursions into the proletarian lifeworld in *Meine Erlebnisse als Bergarbeiter* (1929) and *Deutschland von unten: Reise durch die proletarische Provinz* (1931), might be called a Weimar-era successor of Göhre. Carol Poore discusses the reportages of the so-called Red Count in *The Bonds of Labor: German Journeys to the Working World, 1890–1990* (Detroit: Wayne State University Press, 2000).
20 Quoted by Dieter Schwarzenau, "Die frühen Arbeiterautobiographien," in *Beiträge zur Kulturgeschichte der deutschen Arbeiterbewegung, 1848–1918*, ed. Peter von Rüden (Frankfurt am Main: Büchergilde Gutenberg, 1979), 177. Schwarzenau includes a brief discussion of Göhre's complicated relationship to his worker-writers.

literary conventions might turn off some readers, Göhre in turn uses his introduction to the book to prevent misreadings of the workers' voice: "There are hardly any emotional outbursts, feelings, sentiments, opinions – these are only expressed in the form of actions. One experiences these things by witnessing them. [...] Amusing remarks are entirely missing; big political, religious, economic, scientific, artistic ideas, too; the same holds true for references to his inner life. Of course, no one ever told the man that it would be of any significance."[21] Göhre's conclusion that Fischer "to this day is still not a Social Democrat, still claims for himself a strong religious conviction, and still is filled with reverence for the emperor"[22] may be read as explanation for the author's literary shortcomings or as affirmation of the compatibility of conservative and social reformist positions in the study of the working class.

Encouraged by the critical success of *Recollections*, Göhre used Moritz William Theodor Bromme's *Lebensgeschichte eines modernen Fabrikarbeiters* (1905, Life Story of a Modern Factory Worker) to launch a book series on workers' *Lebensgeschichten* for the Eugen Diederichs Verlag. Known for beautifully designed books and a penchant for neoromantic literature, the publisher initially called the series "Life and Knowledge," in line with its life reform commitments, but then started a new series under the more openly political heading "On the Social Question." Once again, the goal for Göhre was "to spread basic information about the real life of today's proletariat, and do so through the quill of the proletarians themselves."[23] Aware of the mediations necessary for turning the worker-writer into a discursive subject, he early on decided to alter the original title, replacing "Social Democratic factory worker" with "modern factory worker," presumably to make the book more acceptable to a broader readership. By comparing various manuscript versions of a number of workers' life writings, the Germanist Bernd Neumann has reconstructed in great detail what would soon become the norm for most of these projects: changed titles, rearranged sections, extensive cuts, modified dialects, and corrections of orthography, gram-

---

21 Paul Göhre, Introduction to Karl (or Carl) Fischer, *Denkwürdigkeiten und Erinnerungen eines Arbeiters* (Leipzig: Diederichs, 1903), vi. For a close reading of the text, see Jost Hermand, "Carl Fischer, *Denkwürdigkeiten und Erinnerungen eines Arbeiters (1903–1905)*," in *Unbequeme Literatur. Eine Beispielreihe* (Heidelberg: Lothar Stiehm, 1971), 87–106. On Fischer, also see Frank Woesthoff, *Prolet Pietist Prophet. Die "Denkwürdigkeiten und Erinnerungen eines Arbeiters" von Carl Fischer (1841–1906)* (Göttingen: Wallstein, 1995).
22 Göhre, Introduction to Fischer, *Denkwürdigkeiten*, xi.
23 Paul Göhre, Introduction to Moritz William Theodor Bromme, *Lebensgeschichte eines modernen Fabrikarbeiters* (Leipzig: Diederichs, 1905), v–vi.

mar, and style. Interestingly, these revisions are often mentioned in the workers' own accounts of their extensive exchanges with their editors.[24]

For instance, in the introduction to Wenzel Holek's *Lebensgang eines deutsch-tschechischen Handarbeiters* (1909, The Life Story of a German-Czech Manual Laborer), Göhre insists that he knew nothing about Holek's socialist commitments when he invited him to write a follow-up account focused on his adult working life. Given the precarious nature of his own political commitments, it is not surprising that the editor feels compelled "to counter the suspicion that I, as a Social Democrat, was perhaps motivated by the desire to advocate for the cause of my party in this way."[25] Of course, these disavowals do not prevent Göhre in the same introduction from suggesting a natural affinity between Social Democracy and the voice of the people. Drawing on the discourses of folk to emphasize the authenticity of Holek's account, and in the process distracting from his own editorial revisions, he proclaims: "Through these chosen voices, the people are speaking about themselves, their fates, their struggles and joys, their misery, their hope, their painful resignation. Here all veils fall: like soil that has come alive, the people assume form in front of us."[26] Confirming Göhre's investment in the production of authenticity, Franz Rehbein's *Das Leben eines Landarbeiters* (1911, The Life of a Farm Worker), the next volume in the series, offers a very different challenge for the editor. Acknowledging that Rehbein has left behind the hard life on a rural estate to work as a socialist journalist, Göhre goes to some length to assure his readers of the enduring truthfulness of the worker's voice. "No longer does he [i.e., Rehbein] display any signs of awkwardness. He is the full master of his thoughts, images, words, and sentences. Even loanwords he handles with aplomb," notes the proud editor, only to insist, "Nonetheless his language appears extraordinarily authentic, drastically unadorned, in true peasant fashion (*Bauernart*)."[27]

Several of the books edited by Göhre and others identified the authors initially by occupation only – a factory worker, day laborer, or a farmhand. If a book was successful, later editions appeared with the author's name above

---

[24] In his afterword to the 1971 reprint of *Lebensgeschichte* published by Athenäum, Bernd Neumann compares Bromme's stay in a "Hustenburg" near Weimar (for treatment of tuberculosis) to that of Hans Castorp's experiences on the famous "Zauberberg" in Davos.

[25] Paul Göhre, Introduction to Wenzel Holek, *Lebensgang eines deutsch-tschechischen Handarbeiters* (Jena: Diederichs, 1909), iv.

[26] Göhre, Introduction to Holek, *Lebensgang,* i. The book appeared in several revised and expanded editions.

[27] Paul Göhre, Introduction to Franz Rehbein, *Das Leben eines Landarbeiters* (Jena: Eugen Diederichs, 1911), 3.

the title. Mirroring the waves of labor migration within central Europe, Göhre's worker-writers came from diverse regions: Carl Fischer (1841–1906) was a railroad worker and steel miner from Silesia, Moritz Theodor William Bromme (1873–1926) a metal worker from Thuringia, Wenzel Holek (1864–1935) a construction worker and glass blower from Bohemia, and Franz Rehbein (1867–1909) a farmhand from Pomerania who worked on an estate in Holstein. Fischer, Bromme, Holek, and Rehbein all turned to writing after becoming incapacitated due to serious workplace injuries and, with the exception of Fischer, developed their literary voices after joining the workers' movement and its organizations. Like the SPD party leaders, several worker-writers completed their manuscripts during extended stays in prisons or sanatoriums. And like many socialist workers-turned-journalists, involvement with the workers' movement allowed some of these men to turn their new skills as worker-writers into professional careers.[28]

The documented exchanges between worker-writers and their editors attest to an acute awareness of the constructedness of class identities that extends to the emotional attachments forged in the act of reading. The degree to which the problem of reading was always on the minds of editors is confirmed by the introduction of Friedrich Naumann (1860–1919) to *Arbeiterschicksale* (1906, Workers' Fates) by Franz Louis Fischer, a coal miner-turned-dairyman. An influential liberal voice in the debate on social reform, the well-known sociologist believed in the need for better communication across the class divide. Yet Naumann also defended the middle class against accusations of "an egotistical heartlessness that, in reality, is mostly lack of knowledge. It is in fact difficult for the non-worker to form an accurate impression of the living conditions of those who, without financial resources, fight for their survival. [...] Quite a few educated men and women experience their separation from the people as very painful and understand that there is a deep hole in their spiritual and social education."[29] As if responding to Naumann's explanation of middle-class obliviousness, Bruno Hans Bürgel (1875–1948) offered his own reasons for writing down the remarkable success story of *Vom Arbeiter zum Astronomen* (1919, From Worker to Astronomer) in the following way: "I want to show the upper classes how the world looks to someone who is forced to view it from inside a damp basement apartment in a *Hinterhaus* (interior house in a tenement). I

---

28 The biographical information is taken from *Arbeiter über ihr Leben. Von den Anfängen der Arbeiterbewegung bis zum Ende der Weimarer Republik*, ed. and intr. Ursula Münchow (Berlin: Dietz, 1976), 461–481.
29 Friedrich Naumann, Introduction to Franz Louis Fischer, *Arbeiterschicksale* (Berlin: Buchverlag der "Hilfe," 1906), n. p.

want to show how a young worker comes to socialism, how he feels, how he acts."[30]

The written exchanges between worker-writers and editors discussed so far only involve men and male relationships. While women appear in the life writings – as family members, sexual partners, and work colleagues – they never become fully developed figures. Unsurprisingly, the introductions allude to women only when referring to the very different status of sexuality, marriage, and family life in working-class lives. Concerned with the presentation of the worker as a social type and human being, the editors simply assume masculinity and class position to be mutually constitutive, mediated through the dream of an ungendered (but decidedly male) vision of the people or of humankind.

In another context, the life writings of female workers would add further insights in what ways arguments between editors and worker-writers over emotional tones and styles served to establish the function of gender in depictions of the working class.[31] As has been shown, the male worker's desire to assert his individuality against the determinants of class and to recount his personal struggles in the available languages of interiority found expression through bourgeois constructions of masculinity – which also meant that the emancipatory effects of autobiographical writing were not readily available to women workers. More specifically, as the final emanation of the emotional socialism discussed in chapter 4, workers' life writings from the turn of the century made certain that emotions and emotionality could still be claimed for a male-dominated narrative of class. This chapter only allows for a brief mention of the complications of gender and class thematized in Adelheid Popp's critically acclaimed *Die Jugendgeschichte einer Arbeiterin* (1909, published in English as *The Autobiography of a Working Woman*), which appeared, initially without attribution, in a book series called "Life Stories." Radicalized in the workers' movement, Popp (1869–1939) started the proletarian women's movement in Austria and edited the *Arbeiterinnen-Zeitung* during the 1920s. Her account of being socialized in the Viennese

---

30 Bruno Hans Bürgel, *Vom Arbeiter zum Astronomen. Der Aufstieg eines Lebenskämpfers* (Berlin: Im Deutschen Verlag, 1935), 8.
31 Two examples are Gerhard Braun, ed., *Im Kampf ums Dasein! Wahrheitstgetreue Lebenserinnerungen eines Mädchens aus dem Volke als Fabrikarbeiterin, Dienstmädchen und Kellnerin* (1908) and Carl Moszeik, ed., *Aus der Gedankenwelt einer Arbeiterfrau, von ihr selbst erzählt* (1909). Numerous other texts have been included in Richard Klucsaritis and Friedrich G. Kürbisch, eds., *Arbeiterinnen kämpfen um ihr Recht. Autobiographische Texte zu Kampf rechtloser und entrechteter "Frauenspersonen" in Deutschland, Österreich und der Schweiz des 19. und 20. Jahrhunderts* (Wuppertal: Hammer, 1975). On the question of gender and sexuality, see Birgit A. Jensen, "Bawdy Bodies or Moral Agency? The Struggle for Identity in Working-Class Autobiographies of Imperial Germany," *Biography* 28.4 (Fall 2005): 534–557.

working class found a large and receptive readership, especially among Social Democrats; the book saw numerous editions and translations. Like the male worker-writers cited earlier, she experienced a difficult childhood, marked by poverty, hardship, and misery. Yet for Popp, joining the movement meant not only understanding her experiences in class terms but also rejecting the socially prescribed life choices available to women. Perhaps this explains why she chose to present her life in a starkly realistic style – without the stylistic flourishes added by her male colleagues as an integral part of their performances of proletarian masculinity. Popp's highly developed sense of solidarity found expression in sympathetic portrayals of fellow workers and close attention to the unique struggles of working women. It also propelled her to describe her main reasons for writing the book with a view toward its uplifting effects on other women: "What caused me to write down how I became a socialist was solely the desire to cheer on those female workers who yearn for recognition but who always hesitate because they lack the confidence to accomplish something."[32].

Popp's self-effacing tone could not be more different from the eruptions of male suffering and resentment that have been analyzed in this chapter. Karl Kautsky in 1909 wrote a very positive review of *The Autobiography of a Working Woman*, singling out the clarity, simplicity, and sheer optimism of the writing. In the book's preface, August Bebel, too, confessed to having been deeply moved by the author's ethos of "unrelenting self-improvement" and belief in the transformative power of socialism. He was especially impressed by Popp's narrative skills at conveying how social change takes place on the individual level while occurring within a social context. Her unique ability – in Bebel's words, to show "this is how I was, and this is how I am now. What I did, what I had to do – all of you can do something similar, you must only want it"[33] – distinguished her contribution in two equally important ways: through its emphasis on class unity and gender solidarity and through its full identification with Social Democracy. Franz Mehring summarized the opinions of many leading Social Democrats when he recommended that, "workers who wish to publish their life story are well-advised to follow the example of Adelheid Popp and not the tutelage of Göhre."[34]

Worker's life writings continued to be published during and after World War I but failed to reach a large readership. Without a clear social and sociological

---

[32] Adelheid Popp, *Die Jugendgeschichte einer Arbeiterin von ihr selbst erzählt* (Munich: Ernst Reinhardt, 1909), 93. On Popp, see Gerstenberger, *Truth to Tell*, 100–139.
[33] August Bebel, Introduction to Popp, *Die Jugendgeschichte einer Arbeiterin*, v. An English translation titled *The Autobiography of a Working Woman* was published in 1912.
[34] Franz Mehring, quoted in Gerstenberger, *Truth to Tell*, 105.

function, they became more diverse, with titles ranging from Josef Peukert's anarchist memoir *Erinnerungen eines Proletariers aus der revolutionären Arbeiterbewegung* (1913, Recollections of a Proletarian from the Revolutionary Workers' Movement) to Nikolaus Osterroth's Social Democratic conversion narrative *Vom Beter zum Kämpfer* (1920, My Path from Praying to Fighting) to Ottilie Baader's socialist feminist memoir *Ein steiniger Weg* (1921, A Stony Path). In the wake of the October Revolution, the emphasis on communication by editors such as Levenstein and Göhre appeared not only outdated but also ineffectual compared to the confrontational tones and styles promoted by a new generation of radicalized workers. As a product of the nineteenth century, workers' life writings remained indebted to the culture of emotional socialism and reproduced, in the voice of the worker-writers, the tensions between the demands for social reform and the promises of bourgeois subjectivity that could not be resolved in the languages of emotion. A very similar argument can be made for the overdetermined discourses on culture and education that defined the complicated relationship of Social Democracy to the bourgeois heritage and that are the focus of the next chapter.

Chapter 8
The Socialist Project of Culture and Education

> Socialism is more than a mere party program. It is a noble cultural pursuit, a spiritual moral force. It can only succeed when it inspires creative ideas and is able to transform the rich emotional values dormant within into a powerful spiritual experience.
>
> Richard Weimann, "Die sozialistische Bildungsarbeit"

"Cultural," "spiritual," "moral," and "emotional," during the Wilhelmine years, these terms constituted the main building blocks of an emergent – or, to be more precise, imagined – proletarian culture. It was in the Humboldtian sense of *Bildung* (education, formation) as the full realization of human potential that these qualities were called upon to transform the working class into the revolutionary class. It was through recourse to idealist aesthetics and German classicism that socialism – or Social Democracy, with both terms still used synonymously – promised to complete the emancipatory project started by the bourgeoisie through the development of *Kultur* (culture, cultivation) as an entire way of life. And it was through the elusive process of *Veredelung* (refinement, betterment) that culture and education were enlisted in the forging of proletarian identifications as well as socialist commitments.

This chapter reconstructs the socialist appropriation of bourgeois *Kultur* and *Bildung* as part of a larger discourse on class formation, and does so in full awareness of the very different histories of workers' libraries, worker's cultural organizations, and workers' educational associations. Two lines of inquiry will be pursued, the socialist debt to the bourgeois tradition, which hinged on the Marxist appropriation of idealist aesthetics, and the socialist version of cultural nationalism, which included a class-based version of Herder's folk culture. Focusing on the effects of discourse brings into relief the dialogic quality of proletarian culture that was emerging within, through, and against, bourgeois culture and doing so precisely through its proprietary claims on the bourgeois heritage. In other words, the discussions about culture and education will be examined, not as blueprints for actual practices of appropriation, but as acts of appropriation themselves, with their anticipatory functions treated as an integral part of the process, if not its most important characteristic.

The intensely emotional investment that characterized Socialist Democratic debates on culture and education beyond the substantial disagreements on specific points will function once more as a point of entry into the subject matter. Here Richard Weimann's characterization from 1920 of socialism as a "noble cultural pursuit" and "spiritual moral force" perfectly captures the shared sense of spiritual elevation (and moral righteousness) that, for many like him, sustained their political commitments.[1] Even outside observers commented on the intensity of the attachment to bourgeois humanism as a model for class emancipation. For instance, the Austrian anarchist Josef Peukert (1855–1910) noted that in these "workers' associations [...] the worker became aware of his human dignity, cultivated and developed his independent thinking and feeling, and raised his level of consciousness and knowledge in heretofore unimaginable ways."[2] Recalling the years of the Anti-Socialist Laws, the naturalist writer and critic Heinrich Hart (185–1906), too, acknowledged: "Nowhere have I seen a more passionate yearning for knowledge, a more burning hunger for higher learning and cultural refinement than among the comrades who joined the social struggles during the eighties and nineties."

Seventy years later, the West German historian Gerhard Beier had nothing but contempt for this kind of emotional bombast – a first indication that emotions are pivotal even in the scholarly assessment of these larger discourse on (class) formation. Confronting what he saw as a vast repository of bad taste and, worse still, bad emotion, Beier could only conclude: "A workers' education thus conceived was an extracurricular education of the heart, overflowing with the sentimentality of the late romantic variety and the pseudo-pious trivialization of the educational ideals of German classicism – a kitschy harmony of thinking and doing, of doing and thinking in rambling reflections on beautiful appearances."[3] Around the same time, the British communist historian Allen Merson came to very different conclusions in his proud description of a proletarian culture more distinct than in England, the birthplace of the industrial revolution:

> The German working-class movement represented, in the earlier part of the twentieth century, perhaps to a greater extent than in any other capitalist country, a distinct proletarian culture, separate from the culture of the bourgeoisie and based on a highly developed network of class institutions, including not only trade unions and political parties but a vast

---

[1] Richard Weimann, "Die sozialistische Bildungsarbeit" (1920), quoted in Anna Elisabeth Hein and Peter Ulrich Hein, *Kunstpolitische Konzepte der deutschen Arbeiterbewegung. Eine Darstellung am Beispiel von Literatur und Theater* (Münster: Lit, 1983), 12.
[2] Josef Peukert, *Erinnerungen eines Proletariers aus der revolutionären Arbeiterbewegung* (Berlin: Verlag des sozialistischen Bundes, 1913), 5.
[3] Gerhard Beier, "Arbeiterbildung als Bildungsarbeit," in *Beiträge zur Kulturgeschichte der deutschen Arbeiterbewegung 1848–1918*, ed. Peter von Rüden (Frankfurt am Main: Büchergilde Gutenberg, 1979), 59.

range of cultural organisations such as workers' sport clubs, choirs, dramatic societies etc. down to radio circles and esperanto [sic] leagues.[4]

These differences in historical assessment confirm the extraordinary significance attributed to making idealist aesthetics compatible with historical materialism and enlisting bourgeois notions of culture and education for the goals of the socialist movement. Some socialist critics at the time insisted that an authentic working-class culture already existed in the present, while others predicted its inevitable flourishing in a classless society of the future. Many contributors to these debates expressed ambivalence about what earlier chapters have described as conscious acts of cultural appropriation, that is, the transformation of elements of dominant culture for the benefit of subordinate and marginalized groups and in the interest of residual and emergent cultures. All of these possibilities come with larger theoretical questions: Was appropriation a gesture of empowerment or of accommodation? Did it function as an expression of cultural aspiration or a gesture of symbolic expropriation? Was refunctionalization part of other processes of cultural dissemination and hybridization that gave rise to an international democratic mass culture, or did it belong to retrograde struggles over cultural capital that confirmed the validity of high-low divisions and national differences?

Several scholars of the history of socialism have read the intense preoccupation with culture and education as evidence of the political failures of Social Democracy. Hans-Josef Steinberg has called Social Democracy a socialism without workers that, under the cover of exaggerated claims about its ethos of refinement, provided openings for both a vulgar historical materialism in line with Darwinism and an eschatological pseudo-Marxism with strong religious overtones.[5] Along similar lines, political scientist Franz Walter has described the associational culture built around the promise of refinement as a place of self-chosen isolation, an alternative universe that allowed those active in the SPD's organizations to "retreat from the chill of reality" into "the fantasy world of socialist anniversary dramas."[6] There is little to be gained from disputing the po-

---

[4] Allan Merson, "The Struggle for Socialist Consciousness in Nazi Germany," *Marxism Today* (November 1973), 337.

[5] On Social Democracy and the emancipation from theory, see Hans-Josef Steinberg, *Sozialismus und deutsche Sozialdemokratie: Zur Ideologie der Partei vor dem 1. Weltkrieg* (Bonn: Dietz, 1979), 146–150.

[6] Franz Walter, "Auf der Suche nach dem Neuen Menschen. Sozialismus als Solidargemeinschaft und Kulturbewegung," in *Mythen, Ikonen, Märtyrer: Sozialdemokratische Geschichten*, ed. Franz Walter and Felix Butzlaff (Berlin: Vorwärts, 2013), 193 and 194.

litical shortcomings of these parallel projects of cultural refinement and class formation. For that reason, the nineteenth century discourse of bourgeois culture and education will be read as a distinctly German response to what Antonio Gramsci calls cultural hegemony, the establishment of bourgeois values, norms, and beliefs as universal ones and the enlistment of hegemony in the presentation of social and economic inequalities as quasi-natural conditions.[7]

Two speeches by Wilhelm Liebknecht can be used both to reconstruct these discursive constellations in the contradictory terms that confirm them as a product of the nineteenth century and to identify the seemingly incompatible elements of bourgeois heritage, proletarian culture, revolutionary theory, and reformist politics that haunted Social Democracy long into the twentieth century. At the 1874 convention of the SDAP (Social Democratic German Workers' Party of Germany) in Coburg, Liebknecht still insisted on the full politicization of cultural life and called for a new kind of proletarian literature – newspapers, political tracts, and science books – that would allow the party "to force its ideas upon the enemy."[8] Yet after the 1875 Socialist Unity Congress at Gotha, more and more arguments were made in favor of separate cultural and political spheres. Now Liebknecht joined Bebel in his conviction that "during struggles, the muses remain silent" and explained his position as follows: "The proletariat is already being destroyed through social and economic conditions; should we add to that by ruining the body and soul of the children of the proletariat?" Fearing that reading novels might weaken their revolutionary resolve, he had only one conclusion, namely, "a fighting Germany has no time for poetry."[9] Nonetheless, when thinking about the future, Liebknecht remained utterly convinced that, "for the cultural historian of the future, the founding of the smallest workers' club will be of greater value than the battle of Königgrätz."[10]

A clearer sense of the repeated attempts by the party leadership to "solve" the problem of culture, whether proletarian or bourgeois, can be gained from

---

[7] For references, see Antonio Gramsci, *Selections from the Prison Notebooks*, trans. Joseph A. Buttigieg and Antonio Callari (New York: Columbia University Press, 2007).

[8] Wilhelm Liebknecht, quoted by Peter von Rüden, "Anmerkungen zur Kulturgeschichte der deutschen Arbeiterbewegung vor dem Ersten Weltkrieg," in *Beiträge zur Kulturgeschichte der deutschen Arbeiterbewegung, 1848–1918*, ed. Peter von Rüden (Frankfurt am Main: Büchergilde Gutenberg, 1979), 21.

[9] Wilhelm Liebknecht, "Brief aus Berlin," *Die Neue Zeit* 9.2 (1891): 710. The German proverb "Unter den Waffen schweigen die Musen" is based on the Latin "Inter arma silent Musae" attributed to Cicero. The Bebel connection is acknowledged in Hermann Wendel, *August Bebel. Eine Lebensskizze* (Berlin: Verlag für Sozialwissenschaft, 1923), 86.

[10] Johann Jacoby, quoted by Wilhelm Liebknecht, in *Kleine politische Schriften*, 61. Sadowa is an alternative name for the more commonly used Königgrätz.

two earlier Liebknecht speeches, the 1871 "Zu Trutz und Schutz" ("For Opposition and Protection") speech and the 1872 "Wissen ist Macht" ("Knowledge Is Power") speech. Read together, both speeches offer compelling arguments for humanistic education as an indispensable weapon in the struggles of the working class and attest to the simultaneous overvaluation and devaluation of culture as a constitutive part of the relationship to bourgeois culture. Likewise, the almost religious faith in the liberating effect of education and the regular attacks on the institutions of knowledge and power bring out the underlying tension between the political alternatives of revolution and reform that had troubled the socialist movement from the beginning. In "For Opposition and Protection," a speech given on the occasion of the founding of the Crimmitschauer Volksverein, Liebknecht introduced the influential two-culture model that henceforth defined working-class culture in relation to bourgeois culture. "Two worlds now stand sharply opposed to one another," he declared,

> the world of the wealthy and the world of the not-wealthy, the world of capital and the world of work, the world of the oppressors and the world of the oppressed, the world of the bourgeoisie and the world of socialism – two worlds with opposing goals, endeavors, views, and languages, two worlds that cannot exist in harmony with one another, and one of which must make room for the other.[11]

In the late eighteenth century, Liebknecht explained, the emerging bourgeoisie had harnessed the powers of the aesthetic to rise up against the feudal order and demand equal rights. Now the working class was called upon to seize the role of bearer of culture from the bourgeoisie, given its failure to realize the emancipatory goals of the Enlightenment in the political realm. As the redeemer of humanism and humanity, the radicalized working class would be empowered by its deep appreciation for the great works of Weimar classicism and its principled rejection of the nationalist, conservative, and authoritarian culture of Imperial Germany.

In the "Knowledge Is Power" speech, delivered one year later at the founding ceremonies of the Dresden and Leipzig educational associations, Liebknecht further clarified the party's relationship to the legacies of the Enlightenment. He used a well-known phrase attributed to Francis Bacon to outline a socialist position that at once accepted the equation of knowledge with science and attacked the hierarchical structure of bourgeois educational institutions. As "the standard

---

11 Wilhelm Liebknecht, *Zu Trutz und Schutz. Festrede gehalten zum Stiftungsfest des Crimmitschauer Volksvereins am 22. Oktober 1871* (Hottingen: Verlag der schweizerischen Volksbuchhandlung, 1883), 3.

bearer of modern culture," he insisted, the working class could only realize the emancipatory potential of learning under radically democratic conditions:

> If we rely upon political battle, then we also rely upon education, on knowledge. "Through education to freedom," that is the wrong slogan, the slogan of false friends. We answer: through freedom to education! Only in a free people's state can the people obtain education. Only when the people fight for their own political power do the gates of knowledge open to them. Without power for the people, there is no knowledge! Knowledge is power! – Power is knowledge![12]

Confirming the strategic uses of the discourse of culture and education, the two speeches by Liebknecht clearly articulate their anticipatory and performative functions. Against the difficulties of reconciling theory and praxis, the emotionally charged language of aspiration mobilizes the imaginary quality of discourse – in this case, through the redefining of key elements of dominant ideology in the mapping of the socialist master narrative. Of particular relevance to the necessary process of appropriation and refunctionalization is the redefinition of individual practices as collective ones. Alluding to this possibility in his often-cited definition of culture as a whole way of life, Raymond Williams (in one of the founding texts of British cultural studies) concludes that the crucial distinction between bourgeois and working-class culture is not based on particular cultural practices, which in the age of the culture industry anyway tend toward homogenization, but established through the latter's "alternative ideas of the nature of social relationship."[13]

For the case of German Social Democracy, Williams's remark can be read to mean that the references to idealist aesthetics and literary classics should not automatically be treated as evidence of historical inevitability, namely the completion of the dream of bourgeois emancipation by the revolutionary proletariat. Just as the primacy of aesthetic experience in the making of bourgeois subjectivity cannot simply be translated into collectivist or communal terms, the role of autonomous art in the age of secular modernity and competitive individualism cannot easily be transferred to the associational culture of the socialist movement, given its heavy debts to folk culture and mass culture. Conceptually, then, the socialist debates on culture and education are bound to reveal the limits of juxtapositions such as hegemonic versus subversive culture often used by

---

[12] Wilhelm Liebknecht, *Wissen ist Macht, Festrede, gehalten zum Stiftungsfest des Dresdener Arbeiterbildungs-Vereins am 5. Februar 1872 und zum Stiftungsfest des Leipziger Arbeiterbildungs-Vereins am 24. Februar 1872* (Leipzig: Genossenschaftsbuchdruckerei, 1873), 48.
[13] Raymond Williams, *Culture and Society: 1780–1950* (New York: Columbia University Press, 1958), 312.

scholars to validate oppositional and alternative cultural practices. Given the origins of these debates in historically specific class formations, even the demands for access to social, cultural, and symbolic capital remain an integral part of the dynamics of class differences. Accordingly, the speaking about culture and education can be read as either anticipatory or preemptive performances of status and privilege. Under the conditions of Wilhelmine class society, these symbolic performances not only modeled the moral regimes of outraged rectitude that allowed the radicalized workers to make political demands, but also they provided compensatory pleasures by projecting formative experiences of lack – of resources or opportunities – onto the abundance promised by lofty ideas about culture and education.

To further complicate matters, the socialist discourse surrounding culture and education may have functioned primarily as a strategic performance of empowerment, a symbolic gesture of expropriation directed against the ruling classes and their cultural institutions. However, the socialist appropriation of bourgeois heritage also served to contain the growing threat to the humanist tradition from two equally powerful rivals, the world of science and technology and the modern culture industry. In this context, the socialist validation, if not veneration of culture, especially if narrowly defined as literature, sometimes implied a critique of scientific rationality as a dominant epistemology, despite the widespread belief in historical materialism as political philosophy and the embrace of Darwinism as an evolutionary theory of revolution. Meanwhile, the almost habitual tributes to the literary classics legitimated a complete bracketing of the mass cultural diversions that reached the urban masses through new technologies of reproduction, communication, and perception, including early cinema. By equating culture with high culture, and the classics in particular, the socialists could at once critique the commodification of culture in capitalist societies and diagnose the political failure of the bourgeoisie in completing its historical mission. And by reconceiving the project of humanism in collectivist rather than individualist terms, the socialists were able to reunite its aesthetic with its political goals – a connection established first in the writings of Marx and Engels – and to present the appropriation of bourgeois forms and traditions as a first step toward the democratization of culture.

The double meaning in Marxist theory of *Bildung* as both cultivation and formation goes a long way in explaining its prefigurative functions in the imagination of proletarian culture. *Bildung* is accorded this relational quality already in *The Communist Manifesto*, namely through the two meanings that, in the German original, suggest a close connection between humanistic education and class formation. On the one hand, the word *Bildung* refers to the process by which the working class is given access to new *Bildungselemente*, translated into English as "elements of political and general education" or "elements of enlightenment and progress." In both cases, *Bildung* is seen as an integral part of culture.[14] On the other hand, *Bildung* refers to a revolutionary project that aims at the transformation of the workers into an emerging class ready to prevent the expansion of capital. In this explicitly political sense, *Bildung* is always translated as formation. By combining both meanings, the Marxist conception of *Bildung* established the parallel projects of aesthetic education and class formation and defined their contribution to the making of the proletarian dream.

Reread in light of these additional meanings, the two Liebknecht speeches performed the commitment to education as part of the Social Democrats' general response to the profound changes brought about by industrialization, modernization, urbanization, and capitalist development. Hard-fought reductions in working hours and increases in real wages finally allowed industrial workers to take advantage of educational opportunities and pursue professional qualifications. Greater funding for public schools, stricter regulations for parochial education, and new approaches to teaching and learning helped to raise literacy rates and make basic cultural competencies an integral part both of the socialization of the working class and of the reproduction of labor power.

During the early transition from an estates-based society to a class-based one, the promise that "education sets you free" (*Bildung macht frei*), a slogan attributed to Joseph Meyer, founder of the famous *Meyers Konversations-Lexikon*, had served largely stabilizing and integrative functions.[15] The early *Arbeiterbildungsvereine* (workers' educational associations) of the 1840s turned to education to achieve greater equality and opportunity in bourgeois society. Unlike the conservative *Volksbildungsbewegung* (people's education, or adult education movement), which used people's libraries and people's book series to promote social peace and maintain the status quo, the workers' educational associations

---

14 Karl Marx and Friedrich Engels, "Manifest der Kommunistischen Partei" and "Manifesto of the Communist Party," https://www.marxists.org/deutsch/archiv/marx-engels/1848/manifest/ and https://www.marxists.org/archive/marx/works/1848/communist-manifesto/, 1 March 2017.
15 For historical overviews, see Karl Birker, *Die deutschen Arbeiterbildungsvereine 1840–1870* (Berlin: Colloquium, 1973); for a longer period, also see Josef Olbrich with Horst Siebert, *Geschichte der Erwachsenenbildung in Deutschland* (Opladen: Leske + Budrich, 2001). Women played a growing role in the postwar debates on worker's education both inside and on the margins of SPD and KPD initiatives, as can be seen in books such as Gertrud Hermes's *Die geistige Gestalt des marxistischen Arbeiters und die Arbeiterbildungsfrage* (1926) and Hilde Reisig's 1933 dissertation on *Der politische Sinn der Arbeiterbildung* (republished in 1975). The local nature of these educational associations has been documented in Wolfgang Schröder, *Leipzig—die Wiege der deutschen Arbeiterbewegung. Wurzeln und Werden des Arbeiterbildungsvereins 1848/49 bis 1878/81* (Berlin: Karl Dietz, 2010).

emphasized the workers' self-empowerment and the need for social and economic advancement. Many of these associations were founded with the involvement of liberal intellectuals, which explains their ambivalent relationship to industrialization and modernization. Catering especially to craftsmen and journeymen, their organizational structures preserved the traditions of the crafts and trades established through the guild system. The Catholic and Protestant Churches started similar initiatives with a stronger emphasis on Christian values. Far removed from the humanistic education found in gymnasiums and universities, learning in these contexts meant, above all, compensating for the glaring inequities of the class-based school system and promoting the behaviors and competencies (e.g., discipline, cleanliness, reliability) required under the conditions of wage labor and the factory system. The parallel projects of national unification and democratization continued to be the source of many disagreements within the early socialist movement and resulted in sharp debates between those in favor of agitation for class struggle and those interested in compensating for class inequities.

The socialist *Arbeitervereine* (workers' associations) active since the 1860s pursued explicitly political goals within the larger workers' movement – which does not mean that their relationship to the Social Democrats was uncomplicated. Under the Anti-Socialist Laws, when outright bans and repressive measures extended to workers' cultural associations, seemingly "apolitical" singing and gymnastic clubs provided a safe setting for members to continue the free and open discussion of socialist ideas. The new forms of sociability that developed under these conditions ranged from local workers' educational associations to national cultural organizations and eventually included workers' publishing houses, illustrated journals, lending libraries, and countless special interest clubs devoted to everything from singing, boxing, and bicycling, to promoting atheism, preaching temperance, and learning Esperanto.

Together the extensive network of educational and cultural associations and the informal structures of associational life gave rise to a heterogeneous socialist lifeworld that, more or less in alignment with the workers' movement, developed in self-chosen opposition to the institutions of bourgeois culture. Promising to organize workers' lives "from the cradle to the grave," to cite a famous SPD slogan, these organizations and initiatives nonetheless remained an integral part of the Wilhelminian *Obrigkeitsstaat* (authoritarian state) and its version of *Kulturstaat* (cultural state). As the historian Lynn Abrams has shown, the socialist lifeworld may have been built around the (new/old) ethos of class solidarity but still relied heavily on distinctly bourgeois virtues, such as order, discipline, and restraint. Meanwhile it faced growing demands and opportunities for leisure time and entertainment, including pubs, fairs, festivals, circuses, and street performances, and tried to accommodate them within the distinctly local structures of working-class life. According to Abrams, an unshakable belief in the coming revolution grounded in scientific Marxism coexisted with what even some SPD members described as typical German *Vereinsmeierei*, the sentimental cult of community and good cheer mentioned in chapter 3 in conjunction with the workers' choral societies.[16] Last but not least, the workers' associations had to compete with the easy conviviality found in countless neighborhood pubs that took away much time and energy from the daily grind of party politics (or union organizing) and distracted from the larger project of class struggle. In the competition between *Bier* (beer) and *Bildung*, to allude to a book by Horst Groschopp, the latter often lost out.[17]

Beyond the shared investment in culture and education as techniques of formation, a clear consensus on what these terms actually meant and how they shaped working-class lives could never be reached. The idea (rather than the practice) of culture found a receptive audience among members of the so-called labor aristocracy, namely trade union leaders, party bureaucrats, and skilled industrial workers. A few SPD leaders publicly admitted that they had no time to read novels or watch plays, which did not stop them from making sweeping conclusions about the past, present, and future of socialist literature. Key participants in the main literary debates conducted during party congresses rejected tendentious art on principle but called for more politically engaged art. Some believed in an innate class instinct guiding all questions of taste, while others dreamed of a future socialist aesthetic beyond class. Many wrote effusively about the simple people and their love of the classics but railed against the popularity of serial novels and melodramas. Others gushed about the workers' belief in lifelong learning but conveniently ignored the fact that even party leaders had not read Marx. Studies on workers' lending libraries confirm that historical nov-

---

16 Lynn Abrams, *Workers' Culture in Imperial Germany: Leisure and Recreation in the Rheinland and Westphalia* (London: Routledge, 1992). On this point, see Richard Saage, ed., *Solidargemeinschaft und Klassenkampf. Politische Konzeptionen der Sozialdemokratie zwischen den Weltkriegen* (Frankfurt am Main: Suhrkamp, 1986).

17 See Hans Groschopp, *Zwischen Bierabend und Bildungsverein: Zur Kulturarbeit in der deutschen Arbeiterbewegung vor 1914* (Berlin: Dietz, 1987). For three historical studies with very different emphases, see Manfred Hübner, *Zwischen Alkohol und Abstinenz: Trinksitten und Alkoholfrage im deutschen Proletariat bis 1914* (Berlin: Dietz, 1988); Georg Wedemeyer: *Kneipe & politische Kultur* (Pfaffenweiler: Centaurus, 1990); and Dagmar Kieft, ed., *Kirmes—Kneipe—Kino. Arbeiterkultur im Ruhrgebiet zwischen Kommerz und Kontrolle (1850–1914)* (Paderborn: Westfälisches Institut für Regionalgeschichte, 1992).

els, travelogues, pulp fiction, and popular science books were widely read; the classics, whether Marx or Goethe, remained on the shelves.[18]

What really mattered was the sense of legitimacy with which the workers claimed culture and education for themselves and gained social capital from speaking about the larger project of refinement in these terms. In an early study on Social Democracy as a cultural movement, Brigitte Emig documents in great detail how the discourse of *Veredelung* (refinement), with its promises of uplift and betterment, provided a compelling narrative that helped to gloss over many ideological fissures, first under the oppressive conditions of the Anti-Socialist Laws and, sometime later, during the transformation of the SPD from a *Klassenpartei* (class-based party) into a *Massenpartei* (mass-based party). Aided by the integrative rhetorics of folk, or people, shared by institutions such as the Volkshochschule (people's college) and Volksbühne (theater for the people), the ambitious project of "refining" the people thus gave rise to various modes of collective learning in which culture and education functioned as coextensive modes of feeling and being in the world.[19] Many initiatives drew on new pedagogies that promoted the crucial role of education in modern democracies, while others benefitted from scientific studies that confirmed the significance of associational life to civil societies. Important influences included the writings of Swiss educational reformer Johann Heinrich Pestalozzi about the public role of an educated humanity and the philosophical reflections by Johann Gottlieb Fichte on the contribution of education to overcoming political immaturity. Throughout, the socialist project of refinement, according to Emig, was

---

[18] For studies from the period, see August H. Pfannkuche, *Was liest der deutsche Arbeiter? Auf Grund einer Enquête beantwortet* (Tübingen: Mohr, 1900) and Ernst Schneller, *Das Buch des Arbeiters 1930/31. Ein Verzeichnis empfehlenswerter Bücher für den proletarischen Leser* (Berlin: Internationaler Arbeiterverlag, 1931). On the reading habits of the working class, see Dieter Langewiesche and Klaus Schönhoven, "Arbeiterbibliotheken und Arbeiterlektüre im Wilhelminischen Deutschland," *Archiv für Sozialgeschichte* 16 (1976): 135–204; Hans-Josef Steinberg, "Lesegewohnheiten deutscher Arbeiter," in *Beiträge zur Kulturgeschichte der deutschen Arbeiterbewegung, 1848–1918*, ed. Peter von Rüden (Frankfurt am Main: Büchergilde Gutenberg, 1979), 261–280; and Franz Johannson, "Arbeiterlektüre und bibliothekarische Bemühungen vor 1900," in *Literatur und proletarische Kultur. Beiträge zur Kulturgeschichte der deutschen Arbeiterklasse im 19. Jahrhundert*, ed. Dieter Mühlberg and Rainer Rosenberg (Berlin: Akademie, 1983), 310–332.

[19] Brigitte Emig, *Die Veredelung des Arbeiters. Sozialdemokratie als Kulturbewegung* (Frankfurt am Main: Campus, 1980). For an ideology critical reading, see Hildegard Feidel-Mertz, *Zur Ideologie der Arbeiterbildung* (Frankfurt am Main: Europäische Verlagsanstalt, 1972). On competing definitions within Social Democracy, see Christoph Hoeft, "'Wissen ist Macht'—Arbeiterbildung im Kaiserreich und in der Weimarer Republik," in *Mythen, Ikonen, Märtyrer. Sozialdemokratische Geschichten*, ed. Franz Walter and Felix Butzlaff (Berlin: Vorwärts, 2013), 164–171.

sustained by a strong belief in social and political progress and human perfectibility. This meant that aesthetic experiences had to be evaluated together with moral economies, that aesthetic education came with specific assumptions about emotional education, and that a future socialist aesthetics had to treat culture and education not as distinct forms or contents but as part of an all-encompassing social and emotional habitus.

Scholars of Imperial Germany agree on several points: that culture and education – or, rather, the discourses of cultivation, refinement, and betterment – were central to the self-understanding of Social Democracy before World War I; that cultural and educational associations became important mediators between individual socialization in working-class families and collective socialization into a distinct class habitus; and that the appeals to bourgeois heritage functioned at once as a powerful tool in establishing social legitimacy and as a serious obstacle to engaging with modern mass and consumer culture. Furthermore, there exists consensus that the pronouncements on proletarian culture, which more often than not meant literature, often served to gloss over deeper political divisions that first exploded in the revisionism debate, intensified with the war credit debates during the war years, and eventually led to the split between SPD and KPD in 1918/19. Once again, a comparative perspective is helpful in recognizing the European genealogies of this foundational belief in culture as a universal value and considering the socialist initiatives in other countries that likewise gave rise to literary clubs, poetry magazines, autodidact writers, and, last but not least, a worker intelligentsia. The historian Mark Steinberg, in his studies on the proletarian imagination in prerevolutionary Russia, describes remarkably similar arguments, attitudes, and attachments that, drawing on the Kantian sublime as a tool of human emancipation, include the validation of the aesthetic as an expression of community, the reliance on religious symbols and folk traditions, and the belief in individual selfhood and human dignity.[20]

Given the heightened significance attributed to culture since the Enlightenment, it should come as no surprise that its socialist appropriations have been subject to vastly different interpretations. Since the 1970s, social historians and literary scholars have argued passionately, and often with very contemporary investments, about whether the workers' educational and cultural associations emulated, imitated, or transformed bourgeois traditions; whether the socialist faith in progress and science was merely a reflection of the spirit of capitalism or a logical extension of core tenets of historical materialism; and

---

[20] See Mark Steinberg, *Proletarian Imagination: Self, Modernity, and the Sacred in Russia, 1910–1925* (Ithaca, NY: Cornell University Press, 2002).

whether the socialist cult of community offered a valid alternative to bourgeois individualism or merely compensated for the oppressive conditions of workers' lives. Especially during the 1980s, the crisis of the New Left and the rise of new social movements persuaded some scholars to claim nineteenth-century working-class culture as the model for an oppositional or substitute public sphere; a few speculated even how a different aesthetic theory – more materialist or more dialectical – might have saved the proletarian dream from Social Democracy and, ultimately, for Western Marxism.

Historical studies published since have shown that, notwithstanding the self-presentation of the SPD as an inclusive *Kulturpartei* (cultural party), the structure of the party hierarchy and its affiliated organizations institutionalized the homosocial milieu of the workers' movement and perpetuated regional parochialisms and ethnic prejudices at the expense of a living internationalism. The much-vaunted cultivation of moral and intellectual virtues, many scholars now concede, reflected above all the (petty) bourgeois tastes of the party leadership and labor aristocracy and the preponderance of bourgeois academics and worker-intellectuals in the party.[21] Last but not least, the SPD's ritualistic evocation of the classics has to be evaluated as part of more problematic continuities between the "invention" of a national literature in the *Vormärz* period, the struggle for national unity and democratic rule, and the new symbolic politics in the name of nation and empire – continuities that, at every point, involved the workers' movement and that, in the second volume, will have to be followed to the years of National Socialism.

The Enlightenment project of culture and education provided the legitimizing narratives that, institutionalized by schools, universities, libraries, and museums, established what it meant to be German and middle class during the long nineteenth century. The German cult of interiority, with its origins in Protestantism, validated the inner life of the private burgher over and against the civil rights of the citizen. The tastes and sensibilities cultivated during the romantic period developed inseparably from the lack of democratic freedoms in the German states during the first half of the century. At the same time, the belief in aesthetic cultivation as a human right presupposed a critique of the structural inequities in feudal and, later, capitalist societies and laid the groundwork for imagining alternatives – if only in the realm of aesthetic experience. Literary,

---

[21] On the role of intellectuals and academics in the culture of Social Democracy, see Stanley Pierson, *Marxist Intellectuals and the Working-Class Mentality in Germany, 1887–1912* (Cambridge, MA: Harvard University Press, 1993). With a special emphasis on the so-called worker intellectuals, also see Ulrich von Alemann et al., eds., *Intellektuelle und Sozialdemokratie* (Opladen: Leske + Budrich, 2000).

musical, and artistic movements sustained the bourgeoisie during these simultaneous struggles for class emancipation and national unification. The representation of class-based interests as universal values and of the bourgeois habitus as an expression of national character was part and parcel of the desired ideological effects.

The appointment of the working class as the legitimate heir of Weimar classicism meant the completion of the utopian project of culture and education started in the late eighteenth and early nineteenth centuries through the combined forces of idealist philosophy, classical aesthetics, and bourgeois emancipation. These legacies profoundly informed Franz Mehring's views on the relationship between literary form and social relevance that will be used on the remaining pages to examine its manifestations in the context of one body of work.[22] As the author of a monumental history of Social Democracy and the editor of Marx, Engels, and Lassalle, Mehring (1846–1919) came as close as anyone to formulating the official SPD position on proletarian literature and socialist culture. His writings from the 1890s to the 1910s for *Die Neue Zeit*, the party's theoretical organ edited by Kautsky, established the main elements of Marxist aesthetics and articulated the proper relationship between culture, society, and politics. Scholars have explained the tension between historical materialism and idealist aesthetics in his writings as either the result of his bourgeois upbringing and taste or as an indication of the struggles over the place of Marxism in Social Democracy.[23] Like many party leaders, Mehring denounced naturalism as a symptom of decadence even as he acknowledged individual authors' commitment to the social question. He believed in the classical heritage but rejected its normative function in bourgeois culture. He promoted the cause of the people but had mostly contempt for popular culture. And he outlined an ambitious pro-

---

[22] On Franz Mehring, see Hans Koch, *Franz Mehrings Beitrag zur marxistischen Literaturtheorie* (Berlin: Dietz, 1959); Theo Buck, *Franz Mehring. Anfänge der materialistischen Literaturbetrachtung in Deutschland* (Stuttgart: Klett, 1973); and Peter Kiefer, *Bildungserlebnis und ökonomische Bürde. Franz Mehrings historische Strategie einer Kultur des Proletariats* (Frankfurt am Main: Peter Lang, 1986).

[23] For an overview from the West German perspective, see Georg Fülberth, *Proletarische Partei und bürgerliche Literatur: Auseinandersetzungen in der deutschen Sozialdemokratie der II. Internationale über Möglichkeiten und Grenzen einer sozialistischen Literaturpolitik* (Neuwied: Luchterhand, 1972).

For the East German position, see Uta Kösser, "Unter den Waffen schweigen die Musen nicht. Probleme der Theorieentwicklung und Theoriebildung im ästhetischen Denken der deutschen Arbeiterbewegung von 1830 bis 1930. Ein Beitrag zur Geschichte der marxistisch-leninistischen Ästhetik," 2 vols. (PhD diss., University of Leipzig, 1987).

gram for a socialist culture but concluded that a true proletarian art could only flourish after the revolution.

Mehring first presented the Social Democratic position on the classics in an 1893 series of articles on the so-called Lessing legend, that is, the insistence by conservative scholars on a direct connection between the rise of eighteenth-century German literature and the rise of Prussia as a European power during Frederick the Great's rule. The passage is worth quoting at length:

> The work of Lessing's life does not belong to the bourgeoisie, but to the proletariat. In the middle class of the eighteenth century both classes were still united. But the nature and the aim of Lessing's struggle have been relinquished by the bourgeoisie and taken up by the proletariat; the bourgeois class struggle for which Lessing found the refuge of philosophy was taken out of this sphere by Marx and became the proletarian class struggle. As the bourgeoisie rejected the intellectual work of its representatives, this precious inheritance had to become the arsenal from which the working class took their first keen and shining weapons.[24]

The so-called Schiller debate, the next occasion for Mehring to further clarify his position, represented the socialist contribution to the 1905 centennial of the writer's death and involved a critical evaluation of the project of aesthetic education in light of growing doubts about the romance of revolution.[25] Schiller's status as a *Freiheitsdichter* (poet of liberation) and his aura of *Volkstümlichkeit* (folksiness) had made him ideally suited for socialist popularizations and appropriations. His 1794 *Letters on the Aesthetic Education of Man*, in particular, provided an important blueprint for using aesthetic education in reconciling the different aspects of human nature (e.g., the sensual and the rational) and establishing the aesthetic state as the foundation of new forms of sociability. For Social Democrats, the social foundation of art and its significance as an expression of organic growth proved key to their self-understanding as a social movement; the same can be concluded about the role of aesthetic experience in the self-transformation of the working class into the universal class.

All earlier attempts at breaking free of Schiller and his Storm and Stress had failed to produce a socialist aesthetic that acknowledged the complexities and contradictions of modern life. Marx diagnosed this problem early on when he

---

24 Franz Mehring, *The Lessing Legend*, trans. A. S. Grogan. Online at https://www.marxists.org/archive/mehring/1892/lessing/chap6.htm, 1 March 2017. *Die Lessing Legende* was published in book form in 1893.
25 The Schiller debate has been documented in Gisela Jonas, ed., *Schiller-Debatte 1905. Dokumente zur Literaturtheorie und Literaturkritik der revolutionären deutschen Sozialdemokratie* (Berlin: Akademie, 1988).

warned Lassalle, the author of *Franz von Sickingen*, against "using individuals as mere mouthpieces of the spirit of the time" and turning for inspiration to Schiller rather than Shakespeare, but to no avail.[26] Again it was left to Mehring, in *Schiller, ein Lebensbild für deutsche Arbeiter* (1905, Schiller, a Life Story for German Workers), to present the poet's passion for freedom and democracy as an model for the socialist movement but, at the same time, criticize his aesthetic theory as an expression of political resignation.

Intellectual historians continue to evaluate the uniquely German discourse of culture (as opposed to civilization) and use the underlying conceptual binaries (e.g., of spirit vs. matter, freedom vs. necessity) to account for its aesthetic manifestations and political limitations since the late eighteenth century. There exists general agreement that the discourses of culture and education must be read as an integral part of the utopian project of humanism in the transition from an estate-based feudal society to a modern class society. Two recent monographs by Georg Bollenbeck and Wolf Lepenies affirm the formative role of the bourgeoisie in establishing the discourses of culture and education in the nineteenth century and do so in ways that indicate the continued relevance of these discourses in the twenty-first century. Their respective arguments, which make little to no mention of Social Democracy and the working class, can be used to summarize the findings presented in this chapter precisely through the decentered perspectives offered. Bollenbeck's historically oriented study of 1997 provides ample evidence for the contribution of the discourses of culture and education to the emergence of the bourgeois public sphere. In his view, they promoted universalist claims about human nature but also compensated for the lack of political rights and freedoms. Culture and education conveyed knowledge of the world, provided models for interpreting experiences, and defined private values and public behaviors. These discourses accompanied the belated emergence of Germany as a nation-state and affirmed the unique role of the *Bildungsbürgertum* (educated middle class) – sometimes even in opposition to the rationalism of the Enlightenment and its afterlife in economic liberalism.[27] Through their explanatory strengths, Bollenbeck concludes, these discourses helped to clarify social processes, advance political programs, and maintain powerful mechanisms of integration, not least in the name of German nationalism and colonialism.

---

[26] Karl Marx, Letter to Ferdinand Lassalle, 19 April 1859, http://marxists.anu.edu.au/archive/marx/works/1859/letters/59_04_19.htm, 1 March 2017.

[27] Georg Bollenbeck, *Bildung und Kultur. Glanz und Elend eines deutschen Deutungsmusters* (Frankfurt am Main: Insel, 1994), especially Chapter 1.

According to Lepenies's rather broad interpretation of the same nineteenth-century developments, the heightened German investment in culture as part of these processes functioned not simply as a substitute for any sustained engagement with politics but must in fact be seen as evidence of a deep aversion to (parliamentary) politics.[28] The bourgeois revolution established a new culture of progress (e. g., in relation to industry and technology), of liberty (e. g., in the ideology of bourgeois liberalism), and of science (e. g., in its Social Darwinist applications). At the same time, *The Seduction of Culture in German History*, to cite the title of the 2006 book, impeded Germany's belated rise as a modern nation and democracy and legitimated the cultural elites' disdain for political life in general. Lepenies's characterization of German culture as both apolitical and antidemocratic describes parts of the educated middle class during specific historical periods. Yet the implicit equation of German culture with bourgeois culture not only ignores the unique and very different status of culture and education in the lifeworld of Social Democracy and the workers' movement; it also fails to consider the emancipatory function of culture as formation, or refinement, in the highly politicized contexts of socialist and communist movements.

Even a cursory overview of the debates on socialist aesthetics and proletarian culture, including the ones to be discussed in chapter 18, offer plenty of evidence of their intensely political nature – a quality that, to emphasize again, resides less in any particular works or authors but in the self-understanding of the working class as the legitimate heir of the bourgeois tradition. In fact, the claims to this heritage are most political not where they promote tendentious art but where they advocate for a clear separation between art and politics. Thus the socialists' arguments against a politicization of culture bring into sharp relief Bollenbeck's and Lepenies's narrow definitions of culture, and confirm in what ways the discourses surrounding culture and education always involve dominant, residual, and emergent class-based cultures in changing constellations of power and influence. Accordingly, the bourgeois defense of humanistic education during the Wilhelmine years makes sense only in light of its opposition to the workers' educational associations and what they represent: the feared democratization of knowledge and learning. Similarly, the bourgeois conception of culture long after the fall of empire acquires its distinct function as the opposite of politics only in response to the demands on the bourgeois heritage by the representatives of Social Democracy.

---

28 Wolf Lepenies, *The Seduction of Culture in German History* (Princeton: Princeton University Press, 2006), 5–6.

The historically specific discourses of culture and education examined by Bollenbeck and Lepenies and their (distinctly West German) interpretations of these discourses come into even sharper focus through a comparison with the more inclusive definition of culture as a whole way of life proposed by the representatives of (British) cultural studies. Their definition of culture is closer to, though by no means identical with, the German concept of *Zivilisation* (civilization), which refers to the entirety of a people's technical, social, and cultural achievements. Additionally, it describes in more comprehensive ways the rich cultural practices developed in the name of the working class. In the highly charged juxtaposition of culture and civilization that legitimized the self-understanding of Germany's educated elites throughout much of the nineteenth and early twentieth centuries, civilization, as studied by anthropologists and ethnographers, represents the material foundations and belongs entirely to the sphere of activity and utility, including labor and industry. Once removed from the necessities of life, culture in this conceptual division of labor becomes free to devote itself entirely to the pursuit of art and beauty. However, as we have seen, the discourse of culture itself could never free itself from the conditions of its own emergence in the context of Enlightenment thought and its afterlife in the bourgeois heritage.

Historically, culture in Germany acquired its overdetermined status within the project of bourgeois emancipation through sophisticated arguments about its difference from an overly refined, decadent civilization henceforth identified with the aristocracy. Meanwhile, civilization made a return to public debates through the heterogeneous customs, habits, and diversions henceforth associated with modern mass culture. This chapter has shown that these discursive configurations cannot be mapped easily onto the prevailing models in cultural studies that, based on the resistance versus subversion model, tend to align cultural hegemony with dominant ideology and equate popular culture with resistant positions. In the process, they fail to take into account the relational dynamics of high culture, mass culture, folk culture, bourgeois culture, working-class culture, and so forth. Understanding the strategic function of the discourse of (high) culture initially deployed against an estates-based society requires taking into account that which is excluded from such a class-based habitus, namely the cultural practices associated since Herder with the people, or the folk, and, after the rise of the socialist movement, with the working class. Accordingly, the appropriation of the discourses of culture and education by the workers' movement and their institutionalization within the associational culture of Social Democracy represents an important expression of aspiration and gesture of empowerment. The ways in which these key elements of the proletarian dream remained grounded in the nineteenth century will become more apparent in the following chapters about proletarian culture and cultural debates in the Weimar years, which not only feature very different models of proletarian identification but also offer radical alternatives to the promises of upward mobility associated with refinement and cultivation. Marking the beginning of the book's second part, the next two chapters about the revolutionary fantasy in proletarian literature offer first glimpses of the profound changes in the imagination of the proletariat as an emotional community in the wake of the October Revolution.

Part Two: **Weimar Republic**

Chapter 9
Revolutionary Fantasy and Proletarian Masculinity

> He had brought a woman along. Slender, almost haggard, with her black hair cut in a mannish bob and her dark, tight-fitting clothes, she seductively planted herself on top of a box and distracted the young men with her slender legs dangling and her skirt pulled high. Her mannish, angular face looked haggard. Behind her sharp pince-nez sparkled the eyes of a fox, bright and cunning. She was a chain smoker, had barely thrown away the butt of one cigarette when she reached into her blouse and fished out the pack again. Some of the older boys looked at her: that would be something! Fritz was ashamed. She was no comrade! He held back. That hussy only came here to drive the comrades crazy.
>
> Otto Gotsche, *Märzstürme*

"What was it about the fateful month of March?" asked Julian Gumperz (1898–1972) in reflections on what he described as a uniquely German revolutionary calendar. March 1919, the well-known sociologist noted, was "a historical earthquake [...] that covered the land with a smoldering lava mass of political events." March 1920 turned out to be "less fervent but more persistent, less decisive but more responsive." In March 1921, "the formidable movement of the Saxon miners remained isolated," and in March 1922, "things stayed really quiet." Despite these disappointments, Gumperz firmly believed that "a new March, a March of fulfillment, is bound to arrive one day."[1] The emotional nature of his account attests to the powerful need for narratives that could reimagine the political failures of March 1920 and 1921 as the beginning of assured victory in the future. It is the main purpose of this chapter to examine how this revisionist process depended on the realignment of proletarian identifications with the cult of militant masculinity in the aftermath of World War I. The above epigraph from a rather lurid novel about the 1921 March Action by Otto Gotsche (1904–1985) offers a first indication of the ways in which the revolutionary fantasy and, by extension, the proletarian dream depended increasingly on highly gendered and sexualized scenarios.[2]

The protorevolutionary period of the early postwar years described by Gumperz ended in October 1923 with the unsuccessful protests of Hamburg dock-

---

[1] Julian Gumperz, "Vor einem proletarischen März," in *Platz dem Arbeiter!* (Berlin: Malik, 1924), 179–180.
[2] Otto Gotsche, *Märzstürme* (Berlin: Dietz, 1954), 480. His autobiographical novel about the 1921 March Action was originally scheduled for publication in 1933.

workers who saw the instability caused by the hyperinflation and the resulting state of emergency as a welcome opportunity for the KPD to take action. According to Trotskyist historian Pierre Broué, "the fiasco of Germany's 'failed October'" proved especially traumatic in the country that before the war had seen the rise of the largest socialist party in the world and that after the war offered the best chances for a communist revolution in an advanced capitalist society.[3] For KPD leader Ernst Thälmann (1886–1944), the Hamburg Uprising confirmed the party's foremost role in guiding the revolutionary working class and, with the help of trained paramilitary troops, preparing for the dictatorship of the proletariat. To this day, discussions continue on the fringes of the radical left about whether 1923 put into question the very concept of revolution or whether the series of uprisings must be seen as part of an incomplete political project, "the prehistory of a struggle that continues to this day."[4]

Gumperz's reflections on the month of March point to the symbolic significance of short-lived revolts and localized insurrections to the competing proletarian dreams associated during the Weimar years with SPD, KPD, and various other leftist parties and splitter groups. In making sense of these events, the communists found guidance in Vladimir Lenin's prewar writings on the so-called revolutionary situation, which he defines as an intensification of contradictions resulting from the unwillingness of the lower classes and the inability of the upper classes to continue living in the old ways.[5] But can one really speak of what Lenin calls "growing dynamism" in these particular historical instances? Or are these events evidence of the weakness of parliamentary institutions and democratic commitments during the Weimar Republic? In Marxist theory, revolution – as strategy, position, and program – functions as the critical category that distinguishes the proletariat as the agent of history from the working class under conditions of oppression. Accordingly, the failure of revolution threatens to undermine, if not undo, any heroic conception of the proletariat. Compensating for these threats to the revolutionary fantasy, the literary repre-

---

[3] Pierre Broué, *The German Revolution 1917–1923*, trans. John Archer, ed. Ian Birchall and Brian Pearce, intr. Eric D. Weitz (Leiden: Brill, 2005), 899.
[4] Broué, *The German Revolution*, 912. On the later political context, see Hermann Weber, *Die Wandlung des deutschen Kommunismus. Die Stalinisierung der KPD in der Weimarer Republik* (Frankfurt am Main: EVA, 1969); Klaus-Michael Mallmann, *Kommunisten in der Weimarer Republik. Sozialgeschichte einer revolutionären Bewegung* (Darmstadt: Wissenschaftliche Buchgemeinschaft, 1996); and Klaus Kinner, *Der deutsche Kommunismus. Selbstverständnis und Realität. Band 1. Die Weimarer Zeit* (Berlin: Dietz, 2009).
[5] See Vladimir Ilyich Lenin, "May Day Action by the Revolutionary Proletariat," *Collected Works*, Vol. 19: 218–227.

sentations of the March 1920 and 1921 events, the Ruhr Uprising (*Ruhraufstand*) and the March Action (*Märzaktion*), may be read as revisionist narratives that identify causes and effects, reveal obstacles and mistakes, and propose strategies for the future. The novels about these two revolutionary situations try to make sense of the workers' experience of sudden empowerment and unlimited possibility, followed by crushing, devastating defeat, and they do so through the problem of masculinity. The main psychological dilemma addressed by Weimar-era novels about the Ruhr Uprising can be summarized thus: how to live with, and make sense of, failure? The solution offered was revisionist in the political and psychological sense, as authors retold the story of revolution as one of temporary political defeat and inevitable historical victory and, in the process, strengthened proletarian identifications by healing the wound of injured masculinity.

As previous chapters have shown, the proletarian dream had always depended on normative definitions of masculinity in establishing what it meant to be a worker and a revolutionary; this included the sexualization of class struggle as a homosocial project. Measured against the associational culture of prewar Social Democracy, with its own *männerbündlerisch* qualities, the trauma of World War I and the failed German Revolution of 1918/19 required more aggressive – which also means more defensive – scenarios in affirming the primacy of class struggle. Subsequently, all desires and beliefs considered detrimental to the ultimate goal of revolution were projected onto the figure of the sexualized woman, while the theory of revolution itself was sexualized through a cult of militant, ascetic masculinity closely associated with the KPD. No literary works bring out the gendered nature of this kind of revisionism more clearly than several novels written by members of the KPD-affiliated *Bund proletarisch-revolutionärer Schriftsteller* (BPRS, Association of Proletarian Revolutionary Writers).

To briefly summarize the historical events that required such almost compulsive rewriting: On 14 March 1920, in response to the rightwing Kapp Putsch against the elected government, SPD, USPD, and KPD, with support from the unions, had called for a general strike. Emboldened by their initial successes, including the surprise defeat of a Freikorps unit at Wetter and the subsequent conquest of Dortmund by the Red Ruhr Army, workers' councils formed in Essen on 20 March and assumed military and administrative control over the entire Ruhr region. The general strike may have saved Weimar democracy from the first assault by rightwing forces, but after terminating the strike on 22 March, the workers and the government failed to reach a compromise. With fifty to sixty thousand armed men in the Red Ruhr Army, more than three hundred thousand workers still on strike, and the center of the German coal and steel industry in workers' hands, SPD minister Carl Severing made the fateful decision to use the Reichswehr against its own citizens. On 8 April, the Reich regained control over the Ruhr region with brute military force; more than one thousand workers were killed.

From the KPD's perspective, the Ruhr Uprising should have completed what the revolutionary days of 1918/19 had failed to achieve – to establish the dictatorship of the proletariat. Once party functionaries redefined temporary defeat as necessary preparation for the future, March 1920 would be commemorated as a glorious moment in the history of the German working class. The memories of revolution proved especially important during the late 1920s when the KPD pursued a left-radical course of militarization as part of its two-front strategy against National Socialists and Social Democrats. The intense emotions surrounding the Ruhr Uprising – from pride about the organizational competence of the workers' councils to grief about the deaths of the so-called *Märzgefallenen* – tied many workers ever more closely to the dreamworld of communism. The novels channeled these contradictory feelings into gendered scenarios of class that portrayed the bourgeoisie as female or feminized and equated female sexuality with destructive, antisocial tendencies. In the process, the proletarian imaginary became inextricably tied to the problem of modern masculinity and the threat of female sexuality, a process with surprising similarities (on the level of literary tropes and styles) to the autobiographical writings of right-wing Freikorps men and future Nazi leaders.[6]

Beginning in 1925, communist authors produced a steady stream of political analyses, historical recollections, and literary treatments dealing with the immediate postwar years. *Barrikaden an der Ruhr* (1925, Barricades at the Ruhr), a collection of short stories by Kurt Kläber (1897–1959), introduced the Ruhr workers and their struggles to the reading public. The novel was banned because of its alleged threat to public order, despite protests by Thomas Mann, Käthe Kollwitz, and Gerhart Hauptmann; due to space considerations, this work cannot be considered here.[7] Two better-known novels appeared in time for the uprising's ten-year anniversary, Karl Grünberg's *Brennende Ruhr. Roman aus der Zeit des Kapp-Putsches und des Ruhraufstandes* (1928, The Burning Ruhr) and Hans Marchwitza's *Sturm auf Essen* (1930, in English as *Storm over the Ruhr*), and played an important role in the annual *Märzfeiern* (March celebrations) organized by the KPD. Confirming the internationalism of the proletarian imagination during the inter-

---

[6] To what degree both conservative and left liberal authors responded to a crisis of modern masculinity is confirmed by Bernd Widdig, *Männerbünde und Massen. Zur Krise männlicher Identiät in der Literatur der Moderne* (Opladen: Westdeutscher Verlag, 1991).

[7] For a definition of the proletarian novel, see Kurt Kläber, "Der proletarische Massenroman," *Die Linkskurve* 5 (1930): 22–25.

war years, *Storm over the Ruhr* was translated into English and published in New York and London in 1932. Only one year later, all three books were destroyed during the Nazi book burnings, and Kläber, Grünberg, and Marchwitza were forced to flee the country. In East Germany in 1952, Marchwitza published a revised version of *Storm over the Ruhr* that included significant changes; all three novels saw numerous East and West German re-editions during the Cold War and continue to attract interest as part of the local history of the Ruhr region (see figures 9.1 and 9.2).[8]

Fig. 9.1 Karl Grünberg, *Brennende Ruhr* (Berlin: Neues Leben, 1953), dust jacket.

Fig. 9.2 Karl Grünberg, *Brennende Ruhr* (Essen: RuhrEcho, 1999), cover design.

Most fictional and historical accounts of the Ruhr Uprising reduce the main events to a series of military encounters, add drama and suspense to maintain reader interest, and draw on Marxist terminology to explain the broader implications. The lengthy dialogue scenes in the novels often read like editorials from the party press, and the descriptions of armed confrontation in the scholarly works draw heavily on literary conventions. Most leftwing accounts emphasize the heroism of the Red Ruhr Army and the brutality of Freikorps and Reichswehr.

---

8 For instance, note the numerous memorials to slain workers throughout the Ruhr region and the inclusion of the Ruhr Uprising in the "Mythos Ruhrgebiet" theme route 22 of the Route der Industriekultur.

By contrast, rightwing authors tend to focus on the "red terror" and its destructive impact on family, society, and nation. A 1930 book by Erwin Brauer, who was sympathetic to the KPD position, includes chapter headings such as "The Fierce Battle for Essen" and "Düsseldorf in the Hands of the Workers," titles that could just as easily have appeared in the novels by Grünberg and Marchwitza or the writings of Freikorps men, for that matter. In all cases, revolution is translated into the language of war, and the home front transformed into yet another battleground. Two monumental histories of the Ruhr Uprising published in the 1970s, a meticulously researched three-volume work by West German Erhard Lucas and a large tome by East Germans Erwin Könnemann and Hans-Joachim Krusch that carefully toes the SED party line, confirm that the Ruhr Uprising was not merely a predominantly male affair; the experience provided a much-welcomed opportunity for celebrating militancy as an expression of vanguardism.[9] Confirming this point, historians Eric Weitz, Atina Grossmann, and Sara Ann Sewell have examined the cult of hypermasculinity in the communist left with regards to the homosocial bonds forged in the factories and trenches and the anxieties caused by the New Woman and her demands for social and sexual equality.[10]

The insistence by historical participants on the factuality of events and their subsequent transformation into truth events, to use Alain Badiou's term, gives a

---

[9] The standard work is Erhard Lucas three-volume study that includes *Märzrevolution im Ruhrgebiet. Vom Generalstreik gegen den Militärputsch zum bewaffneten Arbeiteraufstand März-April 1920* (Frankfurt am Main: März, 1970) and *Märzrevolution 1920. Der bewaffnete Arbeiteraufstand im Ruhrgebiet in seiner inneren Struktur und in seinem Verhältnis zu den Klassenkämpfen in den verschiedenen Regionen des Reiches* (Frankfurt am Main: Roter Stern, 1973). Together with Ludger Fittkau and Angelika Schlüter, Lucas also published *Ruhrkampf 1920: Die vergessene Revolution: Ein politischer Reiseführer* (Essen: Klartext, 1990). For an East German perspective that presents the GDR as the telos of these historical struggles, see Erwin Könnemann and Hans-Joachim Krusch, *Aktionseinheit contra Kapp-Putsch. Der Kapp-Putsch im März 1920 und der Kampf der deutschen Arbeiterklasse sowie anderer Werktätiger gegen die Errichtung der Militärdiktatur und für demokratische Verhältnisse* (Berlin: Dietz, 1972). Compare Werner Angress, *Stillborn Revolution: The Communist Bid for Power in Germany, 1921–1923* (Princeton: Princeton University Press, 1963).

[10] See Eric D. Weitz, "The Heroic Man and the Ever-Changing Woman: German and Politics in European Communism, 1917–1950," in *Gender and Class in Modern Europe*, ed. Laura Levine Frader and Sonya O. Rose (Ithaca, NY: Cornell University Press, 1996), 311–352 and Atina Grossmann, "German Communism and New Women: Dilemmas and Contradictions," in *Women and Socialism/Socialism and Women: Europe between the Two World Wars*, ed. Helmut Gruber and Pamela M. Graves (New York: Berghahn, 1998), 135–168. On the visual representation of communist masculinity, compare Sara Ann Sewell, "The Party Does Indeed Fight Like a Man: The Construction of a Masculine Ideal in the Weimar Communist Party," in *Weimar Culture Revisited*, ed. John Alexander Williams (New York: Palgrave, 2011), 161–182.

first indication of the discursive strategies necessary in the postrevolutionary rewriting of failure and defeat. This process can be reconstructed through the rhetorical excesses triggered by the specter of female sexuality and the communists' need for its containment. Time and again, in the novels to be discussed, a worker finds his political commitments tested in relationships with three types of women: the mother (or motherly type), the sister (or sisterly type), and, most relevant to this discussion, the sexually threatening woman. Each time, an attractive woman arrives in a revolutionary situation and unsettles the libidinal economy of class struggle; each time, narrative denouement is achieved through her expulsion from the homosocial world of communism. Not dissimilar to a repetition compulsion, the underlying scenarios of attraction/repulsion and attachment/detachment provide the psychological mechanisms necessary for the establishment of communism as a distinct emotional regime. In each case, the preservation of the revolutionary fantasy as a male fantasy requires that the woman be reduced to a projection screen, facilitating change without being part of the solution. Her appearance in the form of images, visions, and hallucinations confirms that what is really at stake is the proletarian dream and its dependence on the convergence of modern masculinity and communist orthodoxy.

Measured by BPRS standards, Marchwitza and Grünberg can be called idealtypical proletarian writers. Both men came from working-class backgrounds and had been soldiers during World War I, with the war experience evident in their detailed descriptions of military strategy. They joined the KPD in 1919/20, became active in the BPRS, and published in KPD-affiliated journals; in fact, it was the German Revolution that turned them into writers. Grünberg (1891–1972) took part in the January 1919 struggles in Berlin; he was unemployed when he wrote *The Burning Ruhr*, joined the communist resistance after 1933, and later in East Berlin, published a memoir about his life as a worker-writer. Marchwitza (1890–1965), the son of a miner, fought in the Red Ruhr Army and the Spanish Civil War and later returned to the GDR to contribute to the postwar mythification of the Weimar KPD. His other novels, set among the miners and steelworkers of the Ruhr region, *Kampf um Kohle* (1931, The Battle over Coal) and *Walzwerk* (1932, The Roller Mill), attest to his close familiarity with the region and its culture.[11]

---

11 On Marchwitza, see Alfred Klein, "Die Arbeiterklasse im Frühwerk Hans Marchwitzas," *Weimarer Beiträge* 18.1 (1972): 73–106. Marchwitza's *Meine Jugend* (1947) offers an autobiographical perspective on the affinities between labor struggles and military battles, from his childhood among the miners of Upper Silesia to his traumatic experiences in the trenches of Verdun.

Both authors wrote as, and for, communists, a point confirmed by the autobiographical references and *Bildungsroman* elements in their novels. At the 1930 Kharkov conference organized by RAPP (Russian Association of Proletarian Writers), Marchwitza proudly declared, "we don't write for the bourgeoisie and its entertainment needs but for the revolutionary proletariat, for the class struggle."[12] In the original version of *Storm over the Ruhr,* this partiality is most evident in a narrative structure that conveys an illusion of mastery by juxtaposing collective action with private feeling. Marchwitza introduces stereotypical figures (e.g., greedy factory owner, reactionary officer, opportunistic politician) to establish clear moral binaries and present the communists as more evolved human specimens. His revolutionaries make decisions based on rational arguments, while their enemies are driven by either selfish motives or irrational fears. Accordingly, the (male) reader's identification with the revolutionary subject is achieved through the reduction of women to sexual objects. Confirming the writers' and the readers' shared emotional investment in the process of masculinization, this ideological interpellation takes place in the heightened registers of melodrama, that is, a quintessential female genre.

Like Marchwitza, Grünberg firmly believed in the value of stereotypical characters as emotional anchors within the revolutionary narrative. Recalling a discussion with workers during a 1929 visit to Moscow, he noted:

> A young student trainee expressed her displeasure that the author had treated the petty-bourgeois student Sukrow [in *The Burning Ruhr*] with much more love than the class-conscious rolling mill operator Grothe. [...] Looking at three hundred pairs of eyes I suddenly knew the answer. [...] For the author, his relationship to his figures resembles that of parents to their children. [...] Without doubt, the indecisive Sukrow required more attention than the class-conscious Grothe who was firmly standing on his own two feet! The long-lasting applause confirmed that I had been understood.[13]

In the introduction to the novel's second 1948 edition, Grünberg elaborated on the need for fictionalizing the historical material and harnessing the emotional power of character identification. After all, he explains, "purely theoretical political books often leave the readers cold. [...] A captivatingly written book that allows the reader to live, love, and suffer with the fictional characters also allows

---

12 Hans Marchwitza, quoted by Werner Ilberg, *Hans Marchwitza* (Leipzig: VEB Bibliographisches Institut, 1971), 27.
13 Karl Grünberg, *Von der Taiga bis zum Kaukasus. Erlebnisse aus den zwanziger Jahren und später* (Halle: Mitteldeutscher Verlag, 1970), 124–125.

him to fight and die together with his heroes."¹⁴ If later accounts can be trusted, Marchwitza himself had learned a few tricks in writing "captivating" literature from an anticommunist pulp novel about the Kapp Putsch, Hermann Dreyhaus's *Lava* (1921).¹⁵ In light of these literary choices and influences, it is only logical that Weimar contemporary Erik Reger, author of a documentary novel set in the Ruhr region, attacked *The Burning Ruhr* for "muddying a great struggle with romantic infatuations, milieu descriptions, and tame lyricisms" and concluded with open scorn that, "the petty-bourgeois heart beating under the red uniform is a matter of fact."¹⁶ A critic from *Die Weltbühne* was even more dismissive, calling the novel "communist kitsch" and its author "the red Courths-Mahler."¹⁷

The unsettling effect of the spectacle of female sexuality on the budding young revolutionary in *The Burning Ruhr* illustrates perfectly how lurid sensationalism could be enlisted in the project of historical and emotional revisionism.¹⁸ Grünberg places the main protagonist between two women, the fascist femme fatale and the communist good girl; both disappear toward the end so that his friendship with a male comrade can be strengthened and the primacy of the collective struggle over personal happiness affirmed. The novel starts with a chance meeting on a train involving the idealistic chemistry student Ernst Sukrow; the beautiful Gisela Zenk, daughter of a factory owner and member of the nationalist, antisemitic Rugard group; and the good-hearted Ruckers, an old miner, union man, and father of a nice, but plain, proletarian girl. The travelers' destination is Sterkrade, a section of Oberhausen (here called Swertrup) and a center of revolutionary activity. Soon the *Werkstudent* (student trainee) Sukrow spends many happy hours with the Ruckers family, including daugh-

---

14 Karl Grünberg, afterword to *Brennende Ruhr. Roman aus der Zeit des Kapp-Putsches*, sec. ed. (Rudolstadt: Greifenverlag, 1948), 257.
15 As claimed by Paul Sielaff, "Karl Grünberg und das Ruhrgebiet. Der Kohlenpott in der proletarischen Literatur," *RotFuchs* (Juni 2010), 24. The work in question is Hermann Dreyhaus, *Lava* (Berlin: Hafen-Verlag, 1921); already a cursory look confirms the novel's strong influence on Marchwitza's equation of the political enemy with an alluring, but dangerous female sexuality.
16 Erik Reger, 1928 review of *Brennende Ruhr*, reprinted in Sabina Becker, *Neue Sachlichkeit, Vol. 1: Die Ästhetik der neusachlichen Literatur (1920–1933)* (Cologne: Böhlau, 2000), 237.
17 Walther Karsch, "Courths-Mahler rot," *Die Weltbühne* 28.39 (1931): 495–497. Hedwig Courths-Mahler was the most successful author of pulp fiction in the late nineteenth century.
18 See Sandra Beck, "Erinnerungen an die Revolution-Konzeptionen der Weiblichkeit: Karl Grünbergs Brennende Ruhr. Roman aus dem Kapp-Putsch (1929)," in *"Friede, Freiheit, Brot": Romane zur deutschen Novemberrevolution*, ed. Ulrich Kittstein und Regine Zeller (Amsterdam: Rodopi, 2009), 163–180. Compare Michaela Menger, "Literatur als 'Waffe' im 'Bürgerkrieg der Erinnerungen.' Ruhrkampf im politisch- propagandistischen Zeitroman der Weimarer Republik," in *Text & Kontext. Jahrbuch für germanistische Literaturforschung in Skandinavien* 36 (2014): 68–97.

ter Mary, and befriends the communist Max Grothe as his fellow worker and mentor; a romantic subplot involving Mary, Grothe, and Sukrow remains undeveloped. Instead the novel focuses on a triangulation of the class struggle that places Sukrow between the proletarian Grothe and the bourgeois Gisela. The trainee's precarious position between classes becomes painfully obvious after his promotion from millwork to lab work; the arrival of Gisela as a coworker – part of a secret rightwing intrigue – introduces further complications.

Throughout the novel, the emotional and rhetorical excesses surrounding the fascist femme fatale serves two functions: to pathologize sexual desire as an obstacle to successful party work and, at the same time, to utilize these erotic energies in the making of the ideal communist worker. The sight of Gisela in the factory lab sets up the basic voyeuristic scenario from Sukrow's point of view: "In the shiny white lab coat, with her rosy cheeks and sparkling deep-blue eyes framed by blond double buns, she appeared to him like a heavenly being. [...] The warm light of the dimmed lamp surrounded the golden parting of this graceful apparition like a halo and was reflected in the fine silky hairs that curled around the beautiful nape of her neck."[19]

Sukrow's hallucination of the woman as an angelic creature soon gives way to an equally hyperbolic description of her witch-like characteristics. The dynamics of attraction and revulsion are harnessed for the class struggle through the tension between two seemingly incongruent iconographies. Tired of Gisela's bait-and-switch tactics, Sukrow tries to forget her during an evening of drinking and dancing with other women. That night, he has a nightmare that, through this wish fantasy of a wedding, attests to deep feelings of class shame and guilt:

> Then they were sitting in a bridal carriage. To their feet lay heavy sacks filled with shimmering gold coins. This was the dowry provided by his father-in-law. When he touched the sacks with his feet, large red spots appeared. "No, this is human blood, I must have shot the workers last night on Ratinger Street," he cried out in fear. But Gisela consoled him: "Whoever wants to love me must be able to shoot workers." (*BR*, 68)

---

19 Karl Grünberg, *Brennende Ruhr* (Bochum: RuhrEcho, 1999), 58–59. The original version was published in Rudolstadt by Greifenverlag in 1928 and reprinted by the same publisher in 1948. Two later West German editions (1974 as part of the Kleine Arbeiterbibliothek and in 1999 by RuhrEcho) confirm the novel's role in the West German discovery during the 1970 of workers' literature and regional history. In the GDR, *Brennende Ruhr* was reprinted several times from the 1950s to the 1980s and became the inspiration for the 1969 two-part television feature *Brennende Ruhr* produced by the DFF (Deutsche Fernsehfunk). Henceforth all quotes from the 1999 Bochum edition will appear in the text in parentheses (*BR*).

During their last attempt at reconciliation, the rightwing seductress spells out the connection between sex and politics as she commands Sukrow: "'Be a man, become one of us! [...] Enter under my command, join the Rugard group!' [and some time later:] 'German-thinking men and women work together for the rebirth of it [i.e., the fatherland] in its new glory. Even if times now seem dark, who knows how soon events will unfold that require men of action? Only such men can win my respect and love.'" (*BR*, 78 and 79) Still unable to extricate himself, he responds with a desperate cry for love: "'Gisela, not like that,' he pleads, 'demand that I kill myself but do not despise me. I love you so much.'" (*BR*, 80)

The dramatic events in the wake of the Kapp Putsch make Sukrow painfully aware of his sexual and political inadequacies. Paralyzed by self-loathing, he ignores the workers' declaration of a general strike and goes into hiding after the arrival of the Freikorps units. Only during a moment of great danger for the Red Ruhr Army does he find the courage to join the armed workers. Having made the commitment, he finally also recognizes Mary as a more suitable companion. However, within the homosocial logic of the proletarian fantasy, the transferal of desire from the wrong to the right woman still requires its mediation by the gaze of Grothe, the ideal proletarian man and, ultimately, the real love object. Mary becomes desirable for Sukrow only because of her appearance in the revolutionary narrative as embodied by his best friend. This is how the narrator presents the proletarian good girl:

> At the entrance to the village, the car with the machine guns stood undamaged. Grothe could hardly believe his eyes: a slender young woman stood tall on the driver's seat, with a carbine in her hand. "Mary? Hey girl, you here? What are you doing?" "I am watching over your machine guns. Without me they would already be in the ditch and your car on the blink," she replied as if it were the simplest matter in the world. (*BR*, 196)

The crude phallic symbolism used by Grünberg implies that Mary functions as an object of male desire only in conjunction with the revolutionary fantasy. Nonetheless, she still has to die in Sukrow's arms during the final battle in order to complete the merging of private and political feeling necessary for the affirmation of communist masculinity. In leftwing and rightwing movements, the homosocial contract is always made over the body of a dead woman. Consequently, the novel's ending finds Sukrow reading the *Sozialistische Republik* in a Cologne café when Grothe walks by, on his way to the train station. First they share fond memories of Mary – "She was a dear, brave fellow (*Kerl*), had the potential to become a comrade in arms" – and vow that "her name will stand at the top of that long list that we will present on the day of reckoning!" (*BR*, 225) Then Sukrow initiates a flirtatious exchange reminiscent of two lovers. Asked by

Grothe to accompany him to the station, he replies: "Don't you want to stay with me for one night? I have a nice room out there in Lindenburg." Grothe declines but leaves open the possibility of a shared future by citing from the well-known folk song "Muß i' denn zum Städele hinaus": "'As for the staying – let's wait until the fall. But when the grapes ripen on the vine, then I'll return to you, my darling (*Schatz*)!'" (*BR*, 226) The closing reference to "storm clouds gathering" and the evocative image of "rapid currents" (*BR*, 227) against which the coal barges on the Rhine travel upriver suggest that the strength of the revolutionary proletariat will depend crucially on men's continuing ability to transfer their sexual energies to the homosocial project of revolution.

Michael Rohrwasser, in the first study on proletarian mass culture, has paid special attention to the highly gendered stereotypes in the popular Rote-Eine-Mark series of novels published by the Malik publishing house.[20] *The Burning Ruhr*, the first book in the series, contains many examples of what Rohrwasser calls the gendered opposition of "communist-young-strong-male" and "Social Democrat-old-impotent-female." As constellations, these stereotypical figures give voice to attitudes and beliefs that, according to Rohrwasser, aim at the denigration of the private sphere in favor of the homosocial milieu of communism. The moral binaries can be read as evidence of the considerable debt of 1920s proletarian literature to nineteenth-century trashy novels. However, the aggressive fantasies projected onto the sexualized woman point to new emotional traumas and ideological divides. In fact, the juxtaposition of the erotically alluring fascist woman and the sisterly communist woman may be closer to the polemical distinction, with the respective reversals, between the red revolver bride and the white nurse identified by Klaus Theweleit as a recurring motif in the autobiographical writings of Freikorps men.[21] In his two-volume study *Male Fantasies*

---

[20] Michael Rohrwasser, *Saubere Mädel, starke Genossen. Proletarische Massenliteratur?* (Frankfurt am Main: Roter Stern, 1975). For a critical response, see Wolfgang Emmerich, "The Red-One-Mark-Novel and the *Heritage of Our Time:* Notes on Michael Rohrwasser's *Saubere Mädel—Starke Genossen: Proletarische Massenliteratur?*," *New German Critique* 10 (1977): 179–189. Compare Paul Günter Krohn and Heinz Neugebauer, ed., *Für Euch ist das Wort. Die Gestalt des Arbeiters in der proletarisch-revolutionären Literatur Deutschlands, 1918–1933* (Berlin: Tribüne, 1962) and, for an overview of Rote-Eine-Mark novels, see Hanno Möbius, *Progressive Massenliteratur? Revolutionäre Arbeiterromane 1927–1932* (Stuttgart: Klett, 1977).

[21] Klaus Theweleit, *Male Fantasies*, 2 vols., trans. Chris Turner, Stephen Conway, and Erica Carter (Minneapolis: University of Minnesota Press, 1987), especially volume 1. Theweleit evokes another lurid Gisela Zenk scene in *The Burning Ruhr* to note similarities between fascist and proletarian texts, but only to then minimize the implications: "If the tendencies we've been discussing seem relatively harmless in proletarian novels as compared with fascist novels, that's because in proletarian novels the central concern is not the aggressive removal of

(1977–1978), Theweleit reconstructs this distinctly fascist genealogy based on the Freikorps men's fascination with, and horror of, female sexuality that, captured in images of floods and streams, attests to their desperate attempts to acquire an armor of masculinity as protection against a thus defined abject other.

The sexualization of war and revolution that appears in both leftwing and rightwing accounts of the Ruhr Uprising points to a shared emotional investment in modern industrialized warfare as a paradigm of political emotions. Describing the "white terror," the KPD's Erwin Brauer includes graphic references to cut-off breasts and vaginal penetrations to make his point: "The white band of soldiers had lost all inhibitions. All gates of sadism and criminality were opened. [...] Now those appeared on the scene who were dying to ram their bayonets into proletarian men and rape defenseless proletarian women."[22] Fixated on the "red terror," the conservative geographer Hans Spethmann used the 15 March 1920 battle in Wetter to observe a complete breakdown of the natural gendered order: "Gruesome scenes took place. [...] Even women participated in the atrocities, taunting the soldiers with the vilest cuss words and spitting on them. [...] Some of the women were not even embarrassed to undress on the castle square and market square, becoming 'fellow fighters,' 'ammunition carriers,' and 'nurses.'"[23] Alluding to "transgressions [...] so horrible that the pen resists recording them,"[24] Spethmann ends his account with effusive praise for the Freikorps troops and deep gratitude to the Reichswehr for restoring law and order.

While these gender stereotypes reveal strong similarities between communist and fascist fantasies of (counter)revolution and point to their shared origins in the traumas of World War I, they should not distract from the considerable differences between the Freikorps men's backward-looking narratives of loss and betrayal and the workers' equally strong fixation on future victory. Having lost everything – their home, country, and community – the Freikorps men in Theweleit's account feel compelled to continue their surrogate battles in civilian

---

women from the scene of the action" (158–159). Lucas briefly discusses the role of women in the Red Ruhr Army in *Märzrevolution 1920*, 81–84.

22 Erwin Brauer, *Der Ruhraufstand von 1920* (Berlin: Internationaler Arbeiter-Verlag, 1930), 94–95. Brauer's book served as a case study on armed uprisings in the MASCH (Marxistische Arbeiterschule) courses organized by the KPD in Berlin until 1933; see Klaus Kinner, *Marxistische deutsche Geschichtswissenschaft 1917 bis 1933. Geschichte und Politik im Kampf der KPD* (Berlin: Akademie, 1982), 435. For a contemporary account of the Ruhr Uprising by a Social Democrat, compare Gerhard Colm, *Beitrag zur Geschichte und Soziologie des Ruhraufstandes vom März-April 1920* (Essen: Baedeker, 1921).

23 Hans Spethmann, *Die Rote Armee an Ruhr und Rhein. Aus den Kapptagen 1920* (Berlin: Reimar Hobbing, 1930), 63 and 77.

24 Spethmann, *Die Rote Armee an Ruhr und Rhein*, 78 and 92.

life. By contrast, the workers long to escape the confinements of factory and tenement for the thrill of demonstrations and street battles. Rightwing fantasies about hardening the soldierly body in military battle may have an emotional equivalent in the communist ethos of discipline and sacrifice, but the latter's dreams of revolution also extend to the processes of massification that cause the Freikorps men's horror of floods, streams, and bodies. In both cases, neither the projections of femininity nor the introjections of masculinity can be reduced to a taxonomy of gendered stereotypes in fictional, autobiographic, and historical writing. Instead, the role of gender as a marker of difference can be utilized to reveal how the revolutionary fantasy is continuously revised in line with changing emotional and ideological needs.

This latter point is confirmed by a comparison of the 1930 and 1952 versions of Marchwitza's *Storm over the Ruhr* and the postwar fate of the story of a young communist worker between two women, a domineering and overprotective working-class mother and a spoiled petty-bourgeois fiancée with a Social Democratic father.[25] In the original version, Franz Kreusat breaks up with his fiancée early on, persuades his mother to pay more attention to politics, and briefly meets up with a pretty *Arbeitersanitäterin* (a red nurse, in Freikorps lingo) working for the Red Ruhr Army before he dies heroically on the battlefield of class struggle. Significantly, the narrator first introduces Franz Kreusat, his best friend Fritz Raup, and their fellow workers as mere supporting characters in the female-dominated world of the tenement. Here women either scream, quarrel, or gossip and generally treat men like children – justification for their subsequent placement outside history and politics. Questioning Franz's masculinity, Theres, the neglected fiancée, resents his friendship with Fritz Raup, while his mother constantly worries about his whereabouts. His opposition to female influences and reactionary forces – both of which seem to have the same detrimental effect on working-class men – begins during a brief imprisonment for political activities: "Franz forgot his mother. He stood still and stared at the stony silent walls. His face lost its soft, tender expression, became hard, and seemed to turn into stone. He clenched his teeth tightly."[26] The camaraderie in the Red Ruhr Army empow-

---

[25] An autobiographical reading might connect the fear of/longing for the maternal in *The Burning Ruhr* to Grünberg's marriage to a widow (with four children) fifteen years his senior; he left her for a younger woman with similar political interests who later became his second wife.
[26] Hans Marchwitza, *Sturm auf Essen. Die Kämpfe der Ruhrarbeiter gegen Kapp, Watter und Severing*, with preface by Frank Rainer (Cologne: Kiepenheuer & Witsch, 1972), 87. Henceforth all quotes from the 1972 edition will appear in the text in parentheses (*SE*). The reprints from 1976, 1979, and 1980 confirm the book's relevance to West German leftist mythmaking and regional Ruhr history.

ers Franz to further establish clear boundaries – that is, to acquire a distinct communist habitus. The passage in which he finally confronts his mother and fiancée deserves to be quoted in full:

> "You will not get away from me anymore," she [Theres] said and reached with heavy hands for the apron ties. "I can't sit at home anymore," he replied, "we have the city, but the battle has not yet ended, we must keep going!" Theres grumbled: "Aren't you tired of it yet? You follow them around like some idiot!" Franz looked at her angrily. "I can't stand back when thousands of others are getting involved! I would be ashamed of myself if I stayed home when I was needed out there!" "Nobody's forcing you?" "Nothing is forcing me, but yet" – he turned to mother – "if only you could understand just this once – none of us are going into the fire for nothing! We cursed when they beat us, when we had to run in front of police bullets! And now we have weapons! We have the city, the police are pulling out because of the armed workers! You should see how happy the guys are! It's as if a storm blew into the fire!" Frau Kreusat turned away tired. "You aren't going anywhere, boy – I believe you, that it is like that, but you're staying here, aren't you?" Franz felt as if he was hitting a rubber wall that kept bouncing him back. "Mother! Don't you understand? I can't leave the battle just for your sake! It doesn't work that way!" Frau Kreusat stared at him. Then she burst into tears again. "Don't you see?" said Theres, "don't you see what you're doing?" "Shut up!" he screamed at her. "Stay out of it! I have to do it, don't you understand? I have to!" (*SR*, 90–91)

Angrily Theres leaves the room, never to appear again. To compensate Franz for this loss, Marchwitza briefly introduces the possibility of love in the figure of a red nurse who hitches a ride with the armed workers. Her description follows the same voyeuristic pattern found in *The Burning Ruhr*, including the moral judgment behind the distinction of shameful male lust and proper heterosexual love that always equates the desiring gaze with others:

> The female medic was pretty. Brazenly and lustily the men's eyes caressed her body. Her full breasts pointed outward taunting them while she was laughing. Coarse hands twitched from the desire to touch them. Several already started grabbing. "Stop that!" the girl shouted indignantly. She leaned out of the car and admonished Franz Kreusat: "What kind of a pigsty do you have here? I am going to get out of here if this doesn't stop." (*SR* 110–111)

Tellingly called Rosa, the young woman offers to accompany him to the front but he objects: "'I fear for your life!' said Franz Kreusat. 'This is not for women'" (*SR*, 120). Significantly, these highly sexualized scenes are missing from the 1952 version of *Storm over the Ruhr*. Rewritten by Marchwitza to reflect what his East German publisher calls "not only his greater literary maturity today, but also the evolving political analyses since 1930,"[27] the new treatment of the Ruhr Uprising emphasizes its mythical status in the history of socialism and fundamentally alters the gendered dynamics in the process. Beyond the ideological revisions that establish clear connections between KPD and SED, most of the changes concern the figure of Theres/Therese, which were made in response to criticisms about Franz Kreusat's lack of a private life. The petty-bourgeois fiancée and the red nurse are combined into one character and the roles of women in the revolutionary struggle greatly expanded – obviously with a view toward East German readers and their more egalitarian views on gender and politics. Now Franz meets a more socially conscious Therese Tauten at a dance and is immediately smitten – as is his mother. Their budding romance survives his heated arguments with her Social Democratic father and her initial annoyance about his many political meetings. Personal and political problems reach their culminating point when Therese informs Franz that they must get married – she is pregnant. Yet these problems are magically resolved once the uprising begins and she breaks with her father and his politics of accommodation. During the decisive battle, Therese even ventures to the frontlines to provide the armed workers with food and medicine: "Therese had overcome her initial fear and sensitivity and carried out her heavy duties with patience and prudence. [...] No, she no longer was the Therese of yesterday; her thinking had completely changed, and her father would probably not have recognized her if he had met her."[28] Franz still has to die a sacrificial death – for the glorious history of communism and the working class. Hope and confidence for the future arrives in the form of a baby boy who, born in 1921, might in fact be reading this revised novel in East Germany as "the first socialist state on German soil." As the next chapter argues, such revisionism was not the only strategy available to communist writers for keeping the proletarian dream alive. Another revolutionary situation, the 1921 March Action, inspired the writer Franz Jung to experiment with alternatives to the gendered narratives of the proletarian novel and reconfigure the constellations of aesthetic and political emotion in the larger context of what this book calls proletarian modernism.

---

27 Afterword of the publisher, Marchwitza, *Sturm auf Essen* (Berlin: Neues Leben, 1952), 361. A two-part 1958 edition appeared in the young-adult Neue Abenteuer series.
28 Marchwitza, *Sturm auf Essen* (Berlin: Tribüne, 1978), 151–152 (177 in the 1952 edition).

Chapter 10
The Revolutionary Fantasy Revisited

> *Voice:* Proletarians! (*moaning*) Proletarians! ...
> *All Choruses:* We are defeated.
> *Voice:* Why are you defeated?
> *All:* Why?
> *Voice:* Were you a vanguard, bold and strong? Steeled, fireproof, one will, one idea?
> *Proletarians:* No, we are not yet a strong party, forged of steel, one will, one idea!
> *Voice:* That's why you were defeated, you brave fighters.
> *Questioning Voice:* Do we always have to be defeated?
> *Voice:* From defeat to struggle to victory.
> *All Proletarians:* From defeat to struggle to victory.
> *Voice:* You must guide the working class in all daily battles, you, the vanguard.
>
> Berta Lask, Leuna 1921

In *Leuna 1921* (1927) by Berta Lask (1878–1967), the striking workers must once again accept the reality of defeat and deal with the contradictory emotions that accompany such experiences: despair, shame, hopelessness, anger, and defiance.[1] And once again, the participation in yet another fateful month of March takes them straight to a compensatory fantasy of future victory. Not publicly performed until 1956, Lask's so-called drama of facts was based on interviews with participants in what is known as *Märzunruhen* or *Märzkämpfe* (March Action). Other literary treatments of the March Action of 1921 follow a similar pattern of emotionalization that promises relief from suffering through identification with the Communist Party. Modelling this process, at the end of his own novel about *Märzstürme* (1933, March Storms), Otto Gotsche, a plumber-turned-writer arrested for participating in the uprisings, helps a young worker named Fritz move beyond morbid thoughts of death and affirm his belief in the revolutionary working class. As Fritz learns, only the life-giving powers of the Party make self-healing possible:

> The hand reached for the heart. Had it stopped? It pounded wildly and eagerly. It beat like the heart of a seventeen-year-old beats, a heart that wants to live, that fears a horrible, torturous death, that desperately seeks the light and stumbles in endless darkness. [...] Good Lord, Fritz! You are not even seventeen years old, are you not ashamed to think of death? Don't be ridiculous! Man can endure so much, much more than you think. And if he desires it, he will survive everything. Willpower is everything. The road to victory is far; it is diffi-

---

1 Berta Lask, *Leuna 1921* (Münster: Kommunistische Texte, 1973), 142.

cult, but it can be taken. The party lives, the working class lives, we will win! Today, tomorrow [...] They live and they will win! And you live, will live, will survive, will be with us! Hold your head high![2]

A third type of communist mourning work, beyond the divine voice from above in *Leuna 1921* and the interior monologue in *March Storms*, can be found in Alexander Abusch's short story *Kampf vor den Fabriken* (1926, The Fight in Front of the Factories). Here the cold rationality of communist vanguardism provides the required emotional scaffolding. Abusch (1902–1982), a KPD (and later SED) politician and editor of *Die Rote Fahne* from 1930 to 1932, introduces a skilled agitator to put the workers' sense of defeat into historical perspective. His arguments are based on the same belief in the inevitability of historical progress that animates the other two works, but he no longer needs to aestheticize suffering to make his point. Reinvigorated by the irrefutable logic of dialectical materialism, Abusch's workers simply leave the meeting softly whistling "The Internationale," mindful of the agitator's final words:

> If we were so strong already that we would no longer have to endure defeats, we could have the victorious takeover of power already today. It is essential that in every part of the struggle we make our male and female colleagues aware that the safeguarding of their basic living conditions is a question of power, that is, of ownership of the factories and political power in the hands of the workers.[3]

The 1921 March Action offered communist writers a second opportunity to return to the main questions asked after the 1920 Ruhr Uprising: how to maintain the revolutionary fantasy, how to deal with feelings of resignation, how not to succumb to an overwhelming sense of hopelessness, and how to make sense of these emotions within the larger narratives of class struggle? Once again it fell to writers associated with the KPD and BPRS to provide dreams of revolution in which the working class could continue to play its designated role as the class for itself and in itself. Furthermore, such fictionalization depended on the projection of individual needs and desires onto the figure of the sexualized woman and the aestheticization of violence in the spectacle of the all-male collective. Only one writer, Franz Jung (1888–1963), in *Die Eroberung der Maschinen* (1923, The Conquest of the Machines), rejected the available gendered tropes and the emotional regimes established in their name. Known for his complicated relationship with communism and his interest in modernism as a distinct technol-

---

[2] Otto Gotsche, *Märzstürme* (Berlin: Dietz, 1954), 166–167.
[3] Alexander Abusch, *Der Kampf vor den Fabriken* (Berlin: Internationale Verlags-Anstalt, 1926), 72.

ogy of emotions, he consciously used the perspective of the working class to challenge basic assumptions about the power of identifications and to enlist decidedly modernist strategies in a conception of collective agency beyond the psychology of suffering and compassion. Introducing perspectives to be developed further in chapters 11 and 17, modernist self-reflection not only afforded Jung a way out of emotional patterns that until that point had defined the revolutionary fantasy in gendered terms, but it also released the proletarian dream from the discourses of masculinity that, time and again, reinscribed its normative effects into the narratives of class struggle. With these qualities, Jung's work belongs to the larger project of proletarian modernism, identified in this study with Franz Wilhelm Seiwert, John Heartfield, Hanns Eisler, and Bertolt Brecht, and distinguished from other modernisms through its open identification with the working class, its close connection to communism, its activist and collectivist approach to culture, and its multimedia practices and international(ist) connections.

In retrospect, the March Action can only be described as a succession of almost tragi-comical events, ill conceived and badly executed, and with catastrophic consequences. "The gun brings the decision," wrote Béla Kun on 17 March 1921 in *Die Rote Fahne*, demanding that workers arm themselves in preparation for a mass uprising in the heavily industrialized area around Mansfeld, Halle, Merseburg, and Bitterfeld.[4] The Hungarian representative of the Comintern arrived at this center of mining and chemical industries to monitor the VKPD's (i.e., the later KPD's) implementation of the new "theory of the offensive," which meant creating a revolutionary situation through insurrectionist actions.[5] Meanwhile, the "communist bandit" Max Hoelz came to Mansfeld Land to organize armed groups of workers just as he had previously done during the Kapp Putsch. Around the same time, the left-communist KAPD (Communist Workers Party of Germany) dispatched Franz Jung from Berlin to take advantage of what turned out to be yet another failed revolutionary situation. A month later, in mid-April, Hoelz was arrested in the capital, and, by mid-May, Jung found himself in a Dutch prison.[6] In fact, it was in Breda where he wrote *The Conquest of the Machines*, a novel haunted by the March Action and, for that rea-

---

[4] Béla Kun, quoted in *Sigrid Koch-Baumgarten, Aufstand der Avantgarde. Die Märzaktion der KPD 1921* (Frankfurt am Main: Campus, 1986), 154.
[5] Vereinigte Kommunistische Partei Deutschlands (VKPD) was the name of the KPD between 1920 and 1922 following the merger with the USPD.
[6] Franz Jung, "Für Max Hoelz," *Feinde ringsum. Prosa und Aufsätze 1912 bis 1963. Werke 1/ Erster Halbband* (Hamburg: Edition Nautilus, 1981), 252. The controversial Max Hoelz inspired the DEFA film *Max Wolz—Leben und Verklärung eines deutschen Anarchisten* (1974) directed by Günter Reisch and Günther Rücker.

son, well suited to confront the failure of revolution once more – but this time through the lens of literary technique.

The March Action had started on 21 March with the VKPD's call for a general strike, allegedly in response to the arrival of *Sicherheitspolizei* (security police, or Sipo) in Mansfeld Land. On 24 March, a state of emergency was declared for Saxony, with the Reichswehr stabilizing the situation around 27 March. Already by 1 April, everything was over. For little more than a week, the possibility of a revolutionary situation meant mass demonstrations, action committee meetings, occupations of factories, clashes with security police and armed forces, and bombings of city halls and rail lines, as well as isolated acts of arson, sabotage, and looting. Not counting small uprisings in Hamburg and parts of the Ruhr region, the March Action remained a regional affair. The outcome: No more than 120,000 workers were on strike at any given time. Most accounts acknowledge 180 fatalities, with thirty-five policemen and 145 civilians among the dead. Numerous arrests, highly politicized trials, and lengthy prison sentences followed, with the state of emergency in Saxony lasting until September.

Compared to the 1920 Ruhr Uprising, the 1921 March Action was little more than an amateurish reenactment of a revolutionary fantasy. Subsequent explanations for the workers' defeat and its political consequences followed predictable patterns of argumentation. The intensification of class conflict prior to the March Action, the more self-serving explanations went, had revealed the underlying contradictions in capitalism, clarified the difference between revolution and counterrevolution, and delivered ever more workers to the movement. In his memoirs, even Hoelz admitted to what was euphemistically called tactical errors.[7] Writing in British exile, former KPD activist Evelyn Anderson disparaged the March Action as "one of the most pathetic chapters in the history of the German Labour movement."[8]

Historical assessments by Heinrich August Winkler and Silvia Koch-Baumgarten put much of the blame on internal struggles among the left radical parties, with VKPD, USPD, and KAPD creating the very conditions to which their competing versions of communism were supposed to offer solutions. Limited mass support, local infighting, bad organization, and a volatile mixture of revolutionary romanticism and left-wing actionism made failure almost inevitable. Today, most scholars agree that the March Action was neither a long-planned putsch attempt by the KPD nor a justified mass response to state violence. In-

---

7 See Max Hoelz, *Vom weißen Kreuz zur roten Fahne. Jugend-, Kampf- und Zuchthauserlebnisse* (Frankfurt am Main: Röderberg, 1984).
8 Evelyn Anderson, *Hammer or Anvil: The Story of the German Working-Class Movement* (London: Gollancz, 1945), 79 and 80.

stead, the events mark the beginning of a deeper crisis of legitimation to which the various parties responded with actionism, dogmatism, and the periodic purging of left and right deviations. These tendencies continued well into the postwar years and became an integral part of the culture of commemoration that, during the GDR, included the March Action among the great moments of working-class history.[9]

Jung's contribution to the revolutionary fantasy breaks with these prevailing models of historical and emotional revisionism by refusing character identification and, similarly, by de-emphasizing the perceptive of gender. A man of many contradictions, Jung was a member of the Munich *bohème* and Berlin Dada, a student of economics and psychoanalysis, and an avid reader of Friedrich Nietzsche and Max Stirner. Jung's life during the Weimar years included periods of intense political activism and repeated prison stays, which he used for uninterrupted writing. His evolving literary style benefited greatly from intermittent work as a business correspondent, which informed his astute analysis of capitalism in *The Conquest of the Machines*.[10] Jung's affinity for outsider perspectives extended to his political commitments as one of the founding members of the KAPD. In favor of spontaneous action, along the lines of Rosa Luxemburg's theory of mass strike, and opposed to the vanguard party model of the KPD, the KAPD was chosen by Lenin as the main exhibit in his trenchant critique of "left-wing communism as an infantile disorder," and it never gained much traction in the political culture of the Weimar Republic.[11]

Nonetheless, for Jung, the KAPD's analysis of the objective conditions for revolution and the subjective obstacles to its realization proved crucial to his own literary reconceptualization of proletarian subjectivity. The same can be said for his close attention to questions of form in addressing what the party's

---

9 The Weimar-ear KPD celebrated the March Action as part of local struggles going back to the Peasant Wars; see Otto Kilian, *Warum die Kirschbäume in Mansfeld im Herbst blutrote Blätter haben. Bilder aus der Geschichte des Mansfelder Lands in Verehrung seines tapferen roten Proletariats* (Leipzig: Uns-Produktivegenossenschaft, 1925); reprinted in 1975. In the GDR, the March Action was commemorated as part of the heroic history of the German working class. Thus the year 1971 saw the publication of yet another version of Gotsche's *Märzstürme* and a pamphlet on *Die Märzkämpfe 1921. Eine ruhmvolle Kampfaktion des mitteldeutschen Proletariats* published by the local SED branch in Aschersleben.
10 The best introduction to Jung can be found in Wolfgang Rieger, *Glückstechnik und Lebensnot. Leben und Werk Franz Jungs* (Freiburg im Breisgau: Ça Ira, 1987). A recent reading of *Eroberung der Maschinen* as part of a reassessment of realism can be found in Devin Fore, *Realism after Modernism: The Rehumanization of Art and Literature* (Cambridge, MA: MIT Press, 2012), 87–115.
11 Vladimir Ilyich Lenin, "'Left-Wing' Communism: An Infantile Disorder," *Collected Works* (London: Lawrence & Wisehart, 1964–70), 31: 17–118.

official program called "the problem of the German proletariat's development of consciousness."[12] Consequently, just as the KAPD decided to create a revolutionary situation by cutting through the layers of party bureaucracy, appealing instead to the spontaneity of the masses, Jung sought to liberate his readers from the strictures shared by bourgeois ideology and its favorite vehicle, the realist novel, and to experiment with forms of collective agency beyond the surrogate pleasures found in psychological interiority.

Jung's novellas from his so-called red years comment almost compulsively on the conditions necessary for a revolutionary situation while continuously sharpening his critical terms for analyzing the causes and effects of the revolution's repeated failures. *Proletarier* (1920, Proletarian) takes place in the aftermath of the October Revolution, while *Die Rote Woche* (1921, The Red Week) depicts the workers' response to the Kapp Putsch. *Arbeiterfriede* (1922, Workers' Peace) tests the limits of communitarianism, and *Arbeiter Thomas* (Worker Thomas), written in 1930, uses a 1921 uprising in Upper Silesia for an exercise in communist self-reflection. Written "with purpose and without artistic ambition,"[13] these novellas share many formal and thematic elements with the then-popular reportages from the working world. In their innovative use of literary technique, however, they function above all as models for a very different politics of identification. All of the works describe emotional trajectories from hope to disillusionment, with brief moments of togetherness followed by extensive periods of isolation, but they do so without ever resorting to the emotional scripts of melodrama or pathos. Instead the narrative strategies reenact the tension between social reality and utopian possibility through the means of literary intensifications that include sensations, perceptions, and observations, all the while guarding against the dangers of character identification, whether empathetic or sympathetic.

The refusal of emotional engagement made Jung a difficult writer especially in leftist milieus sustained by clear emotions and strong passions. Literary scholars, too, have struggled to evaluate a body of work that can be grouped neither with the historical avant-gardes nor with the Communist BPRS writers. Critical

---

[12] Program of the KAPD of May 1920, reprinted in Hans-Manfred Bock, *Syndikalismus und Linkskommunismus von 1918–1923* (Meisenheim: A. Hain, 1969), 410. For historical overviews, see by the same author, *Geschichte des "linken Radikalismus" in Deutschland: Ein Versuch* (Frankfurt am Main: Suhrkamp, 1976).

[13] Franz Jung, "Lebenslauf," *Abschied von der Zeit* (Werke 9.2), ed. Lutz Schulenburg (Hamburg: Edition Nautilus, 1997), 30. The quote is taken from his application for a visa to the United States after 1946.

responses from the orthodox left established the pattern early on, with Gertrud Alexander, in her review of *The Conquest of the Machines*, confessing to yet another disappointment in her ongoing quest for the great proletarian novel. By rejecting individualization as a feature of bourgeois literature, she complained, Jung ends up showing political struggles without the individuals that make them possible. Instead of engaging his readers emotionally, Jung confronts them with chilly detachment and dry factuality; hence Alexander's conclusion: "This coolness will be incomprehensible to a revolutionary worker."[14] A few critics welcomed the honesty with which the author posed the all-important question "Well then, what should we do?" and laid out modest proposals for provisional "attempts at a revolutionary life."[15] The shadows of left communism continued to haunt the negative reception of Jung well into the 1970s, with Walter Fähnders and Martin Rector taking issue with his actionism and utopianism. Depicting the worker not as the subject but the object of history, *The Conquest of the Machines* in their view amounted to little more than a "compendium of left-communist theory" and achieved nothing but "the self-annulment of the aesthetic project."[16]

All these complaints are responses to the provocative gesture of refusal performed in, and by, the text itself: refusal of psychologically developed characters and, with it, of interiority, immersion, and identification. In their place, the novel introduces social types with personal choices but without individual agency, with even the state representatives appearing as mere functionaries within a larger system. Moreover, the absence of revolutionary romanticism deprives the reader of any compensatory fantasies or surrogate identities, including the homosocial scenarios found in almost all novels by the BPRS writers. Without recourse to the dangerous sexual attractions and pathos-laden speeches offered up by fellow communists from Grünberg to Lask, Jung is able to concentrate on the formal elements and techniques that best establish the conditions for radical change; this includes a reconsideration of the relationship between authors and readers and between literature and politics. That his call for turning art into a weapon can be taken quite literally is confirmed by John Heartfield's cover design for the Malik edition of *The Conquest of the Machines* (see figure 10.1).

---

14 Gertrud Alexander, 1923 review of *Die Eroberung der Maschinen*, rpt. in *Vom "Trottelbuch" zum "Torpedokäfer." Franz Jung in der Literaturkritik 1912–1963*, ed. Walter Fähnders and Andreas Hansen (Bielefeld: Aisthesis, 2003), 126.
15 Anon. "Was soll der Proletarier lesen? Franz Jung," *Die Rote Fahne*, 23 July 1922.
16 Walter Fähnders and Martin Rector, *Linksradikalismus und Literatur. Untersuchungen zur Geschichte der sozialistischen Literatur in der Weimarer Republik*, 2 vols. (Reinbek: Rowohlt, 1974), 1: 218.

Fig. 10.1 Franz Jung, Die *Eroberung der Maschinen* (Berlin: Malik, 1929), cover design by John Heartfield. Copyright 2017 The Heartfield Community of Heirs/Artists Rights Society (ARS), New York.

The Conquest of the Machines opens with the description of a workers' uprising obviously modeled on the March Action that brings together the main elements of Jung's literary technique, including his strategic use of an undifferentiated third person plural subject called "they," and, for that reason, deserves to be cited at length:

> Now the following happened: When armed police marched into the courtyard, they hit the workers like a flash in the bones. After a couple of minutes, they couldn't even wait for the break. The director gave evasive comments; the plant managers acted very surprised themselves. In the meantime, the greens (i.e., *Sicherheitspolizei*) settled in. One hour later the entire factory stood still. People gathered outside. Became more and more threatening. Finally, their anger came out. Before the greens thought about it, the workers were back in the courtyard. Anyhow, they were a few thousand men, and then they let loose on the soldiers. Dazed but willing they handed over their weapons. These guys were let go. Then onward to the office building, from which most of the administrators had already fled, and there everything was smashed to pieces. But in their rage, they paused: elected a workers council; took over all divisions of the business, including inventory and all that; and split up into groups, some for security, some for production, and some for outside agitation. Immediately a group departed for the industrial town. All of this happened entirely without discussion and commotion. It was the work of a few hours. Even before the sun passed

its highest point above them, one could see groups of workers marching and exercising, loosening up their bones made stiff from laboring.[17]

In a well-known exchange with Bertolt Brecht from the early 1930s, Georg Lukács faults the literary genre of reportage for focusing on the appearance of physical reality without grasping the totality of social reality.[18] His criticism could also be applied to the cited passage and its deliberate refusal to center the narrative on individuals with personal names and, hence, biographies. Illustrating this point, the many temporal conjunctions (e. g., "when," "then," and "after") and temporal adverbs (e. g., "finally," "immediately") suggest a surfeit of continuity but a lack of causality. In this way, the writing style preempts any efforts by author or reader at forcing the distinct parts into a meaningful whole. All Jung seems to be doing is recounting a series of actions and reactions in a telegram style similar to that of expressionist prose but devoid of its emphatic, declamatory style. Any references to the emotional energies behind the uprising are limited to basic emotions such as anger and fear that are observable from a distance as they assume form through, and in, the body – "in the bones," for example. The ways in which Jung strategically enlists these structuring absences in his representation of class struggle become even more apparent during the brutal suppression of the uprising:

> Revenge erupted. Like something that explodes after having gathered momentum. Far and wide, every place was controlled by soldiers. Everything calm. In the industrial centers, all strike attempts were nipped in the bud. All efforts at organization were broken up, split up, burst apart. Then the arrests started. Arbitrarily and massively. The henchmen followed certain lists put together beforehand. The workers had been used to it for some time. They cowered, submitting to their fate. Thus ended the uprising out there in the lands where not even an attempt could gather any traction. But in the mining area, the bloodhounds applied even harsher methods. House after house was searched. Men were arrested. Stood facing the wall for hours, hands raised – until it was decided what punishment they should receive. Many hundreds were sent to prison. Were interrogated and threatened for days. Everything and anything was dug up. Even a woman who had given coffee to a worker was arrested. Local officers who had sympathized with the workers were rounded up separately. During evacuations were simply gunned down. There was no special order, whether for that one or the other. The troops' commanding officers acted on their own; the soldiers too. An outpouring of revenge, a rabid hatred had taken hold of these people. They would have mowed down everything, women and children (*CM*, 41).

---

17 Franz Jung, *Die Eroberung der Maschinen*, Werke 4 (Hamburg: Edition Nautilus, 1989), 14. Henceforth quoted in the text in parentheses (CM).
18 Georg Lukács, "Reportage or Portrayal," in *Essays on Realism*, ed. Rodney Livingstone, trans. David Fernbach (Cambridge, MA: MIT Press, 1981), 47–75.

Despite his description of narrative events as if observed from a distance and without commentary, Jung can hardly be called a typical representative of the reportage novel. His utopianism is materialist to the core for he treats hopes and fears as an integral part of social reality, and not just as emotional rewards added to maintain reader interest. Accordingly, the mistreatment of the workers in the passage cited above is reenacted and made available to critical analysis through their reduction to an anonymous mass identified as "they." The violence of the police is reproduced in the fragmented sentence structure, and the excessive use of passive voice mirrors the anonymity of existing power structures. Meanwhile, in the hopeful vision of the prisoner at the end of *The Conquest of the Machines*, the force of conviction is conveyed not through pathos or sentiment, but in anticipation of a long and arduous march into life:

> Now the prisoner saw the march into life that the mass of workers began centuries ago. Many stay behind along the way, are mowed down in rows, but the march cannot be stopped. In every breach steps a new fighter. [...] Then the prisoner's memories set free a new force. A burden weighing for hours on the heart lifts. Nothing is coincidental. [...] The feeling of being irrevocably lost disappears. Like the sun appearing from behind a bank of fog and chasing away the thick swaths of mist. That is what the prisoner felt: the rhythm that, in the midst of the struggle and the expectation of immediate results, seems lost and buried is alive after all. It animates the enormous masses of workers, setting them into motion, into beats and steps. In the loneliness of remembrance, it becomes all-powerful, filling the prisoner's soul, and enlarging its narrow vessel. Indeed, the proletariat of the world is on the march, the blood of those hoping in their loneliness, hesitating, breaking under pressure. With feverish pulse, a cry yearning for release, born of confidence and a sense of happiness. [Hence the prisoner's final vision:] He felt happy and free. He drew himself up. He felt that everything keeps moving and runs its path. The lockstep of the workers can be heard, growing stronger and stronger. Some of the circumstances are still unclear. Those coming after us will know better. Our victory is like an iron law of nature. In our field of vision, the happiness of free people already appears. It does not matter whether today or tomorrow. But it will. And it is! (*CM*, 160 and 162)

Jung's self-reflexive comments in his other works provide a conceptual framework for this miraculous transition from scenes of working-class struggle to visions of collective happiness.[19] In a 1919 article, he describes class consciousness as "the feeling of community (*Gemeinschaftsgefühl*) among those who are oppressed and dominated [...] and who commonly feel the effects of oppression and domination. [...] And it is embodied by the workers precisely because the sum of oppression and domination becomes most noticeable among the work-

---

[19] See Annette Graczyk, *Die Masse als Erzählproblem unter besonderer Berücksichtigung von Carl Sternheims "Europa" und Franz Jungs "Proletarier"* (Tübingen: Niemeyer, 1993).

ers."[20] For Jung, a thus defined *Gemeinschaftswillen*, which denotes the will of, and for, community, functions as an essential and integral part of the human search for happiness. It finds expression in lived experiences of solidarity and, by extension, growing awareness of the reality of class conflict. Based on his analysis of the condition of modernity, this experience can no longer be captured by traditional literary forms; it can only be imagined by the reader and, ultimately, realized in collective action. Jung's definition of revolution, an "event turned into a rhythmical living community,"[21] reaffirms his left-communist belief in the formative power of events (i.e., in producing revolutionary facts). Yet by inviting the kind of cooperation that blurs the lines between author and reader, his narrative voice also draws attention to the ethos of brotherliness promoted by utopian socialists and combines it with the critique of subjectivity spearheaded by the modernists.

Worker's Peace, published one year before *The Conquest of the Machines*, reflects openly on this dialogic relationship between author and reader and makes it a precondition of political radicalization as well as literary innovation. Giving reading instructions that are applicable to other prose texts by Jung, the author/narrator announces his intentions early on: "Before I begin, I would like to tell the reader what I want and where the technical problem lies. While reading, he [i.e., the reader] should actively help with the solution and presentation [...] and establish between author and reader the connection that constitutes the most substantial contribution of this book."[22] The remarkable passage ends with an affirmation of the power of emotions but not necessarily in the familiar registers of the melodramatic or sentimental. As the narrator explains, "we want to do everything to eliminate the flood of words and instead open up the heart. The social revolution, that colossus, is pushed into the world and into the nation not by forces from the outside, but from the inside, from our beliefs and our sacrifices. That is the power we seize."[23]

In *Workers' Peace* Jung clearly spells out what *The Conquest of the Machines* intends to do: to release the reader into a world without empathy but with solidarity. But how do these literary strategies help to mitigate the experience of political defeat? How does proletarian literature engage a different set of sensations and perceptions unencumbered by the existing discourses of emotion? How does it offer new insight into the causes and effects of powerlessness? According to

---

20 Jung, "Zweck und Mittel im Klassenkampf," in *Feinde ringsum*, 226.
21 Jung, *Die Technik des Glücks, Werke* 6, 20.
22 Jung, "Arbeitsfriede," in *Werke* 2, 105. We find similar self-reflexive passages in *Proletarier*.
23 Jung, "Arbeitsfriede," 208.

Jung, these questions can be answered by treating reading as a dialogic process, a process based on the refusal of identification in the traditional sense, and even more importantly, through the advancement of collective feeling and thinking. After all, a fictional work is "not just exclusively plot plus narrative structure but an integral part of our selves, the events in and with us, our feelings, that sense of being linked together as a living community."[24] Asserting that all art "is and must only be the product of class, of class ideology, and of class difference,"[25] Jung recognizes the obstacles to the development of a proletarian art in the present. He also expresses absolute certainty about its full emergence after the victory of the revolutionary working class. In the meantime, he concludes, proletarian literature in particular must strengthen "the idea of community in an oppressed class that not only thirsts after fighting the oppressors but already builds the new through its own creative energies."[26] It is precisely this anticipatory quality that distinguishes Jung's reconstruction of the revolutionary situation from the revisionist accounts offered by the proponents of strong identifications. And it is this strong belief in modernist technique as an instrument of proletarian mobilization that he shares with Franz Wilhelm Seiwert of the Cologne Progressives, the subject of the next chapter. Last but not least, it is the fundamentally different approach to artistic technique and political emotion that makes the four case studies on proletarian modernism presented in chapters 10, 11, 17, and 18 so essential to a critical reassessment of the productive encounter between modernism and communism, which sustained the artistic and political avant-gardes from the late 1910s to the early 1930s, including through their activist, collectivist, and internationalist commitments.

---

24 Jung, "Arbeitsfriede," 105.
25 Jung, "Proletarische Erzählkunst," *Feinde ringsum,* 241.
26 Jung, "Proletarische Erzählkunst," 242.

Chapter 11
Franz Wilhelm Seiwert's Critical Empathy

> An art form that relates to a particular social class does not exist, and if it did, it would be entirely irrelevant to life. We ask those who want to create proletarian art: What is proletarian art? Is it an art created by the proletarians themselves? Or an art only in the service of the proletariat? Or an art intended to arouse proletarian (revolutionary) instincts? There exists no art created by proletarians because a proletarian who creates art no longer remains a proletarian but becomes an artist.
>
> Theo van Doesburg, Hans Arp, and Kurt Schwitters, "Manifest Proletkunst"

The spirited defense in 1923 of autonomous art by Theo van Doesburg (1883–1931), Hans Arp (1886–1966), and Kurt Schwitters (1887–1948) and their denunciation of "proletarian" as the symptom of all that was wrong with politically engaged art originated in the intense conflicts and deep divides that characterized the culture and society of the Weimar Republic.[1] According to van Doesburg, the founder of the De Stijl movement, a worker transcended his class origins when he became an artist. But could an artist also decide to stand with the working class? Famous Weimar artists, from Otto Dix (1891–1969), George Grosz (1893–1959), and Käthe Kollwitz (1867–1945) to lesser-known ones such as Otto Nagel (1894–1967), Curt Querner (1904–1976), Oskar Nerlinger (1893–1969), and Alice Lex-Nerlinger (1893–1975), would have answered with an enthusiastic "yes," including those who, like Nagel and Querner, did not come from working-class backgrounds. Working in realist, expressionist, constructivist, and New Objectivist styles, all of them used artistic technique to critique the structures and conditions of modern class society.

As will be argued on the pages that follow, Franz Wilhelm Seiwert (1894–1933) and John Heartfield (1891–1968) were most consistent in forging proletarian identifications through modernist techniques, Seiwert through what he called figurative constructivism and Heartfield through the means of photomontage. Even more important for our purposes, these artists significantly expanded the emotional registers of modernism, with Seiwert using critical empathy to model a habitus of class solidarity and Heartfield by drawing on what his brother called productive rage to promote the cause of class struggle. The fact that both artists relied on performances of the classed body – groups of workers united in

---

[1] Theo van Doesburg, Hans Arp, and Kurt Schwitters, "Manifest Proletkunst," *Merz* 2.1 (April 1923): 24.

struggle and individual hands turning into fists, respectively – confirms once more the importance of (gendered) embodiments in the making of the proletarian dream.²

Defining proletarian art from a communist perspective meant, first of all, establishing alternatives to the institutions of bourgeois art. As Heartfield's brother, Wieland Herzfelde (1896–1988), explained: "The artist is a worker and, like others, exploited. Nonetheless, he is no proletarian. […] He has no comrades but only rivals and competitors; his existence is bourgeois."³ Changing the conditions of artistic production for Seiwert and Heartfield meant to become active in artists' groups – the Cologne Progressives and Berlin Dada, respectively – and to align the project of the artistic avant-garde with that of the communist vanguard. Accordingly, they approached artistic innovation as a collective project, showing their work in group exhibitions and nontraditional venues and publishing in new art journals and party newspapers. Expanding the parameters of aesthetic experience also meant making extensive use of new mass media and techniques of mass mobilization and developing the elements of a truly modern *Volkskunst* (popular art). The combination of these artistic, institutional, and ideological interventions will henceforth be called proletarian modernism in recognition of its class-based perspective, collaborative ethos, interventionist method, multimedia aesthetic, and internationalist orientation.⁴

---

2 See Debbie Lewer, "Revolution and the Weimar Avant-Garde: Contesting the Politics of Art, 1919–1924," in *Weimar Culture Revisited*, ed. John Alexander Williams (New York: Palgrave, 2011), 1–22. The best introductions to Weimar leftwing art and politics can be found in two monographs on George Grosz, Beth Irwin Lewis, *George Grosz: Art and Politics in the Weimar Republic* (Princeton: Princeton University Press, 1991) and Barbara McCloskey, *George Grosz and the Communist Party: Art and Radicalism in Crisis, 1918 to 1936* (Princeton: Princeton University Press, 1997). On the marginal role of the visual arts in the labor movement and its historiography, see W. L. Guttsman, "Bildende Kunst und Arbeiterbewegung in der Weimarer Zeit: Erbe oder Tendenz," *Archiv für Sozialgeschichte* 22 (1982): 331–358.
3 Wieland Herzfelde, "Gesellschaft, Künstler und Kommunismus" (1921), reprinted in *Zur Sache. Geschrieben und gesprochen zwischen 18 und 80* (Weimar: Aufbau, 1976), 66.
4 Proletarian modernism is a scholarly term used to describe the proletarian art and literature produced during the late 1920s and 1930s in the United States, Latin America, and East Asia and examined in several monographs on the so-called proletarian moment or wave cited in the introduction (fn. 6). The absence of an equivalent term in the German context suggests continued adherence to the standard histories of modernism and the avant-garde. For an early German study on the Soviet Proletkult movement, see Peter Gorsen and Eberhard Knödler-Bunte, *Proletkult*, 2 vols. (Stuttgart: Friedrich Frommann-Holzboog, 1974–75). A recent example focused on the British context is Benjamin Kohlmann, *Committed Styles: Modernism, Politics, and Left-Wing Literature in the 1930s* (Oxford: Oxford University Press, 2014).

The fault lines separating political and artistic avant-gardes have often been examined through the latter's representational strategies, beginning with the distinction between figuration and abstraction. The definition of modern art espoused by van Doesburg and others privileged formal innovation – in this instance, abstraction – as a mark of aesthetic autonomy and hailed modern art as liberation from social determinations, national differences, and historical traditions. Meanwhile, influential communist critics defined politically engaged art as synonymous with figurative art, outlining ideological positions that continued both in their promotion of social realism and, later, socialist realism and in their antimodernist stance in the formalism debates of the early 1930s and beyond. The arguments over modernism, to which the book will return in chapter 18, were first articulated during the prewar debates on Social Democracy concerning socialist literature and the bourgeois heritage and bear witness, above all, to the conservative tastes of the party leadership.

What would Franz Mehring, Clara Zetkin, or Gertrud Alexander make of communist artists who not only expanded the boundaries of realism with the help of modernist techniques but also rejected the emotional regimes that had dominated politically committed art during the Wilhelmine years? Instead of relying on compassion or pity as conduits to class solidarity, enlisting melodramatic and sentimental modes for proletarian identifications, or promoting working-class pride through allegory and mythology, they drew on distinctly modernist strategies to uncover the mechanisms of class rule and propose emotional strategies for political resistance and critique. Discussing photographs of the Krupp and AEG factories, Bertolt Brecht once famously declared that a mere reflection of reality no longer reveals anything about social reality because the truth about power relations has disappeared into the functional and, as a result, seeing can no longer be equated with knowing.[5] The same argument applies to the conditions under which political emotions could be expressed and developed through artistic means. With the preferred emotional and aesthetic modalities of working-class culture – pathos and sentimentality – no longer able to sustain the revolutionary fantasy in the wake of the October Revolution, the terms of emotional engagement had to be redefined as well. Notwithstanding the frequent association of the modernist aesthetic with coldness, as in the cool conduct analyzed by Helmut Lethen in his evocative reflections on a Weimar-era culture of distance, it would be counterproductive to describe the figurative constructivism of the Co-

---

5 Bertolt Brecht, "The Threepenny Lawsuit," in *Brecht on Film and Radio*, ed. and trans. by Marc Silberman (London: Methuen, 2001), 164–165.

logne Progressives in these terms.[6] Their rejection of sentiment and pathos did by no means signal emotional detachment or, still less, the kind of cynical reason diagnosed by Peter Sloterdijk in his influential study on Weimar mentalities. On the contrary, detachment opened up the possibility for a different kind of engagement based on the recognition of similarity – which also means solidarity – shared by the unified figures within the picture frame and the radicalized artists and workers themselves. It should be clear that retrieving this habitus of critical empathy is only possible through an expanded definition of proletarian modernism that takes into account its interventionist and collectivist qualities.

Fig. 11.1 Franz Wilhelm Seiwert, *Sozialistische Republik*, 30 April 1925, front page.

On 30 April 1925, the day before the annual May Day celebrations, the *Sozialistische Republik*, a communist newspaper in Cologne, featured an illustration by Seiwert on its front page that can be used to introduce Seiwert's own lifelong quest for an oppositional aesthetic beyond verisimilitude and sentimentality. The image shows a large group of workers marching together during a demonstration, with the hammer and sickle flags identifying them as communists. The

---

6 See Helmut Lethen, *Cool Conduct: The Culture of Distance in Weimar Germany*, trans. Don Reneau (Berkeley: University of California Press, 2002) and Peter Sloterdijk, *Critique of Cynical Reason*, 2 vols., intr. Andreas Huyssen, trans. Michael Eldred (Minneapolis: University of Minnesota Press, 1988). For the Anglo-American context, see Jessica Burstein, *Cold Modernism: Literature, Fashion, Art* (University Park, PA: Penn State University Press, 2012).

men in the front have individual facial features, while the increasingly smaller and faceless heads in the background suggest a large group merging into one unified body. On the left, two policemen watch the marchers with suspicion. The caption reads: "Masses out on the streets! [...] Watchword for Cologne: To the KPD rally" (see figure 11.1).[7]

In an article published in the same newspaper a couple of days later, Seiwert explained his artistic choices, aware that communist readers might respond negatively to his use of abstraction. "I was not interested in reproducing a fleeting reality but to create a symbol (*Sinnbild*) of what today is happening all over the world," he explained:

> Everywhere proletarians will gather around the red flag, and everywhere the representatives of law and order will stand around waiting to see whether they can do something about it. Fleeting reality doesn't really matter, the small pockmark and the "correct" nose in the face of the "correctly" drawn demonstrating worker. Instead, what matters is to convey an image of the proletariat in its incalculable multitude.[8]

A recurrent motif since the early workers' movement, demonstrations, rallies, and marches have allowed artists to support struggles for democratic freedoms and civil rights, commemorate violent confrontations during strikes and uprisings, and establish visual conventions for decidedly modern mise-en-scènes of resistance and revolution. Eugène Delacroix in the famous *Liberty Leading the People* (1830) modeled how to draw on realist and allegorical elements in celebrating the continuities between the French Revolution and the July Revolution. Using a similar frontal composition, Giuseppe Pellizza da Volpedo's monumental oil painting *The Fourth Estate* (1901) combined realist and impressionist techniques in transforming a large group of Piedmontese rural laborers into the harbinger of the modern working class.[9] In *Die Internationale* (1928–1930, *The Internationale*), Otto Griebel (1895–1972) restaged the same moment of confrontation with a more unified group of industrial workers in the hyperrealist style of New

---

7 *Sozialistische Republik*, 30 April 1925. Gerd Arntz created a very similar image in support of the AAUE's program of council communism for the title page of *Die proletarische Revolution* 2.23 (1927).
8 Franz Wilhelm Seiwert, "Unser Maibild," *Sozialistische Republik* 103, 4 May 1925. Reprinted in Uli Bohnen and Dirk Backes, eds., *Der Schritt, der einmal getan wurde, wird nicht zurückgenommen. Franz W. Seiwert. Schriften* (Berlin: Karin Kramer, 1978), 47. Other paintings of demonstrations from the Weimar period include Hans Baluschek's *Proletarier/Streik* (1920) and Curt Querner's *Demonstration* (1930).
9 The fourth estate refers to working class that, in modern class society, challenges the three estates of feudal societies, the aristocracy, clergy, and peasantry.

Objectivity. Establishing a predominantly male iconography of labor, the realist tradition continued throughout the 1930s, giving rise to both the Mexican muralist tradition and the doctrine of socialist realism. With the promotion of a fascist imaginary of the worker in German and Italian art, the modernist elements eventually disappeared and, with them, the possibility for a very different aesthetics and politics of solidarity.

Fig. 11.2 Franz Wilhelm Seiwert, *Demonstration* (1925), oil on canvas. With permission of Merrill C. Berman Collection.

Seiwert's interest in the revolutionary proletariat, and in the process of becoming, found fullest articulation in a group of prints and paintings that share the frontal figure constellations so distinctive of his work produced between 1920 and 1933. In fact, we can use *Demonstration* (1925, oil on canvas) to reconstruct how he translated the specificity of the 1925 May Day scene published in *Sozialistische Republik* into more conceptual and painterly terms (see figure 11.2). In the painting, a group of six workers dominates the frame; they are led by a central figure whose angular shape captures the internal strength and forward thrust of the group's movement.[10] The symmetrical composition includes a middle-aged burgher with old-fashioned *Vatermörder* high collar and bowler hat and a policeman with *Tschako* (shako, or military cap) and pulled gun as the representatives of law and order, easy targets for the kind of social caricature usually associated with Grosz. The workers' faces are reduced to basic ovals (with caps or hair) and simple features (eyes, mouths) that distinguish them as human beings; vertical lines suggesting noses add spatial depth through the use of shading. Meanwhile, any references to their masculinity, still visible on the front page of *Sozialistische Republik*, have been removed from the uniform geometrical figures whose gender is nonetheless beyond doubt. The similarities of shapes and their staggered arrangement inside the frame present the group as the sum of individual bodies and a social class in the moment of formation. The warm and vibrant colors – browns, oranges, and reds – infuse this collective body with a semblance of life, with the red half circles in the center, a reference perhaps to flags, adding a distinct communist halo: confirmation that the demonstrators are to be read as saviors fighting for a future classless society rather than as mere social types trapped in the capitalist present.

On the one hand, *Demonstration* and similar works can be interpreted as a paradigmatic scene of class struggle. The workers claim their right to the street, that is, to freely assemble and state their demands. Their strength is conveyed through the introduction of obstacles, and their determination heightened by the overall sense of stillness. On the other hand, these mise-en-scènes suggest a powerful moment of (self-)recognition. As if standing in front of a mirror, viewers are invited to recognize their similarities to individual workers and the group as a whole. The Marxist dialectic of the particular and universal is essential to such classed identifications. These scenes of recognition recall the work of Axel Honneth and his insistence on the importance of *Anerkennung* (recognition) and its absence, *Mißachtung* (disrespect), as a driving force behind all social struggles.[11] What Honneth describes as networks of solidarity and institutional-

---

10 In a particularly crass example of Cold War revisionism, *Demonstration* is renamed *Arbeitgeber, Arbeitnehmer und Polizei* in Carl Oskar Jatho, *Franz Wilhelm Seiwert* (Recklinghausen: Aurel Bongers, 1964), 39. On the art historical reception of the Cologne Progressives during the Cold War, see the catalogue *Hoerle und Seiwert. Moderne Malerei in Köln zwischen 1917 und 1933: Eine Monographie* (Cologne: Kölnischer Kunstverein, 1952).
11 Axel Honneth, *The Struggle for Recognition: The Moral Grammar of Social Conflicts*, trans. Joel Anderson (Cambridge: Polity, 1995). On the debate, see Nancy Fraser and Axel Honneth, *Redistribution or Recognition? A Political-Philosophical Exchange*, trans. Joel Golb, James Ingram, and

ized relations of respect are made visible here through a compositional approach that emphasizes the mutually constitutive processes of individuation and socialization. Solidarity, in Honneth's terms, presupposes the culture of belonging in which self-esteem becomes possible. In Seiwert's work, this shared experience is captured in the quiet spirit of determination that, as enacted through the formal means of repetition and reduction, is sustainable even in moments of defeat. At the same time, the workers' demand for recognition is inseparable from what Nancy Fraser, in her famous 2003 debate with Honneth, calls the "demand for redistribution" – still called class struggle in 1925 – and what remains the thematic focus and organizing principle throughout Seiwert's entire oeuvre.

In 1920, Franz Wilhelm Seiwert, together with Heinrich Hoerle (1893–1936), Gerd Arntz (1900–1988), and several others, founded the artists' group called the Cologne Progressives. Like many artists of their generation, they were radicalized by the traumatic experience of World War I and the pervasive sense of crisis and possibility after the revolutionary uprisings of 1918/19. For them, the new world of mass mobilizations – in the trenches, factories, and big cities – required radically different modes of representation and, by extension, forms of engagement. As Cologne-based painters, photographers, architects, and graphic artists, they responded in particular to the profound sense of political instability that made the Rhineland a symbol of German defeat for the nationalist right, and that transformed the adjacent Ruhr region, home to Germany's coal and steel industries, into a center of revolutionary ferment. Brought together in their desire, to paraphrase Arntz, to unite the politically revolutionary with the formally revolutionary, the painters in the group made the working class their main artistic subject and object depicting workers in the factories and daily life in the tenements and uncovering the social and economic inequities produced by modern capitalism.[12] Convinced of the emancipatory potential of modernist forms and techniques, they relied specifically on the clarifying function of clear lines and geometric forms to define the meaning of social types and explore the formation of collective bodies. In the words of Seiwert, their overarching goal was to "represent a reality stripped of all sentiment and arbitrariness and to

---

Christiane Wilke (London: Verso, 2003). On Honneth's reevaluation of socialism, see *The Idea of Socialism: Towards a Renewal*, trans. Joseph Ganahl (Cambridge: Polity, 2016).

12 Gerd Arntz, quoted by Lynette Roth, *Painting as a Weapon: Progressive Cologne 1920–33. Seiwert—Hoerle—Arntz*, trans. Uta Hoffmann (Cologne: Walther König, 2008), 17. On art and culture in Cologne during the 1920s, also see Wulf Herzogenrath, ed., *Von Dadamax zum Grüngürtel. Köln in den zwanziger Jahren* (Cologne: Kölnischer Kunstverein, 1975). Aside from the work of Bohnen and Backes, Roth's catalogue for the 2008 exhibition at the Museum Ludwig in Cologne remains one of the few scholarly assessments of Seiwert in recent years.

make visible its meaning, its underlying principle, its relationships and tensions through the formal laws within the pictorial frame."[13] In addition to *Demonstration*, two other works from the year 1925 confirm that "stripped of all sentiment" does not mean without feeling – on the contrary. A 1925 linocut print titled *Klassenkampf (Class Struggle)* published in the expressionist journal *Die Aktion* uses the same confrontational composition to at once show the workers' anger and determination, celebrate their unity and strength, and promote solidarity with, and understanding for, their cause. Here medieval artistic techniques are combined with modern strategies of abstraction to present the class struggle as part of a longer fight for justice and demand for recognition (see figure 11.3). The inscription in *Die Arbeitsmänner* (1925, The Working Men) clearly identifies the strategies of emotional and political interpellation that make "workers" and "class struggle" synonymous terms and equate both with a particular habitus of standing: resolute, united, confident, and empowered (see figure 11.4).

Fig. 11.3 Franz Wilhelm Seiwert, *Die Arbeitsmänner/ The Working Men* (1925), oil on canvas, Museum Kunstpalast Düsseldorf.

Fig. 11.4 Franz Wilhelm Seiwert, "Klassenkampf/Class Struggle," linocut, *Die Aktion* 12.43/44 (1922), front page. With permission of Merrill C. Berman Collection.

The Cologne Progressives turned to abstraction precisely in order to reaffirm the utopian qualities of aesthetic experience and to harness its powers of prefiguration, i.e., the modeling of emergent identifications in, and for, the present.

---

13 Franz Wilhelm Seiwert, quoted in Annedore Scherf, *Franz Wilhelm Seiwert und die rheinische Tradition. Seiwerts Bildsprache zwischen Tradition und Moderne* (Norderstedt: Books on Demand, 2013), 53.

However, they also reaffirmed the importance of figuration as a conduit for the powerful attachments that connected the working class to older formations of the people and the folk. They recognized that combining both modalities could only be achieved through an active engagement with Marxist thought, a process that required a clear understanding of the role of artists and the institution of art in bourgeois society. For that reason, their pictorial method (or style) must be evaluated as an integral part of their political critique, their typological approach analyzed as a process-based method of class empowerment, and their formal intervention seen as a prefiguration of new social relations and emotional connections.

Some of the reasons for the scholarly neglect of the Cologne Progressives have to do with the kind of regionalism that does not fit easily into Berlin-centric narratives of Weimar politics and culture. Other explanations involve the dominant narrative of art history that still classifies modern German art according to apolitical postwar definitions of modernism and the avant-garde. The continuing political provocation of the Cologne Progressives can be traced from an early West German reception that appropriated Seiwert and his colleagues for existentialist humanist interpretations and nostalgic local histories to the group's recent denunciation as silly Legoland artists in the sectarian DKP party press.[14] In the two main scholarly studies on the Cologne Progressives, art historians Uli Bohnen and Lynette Roth have provided rich accounts of the unique historical and geographic conditions that made Cologne both a provincial center and a European city with strong ties to Belgium and the Netherlands. In the city's artist studios and exhibition spaces, transnational experiments in modern design and social reform met with a distinct brand of left-radical communism and Rhenish Catholicism. It is easy to see how Seiwert's didactic exploration of image-text relations references popular treatments of the Passion of Christ and the lives of the saints. Closely related, Bohnen notes strong similarities to the medieval *Blockbuchtechnik* (block-book technique).[15] As Dirk Backes has shown, Seiwert, Hoerle, and Arntz later disagreed on whether an aesthetic of resistance could be developed through the resistant qualities inherent in visual forms, with Hoerle eventually turning to portraits and still lives and with Arntz (together with Otto Neurath) developing an almost scientific system of pictorial statistics. Nonethe-

---

14 The recent reference appears in Dietmar Spengler, "Klassenkampf im Legoland," *Unsere Zeit*, 28 March 2008. http://www.dkp-online.de/uz/4013/s1301.htm, 1 March 2017. The Deutsche Kommunistische Partei (DKP) is the successor part of the West German KPD. Legoland obviously refers to the famous plastic construction toys.
15 Uli Bohnen, *Franz W. Seiwert 1894–1933. Leben und Werk* (Cologne: Kölnischer Kunstverein, 1978), 17.

less, their original experiments with the enduring power of figuration within the framework of abstraction offer an important corrective to the conventional association of proletarian identifications with realistic paradigms and of political emotions with figurative practices.[16]

Notwithstanding their commitment, as modernists, to abstraction as an empowering cognitive principle, the Cologne Progressives insisted that figuration, with its grounding in referentiality, remained the most promising strategy for reaching radicalized workers and advancing a proletarian culture. Convinced of the liberating potential of modernism, they set out to develop aesthetic, political, and emotional alternatives to the two prevailing modes of engagement with the working class: the mixture of humor and sentimentality that turned the proletarian lifeworld into a modern idyll (Heinrich Zille) and the ethics of suffering that permeated naturalist and realist depictions of the urban underclass (Käthe Kollwitz, Hans Baluschek). Searching for a middle ground between abstraction and figuration, Seiwert and his colleagues rejected the ecstatic pathos of expressionism and playful nihilism of Dada as corresponding manifestations of bourgeois individualism. Yet they also sought to distinguish their visual style from the cool detachment of New Objectivity, which they saw as a sign of political resignation. Their shared interest in establishing forms and practices of proletarian modernism outside the restrictive modern-traditional, and innovative-conventional binaries is especially evident in the ways Seiwert, Hoerle, and Arntz utilize elements from advertising and poster design in their approach to text-image relationships in the woodcuts and advance the didactic and agitational qualities of print media (posters, fliers) through the engagement with medieval religious and regional folk art.[17]

The Cologne Progressives diagnosed the deindividualization and dehumanization of the workers through formal (rather than affective) means and turned a result of capitalist exploitation (i.e., massification) into a powerful weapon in the struggle of the revolutionary working class. The attendant process of depsy-

---

16 See Dirk Backes, *Heinrich Hoerle, Leben und Werk 1895–1936* (Cologne: Rudolf Habelt, 1981).
17 This point can be illustrated through a comparison to the woodcuts in the Mexican journal *El Machete*, as examined in John Lear, *Picturing the Proletariat: Artists and Labor in Revolutionary Mexico, 1908–1940* (Austin: University of Texas Press, 2017), chapter 3. Similar connections between local folk traditions and an internationalist cultural leftism characterize the proletarian art of Japan and Korea, as examined by Heather Bowen-Struyk, "Proletarian Arts in East Asia: Quests for National, Gender and Class Justice," in *Positions: East Asia Cultures Critique* 14.2 (2006): 251–278. For another example for the productive alliances among counterhegemonic positions across the modern-traditional, North-South divides, see Barbara McCloskey's reading of the Peruvian artist José Carlos Mariátegui in "The Face of Socialism: George Grosz and José Carlos Mariátego's *Amauta*," *Third Text* 22.4 (2008): 455–465.

chologization is most apparent in Seiwert's systematic exploration of types, groups, masses, and multitudes and his visual allusions to the models, casts, and prototypes found in industrial production. These constructivist elements, which, in the imagination of a fully rationalized society, draw on the world-building powers of geometry, could be read as a comment on the complete determination of individuals by social structures and economic conditions. However, the rejection of psychological explanations and compensations should not be confused with lack of emotion, whether in the mode, form, or content of representation. On the contrary, Seiwert's refusal of psychological interiority attests to an acute awareness of the limits of bourgeois individualism in capturing the conditions under which the workers are, in fact, constituted as a faceless mass; this is the reason for the many images of man-machines and war-wounded. More significantly, the implicit critique of psychology as ideology opens up the world of emotions toward the possibility of solidarity within the working class. Under such conditions, the formal choices of type and serialization must be read not as symptoms of loss of individuality but as conduits to the greater power of community and collectivity.

Seiwert's declaration that "proletarian culture is the intensification of the life of *all* people"[18] not only announces his identification with the workers but also affirms his belief in their designated role as the embodiment of humankind. These positions were not just intellectual ones grounded in his reading of key socialist and anarchist texts. Seiwert's affinity with the working class as the suffering class had strong biographical elements; the same could be said about Hoerle. Both men experienced debilitating illnesses as children, Seiwert after a failed X-ray treatment that left him with seeping wounds and led to his early death at thirty-nine, and Hoerle through recurring bouts of tuberculosis to which he succumbed at the age of forty.

The urgent tone in Seiwert's writings suggests that intensification meant not only the above-mentioned transformation of suffering into solidarity and of empathy into solidarity, but also included the kind of destructive energies associated more typically with John Heartfield. In several articles, Seiwert denounced the art market as an extension of capitalist society, predicted the disappearance of professional artists in communist society, and speculated on the inevitable transformation of art into a public good. He was greatly inspired by the writings of Gustav Landauer and shared his religious mysticism and anarchist insurrec-

---

18 Franz Wilhelm Seiwert, "Aufbau der proletarischen Kultur," *Die Aktion* 10.51/52 (1920): 721. For a comparison, see Herbert Anger's *Revolution* on the cover of *Die Aktion* 9.45/46 (1919) or Conrad Felixmüller's *Es lebe die Weltrevolution* on the cover of *Die Aktion* 10.17/18 (1920).

tionism. Like Arntz, he sympathized with the antiparliamentarian Allgemeine Arbeiter-Union (AAUE, General Workers' Union) and the left-communist KAPD. At the same time, the emotional habitus that gave his body of work spiritual intensity and depth is inconceivable without the enduring influence of the culture of Catholicism. Suffering for Seiwert was an integral part of the human condition, and loving others, expressed through *caritas* (charity) and *agape* (compassion, love), remained a moral obligation. It is as part of these traditions that the agitational woodcuts and linocuts made to commemorate the "martyrs" of the failed 1918/19 German Revolution, Karl Liebknecht und Rosa Luxemburg, draw on an established Christian iconography of suffering and redemption. Similarly, Seiwert's contribution to the memory of the 1920 Ruhr Uprising, *Christus im Ruhrgebiet* (1922, Christ in the Ruhr Region), enlists a familiar chiliastic eschatology to promote an insurrectionist strategy along the lines of council communism.

Demonstration, the clearest articulation of Seiwert's bold artistic and political vision, may have established the terms under which the representation of the working class could be accomplished through revolutionary art and politics. Nevertheless, it was an actual armed confrontation and its very tangible impact on a work of art – in the form of a bullet – that revealed to him the class-based nature of bourgeois culture in what has become known as the *Kunstlump* (Art Scoundrel) debate. During street battles in Dresden between Reichswehr and striking workers in response to the 1920 Kapp Putsch, a stray bullet had hit Peter Paul Rubens's *Bathsheba* in the Zwinger Museum, prompting Oskar Kokoschka to request that all fighting be conducted at a safe distance from the art treasures. In response, George Grosz and John Heartfield wrote an angry polemic in the appropriately named journal *Der Gegner* (The Enemy). Denouncing the ideological function of bourgeois art, they mockingly asked, "Well, what good does art do the workers? Did the painters give their paintings the contents that correspond to the struggle for liberation of the working people and that teach them how to throw off the yoke of a thousand years of oppression?" Their answer was a defiant "no" that allowed for only one conclusion: "There is only one task: to accelerate the collapse of this culture of exploitation with all means possible."[19] Ignoring accusations of vandalism against Heartfield and Grosz in the communist press, Seiwert came to very similar conclusions:

> We cannot destroy enough of "culture" in the name of culture. We cannot destroy enough "works of art" in the name of art. Everything true, everything authentic is indestructible.

---

19 John Heartfield and George Grosz, "Der Kunstlump," *Der Gegner*, 1.10/12 (1920): 48–56; available at http://www.dada-companion.com/heartfield_docs/hea_kunstlump_1920.php, 1 March 2017.

> [...] But that which can be destroyed in these works attaches itself to us, burdens us, robs us of the courage to act. Therefore: off you go! [...] Cut down the old idols! In the name of the coming proletarian culture![20]

Seiwert's announcement of a new proletarian culture proved premature, with the revolutionary enthusiasm of the postwar years soon giving way to the disillusionment of the stabilization period. Fully in line with his contribution to the *Kunstlump* debate, a 1921 article in Franz Pfemfert's *Die Aktion* still repeated the assertion that art is only proletarian "when content *and* form are proletarian" and when both support the building of class consciousness.[21] Yet in the end, the hegemony of the bourgeoisie and its corrosive effect on working-class culture proved too formidable an obstacle. "There is no proletarian art," Seiwert conceded in 1925, the same year he completed *Demonstration* and two years after the antiproletarian manifesto published by van Doesberg and others:

> Because art is the expression of a culture, the visible intensification of a feeling of life. And the proletariat has no culture. [...] The proletariat will never have its own culture, for the concept of the proletariat is inseparably tied to the concept of the capitalist economy. With its disappearance, the proletariat disappears, making room for the classless society that brings forth its own unique, incomparable culture.[22]

Seiwert's experiments with figuration and abstraction in the service of proletarian identifications found a logical continuation in Gerd Arntz's *Bildstatistik* (pictorial statistics) and his very similar approach to figuration, abstraction, and emotion. Working under the unique circumstances that produced the ambitious social and architectural programs known as Red Vienna, Arntz ended up creating a minimalist language of pictograms, later called Isotypes, or the International System of Typographic Picture Education.[23] In Cologne, Arntz had made

---

20 Seiwert, "Das Loch in Rubens Schinken," *Die Aktion* 10.29/30 (1920): 418.
21 Seiwert, "Offener Brief an den Genossen A. Bogdanow!," *Die Aktion* 11.27/28 (1921): 373.
22 Seiwert, "Zeichen—Versuch der Aufzeichnung einer dialektischen Entwicklung in der Darstellung des Gesichtes der Welt," *Die Aktion* 15.9/10 and 11/12 (1925): 313. Republished as "Die Kunst und das Proletariat," *Die proletarische Revolution* 2.16 (1927), together with the linocut "Erkenntnis der Welt treibt zur Änderung der Welt." A revised version of the article, "Die Kultur und das Proletariat," appeared in *A bis Z. Organ der Gruppe Progressiver Künstler Köln* 21 (1932), 83–84.
23 For an introduction, see Christopher Burke, Eric Kindel, and Sue Walker, eds., *Isotype: Design and Contexts 1925–1971* (London: Hyphen Press, 2013). On the connection to workers' education initiatives, see Flip Bool, "Figurativer Konstruktivismus und kritische Grafik von 1924 bis 1971," in *Arbeiterbildung in der Zwischenkriegszeit*, ed. Friedrich Stadler (Vienna: Löcker, 1982), 219–226.

woodcuts that restaged scenes of everyday life under capitalism in a graphic style reminiscent of Frans Masereel. In 1929, he moved to Vienna to work for the Gesellschafts- und Wirtschaftsmuseum headed by Otto Neurath (1882–1945), a political economist, philosopher of science, and member of the Vienna Circle.[24] The empirical materialism of the Vienna Circle brought proponents of an antimetaphysical worldview together with socialist activists involved in workers' education. Interested in the methods of rationalization promoted in the name of Fordism and its socialist variants, Neurath attempted nothing less than to show that science and socialism were mutually compatible epistemologies and, furthermore, to establish the scientific worldview as the foundation of a radical socialist politics. This ambitious project, all agreed, was dependent on effectively communicated information, including visual propaganda. Through the use of pictorial statistics, Neurath and Arntz set out to increase public awareness of the problems in capitalist economies (e. g., in the form of traveling exhibitions with charts and posters) and promoted new social policies through representational formats that recognized the primacy of vision and visuality in modern mass culture.

At first glance, Isotypes seem little more than a pictorial response to the sign character of modern life and the ascendancy of advertising and graphic design. Typical Isotypes depict social and economic relations through pictograms and rely on a highly developed system of simple figures that builds on the kind of typization explored first by the Cologne Progressives. This is how art historian Benjamin Benus describes the practice: "Human anatomy is reduced to simple shapes. Facial characteristics, where they do occur, are limited to one or two circulate forms and lack any individualizing characteristics. Figures are set in frontal or profile views; and forms are generally composed along vertical and horizontal axes."[25] A comparison between Arntz's 1931 linotype *Fabrikbesetzung* (Occupation of a Factory) and the Isotypes produced in his collaboration with Neurath for a 1930 statistic on unemployment confirms the origins of pictorial statistics in the radical politics of the Cologne Progressives and demonstrates their shared focus on the standardized human form in the representation of

---

24 See Gerd Arntz, *Zeit unterm Messer. Holz- & Linolschnitte 1920–1970* (Cologne: C. W. Leske, 1988) and *Holzschnitte* (Cologne: Museum Ludwig, 2008). Another example of the continuities in Arntz's work is *Fabrikbesetzung* (1931, Occupation of a Factory), which depicts concurrent scenes of action: threatening the factory owner, discussing strategy in the factory hall, drawing a hammer and sickle on a wall, and so forth.
25 Benjamin Benus, "Figurative Constructivism and Sociological Graphics," in *Isotype: Design and Contexts*, 219. For the larger argument, see his "Figurative Constructivism, Pictorial Statistics, and the Group of Progressive Artists, c. 1920–1939 (PhD. diss. University of Maryland, 2010).

labor under capitalism (fig. 11.5 and 11.6). In both contexts, the creative tension between figuration and abstraction is put in the service of workers' education and political agitation. In Vienna and, later, in the Netherlands, Arntz continued the original project of the Cologne Progressives in the realm of visual education, with the dream of proletarian culture preserved in pictorial statistics as ideology critique. The promise of representation, understood in the artistic and political sense, is once again given to the people – with a clear understanding of the key role played by form and technique in facilitating new experiences of community.

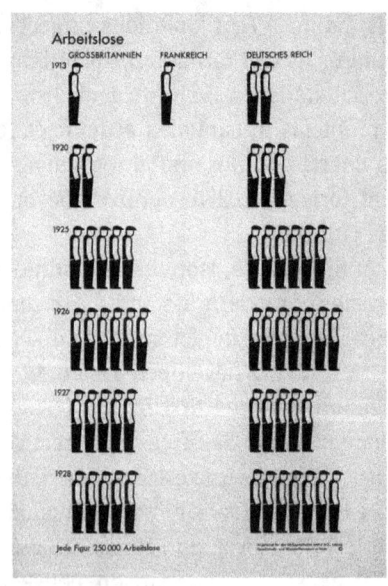

Fig. 11.5 Gerd Arntz, "Arbeitslose/Unemployed" (1931), woodcut, Neuer Berliner Kunstverein. Copyright *2017* Artists Rights Society (ARS), New York c/o Pictoright Amsterdam.

Fig. 11.6 Gerd Arntz, "Arbeitslose/Unemployed," Isotype, in Otto Neurath, *Gesellschaft und Wirtschaft* (Leipzig: Bibliographisches Institut, 1930), 87.

In lieu of a conclusion, it might make sense to enlist Neurath in defining how the proletarian modernism of the Cologne Progressive could be situated within the larger educational, scientific, and political initiatives that made up working-class culture during the late 1920s and early 1930s. At one point in *Lebensgestaltung und Klassenkampf* (1928, The Art of Living and the Class Struggle), Neurath explicitly (and perhaps surprisingly) describes statistics as "a tool in the proletarian struggle! A component of socialist economics, a source of joy for the victorious proletariat, and last but not least, the foundation of human empathy."[26] He later explains that statistics "does not move away from the living human being; it leads toward the living human being. It shows where the individual can feel compassionate, where he can feel joy. One can only feel part of a community with others when one can visualize how that entity suffers and rejoices."[27] What could describe better the enlistment of figuration *and* abstraction, and of emotion *and* cognition, presented by Franz Wilhelm Seiwert and the Cologne Progressives as the basis of proletarian identifications? After 1933, Arntz and Neurath in exile continued to promote the benefits of pictorial statistics to solve the problems of modern class society and industrial modernity, whereas the Cologne Progressives were denounced as representatives of degenerate art. It was a very different tradition of class solidarity, associated with much older notions of community, that gained remarkable visibility during the Weimar years. The next chapter on the *Sprechchor* will identify some of its performative qualities and emotional regimes.

---

26 Otto Neurath, *Lebensgestaltung und Klassenkampf* (Berlin: E. Laub, 1928), 124.
27 Neurath, *Lebensgestaltung und Klassenkampf*, 280.

Chapter 12
Social Democracy and the Performance of Community

> Alone we are nothing.
> Together we are everything.
> You and you and you,
> belong to us too.
> Take this hand, you're also a prole (*Prolet*).
> We are the storm troops
> conquering the world,
> We! We! We!
>
> R. Barthel, *"We!"*

Social and political movements are propelled forward by the shared desire of their members to say "we," "us," and "our."[1] Shouted in anger, uttered with pride, and whispered in fear, the first-person plural gave form and function to a theatrical genre or, rather, event unique to the socialist lifeworld of the 1920s and early 1930s, the *Sprechchor*, with the term usually translated as speaking chorus, choral play, or choric drama. The pronouncement of "we" by choral players speaking and moving in unison created an emotional community through highly ritualized performances of *Gemeinschaft* (community) and established the emotional regimes necessary for performers as well as audiences to proudly identify as "proletarian." The *Sprechchor* became an important vehicle especially in Social Democratic cultural organizations for developing a socialist alternative both to the *völkisch* version of community instrumentalized by the NSDAP and to the vanguard model of the party promoted by the KPD and its allied organizations.[2] Within these parameters, the *Sprechchor* movement allowed socialist activist writers, actors, dancers, musicians, and composers to respond to new experiments in modern theater and dance, introduce mass bodies as *dramatis personae*, and, for a brief moment during the interwar years, imagine the arrival of the revolutionary working class – if only in performative terms. More problematically, the *Sprechchor* offers the strongest evidence for the con-

---

[1] R. Barthel, "Wir!," *Kampflieder*, Blatt Nr. 1 (1931), Reichsarbeitsgemeinschaft der Kinderfreunde, Archief Hendrik de Man, 112, International Institute of Social History Amsterdam (IISH).
[2] For a recent reassessment of the discourse of community, see Roberto Esposito, *Communitas: The Origin and Destiny of Community*, trans. Timothy Campbell (Stanford: Stanford University Press, 2009).

tinuities between Weimar and Nazi era performances (e.g., in the *Thingspiel*) of the working class as an imagined emotional community and the most compelling argument for reconstructing the historical configurations of nationalism, socialism, and populism through the shared investment in emotionally charged public performances of "we" (see figure 12.1 and 12.2).

Fig. 12.1 Bruno Schönlank, *Der gespaltene Mensch, Spiel für bewegten Sprechchor*, Sprech- und Bewegungschor der Volksbühne Berlin, 1928. With permission of Archiv der deutschen Jugendbewegung, Witzenhausen, AdJb, F 1 Nr. Seriennr. 289/Bildnr. 09.

Fig. 12.2. Erno Peiser, *Wir Masse*, Sprech- und Bewegungschor der Volksbühne Berlin, 1928. With permission of Archiv der deutschen Jugendbewegung, Witzenhausen, AdJb, F1 Seriennr. 269/Bildnr 04.

Whether on the theatrical stage or at a political rally, the first-person plural pronoun during the first decades of the twentieth century served three interrelated psychological and discursive functions: as a declaration of group belonging that established clear distinctions between self and other; as a collective mode of enunciation that presumed full agreement between performers and spectators; and as a gesture of empowerment that defined the very terms of speaking, moving, and acting in a public space. At times, saying "we" involved an act of professing in front of a community of believers; in such cases, the dividing line between spectacle and audience had to be preserved in order to guarantee the desired effect of self-mirroring. At other times, the mass spectacle turned into a demonstration of shared political will that, at any point, could spill over into the streets.[3] Within the highly politicized theater of the Weimar Republic, establishing the conditions under which performances of "we" became possible required the mobilization of all artistic means in the making of a thus defined proletarian *Gesamtkunstwerk* (total work of art). The *Sprechchor* staged multitudes, moved collectivities, and forged communities – goals that, on the following pages, will be examined through the lens of emotions and their contribution to the performance of the proletarian dream. Few plays are better suited to shed light on these performances and situate them in the larger context of socialist theater and mass spectacle than *Wir! Ein sozialistisches Festspiel* (1932, We! A Socialist Festival) by the Belgian-born Hendrik de Man (1885–1953).

Assessing the contribution of the *Sprechchor* to socialist event culture requires that mass spectacles be treated as a form of public practice and a production of community. Concretely, this means that the entire range of aesthetic means (theater architecture as well as lighting, sound, music, costume, and set design) is enlisted in a performance-based understanding of class identifications. Naturally, such an approach cannot be developed on the basis of scripts, notes, sketches, photographs, and reviews alone. It requires further engagement with the performative categories first introduced in chapter 4 on the workers' choral societies.[4] Fortunately, growing interest in performance and performativity as critical categories has brought renewed attention to forgotten or neglected practices that have always existed outside the institution of bourgeois theater and that continue to challenge standard histories of the rise of postdramatic theater out of 1960s avant-garde practices. In emphasizing the performed (i.e., constructed) nature of identities and acknowledging the role of embodiment in

---

[3] On the people as a dramatic subject, see Hannelore Schlaffer, *Dramenform und Klassenstruktur: Eine Analyse der dramatis personae "Volk"* (Stuttgart: Metzler, 1972).
[4] There has been renewed interest in the *Sprechchor*, as evidenced by the 2013 performance of parts of Bruno Schönlank's *Der gespaltene Mensch* at the Mousonturm in Frankfurt am Main.

imaginary communities, the so-called performative turn has allowed scholars to be more attuned to public practices that emerged before, outside, and against the normative effects of bourgeois subjectivity in the theater and beyond, especially the class-based practices developed by the *Sprechchor* movement. This is not the place to use the socialist event culture of the late nineteenth and early twentieth century to imagine a suppressed, if not alternative history of public performances rooted in folk culture and religious culture. However, rethinking socialist performance along these lines means to include ludic and cultic elements in an expanded definition of the public sphere and to see the Kantian free play of the imagination as an important mediator between romantic notions of expressive individuality and collectivity.

Revisiting modern performance practices from these perspectives, theater historian Matthias Warstat and dance historian Yvonne Hardt have studied emotional communities in official Wilhelmine culture, including its national ceremonies and anniversaries, as well as in Weimar consumer culture, youth culture, and body culture. Their analyses of public performances, rituals, and events have shed new light on a modern body politic that facilitated socialist and communist reclamations of the people and the public sphere – and, after 1933, gave rise to the aestheticization of the racial community in the fascist *Gesamtkunstwerk*.[5] According to Warstat, the shift from text-based to body-based cultures of community that occurred around the turn of the century must be seen not just as a response to the bourgeois crisis of language, a critical cliché of modernism studies, but primarily as a continuation of well-established practices in the workers' movement and, one might add, even older traditions ranging from medieval mystery plays to regional folk festivals.

Once community is described as a historically specific performance, the particular contribution of the *Sprechchor* and its dance-based variant, the *Bewegungschor* (movement chorus), in establishing the emotional regimes identified with socialism comes into clearer view; this includes the gendered divides that define community as either all-male or equated with a position of masculinity. On 1 May 1932, twenty thousand people gathered in the Städtische Festhalle in

---

5 See Yvonne Hardt, *Politische Körper. Ausdruckstanz, Choreographien des Protests und die Arbeiterkulturbewegung in der Weimarer Republik* (Münster: Lit, 2004) and Matthias Warstat, *Theatrale Gemeinschaften. Zur Festkultur der Arbeiterbewegung 1918–33* (Tübingen: Francke, 2004). For a short English-language version, see Warstat's "Community Building within a Festival Frame—Working-Class Celebrations in Germany, 1918–1933," in *Festivalising! Theatrical Events, Politics and Culture*, ed. Temple Hauptfleisch et al. (Amsterdam: Rodopi, 2007), 242–260. Theatricality, the term preferred by many German theater historians, and performativity, the one prevalent in Anglo-American scholarship, can be used synonymously.

Frankfurt am Main to watch a cast of two thousand perform de Man's only play. Herbert Graf, who later gained notoriety as Sigmund Freud's Little Hans, was in charge of the production; Ottmar Gerster, who taught at the Folkwangschule in Essen, wrote the musical score. The Frankfurt-based Kulturkartell (cultural cartel), a socialist cultural organization, had commissioned *We!* to celebrate May Day in the form of a *kultische Feier* (mass ritual) and, as was hoped, repeat the phenomenal success of Lobo Frank's *Kreuzzug der Maschine* (1930, Crusade of the Machine) with its more than one thousand lay actors. Cultic celebrations like these promised to eliminate the fourth wall of the traditional proscenium stage and, in so doing, expand the boundaries of political theater beyond the available choices (in the Aristotelian tradition) of imitation and identification. As the author of *We!* said, the ultimate goal was to stage "a performance of the masses eager to announce their collective will in the fight for socialism and, through this performance, to give their commitment a more explicit and compelling form."[6]

Today primarily known as the collaborationist uncle of Paul de Man, Hendrik de Man at the time was widely recognized as an original socialist thinker who taught in workers' education associations and lectured on social psychology at the University of Frankfurt. His evolving critique of Marxist historical materialism and Social Democratic reformism found expression in a distinct, if not idiosyncratic cultural socialism based on individual ethical principles. During the 1930s, he contributed to the statist labor policies and public works projects promoted throughout Europe and the United States with his own proposal for a New Deal in Belgium, the so-called 1933 Plan de Man. Notwithstanding his later fascist affiliations, his critical writings from the 1920s, and his observations on an emotionally based understanding of socialism in particular, are very much informed by his active involvement in Social Democratic initiatives in Frankfurt.

One of the initiatives receptive to de Man's concept of emotional socialism was the above-mentioned Kulturkartell, which was founded in Frankfurt in 1925 to coordinate cultural events among the USPD, SPD, SAJ, ADGB, and other left-leaning groups. Their shared belief in culture (and, by extension, education) as a powerful source of class mobilization enabled the representatives of *Kultursozialismus* (cultural socialism) to realize aspects of an authentic working-class culture already under capitalist conditions. Intent on making culture the third pillar of the proletarian lifeworld – the other two were the party and the union – the leader of the Kulturkartell, Conrad Broßwitz (1881–1945), defined

---

[6] Hendrik de Man, *Wir! Ein sozialistisches Festspiel* (Berlin: Arbeiterjugend-Verlag, 1932), 2. Henceforth cited in parentheses in the text.

the organization's goal as follows: "The proletariat must arrive at its own culture. The life of the proletariat, their suffering, their struggle, and their victory must find expression in cultural work. [...] Proletarian cultural work moves toward community, which is the true meaning of all socialist cultural activities."[7] Only a "socialist emotional education," SPD politician Paul Franken (1894–1944) insisted, could provide the proper foundation for a socialist "mental education."[8] Considering the practical implications, Gustav Radbruch (1878–1949), another SPD member of the Reichstag, added a more cautious perspective when he reminded his colleagues that economic forces determined all cultural works and practices, including in bourgeois culture. Among other things, his comment implied that the new socialist *Gemeinschaftskultur* (culture of community) had to move beyond the fixation on the individual work shared by bourgeois high culture and commercial mass culture and foreground the collective, communicative process of cultural production. "Proletarian culture," Radbruch concluded, "socialist culture in the making, can only be a culture of the masses. But we call these refined masses community."[9] Of course, the mysterious element capable of transforming the infamous modern masses into the ideal socialist community was the feeling of community (*Gemeinschaftsbefühl*) that, through the performative qualities of "we," promised the imaginary reconciliation of the competing discourses of mass, folk, and class.

In aiding this process, the Frankfurt production of *We!* presented the performers in matching uniforms, surrounded by dramatic lighting, and on a minimalist stage set reminiscent of a step pyramid. Popular songs, dance numbers, and film clips added to the celebratory mood of this enormous mass spectacle. Responsible for the choreography, Otto Zimmermann (1894–1956) described his primary objective in ways that could be applied to the *Sprechchor* as a whole: "At the end of the event, performers and audiences were to become one big 'we,' thinking, feeling, and acting as a unit."[10] Contemporary reviewers were effusive in their praise for the production's mixture of dramatic, visual, and musical elements. In the words of one reviewer, de Man realized the full potential of the

---

[7] Quoted by Rainer Stübling, *Kultur und Massen. Das Kulturkartell der modernen Arbeiterbewegung in Frankfurt am Main von 1925 bis 1933* (Offenbach am Main: Saalbau-Verlag, 1983), 27.
[8] Paul Franken, *Vom Werden einer neuen Kultur. Aufgaben der Arbeiter-Kultur- und -Sportorganisationen* (Berlin: Laube, 1930), 39.
[9] Gustav Radbruch, *Kulturlehre des Sozialismus. Ideologische Betrachtungen* (Berlin: Dietz, 1927), 22. For an influential critique of the discourse of community from the Weimar period, see Helmuth Plessner, *Grenzen der Gemeinschaft. Eine Kritik des sozialen Radikalismus* (Bonn: Friedrich Cohen, 1924); the book was republished by Suhrkamp in 2002.
[10] Otto Zimmermann, "Inszenierung des Festspiels *Wir!*," Archief Hendrik de Man, 170.

Sprechchor "by showing the tension between positive and negative forces that brings forth the commitment to socialism through the experience of contemporary man – that is, the suffering and struggle of the proletariat."[11] Originally called *Erlösung* (Redemption), *We!* may have failed to deliver on the promise of socialist revolution, but the yearning for spiritual renewal survived and thrived in National Socialist terms. Only one year later, in 1933, the official *Kampftag* (day of struggle) of the working class was renamed "day of celebration of national labor," the figure of the revolutionary worker claimed for the racial community, and the proletarian subject of the *Sprechchor* integrated into the *völkisch* dream world of the *Thingspiel*, the Nazi version of cultic ritual performed in specially designed outdoor amphitheaters during the early 1930s and discussed in detail in the second volume.

There is still a widespread tendency in literary and historical scholarship to equate the term "community" with reactionary and *völkisch* ideologies and, for that reason, attribute prefascist tendencies to all references to community in Weimar-era texts and practices. In fact, the performances of "we" in the *Sprechchor* built on the complex and contradictory meanings of one of the most important concepts in the social imaginary of nineteenth-century German thought, that of community. Through ritualistic acts and cultic forms, the productions referenced precapitalist forms of sociability and redirected their emotional residues toward postcapitalist models of community. Though presented as a radical alternative to both bourgeois class society and modern mass society, this imagined socialist community never broke free of the heterogeneous influences that account for the term's problematic compatibility with the political alternatives to society proposed in the name of the people. Ferdinand Tönnies's famous distinction between the organic ties present in "community" and the formal relations existing in "society" and his corresponding juxtaposition between authentic German culture and European civilization captured the widespread anxieties in Imperial Germany caused by capitalist modernization and rapid urbanization. During the Weimar years, the discourse of community, especially in the form of romantic anticapitalism, continued to generate emotionally charged binaries for the conservative revolution that extended from the prewar "reflections of a nonpolitical man" by Thomas Mann to the racial theories of Nazi ideologue Alfred Rosenberg. Even for socialist theorists from de Man to Gramsci, the notion of community, often in conjunction with solidarity, remained *the* central category for imagining another kind of society and a different form of politics, a point confirmed by Gramsci's insistence on the importance of folk culture to the rev-

---

11 Anon, Review of *Wir!*, Archief Hendrik de Man, 170.

olutionary working class and by de Man's close attention to a mass-based psychology of socialism.

Brought forth by these traditions and discourses, the community in *We!* proudly declares the pursuit of happiness and the joy of work as equally important and mutually constitutive forces in the making of socialist commitments. For de Man, the process of forming a community means engaging the elementary *Gefühlsspannungen* (emotional tensions) shared by all human beings, their hopes and doubts, joys and sorrows. *We!* stages these emotional states through a series of confrontations between the great speaking chorus of workers and several smaller choruses called Nature, Technology, and Religion. The play opens with a group of male workers declaring that "We can't!" an admission of defeat that identifies the obstacles, both external and internal, to a self-determined life. In accordance with its agitational purposes, the triumphant ending offers a joyous celebration of unity, freedom, and democracy under a new kind of "rule of work." Once the workers recognize the exploitation of labor under capitalism as the source of their unhappiness, they are able to state their demands: "We want joyful work!/ We want healthy apartments!/ We want cheerful wives!/We want happy children!/ We want free time!/ We want knowledge and beauty!/ We want human dignity!/ We want unity of the world!" (23). The ending makes clear that the realization of these demands requires collective action: "We! We! We!/ We all want to rise together!/ We all want to join hands! We all want to sing together!" (30–31). The shared singing of "Brothers, to the Sun, to Freedom!," the well-known communist tune adapted from the Russian by Hermann Scherchen, implies that only the socialist movement could fulfill the promise of individual happiness on earth.

The rousing finale of *We!* reads like a stage adaptation of de Man's *Der Kampf um die Arbeitsfreude* (1927, The Struggle for the Joy of Work), which discusses the emotional rewards gained from work as an essential part of modern life and a key requirement in the achievement of labor peace.[12] The play rehearses key arguments about socialism as the promise of happiness first presented in *Zur Psychologie des Sozialismus* (1926, translated as *The Psychology of Socialism*), an influential work discussed by Gramsci and others. In both books, de Man examines and validates the workers' spiritual needs, analyzes the emotional regimes specific to capitalism, and reassesses the latter's detrimental effect on working-class lives from the perspective of class psychology. Against the economic determinism

---

[12] Hendrik de Man, *Der Kampf um die Arbeitsfreude. Eine Untersuchung auf Grund der Aussagen von 78 Industriearbeitern und Angestellten* (Jena: Eugen Diederichs, 1927). In light of de Man's collaborationist activities during the Nazi occupation of Belgium, it would be easy to compare his proposals to the "Strength through Joy" organization of the Reich Labor Service.

and historical materialism of orthodox Marxism, he introduces the ambitious program of a culture of socialism based on, and sustained through, class unity, harmony, and solidarity – that is, the positive feelings flowing from real and imagined experiences of "we."[13] Rejecting arguments that the problem of culture can only be addressed after the revolution, de Man points to the original meaning of culture as a form of cultivation – in short, a way of life. Socialism for him represents nothing less than a new art of living and a new attitude toward life best described as "a spiritual experience" and "a uniquely communitarian way of feeling."[14] Making workers part of the long history of the people, this unique feeling is a

> direct expression of the deeper layers of existence where emotional bonds are forged that connect people to their ancestors, their fellow human beings, and their own times. Reason helps us to recognize and realize our life goals, but it does not set them for us. Everyone among us holds in his mind an ideal image of life that he tries to realize on the basis of a clear feeling about what is worth and not worth fighting for.[15]

In *We!*, proletarian identifications are achieved through choral speaking, singing, and dancing, and the self-transformation of the collective speaking subject through the rhetorical means of oration and declamation. In the text, the community in the act of becoming is alternately described as "The Great Chorus," "Everyone," or "One and All." But are they a social class or a political movement? A community or a collective? The multitudes or the masses? As a theatrical genre, the *Sprechchor* typically draws on a limited number of *dramatis personae* and presents them in predictable constellations. Tensions are introduced through antagonists against whom the ubiquitous "we" asserts its affective charge and critical stance. Predictably, these antagonists include exploitative factory owners, greedy bankers, and the representatives of what Louis Althusser calls state apparatuses (e.g., police, church, school). Equally important for the process of class formation are the historical precursors that, by representing earlier stages of awareness, bear witness to the psychological obstacles to class con-

---

[13] Hendrik de Man, *Der Sozialismus als Kulturbewegung* (Berlin: Arbeiterjugend-Verlag, 1926), 8 and 37. For an introduction and selection of key texts, see Peter Dodge, *A Documentary Study of Hendrik de Man, Socialist Critic of Marxism* (Princeton: Princeton University Press, 1979). For a historical assessment of de Man's writings from the prewar years, also see chapter 5 in Gerd-Rainer Horn, *European Socialists Respond to Fascism: Ideology, Activism, and Contingency* (Oxford: Oxford University Press, 1996). And on de Man as a lapsed Marxist, see chapter 2 in Stanley Pierson, *Leaving Marxism: Studies in the Dissolution of an Ideology* (Stanford: Stanford University Press, 2001).
[14] de Man, *Der Sozialismus als Kulturbewegung*, 11 and 37.
[15] Hendrik de Man, *Zur Psychologie des Sozialismus* (Jena: Eugen Diedrichs, 1926), 13.

sciousness. These range from defeatist behaviors and compensatory beliefs born of oppression to the individual longings located in the private sphere and often expressed by smaller choruses such as "The Women" or "The Children." With these two groups classified as part of "nature," the celebration of the worker as the incarnation of true humanity once again affirms the male position as the universal one – with the implicit assumption that the absorption of the individual into the collective would eventually resolve any remaining conflicts arising from the gendered division of labor.

Speaking choruses ranged from small amateur groups reciting poems and playing short scenes to large semiprofessional groups of up to two hundred rehearsing under professional direction. These choruses regularly participated in socialist mass spectacles featuring groups of singers, musicians, dancers, and athletes. All formats foregrounded the performative aspects of community, with the potential conflict between the openness toward audience participation and the disciplining function of public ritual an inevitable side effect of such proletarian mobilizations. The tensions between theatricality and authenticity inscribed in these practices – and ideally resolved through the transindividual, transhistorical perspective inherent in the cultic format – functioned as a constitutive part of this process as they foregrounded the social and economic determinations of class society. To what degree the *Sprechchor* achieved audience participation or raised class consciousness beyond the actual theatrical event cannot be determined based on formal analyses or critical reviews. For the purposes of this study, the belief in such transformations is ultimately more relevant to the reconstruction of the proletarian dream than any empirically confirmed political conversions.

The heavy dependence of the *Sprechchor* on bodies rather than characters is even more pronounced in the *Bewegungschor*. In the words of one contemporary: "Here, in the *Bewegungschor*, we experience the renewal of the awareness of the body, which is the result of emotional movement toward the outside world. Love and hate, sorrow and joy, roused by the music, become visible and resonate strongly in the rhythmical choreographies of human limbs."[16] Drawing on influences from workers' sport and modern dance, these mass choreographies developed further the performative potential of the classed body as a site of oppression as well as resistance. Staging groups of dancers contracting and expanding, retreating and advancing, and taking possession of public spaces, the *Bewegungschor* functioned like an embodiment and pre-

---

[16] Quoted by Stübling, *Kultur und Massen*, 32. Stübling's book contains a brief discussion (and several sketches from the production) of *Wir!* (49–55).

figuration of the revolutionary working class. With emotion equated with motion, physical movement came to stand in for political movement in general. Choreographies often alluded to the hardships of industrial labor, with some even emulating the repetitive work on the conveyor belt and the reduction of human beings to mere automatons. Rhythm, tempo, and repetition not only revealed the harmful effects of alienated labor on the working body but also modeled simple forms of collective resistance. According to Martin Gleisner, these mass choreographies were "best suited to convey mass and community feelings through important basic constellations: opposition and unification, division and unity, weakness and strength."[17] From the participants' perspective, the transition from *Sprechchor* to *Bewegungschor* could be challenging, he conceded, and a successful contribution to this "nonindividual, supraindividual theater" required specialized training in acting and dancing that could not be made available to everyone.[18]

Several manuals written for directors and conductors addressed the difficulties of staging mass spectacles without compromising artistic quality. Time and again their authors confirmed emotions as the driving force behind the desired trajectory from theatrical performance to political action. The prolific Bruno Schönlank (1891–1965), the author of many *Sprechchor* plays, described the performers as stand-ins for the audience, functioning as "herald of their longings, their desire for battle, but also their desperation."[19] Similarly, Adolf Johannesson emphasized the power of embodied emotions in imagining a future socialist society. Modeled on the ancient Greek drama as a microcosm of Athenian democracy, the new mass performances in his view reconciled earlier conceptions of the people as the original folk with Marxist notions of the working class as the universal class. "Just as the proletariat took the first step toward the creation of a true folk community," he explained, "it also created the first community of experience (*Erlebnisgemeinschaft*) by appearing on the stage [...] and giving expression to its feelings and longings."[20]

The above-mentioned Otto Zimmermann went one step further by declaring the audience – and, by implication, the conditions of reception – as the primary

---

[17] Martin Gleisner, "Der Bewegungschor," *Kulturwille* 7.1 (1930): 9–10.
[18] Martin Gleisner, "Das Zusammenwirken der Künste in der Festgestaltung," *Sozialistische Bildung* 2 (1929): 25.
[19] Bruno Schönlank, *Der Moloch* (Leipzig: Arbeiter-Theaterverlag A. Jahn, 1930), n. p.
[20] Adolf Johannesson, *Leitfaden für Sprechchöre*, third ed. (Berlin: Arbeiterjugend-Verlag, 1929), 7. It would be interesting to compare these guidelines for socialist choral directors with one from the Nazi era such as Richard Noethlichs's *Der Sprechchor. Eine Anleitung für den Chorführer* (1934).

site of political mobilization. Based on his experiences working with various Leipzig-based amateur groups, he described the main goal of the *Sprechchor* movement as "the manifestation of rousing political insights through the performers' bodies, with the ultimate goal of propelling the audience into action."[21] The growing significance of body culture in everyday life confirmed his belief in what he called the primacy of rhythm – especially its prelinguistic, preindividual qualities – in facilitating proletarian identifications.[22] If treated as an integral part of these bodily regimes, choral speaking would eventually overcome the divide between "passive majority" and "active minority" and fully integrate the audience into the aural, visual, and kinetic effects of the movement chorus turned mass movement. Of course, the realization of the proletarian *Gesamtkunstwerk* required extensive training of all participants, Zimmermann admitted, including gymnastic exercises that achieved complete unity and synchronicity in group movements and breathing and speaking exercises that trained the performers in precise diction, rhythm, and volume.[23]

The *Sprechchor* movement began as part of the socialist mass festivals organized in Leipzig around the turn of the century and reached an initial high point in January 1920 with the staging of the historical slave revolt of *Spartacus* on a cycle-racing track during a trade union festival in front of fifty thousand spectators. Mass dances, songs, and pantomimes had always played an important part in the dramatization of revolutionary moments, with the preference for open-air theaters discouraging illusionist tendencies and expanding the boundaries of theater as a public space. On the remaining pages, it may make sense to situate the emergence of the collective subject as part of a longer nineteenth-century history of socialist theater in critical dialogue with bourgeois theater and older dramatic forms and traditions. Introducing the *dramatis personae* of the worker's movement, titles such *Tag des Proletariats* (1924, Day of the Proletariat) by Ernst Toller, *Arbeiter, Bauern, Soldaten* (1924, Workers, Peasants, Soldiers) by Johannes R. Becher, and *Liebknecht Luxemburg Lenin* (1927) by Hans Lorbeer proudly declared the Marxist orientation of this emerging collective

---

[21] Otto Zimmermann, "Dramatischer Chor?," *Kulturwille* 7.5 (1930): 93–94. For a similar argument, see Walter Zeiler, "Unsere Jugendweihen," *Sozialistische Bildung* 1 (1932): 14–16.

[22] Otto Zimmermann, "Gymnastik und Tanz vom Standpunkt des Arbeiters," *Kulturwille* 5.1 (1928): 4–5. Zimmermann wrote the standard works on this variant of the *Sprechchor*, the two-part *Der Sprechbewegungschor* (Leipzig: Arbeiter-Turnverlag, 1929–30) and, together with Hermann Heyer and Georg Benedix, *Maschine und Arbeit in Gestaltungen für Laientanz-, Sprech- und Bewegungs-Chor* (Leipzig: Arbeiter-Turnverlag, 1930).

[23] Otto Zimmermann, *Der Sprechbewegungschor. Theoretische Grundlagen* and *Hinweise für die Praxis* (Leipzig: Arbeiter-Turnverlag, 1929).

mythology and socialist modernity. Stylistically, the ecstatic utopianism of early expressionism prevailed, notwithstanding occasional experiments with the cool factuality of New Objectivity and the aggressive militancy of communist agitprop. The spiritualization of working-class suffering through a Christian iconography and its aestheticization in an expressionist staccato (or telegram) style were especially pronounced in contributions by Schönlank, including *Großstadt* (1923, Big City), *Der gespaltene Mensch* (1927, Divided Man), and *Seid geweiht!* (1927, Be Blessed!). Karl Bröger's *Rote Erde* (1928, Red Earth), written for the Sozialistische Arbeiterjugend (SAJ, Socialist Workers' Youth), and Max Barthel's *Ins Leben hinein* (1929, Forward into Life), written for the nondenominational *Jugendweihe*, a socialist version of the Christian rite of Confirmation, attests to the *Sprechchor*'s frequent enlistment in secular initiation rituals directed specifically at working-class youth. By contrast, the modernist proletarian ballad *Mann im Beton* (1932, Man in Concrete), with music by Walter Gronostay and words by R. A. Stemmle and Günther Weisenborn, attests to the strong influence of the Brechtian *Lehrstück* (teaching play) on the *Sprechchor* movement. Throughout, the theater of ancient Greece, its architectures and choreographies, remained an important inspiration, with the patterns of rediscovery extending all the way to the Delphic Festivals of 1927 and 1930 that included a performance of *Prometheus Bound*.

In making community the preferred category of class analysis, the *Sprechchor* does not fit easily into standard accounts of Weimar drama and theater based on leftwing and rightwing distinctions.[24] In addressing the problem, Uwe Hornauer has proposed two concepts, "refunctionalization of bourgeois traditions" and "anticipation of the socialist community,"[25] to evaluate the unique

---

24 For a general English-language account of modern German theater, see Michael Patterson, *The Revolution in German Theatre, 1900–1933* (London: Routledge & Kegan Paul, 1981). The best overviews of proletarian theater during the Weimar Republic published in the GDR are Ludwig Hoffmann and Daniel Hoffmann-Ostwald, eds., *Deutsches Arbeitertheater 1918–1933*, 2 vols., third ed. (Berlin: Henschel, 1977) and Ludwig Hoffmann and Klaus Pfützner, eds., *Theater der Kollektive. Proletarisch-revolutionäres Berufstheater in Deutschland 1928–1933: Stücke, Dokumente, Studien*, 2 vols. (Berlin: Henschel, 1980). In both collections, the *Sprechchor* is treated as a marginal phenomenon because of its association with Social Democracy. Compare, from a West German perspective, Richard Weber, *Proletarisches Theater und revolutionäre Arbeiterbewegung 1918–1925* (Cologne: Prometh, 1978). On the *Sprechchor* movement in the extensive scholarship on Weimar theater, see Richard Sheppard, "Proletarische Feierstunden and the Early History of the Sprechchor 1919–1923," *Internationales Archiv für Sozialgeschichte der deutschen Literatur* 8 (1997): 147–185.
25 Uwe Hornauer, *Laienspiel und Massenchor. Das Arbeitertheater der Kultursozialisten in der Weimarer Republik* (Cologne: Prometh, 1985), 35 and 39. For an introduction to the *Sprechchor*

contribution by the cultural socialists. Meanwhile, Dieter Klenke has highlighted the close connections between theatrical and musical practices that, since the workers' choral societies of the mid-nineteenth century, defined socialist culture as an event culture indifferent to the pressures of normative poetics.[26] While there exists widespread agreement on the multimedia qualities of the *Sprechchor* and related mass spectacles, scholarly assessments tend to reproduce official party positions when they distinguish all too clearly between the educational theater of the SPD and the agitational theater of the KPD. A comparison of actual plays and productions cannot confirm such clear and simple ideological divides. For this reason, in these remaining pages, the unique contribution of the *Sprechchor*, whether socialist or communist, will be evaluated as part of the longer history that brought the working class to the theatrical stage: first in the form of social types and, eventually, as a collective body.

In most literary histories, the appearance of workers on the modern stage is equated with the formal and political provocation of Gerhart Hauptmann's *Die Weber* (1892, *The Weavers*) about the 1844 Weavers' Revolt in Silesia.[27] Few accounts mention an earlier treatment of the Weavers' Revolt, Julius Leopold Klein's never performed *Cavalier und Arbeiter* (1850, Squire and Worker), which contains the first depiction of class struggle in a German-language drama. The early socialist movement after the Revolutions of 1848 produced numerous largely forgotten plays (of negligible quality), typically written by workers turned activists, performed during socialist festivities and anniversaries, and concerned above all with labor struggles and social conflicts.[28] Publishers Adolf Hoffmann in Berlin and Richard Lipinski in Leipzig printed these plays primarily for use by amateur theater groups – a situation that changed only with the turn toward a more professional workers' theater in the early 1900s. Lengthy dialogues and monologues on the social question and stereotypical characters without psychological depth are the two main reasons for the plays' lack of reception beyond socialist associations; another factor that would become obvious only in retro-

---

movement through the work of its most active proponent, see Jon Clark, *Bruno Schönlank und die Arbeitersprechchorbewegung* (Cologne: Prometh, 1984).

26 On this connection during the Weimar years, see Dietmar Klenke, *Arbeitersänger und Volksbühnen in der Weimarer Republik* (Bonn: Dietz, 1992).

27 For an overview of the Wilhelmine period, see Andrew Bonnell, *The People's Stage in Imperial Germany: Social Democracy and Culture 1890–1914* (London: Tauris, 2005).

28 The contradictions in the SPD's approach to theater before World War I can be studied exemplarily in Rudolf Franz, *Theater und Volk: Nebst einem Anhange. Die Debatten des Sozialdemokratischen Parteitages in Gotha 1896 über Kunst und Proletariat* (Munich: G. Birk, 1914). On Franz, see Gerhard Engel, *Dr. Rudolf Franz (1882–1956). Zwischen allen Stühlen – ein Leben in der Arbeiterbewegung* (Berlin: edition bodoni, 2013).

spect was their inability to imagine the working class outside the dramatic conventions of bourgeois individuality.

A brief overview of early socialist plays confirms this constitutive tension between provocative topic and traditional form and reveals the shortcomings of a thus defined theater of ideas that the *Sprechchor* movement tried to overcome through its emphasis on collective performances. In a "national economic humoresque" titled *Ein Schlingel* (1867, A Prankster), written by ADAV president Johann Baptist von Schweitzer, a socialist worker suddenly appears on the scene and starts a heated discussion on surplus value with the local factory owner. In August Otto-Walster's farce *Ein verunglückter Agitator* (1874, An Accidental Agitator), two students arrive in a picturesque village and, pretending to be socialist agitators, raise the problem of landownership. In Heinrich Bulthaupt's social tragedy *Die Arbeiter* (1877, The Workers), the confrontation between a working-class family and a factory owner ends tragically with a mass riot and a burning castle. Dramatizations of strikes, revolts, and revolutions increased significantly after the rescinding of the Anti-Socialist Laws. Friedrich Bosse's agitational play *Im Kampf* (1892, In the Struggle) dramatizes the various stages of a strike in order to showcase the workers' growing power. In the drama *Familie Wawroch* (1899, The Wawroch Family), Franz Adamus (pseudonym Ferdinand Bronner) has a Jewish socialist agitator arrive in a small Austrian town on the verge of a labor strike. Meanwhile, the naturalist approach to working-class milieus continues in Emil Rosenow's *Daheim* (1894, At Home) and Ernst Preczang's *Im Hinterhaus* (1903, In the Rear Building), two tenement-centric stagings of the Marxist immiseration theory. In an unpublished manuscript, Preczang describes his approach in ways that capture the prevailing view of workers as *dramatis personae* and highlight the strong reliance by all socialist playwrights on emotion as a mobilizing force: "My interest lies primarily in the emotional dimension of the movement and its contribution to a new spiritual culture, [...] freedom, equality, justice – these are and were for me not only political but also human and ethical postulates."[29]

After the turn of the century, the gradual opening of socialism toward modernism established the conditions for the imagination of collective subjectivities beyond the constraints of individualism and psychologism. Two early expressionist dramas, Paul Mehnert's *Golgatha* (1908) about a 1905 miners' strike in the Ruhr region and Lu Märten's *Bergarbeiter* (1909, Miners), performed during a miners' strike in 1911, modeled the all-important transformation of disempo-

---

[29] Ernst Preczang, "Rückblick," quoted in Georg Bollenbeck, *Zur Theorie und Geschichte der frühen Arbeiterlebenserinnerungen* (Kronberg: Scriptor, 1976), 50.

werment to empowerment, which was meant to result in the revolutionary deed. During the early postwar years, Ernst Toller's *Masse Mensch* (1921, translated as *Masses and Man*) and *Die Maschinenstürmer* (1922, The Machine Wreckers) not only connected the historical battle between capitalism and socialism to the contemporary traumas of war and revolution but also imagined the future of modernity in alternatively chiliastic and apocalyptic tones. Significantly, channeled through the expressionist sensibilities of Toller, the mass chorus still expressed the desire to become a class in the form of a question: "From the abysses of the factories we cry: When shall we live in love? When shall we work at will? When is deliverance?"[30]

The workers had to wait for the cultural organizations of the SPD and KPD founded during the Weimar years to create public spaces in which these emotional needs could be addressed as part of the parties' respective reformist and revolutionary strategies; as this chapter has shown, that distinct emotional and performative space was claimed by the *Sprechchor* movement. Its cult of community may have appealed to writers, performers, and audiences across the divisions in the Weimar left; but it also found its most outspoken critics in the cult of the collective developed in the context of communist agitprop and its very different performance practices and emotional regimes.

---

30 Ernst Toller, "Masses and Man," trans. Vera Mendel, in *German Expressionist Plays*, ed. Ernst Schürer (New York: Continuum, 2005), 212.

Chapter 13
Taking a Stand: The Habitus of Agitprop

> A proletarian whose facial expressions convey submission and resignation makes for an embarrassing and shameful sight. By contrast, in the gestures of protest, he comes across as appealing, inspiring, heroic even. And because the importance of setting an example, of encouraging through suggestion, must not be underestimated, the rebellious proletarian is without doubt not only more likeable and more beautiful but also more valuable to the class struggle than the proletarian who has turned bourgeois.
>
> <div align="right">Otto Rühle, <i>Illustrierte Kultur- und Sittengeschichte des Proletariats</i></div>

Proletarian identifications allowed individuals to imagine themselves as part of the collectivities visualized by the Cologne Progressives (of chapter 11) and performed by the *Sprechchor* movement (of chapter 12). As previous chapters have shown, the interpellation of the revolutionary working class depended on the constitutive tension between figuration and abstraction that channeled anger and indignation into highly formalized – which also means, highly politicized – terms. For communist artists and writers, especially those affiliated with the KPD, the declared goal was to transform physical bodies into classed bodies: by identifying antagonists and obstacles, by modeling the process of moving and feeling as one, and by expressing the various stages of transformation through specific emotions.

Given the importance attributed to the right (and wrong) ways of standing in these paradigmatic scenes of political mobilization, taking a very literal approach to the making of communist bodies might prove useful and productive. In reconstructing the proletarian dream through its emotional regimes, this time through the lens of embodied emotions, this chapter draws on three very different artistic practices and examines in what ways the act of standing becomes a public performance of political habitus. The argument is developed through the representation of the agitator in paintings by Curt Querner, Magnus Zeller, and Käthe Kollwitz and continues with the equation of class consciousness with masculinity in two solo dance pieces by Jean Weidt and Jo Mihaly. The instructions on the right ways of standing (and speaking) by the agitprop troupe Das rote Sprachrohr (The Red Megaphone) extend the conception of embodied emotions toward the relationship between body and voice and its implications for the articulation of what in Marxist theory is called *Klassenstandpunkt* (class standpoint).[1]

In the increasingly polarized atmosphere of the late Weimar Republic, the many acts of standing in political or politicized settings functioned as the most visible manifestation of what dance historian Hannah Kosstrin calls embodied ideology.[2] As a physical activity, standing signifies the opposite of moving (or sitting, for that matter), but it also marks the beginning and end of any movement. For the communists, taking a stance under the condition of intensified class struggles meant to define movement in the literal and figurative sense. During the early 1930s, KPD agitators appeared on the streets to articulate their own stance in the confrontational terms both of class struggle and party politics, including against Nazis and Social Democrats. In the groups and initiatives dominated by the KPD, a thus defined *Klassenstandpunkt* functioned very much in the sense of what Pierre Bourdieu calls embodied habitus, a "political mythology realized, *em-bodied*, turned into a permanent disposition, a durable manner of standing, speaking, and thereby of *feeling* and *thinking*."[3] In relying so heavily on such embodied performances of class consciousness, communist artists, actors, musicians, dancers, and agitators were able to draw on a long tradition of embodied habitus and its rhetorical uses in religious, political, and legal confrontations. This tradition can be traced from Martin Luther's (apocryphal) declaration "Here I Stand" at the Imperial Diet of Worms, which expressed his unwillingness to yield to authority and renounce his faith, to a legal term like *locus standi* (literally "place to stand"), which denotes the right to be heard and appear before an official body and, more generally, to claim the rights to free speech. The same connections between physical body and religious or political conviction inform the meaning of words, such as stand, stance, standpoint, standing, and so forth.

"Habitus" is closely related to the German *Haltung*, a term denoting posture, bearing, attitude, or demeanor. Significantly, the gestural codes that produce *Haltung* on the theatrical stage have played a key role in the development of antipsychological approaches favoring mechanistic models in Soviet psychology and modern performance practices. Delineating its potentialities in Bertolt

---

[1] The ways in which these modalities also informed the mass spectacles of workers' sport and continued in Nazi organizations such as the Reich Labor Service will have to be examined in greater detail in the second volume.

[2] Hannah Kosstrin, "Inevitable Designs: Embodied Ideology in Anna Sokolow's Proletarian Dances," *Dance Research Journal* 45.2 (2013): 5–23.

[3] Pierre Bourdieu, *Outline of a Theory of Practice* (Cambridge: Cambridge University Press, 1977), 93–94. Here Bourdieu uses the Greek word *hexis* to describe the embodied habitus.

Brecht's instructions for the *Lehrstücke* (teaching plays), Darko Suvin in fact designates *Haltung* as the "terminus technicus of a Marxist theory of behavior."[4] According to Suvin, *Haltung* and its cognate *Verhalten* (behavior) are closely related to discourses of control and strength – especially, one might add, whenever power remains beyond reach. Whether identified with an individual or a group, the term establishes a relationship between bodies and ideas in performative terms. It is inseparable from norms of public behavior and, while typically equated with an ethos of resistance, just as often associated with an attitude of inflexibility. In all cases, *Haltung* implies a strong sense of conviction that, by choosing steadiness over adaptability, promotes a tendency toward dogmatism. And precisely through this unwillingness to yield, *Haltung*, according to Suvin, is well suited for articulating a political position or, in this case, defining an agitational style.

At first glance, *Haltung* has much in common with the Brechtian practice of *Gestus*, which treats physical gestures as manifestations of political attitudes. Both modalities, in turn, are inseparable from the body cultures developed in the context of workers' sport, industrial labor, and military training and, in their insistence on influencing attitudes and behaviors through physical regimes, far removed from bourgeois notions of psychological interiority. However, *Gestus* typically involves a much more dialogic, process-based practice. As Marc Silberman points out, its function is to foreground the historical nature of social structures and institutions and to emphasize their availability to critical analysis and political critique.[5] By contrast, the performances of *Haltung* examined in this chapter preclude the possibilities for open dialogue as they follow highly normative definitions of political emotions and make clear distinctions between constructive and destructive ones. In defining the terms and conditions of standing like a communist, KPD agitprop not only articulated official party positions; of special relevance to this discussion, it also presented radicalization as a process of masculinization. To what degree the equation of class consciousness with masculinity drew on tropes of militancy formed in the crucible of war and revolution has already been discussed in chapters 9 and 10. In what ways this gendered model of proletarian identifications nonetheless opened up a space for

---

[4] Darko Suvin, "Haltung," in *Historisch-kritisches Wörterbuch des Marxismus*, ed. Wolfgang Fritz Haug, 7 vols. (Berlin: Argument, 2001), 5: 1134. Also see his "*Haltung* (Bearing) and Emotions: Brecht's Refunctioning of Conservative Metaphors for Agency," in *Zweifel—Fragen—Vorschläge. Bertolt Brecht anlässlich des Einhundertsten*, ed. Thomas Jung (Frankfurt am Main: Peter Lang, 1999), 43–58.

[5] Marc Silberman, "Gestus," in *Historisch-kritisches Wörterbuch des Marxismus*, 5: 659.

women, for instance through the habitus of androgyny, will be considered in greater detail in chapter 18.

Proletarian identifications were formed both through propaganda as a technique of persuasion and through agitation in the sense of physical and emotional stimulation. During the later Weimar years, agitprop emerged as the KPD's preferred method of mass mobilization and found privileged expression in the ubiquitous figure of the agitator. A portmanteau word, "agitprop" is usually defined as a musical or theatrical performance distinguished by its improvised sets and settings, short pieces and mixed forms, and heavy reliance on parody, satire, and the grotesque. Combining posters, songs, speeches, dances, skits, and film clips in short programs and longer revues, agitprop troupes addressed typical working-class problems, such as labor struggles, low wages, family strife, unemployment, homelessness, poverty, and so forth. These groups developed programs in solidarity with the Soviet Union and appeared at KPD election rallies, RFB mass demonstrations, RGO factory cell meetings, and events organized by the KJVD (Communist Youth Association of Germany). Beyond these political contexts, agitprop at the time also defined a particular mode of enunciation, or form of presentation, adopted across a wide range of body practices in modern theater, music, and dance. Historian Richard Bodek rightly insists on the importance of proletarian performances to Weimar modernism as a whole. Communication scholar Robert Heynen makes a similar point about the class politics of embodiment and its little understood role in (the critique of) capitalist modernity.[6] Precisely by linking the spheres of the aesthetic and the political, both scholars conclude, agitprop served radicalizing functions in the highly politicized culture of the Weimar Republic.[7]

In the Soviet Union, agitprop had been introduced originally as a coordinated propaganda effort in support of new Bolshevik initiatives and policies. Its forms and techniques were developed within the Proletkult movement that provided agitational visual, literary, theatrical, and educational materials from a proletarian point of view, that treated proletarian culture as a privileged site of socialist modernity and industrial modernization – and that eventually clashed

---

6 See Richard Bodek, *Proletarian Performance in Weimar Berlin: Agitprop, Chorus, and Brecht* (Columbia, SC: Camden House, 1997) and Robert Heynen, "Revolution and the Degeneration of the Weimar Republic: Worker Culture and the Rise of Fascism," in *Degeneration and Revolution: Radical Cultural Politics and the Body in Weimar Germany* (Leiden: Brill, 2015), 496–583.
7 For a brief introduction to Weimar-era agitprop, see Erika Funk-Hennigs, "Die Agitpropbewegung als Teil der Arbeiterkultur der Weimarer Republik," *Beiträge zur Popularmusikforschung* 15–16 (1995): 82–117.

with the leadership claims of the Bolsheviks as the vanguard party.[8] Under the influence of this proletarian moment, the most famous Soviet agitprop troupe, the Blue Blouse collective, perfected a unique style of speaking usually described as hard-hitting and assault-like; mental and physical alertness were essential components of their rehearsal practices and performance styles. Their highly anticipated appearance at Erwin Piscator's Theater am Nollendorfplatz in 1927 and their subsequent German tour led to the founding of numerous agitprop troupes, such as Rote Raketen and Kolonne Links in Berlin, Rote Fanfaren in Stuttgart, Rote Rebellen in Chemnitz, Rote Ratten in Dresden, and so forth; a group of children even agitated under the name Rote Trommler.[9] Gustav von Wangenheim's productions with Truppe 1931 (Troupe 1931) and, before that, his experiments with choral plays and mass pantomimes confirm the strong influence of Proletkult on theatrical practices that combine agitation, information, and entertainment. Following the example of Piscator's Revue Roter Rummel (1924, Revue Red Rabble), agitprop troupes often sought inspiration from distinctly urban diversions, including as variety shows, and produced a barrage of stimuli sometimes compared to hammering and drumfire.[10] Their performances became more propagandistic and less imaginative after Stalin's consolidation of power after the death of Lenin in 1924. At the request of the Comintern, the IAH-funded Kolonne Links and other troupes soon created entire programs in support of the Soviet Union, with the result that the playful elements that had made agitprop part of a staged multimedia aesthetic gradually disappeared and gave way to predictable exercises in political indoctrination.

Through agitprop, key ideas of the Proletkult movement gained entrance into the international debates on proletarian culture, including behaviorist models of human behavior and conditioning inspired by Pavlovianism. Against the classic Marxist formulation provided by Georgi Plekhanov, "that social consciousness is determined by social existence" and that art "expresses the striv-

---

8 For a comprehensive account of proletarian theater, including agitprop during the early Weimar Republic, also see Richard Weber, *Proletarisches Theater und revolutionäre Arbeiterbewegung 1918–1925* (Cologne: Prometh, 1976). On Proletkult and its agitational practices, see Peter Gorsen and Eberhard Knödler-Bunte, *Proletkult*, 2 vols. (Stuttgart: Frommann-Holzboog, 1974–75).

9 Two lesser-known agitprop troupes are the focus in Susanne Seelbach, *Proletarisch-revolutionäres Theater in Düsseldorf 1930–1933: Die Bühne als politisches Medium* (Frankfurt am Main: Peter Lang, 1994). For more personal recollections, see Daniel Hoffmann-Ostwald, ed., *Auf der roten Rampe. Erlebnisberichte und Texte aus der Arbeit der Agitproptruppen vor 1933* (Berlin: Henschel, 1963).

10 Erwin Piscator, "R. R. R. (Revue Roter Rummel)," *Das politische Theater*, ed. Ludwig Hoffmann (Berlin: Henschel, 1968), 60–62.

ings and the mood of a given society, or, if we have to do with a society divided into classes, of a given social class," the leading proponents of proletarian culture emphasized the ability of culture to train new political attitudes and reorganize social experiences – including through the regimes of the body. In the words of Alexander Bogdanov, "Art organizes social experience by means of living images, not only in the sphere of cognition, but also in that of feelings and desires. As a consequence it is a most powerful weapon for the organization of collective forces, and in a class society, of class forces."[11]

Whether in the theater or on the street, agitprop sought to reorganize social experiences through confrontational performances that relied heavily on physical and psychological techniques. In addition to rhetorical devices such as repetition, simplification, and direct address, aggressive body postures and gestures and forceful modes of speaking were considered essential to the conditioning of proletarian strength and communist militancy. Identifying the constitutive elements, especially as regards their emotional energies, requires closer consideration of diverse body practices and their compensatory and disciplining effects. KPD agitprop may have looked and sounded aggressive, but it developed its militant stance from a defensive position within the left- and rightwing divides of the late Weimar years. The precarious position of the party during the final years of the republic thus attest also to the emotionally charged function of agitprop in a country where the revolution had failed and where a subsequent series of failed revolts (discussed in chapters 9 and 10) had only increased the factionalism and dogmatism that would continue to haunt the Weimar left. The agitator appeared on the scene as the very embodiment of these larger struggles over correct positions and gave a body and a voice to the communist *Kampfkultur* (militant culture) and its masculinist emotional regimes.

The description by Otto Rühle (1874–1943) of the "rebellious proletarian" illustrates the functioning of a thus defined embodied ideology and can be used to introduce the discussion of the examples through a few deceptively simple questions:[12] What did the ideal proletarian look like – aside from the fact that he was young and male? What made him appear likable, valuable, and, yes, beautiful? How did his incarnation in the figure of the agitator establish a repertoire of typical gestures and postures? And how did the agitator – and, by extension, the larger project of communism – come to occupy a place, control a space, and move as part of a group or inside a crowd? To begin with, the ideal proletarian

---

[11] Quoted by Edward J. Brown, *The Proletarian Episode in Russian Literature, 1928–1932* (New York: Columbia University Press, 1953), 7.
[12] Otto Rühle, *Illustrierte Kultur- und Sittengeschichte des Proletariats* (Berlin: Neuer Deutscher Verlag, 1930), 29.

was not supposed to look like council-communist-turned-anarchist Rühle (see figure 13.1), portrayed with bulging, bloodshot eyes by Conrad Felixmüller in *Der Agitator/Otto Rühle spricht* (1920, The Agitator, O.R. Speaks). At the same time, the communist scene of agitation was not to be confused with George Grosz's caricature of a rightwing agitator in *Der Agitator* (1928, The Agitator). On the contrary, the examples presented on the following pages suggest that communist agitprop sought to move beyond the pathos and ecstasy of the early postwar years and align the Bolshevik concept of vanguardism more closely with what Ernst Bloch once called the cold stream within Marxism – that is, an unemotional approach that promised self-control and control of others.

Fig. 13.1 Conrad Felixmüller, *Der Agitator. Otto Rühle spricht/The Agitator. Otto Rühle Speaks* (1920), oil on canvas. Nationalgalerie Berlin, 1946 reproduction. Copyright 2017 Artists Rights Society (ARS), New York/VG Bild-Kunst Bonn.

Fig. 13.2 Curt Querner, *Agitator* (1930), oil on canvas, Nationalgalerie Berlin. Copyright 2017 Artists Rights Society (ARS), New York/VG Bild-Kunst Bonn.

And indeed, the most compelling personification of communist cool can be found in a large-scale oil painting, titled *Agitator* (1931), by the Dresden-based Curt Querner (1904–1976), a metalworker-turned-artist who worked in the New Objectivity style of his teacher Otto Dix (see figure 13.2). The work in question depicts a slender man in his thirties standing alone on a street corner in what looks like a working-class neighborhood. The cobblestone street and the gray walls, drainpipe, and houses in the back conjure a mood of deprivation and desolation.

Despite the drab setting, the man's posture, his legs slightly apart and knees tightly locked, conveys confidence and strength. His arms are extended forward, with both digit fingers pointing at an imagined audience beyond the frame. His wide corduroy pants and short light-brown jacket are not typical sartorial choices for a factory worker and suggest a party functionary. For Querner, an active member of KPD and ASSO, the proletariat was inseparable from its uniforms – the pea coats, simple tunics, and soft caps worn by the marching workers in his best-known work, *Demonstration* (1930), and the overalls and smocks donned by the artist himself in several probing self-portraits. Perhaps the agitator's mountaineering-type jacket is an allusion to communism's heroic climb to the summit of world history, and his chiseled face and tight lips an expression of the self-control required of all party members. In either case, Querner was interested less in the representation of a particular social milieu or political type than in the performance of an ideological position. The fact that the agitator does not even require the visible presence of an audience strengthens the implied connection between communist orthodoxy and aggressive militancy and adds some credence to the claim by Hellmuth Heinz that an earlier, larger version of the painting included a worker's hand wielding a gun.[13]

The gendered nature of the communist habitus becomes glaringly obvious through a comparison of *Agitator* to earlier treatments of scenes of agitation that explicitly draw on Christian iconographies of suffering. These are on full view in Magnus Zeller's expressionist *Agitator/Volksredner* (1920, Agitator/Orator, oil on canvas), which relies on religious tropes and symbols to depict agitation as a state of ecstatic communitarianism (see figure 13.3). In choosing the subject matter, Zeller (1888–1972), who studied with Berlin Secession member Lovis Corinth, drew on his personal experiences during the revolutionary uprisings in the capital and his close familiarity with the conventions of the expressionist stage. His reenactment of the transformative effect of agitation centers on a preacher-like figure, a young, slender man in a garish green suit, who is surrounded by an enraptured audience in what could be a religious revival – were it not for a large silhouetted man in the foreground ominously shaking his fist. The danger emanating from the scene is captured in the raw emotions on the faces of the worshippers and the formal dynamism of stark contrasts, diagonal lines, and elongated shapes. The constitutive tension between reverie and revolt, to cite the title of a related portfolio of Zeller lithographs, foregrounds

---

13 Hellmuth Heinz, *Curt Querner* (Dresden: Verlag der Kunst, 1968), 24. On the figure of the agitator (also from a GDR perspective), see Dieter Schmidt, "Die Figur des Agitators in der proletarisch-revolutionären Kunst," *Bildende Kunst* 11 (1964): 576–83.

what, for many expressionist artists, constituted the deeply religious and intensely emotional qualities of modern mass mobilizations.[14]

Fig. 13.3 Magnus Zeller, *Volksredner/Agitator* (1920), oil on canvas, Los Angeles County Museum of Art (LACMA). Copyright 2017 Artists Rights Society (ARS), New York/VG Bild-Kunst Bonn.

Fig. 13.4 Käthe Kollwitz, *Der Agitationsredner/The Agitator* (1926), lithograph, Käthe-Kollwitz Museum Berlin. Copyright 2017 Artists Rights Society (ARS), New York/VG Bild-Kunst Bonn.

Taking a very different approach, Käthe Kollwitz (1867–1945), in the lithograph *Der Agitationsredner* (1926, The Agitator), focused on the distance between speaker and audience in inviting empathy for the workers and their plight (see figure 13.4).[15] Her composition focuses on a haggard man with sunken face whose raised shoulders and clenched fists suggest anguish and defeat. He stands timidly in front of a small group of (bourgeois) men identified only through their hats – evidence of the difficulty of real dialogue across the class divide. The isolated speaker figure displays the marks of abjection in the profoundly humanist ways that characterized Kollwitz's identification with the powerless and oppressed throughout her career. And because of his "unmanly" posture, Kollwitz's agitator by the mid-1920s appeared to many communist workers and activists as a pitiable character from the naturalist imagination, a victim and

---

14 The terms refer to the title of the exhibition catalogue *Magnus Zeller, Entrückung und Aufruhr*, ed. Dominik Bartmann (Berlin: Stiftung Stadtmuseum, 2002).
15 Another version of *Agitationsredner* (charcoal on paper) stages a more militant scene that includes (cap-wearing) workers raising their fists.

a supplicant. To them, his abject stance not only represented the failed project of social reform and liberal humanism but also the dangers of the politics of empathy and compassion against which KPD artists promoted their cult of masculine militancy.

The evolving artistic discourse on position, stance, and posture proved very important to a highly politicized body culture that drew on well-established traditions and conventions and relied on extensive commentary (e.g., in manuals for agitprop troupes) to achieve the desired interpellative effects. In defining a communist habitus, agitprop performers found rich inspiration in the visual arts, including the classical ideal of the male body as perfected in Greek and Roman sculpture. The bodily regimes shared by the modern penal system and industrial management and appropriated by the workers' movement in the context of workers' sport provided important contemporary points of reference. As Sander Gilman has shown, extensive medical research was conducted during the age of industrialization to prove the importance of good posture.[16] Related assumptions about physical exercises and psychological dispositions helped to compel children, soldiers, as well as workers to willingly submit to the body politic of state authority and class hierarchy. In light of these connections, Max Blumtritt's definition of the ultimate goal of workers' sport can easily be applied to agitprop as well: "The goal is to be *fresh* in struggle,/ *free* of prejudices and weaknesses,/ *strong* in faith in yourself and your own power/ and to stand *firm* for the cause of the proletariat." In fact, the SPD politician's appeal to workers "to be healthy and physically beautiful, fully realized human beings" adds a troubling equation of physical and mental health to the earlier description of proper standing by Rühle (but certainly not of Rühle). This time through prescriptions for a healthy classed body, class consciousness is once again defined as an embodied habitus based on the body of the male industrial worker and worker athlete.[17]

The difficulties of contributing to the performance of classed bodies while avoiding their gendered inscriptions are on full view in the work of two communist dancers, Jean Weidt and Jo Mihaly. Descriptions, photos, and reviews of their choreographies suggest that Weidt and Mihaly drew upon a limited register of motion and emotion to present the worker as a distinct social and physical type and doing so in the registers of modern dance. The fact that Mihaly bound her breasts to pass as a male worker, thereby signaling the primacy of

---

16 See Sander Gilman, "'Stand Up Straight': Notes Toward a History of Posture," *Journal of Medical Humanities* 35 (2014): 57–83.
17 Max Blumtritt, *Arbeitersport und Arbeiterbewegung. Ein Weck- und Mahnruf* (Leipzig: Arbeiter-, Turn- und Sportbund, 1926), 19 and 15.

class over gender, confirms the degree to which masculinist body practices sustained the revolutionary fantasy, and that despite the Weimar-era myth of the New Woman or the fashion of androgyny. In fact, Mihaly's ability to make this choice without causing a scandal underscores the attractiveness of a male habitus even to women.

Fig. 13.5 Jean Weidt, "Der Arbeiter/The Worker" (1925), Sammlung Weidt. With permission of Universitätsbibliothek Leipzig, Tanzarchiv, Slg. Weidt.

Fig. 13.6 Jo Mihaly, "Arbeiter/Worker" from "Feierliche Tänze," c. 1926, Photo: Atelier Stone. With permission of Deutsches Tanzarchiv Köln.

Jean (originally Hans) Weidt (1904–1988), known as "the red dancer," grew up in the Hamburg working class, worked as a gardener and a coal trimmer in the harbor, and became one of the few communists in the world of German *Ausdruckstanz* (expressionist dance). In 1925, he created a solo dance called *Der Arbeiter* (The Worker) that drew on his own experiences as a physical laborer. In his memoirs, Weidt describes the difficulties during the rehearsal phase of creating a dance piece that could at once be descriptive and prefigurative:

After all, I myself worked as a professional gardener for eight to ten hours a day and felt it in my bones. But I did not want to present the worker who toils and labors but the worker who builds a more beautiful life. [...] I worked until I was ready to acknowledge that the worker should not be danced with a bowed head but that he has to be shown as proud, oriented toward the future.[18]

With his body not only marked by daily experiences of exploitation but also animated by his belief in radical change, Weidt sought to capture the movement, in the words of Marion Reinisch, "from feeling socially [...] to thinking politically."[19] Photographs from the performance at Hamburg's Komödienhaus show a slender man dressed in simple gray pants and an open shirt, with his bare feet signaling his modern dance credentials (see figure 13.5). His right arm is extended upward, and his left arm bent sideways across his chest – choices that recall the scene of agitation in Querner. While his downward glance conveys a feeling of hesitation or concentration, the clenched fists and legs ready to jump suggest an unfurling of revolutionary energy. Despite negative reviews – one critic dismissively referred to him as the Ernst Toller of dance – Weidt was able to build on these early experiments in his later choreographic work with the Berlin-based Die roten Tänzer (Red Dancers) and in his collaboration with Erwin Piscator on the ambitious program of political theater at the Theater am Nollendorfplatz. The goal of the proletarian dancer, Weidt would later explain, was "to visualize the surrounding world with the means of his body so that his embodied experience gives his fellow human beings spiritual nourishment!" His conclusion can be read as a succinct definition of the communist habitus: "Dance is struggle, and struggle is our language."[20]

In 1926, the Berlin-based dancer and poet Jo Mihaly (1902–1989) created a similar piece also called *Der Arbeiter* (see figure 13.6). One newspaper review described a performance "in which the arduous life of the working proletarian and his breaking under the weight of oppression were brilliantly depicted."[21] Photo-

---

18 Jean Weidt, *Der Rote Tänzer. Ein Lebensbericht* (Berlin: Henschel, 1968), 10.
19 Marion Reinisch, Preface, *Auf der großen Straße. Jean Weidts Erinnerungen. Nach Tonbandprotokollen aufgezeichnet und herausgegeben von Marion Reinisch* (Berlin: Henschel, 1984), 5. For a comparative perspective, see Ellen Graff, *Stepping Left: Dance and Politics in New York City, 1928–1942* (Durham: Duke University Press, 1997) that includes a discussion of Edith Segal's Red Dancers.
20 Reinisch, *Auf der großen Straße*, 184 and 186.
21 Quoted in Yvonne Hardt, *Politische Körper. Ausdruckstanz, Choreographien des Protests und die Arbeiterkulturbewegung in der Weimarer Republik* (Münster: Lit, 2004), 87. For the only English-language article on Weidt, see, by the same author, "Ausdruckstanz, Workers' Culture, and Masculinity in Germany in the 1920s and 1930s," in *When Men Dance: Choreographing Masculin-*

graphs show a slender woman re-enacting proletarian masculinity through the tension between oppression and resistance. Knowledge of the dancer's gender only heightens the underlying sense of provocation. With her dark hair closely cropped and her breasts tightly bound, Mihaly conveys both strength and vulnerability; in so doing, she foregrounds the conventions that define the working class in highly gendered terms. Even as the fists raised to protect the chest suggest a defensive gesture, the feet firmly planted on the ground express a sense of stability. She is clearly prepared for assaults by imagined enemies, including by those provoked by such a bold assumption of male privilege.

In their performances of class struggle, Weidt and Mihaly contributed to what dance historian Gabriele Brandstetter, building on Aby Warburg's notion of pathos formulas, has described as a selective appropriation of the discourse of pathos by the historical avant-gardes.[22] Pathos formulas, as defined by Warburg, are the primeval vocabulary of passionate gesticulation; in the arts, they establish highly codified (and universally valid) connections between emotions and bodies, especially in the form of body gesture and facial expression. In Brandstetter's reading, these pathos formulas were claimed for a modernist aesthetic arising out of the tension between body language and textual corpus. Very similar processes can be observed at the intersection of class performance and politics in the context of communist agitprop and its proletarian modernist credentials. Here, however, pathos formulas always aim to escape the confines of bodies and texts and use expanded notions of performativity to affect real political change. Their meaning is always defined in relational and referential terms. Developed within the divided political landscape of the late Weimar Republic, particular gestures thus mean something very different, depending on whether they are performed in middle-class or working-class settings, whether they address KPD, SPD, or NSDAP audiences, and whether they focus on embodied emotions as part of the political instrumentalization or radical transformation of the work of art.

One way of assessing the communist appropriation of pathos formulas involves looking at the instructions by practitioners of agitprop about the right (and wrong) ways of standing and speaking. The Rote Sprachrohr (Red Mega-

---

ities Across Borders, ed. Jennifer Fisher and Anthony Shay (Oxford: Oxford University Press, 2009), 258–275. For a then-contemporary overview of modern dance from a working-class perspective, also see John Schikowski, *Geschichte des Tanzes* (Berlin: Büchergilde Gutenberg, 1926).
22 See Gabriele Brandstetter, *Poetics of Dance: Body, Image, and Space in the Historical Avant-gardes*, trans. Elena Polzer (Oxford: Oxford University Press, 2015), especially the introduction. It should be noted that pathos formulas, which Warburg describes as visual tropes, have nothing in common with the pathetic as defined by Schiller.

phone) agitprop theater troupe offered very concrete recommendations for fellow performers in the art and science of embodied ideology. Founded in 1929 by the actor and director Maxim Vallentin (1904–1987), the Rote Sprachrohr played a key role in turning agitprop into a multimedia practice that included extensive commentary on the proper class habitus. For Vallentin, agitprop meant direct intervention into current political crises and critical engagement with the structural problems of capitalist societies. It also meant to model the process of hardening and strengthening in posture, gesture, and tone considered so necessary to proletarian mobilizations; this included the obligatory rituals of communist self-critique, with several skits addressing residues of petty-bourgeois attitudes in working-class lives. Their journal, also called *Das rote Sprachrohr* (1929–1933), published songs and scenes about labor struggles, political confrontations, and family problems and offered detailed advice on the types of programs most suited for factory settings, neighborhood events, and large rallies.

Fig. 13.7. Das rote Sprachchor, *Kuhle Wampe*, DVD capture.

When a makeshift stage was not available, the Rote Sprachrohr performed on top of flatbed trucks, like construction workers on assignment. Their use of musical instruments familiar from folk songs and marching songs – namely, accordion, mandolin, and snare drum – reflected the troupe's decision to convey a militant message with popular appeal. Easily recognized by their dark blue unisex overalls, known as *Kesselanzüge* (boilersuits), male and female performers cultivated the confrontational tones and gestures that, according to Vallentin, best conveyed the perspective of class struggle. Approvingly, a contemporary observer of the Rote Sprachrohr noted "a distinct toughness, a sharp awareness in their performance; their momentum resembled the blows of a hammer; their restraints had something of the reflective polish of metals and glass."[23] Speaking in general terms, Hanns Eisler identified as the distinctive characteristic of agitprop its "very tight, rhythmical, precise singing" and a "cold, sharp, and cutting delivery" more typical of political lectures.[24] Very few film recordings by the Rote Sprachrohr have survived, but their distinct style is on full display in *Kuhle Wampe* where they perform a short skit about the eviction of a working-class family during a workers' sport festival (see figure 13.7). The inclusion of this live performance in a feature film confirms that agitprop was conceived to translate stances into actions – in this case, by having the actual workers (and the actors playing workers) join together in singing "The Internationale" on their return to Weimar Berlin.

In a little-known song on the wrong ways of standing, the Rote Sprachrohr addressed the difficulties of mass mobilization by introducing the figure of a timid, passive bystander called "you" (i.e., the audience) who resists all invitations by a collective "we." Under the title "Doch du stehst da am Fenster" ("But There You Stand at the Window"), the song opens in the voice of a disheartened worker complaining about mass unemployment. The refrain has him linger at the window, passively watching events outside unfold. That is when the voice of communist agitprop admonishes him: "But you are standing at the window/ grumbling once in a while./ When things get going, you are cool with it./ But until that point, you just don't feel like it."[25]

These stern admonitions were part of a systematic training of embodied habitus meant to distinguish the Communists from the Social Democrats, including through vocal intonation and enunciation. Already in the early 1920s, Gustav von Wangenheim (1895–1957), in instructions for *Chor der Arbeit* (1923, Chorus of Labor), proposed different modes of speaking for characters representing the rivaling leftist parties. "The KPD always speaks tersely and energetically, the SPD broadly and comfortably," he informs his actors and explains how to ridicule Social Democrats by giving them soft, effeminate voices. Not surprisingly, the strength of the KPD in that performance is announced through different vocal pitches, with "the masses [on the stage] once again separated into placidly

---

[23] Quoted in Dieter Steinke, *Die Entwicklung der Agitprop-Truppe "Das Rote Sprachrohr"* (Leipzig: Zentralhaus für Volkskunst, 1958), 17. For a personal account, see Hannes Küpper and Maxim Vallentin, *Die Sache ist die* (Potsdam: Gustav Kiepenheuer, 1924).
[24] Maxim Vallentin, "Agitpropspiel und Kampfwert," *Linkskurve* 2.4 (1930): 15–16 and Hanns Eisler, "Einige Ratschläge zur Einstudierung der Maßnahme," in *Musik und Politik. Schriften 1924–1948*, ed. Günter Mayer (Leipzig: Deutscher Verlag für Musik, 1973), 168.
[25] "Doch du," in Lammel, *Lieder der Agitprop-Truppen*, 28.

thrashing SPD and quickly striking KPD."[26] In line with this kind of aggressive language (e. g., cold, sharp, tough, terse, energetic), impatient calls for more emotional restraint became a recurring feature in critical comments on proletarian performance, with too much expressivity seen as a sign of bourgeois decadence and social reformism and with discipline, steadfastness, and self-control extolled as essential communist virtues.

To offer a few examples from the instructional manuals of communist theater and agitprop, the actors in a play by Hans Marchwitza were instructed not to succumb to sentimental or melodramatic impulses and to "deliver all sentences in a clear, hard, untheatrical tone."[27] Elsewhere Johannes R. Becher (1891–1958) warned performers not to present political slogans as if frozen in time and place. Instead he recommended: "Add movement. But only movements modeled on reality. Don't stage symbolic dances."[28] It was as part of a coordinated campaign against too much emotion that *Der Agitator* (1931–1932, The Agitator), a short-lived journal published by the Rot Front organization, offered practical advice on effective public speaking and street agitation. No detail was deemed irrelevant, with one program for the KPD's 1932 election campaign even offering tips on how not to extend one's hand: "A class-conscious worker will never extend his hand, never! Because he cannot be found begging; instead, he must demand. I tell you again, you must understand that you demean yourselves endlessly in the eyes of the bourgeoisie, the ruling class, when you stand in front of their doors and ask for scraps from their tables."[29]

The Nazi takeover of power in 1933 resulted in the violent suppression of the communist habitus in political life and public performance. One of the last issues of *Das Rote Sprachrohr*, already produced under conditions of illegality, contains the haunting image of a worker standing in front of a wall, with his raised hands suggesting a scene of execution, and a desperate plea written across the page: "It cannot end that way!" By the end of the year, almost all of the artists and performers mentioned in this chapter had left the country. After 1945, the majority returned to East Germany to once again lend their expertise to the definition of the correct *Klassenstandpunkt*. As one of the first, Maxim Vallentin arrived from the Soviet Union to train a new generation of actors at the Deutsche Theaterinstitut in Weimar and build up a distinctly socialist German

---

26 Gustav von Wangenheim, *Chor der Arbeit* (Berlin: Vereinigung Internationaler Verlagsanstalten, 1924), 110.
27 Hans Marchwitza, "Die rote Schmiede," *Das rote Sprachrohr* 1.4 (1929): 10.
28 Johannes R. Becher, "Die Partei," *Das rote Sprachrohr* 1.4 (1929): 4.
29 *Das rote Sprachrohr. Material für Agitproptruppen und Arbeiter-Theatervereine* (Berlin: Zentralagitprop der KPD und des KJVD, 1932), 16.

theater repertoire as the director of the Maxim-Gorki Theater in East Berlin. Jean Weidt came from Paris to train new dance ensembles at the Volksbühne and the Komische Oper. Notwithstanding these prestigious appointments, the performative registers of communist agitprop struggled to find recognition in the new workers' and peasants' state. In fact, when Felixmüller, who taught at the University of Halle, repainted his 1920 portrait of Otto Rühle in 1946, he smoothed out the irregularities on the face of this forgotten representative of left communism. Meanwhile, Querner, who after 1933 had limited his output to idyllic scenes of everyday life, was rediscovered as a major proletarian painter during the 1960s in what must be considered the first of several waves of nostalgia for communism, including for the confrontational ways of standing codified during the 1920s and early 1930s. In the larger context of this book, these revisionist tendencies confirm the overdetermined function of embodied habitus as part of the very different models of proletarian culture promoted by the Communists and the Social Democrats during the Weimar years. As the next chapter argues, the underlying discourse of *Kampfkultur* was not limited to agitprop and its unique performative forms and techniques but, in fact, found its clearest articulation in literary theory and criticism. In delineating these connections made in the name of militancy, the debates in the KPD's *Linkskurve* offer privileged access to the underlying assumptions about proletarian literature as a method of emotional conditioning and the highly gendered proposals for increasing its effectiveness in the class struggle.

Chapter 14
Marxist Literary Theory and Communist Militant Culture

> The "literary writer" glorifies the proletarian because he, a declassed rabbi, is only capable of fighting for gods. When a revolutionary shows him the weaknesses of proletarians, he shouts "traitor and counterrevolutionary!" Not because he defends the proletarians but because he defends his cult.
>
> Ernst Toller, "Splitter"

Marxist literary theory and criticism is never just concerned with narratives, characters, themes, or styles. On the contrary, these categories convey competing views on the political function of literature and serve as indicators of wider social and cultural changes. Writing about literature means establishing connections between dominant and oppositional emotional regime, on the one hand, and literary devices such as character identification and narrative point of view, on the other. Unspoken assumptions and value judgments about the place of emotion in literature inform literary criticism in multiple ways: in the demand for moving stories and convincing characters, in the gendered hierarchy of literary genres based on their moods and styles, in the prescriptions for appropriate forms of reading, and so forth. In all instances, the criteria of literary evaluation tend to reproduce not only dominant discourses of class but also prevailing attitudes about literature as both a site of psychological interiority and a laboratory for new emotions and sensibilities.

Unsurprisingly, this connection proved of great interest to the writers, critics, and functionaries who set out to define proletarian literature in line with Marxist theory and party policy. Reread through the lens of political emotions, the literary debates in the SPD and KPD press, preoccupied on the surface with questions of authorship, narrative, realism, and tendency, offer privileged access to the intensifying struggle over competing models of proletarian identifications between the visions of precapitalist and socialist community that had inspired nineteenth-century Social Democracy and the decidedly modern forms of collectivity emerging after World War I and the October Revolution.

In the epigraph, Ernst Toller (1893–1939) mocks fellow leftist writers who claimed the label "proletarian" for their own fantasies of literature and revolution. As the author of several expressionist plays about the modern masses and an active participant in the short-lived Bavarian Council Republic, he may have even been describing a former version of himself; in fact, these lines were written during his imprisonment for high treason.[1] In light of the compensatory and anticipatory function of much leftwing literary criticism, including the romantic notion of the writer as a vessel of the collective will to revolution, it might therefore be best to focus not on what such comments imply about literary practices in the past and present, but on what they reveal about emotional attachments to social movements and political utopias. The implicit and explicit assumptions about the power of emotions are especially noticeable in the seemingly endless debates about proletarian literature, what it is and what it could and should be.

During the Wilhelmine and Weimar years, the search for suitable formal registers and appropriate thematic choices – in short, a socialist version of normative aesthetics – served two distinct purposes: to forge proletarian identifications through the mutual instrumentalization of aesthetic and political emotions and, in the name of tendency or partiality (with its changing definitions), to enlist literature in the fight for a classless society. The enduring belief in the unique ability of literature to capture modern life in all of its complexities is evidence of the unwillingness of most critics to seriously consider the challenges of new media technologies and forms of cultural consumption. The resistance to what Walter Benjamin calls the age of mechanical reproduction attests to their anxieties that the working class might be lost to decidedly nonliterary diversions – anxieties than can only be understood once literary theory is untangled from literature and both treated as separate discourses concerned with narratives, characters, identifications, and attachments but for very different reasons.

Earlier commentators on the heated debates in the leading SPD and KPD publications have either noted the enduring influence of bourgeois culture, including its veneration of the classics, or pointed to the radical experiments modeled on developments in the Soviet Union. Most scholarly studies on the subject treat literary criticism as a prescriptive or evaluative discourse – one in which literary practices are described, assessed, and examined and the proper connection between literary form and Marxist theory established. By contrast, this chapter takes advantage of the almost compulsive speaking about literature to shed light on the two emotional cultures imagined in the name of the proletariat during the Weimar years. Roughly identified with the Social Democrats and Communists, these two models conceived of the proletariat either as a community sustained through unity and harmony or as a collective forged in resistance and conflict. Given the extensive discussion of Social Democratic performances of community in chapter 12, the main part of this chapter focuses on the Commu-

---

[1] Ernst Toller, "Splitter," *Kulturwille* 1.1 (1924): 16.

nist militant culture introduced in chapter 13 through the embodied habitus of agitprop and examined here through the literary debates in the KPD journal, *Die Linkskurve*.

Hans-Joachim Schulz has perceptively described the literary criticism that defined the increasingly antagonistic relationship between SPD and KPD as a form of excessive discursivization. The conflation of literature with literary theory and, ultimately, Marxist theory, he observes, was unfortunately reduplicated in the leftist scholarship from the 1970s that tended to treat theory as a superior form of knowledge.[2] With ideology thus reduced to questions of hermeneutics, one unintended outcome has been the affirmation of two kinds of canons, with Marx and his exegetes on the one side and the literary classics on the other; another has been the overvaluation of the role of the literary critic in the left's major and minor ideological battles. Schulz rightly warns against confusing the programmatic statements on literature with the actual writings of real workers, recommending that scholars instead concentrate on normative functions and disciplinary effects. His diagnosis of "excessive" makes perfect sense within an analysis of Marxist orthodoxy. With regard to the underlying assumptions about emotions that are the main concern here, it might be more useful to call these debates productive – because they create powerful fictions in their own right.

After World War I, the discourse of community allowed Social Democrats to build on the associational culture established during the Wilhelmine years and to reaffirm their commitment to culture and education under the very different conditions of their party's active participation in government. The reformist positions promoted in the name of *Kultursozialismus* (cultural socialism) found an almost perfect platform in the Leipzig-based journal, titled *Kulturwille: Monatsblätter für Kultur der Arbeiterschaft* (1924–33). As the official organ of the Arbeiter-Bildungsinstitut (ABI, Workers' Educational Institute), *Kulturwille* (literally: the will to culture) continued the nineteenth-century project of education as self-cultivation that, as argued in chapter 8, long sustained Social Democratic narratives of class and community. Valtin Hartig (1889–1980), the editor of *Kulturwille*, was an outspoken proponent of the so-called three-pillar theory that conceived of culture as the third column, next to party and unions, in the thus defined big house of socialism. Praising the advantages of this division of labor, he explained how "such a division within the movement is a gain for the party to pursue political goals politically; it is a gain for the cultural move-

---

[2] Hans-Joachim Schulz, *German Socialist Literature 1860–1914: Predicaments of Criticism* (Columbia, SC: Camden House, 1993), 1–8.

ment to preserve a pure ideal that would otherwise be tainted and damaged by the demands of politics."[3]

The communitarian ideals of the cultural socialists, in turn, were inseparable from the corresponding fantasies of an older folk culture and a bourgeois high culture that had sustained the SPD during the years of the Anti-Socialist Laws but that, after the cataclysms of war and revolution, looked increasingly like withdrawal to a self-sustaining proletarian lifeworld – complete with nineteenth-century utopian tendencies, conventional tastes, and provincial attitudes. In line with Marx's characterization of the working class as the universal class, the cultural socialists defined an emerging proletarian culture not as the culture of a specific class but of all of humankind. Insisting on the utopian potential of the aesthetic, they appropriated the bourgeois concept of autonomous art for the self-definition of this socialist cultural movement as "a transhistorical force beyond class divides." In the words of Kurt Heilbut, "the bourgeois man puts things (money, factories, material goods) before people. The socialist puts people before things. The bourgeois places the individual at the center (individualism), the socialist the community (collectivism)."[4] Against the Communist version of the collective, the cultural socialists upheld romantic visions of a past and future folk community and promised the integration of the traditions of bourgeois individualism into a superior socialist communitarianism. Their ultimate aim, in Hartig's words, was the cultivation of the individual as part of the community. "What is the ideal of socialism as a cultural movement?" he asked: "It wants community. However, community is experienced by the individual and must be experienced as a shared value that incorporates the personal. In other words, community must be experienced as being conducive to one's own personality."[5]

By the mid-1920s, two distinct models of proletarian culture vied for dominance, Social Democratic *Gemeinschaftskultur* (communitarian culture) and Communist *Kampfkultur* (militant culture). While critics writing for SPD-affiliated publications drew on arguments formulated during the years of the Anti-Socialist Laws, KPD functionaries increasingly sought inspiration and guidance from the Soviet Union. The terms "communitarian" and "militant" in these cultural contests capture the complicated relationship between the SPD as a reform

---

[3] Valtin Hartig, "Über die Möglichkeit proletarischer Kultur," *Kulturwille* 1.1 (1924): 1. Similar arguments were made by the prolific Paul Kampffmeyer in "Die Arbeiterbewegung als Faktor der allgemeinen Kulturentwicklung," *Sozialistische Monatshefte* 16–18.1 (1912): 30–32 and "Auf dem Weg zur sozialistischen Kultur," 3 parts, *Kulturwille* 2.6,7, and 8 (1925): 113–115, 146–148, 164–166.
[4] Kurt Heilbut, "Sozialistische Festkultur," *Sozialistische Bildung* 22 (1930): 51.
[5] Valtin Hartig, "Kulturbewegung im Sozialismus," *Die Tat* 16.12 (1925): 885 and 886.

party and the KPD as a vanguard party of the Leninist type and articulate the aspirational values of these competing models in recognizable emotional terms. As to be expected, the symbiotic relationship between working-class culture and masculinity, with the SPD offering primordial brotherhood and patriarchal father figures and with the KPD celebrating the worker-functionary-engineer as the ideal of the New Man, remained largely unaffected by these ideological divides.

Promising social harmony and a sense of belonging, "community" in these contexts represented the more established, broader term and is closely tied to older ideas about folk, race, and nation. As shown in chapter 1, the nineteenth-century discourse of community was the product of a two-front battle within the social imaginary against the specter of massification associated with the working class and the divisions in class society produced by capitalism. Accordingly, the conceptualization of communitarian culture involved terms such as unity, stability, continuity, harmony, and, above all, forms of sociability free of the competition, isolation, and estrangement experienced in modern capitalist societies. By contrast, the term "militant," which translated all relationships into antagonistic terms, gained its legitimacy from those revolutionary moments – the Paris Commune, the October Revolution, and the German Revolution of 1918/19 – when long existing social problems exploded in violent solutions. As a political habitus, confrontation only needed an initial decision to place the imaginary proletariat in the midst of battle, surrounded by enemies on all sides. In order to maintain this momentum, however, militant culture required the acceptance of authority and hierarchy, with party discipline strictly enforced in line with the vanguard principle. As seen in chapters 9 and 10, its coolly masculinist attitude took inspiration from the battlefields of modern war and industry and drew heavily on the iconography of the military to maintain internal coherence and convey external strength. Confirming its Bolshevik genealogy, this KPD *Kampfkultur* had little in common with older traditions of militancy, such as Georges Sorel's reflections on violence and its eruption in the general strike or Rosa Luxemburg's writings on spontaneous mass action and the mass strike as a political tool.

Not surprisingly, the battle cry of *Kampf*, to be translated as conflict, fight, or struggle, became a recurring theme in the various initiatives overseen by the KPD. In 1925, Karl August Wittfogel (1896–1988) established the party's new militant stance when he declared that, in light of the inevitability of class struggle under capitalism, "the emerging revolutionary proletarian culture is, by necessity, a *Kampfkultur*."⁶ Antagonism under these conditions meant conflict with not only the democratic institutions of the Weimar Republic but also the SPD as the party of political defeatism and, in the heated rhetoric of the times, social fascism. In the years that followed, "battle" became the motto for a wide range of cultural groups. The KPD formed its own Arbeiter Theaterbund Deutschlands (ATBD, Worker Theater Association of Germany) under the heading of *Kampftheater*. Several musical splinter groups organized in the Kampfgemeinschaft der Arbeitersänger (KdAS, Agitational Unit of Workers' Choral Singers) to promote the sounds and rhythms of *Kampfmusik*. Communist athletes in 1928 formed the Kampfgemeinschaft für Rote Sporteinheit (KG, Agitational League for Red Sport Unity, or short: Rotsport) after their exclusion from the Arbeiter-Turn- und Sportbund (ATSB, Workers' Gymnastics and Sports); its largest club, the Berlin-based ASV "Fichte" even published its own journal, predictably called *Kampfgenoss* (1926–1930, Fighting Comrade).

The Stalinization of the KPD in the late 1920s was the main reason for the party's increasingly confrontational stance toward the SPD.⁷ The same can be said about the repeated attacks in KPD publications on modernism as a phenomenon of bourgeois decadence. Scholars have explained the party's promotion of classical realism and, later, the doctrine of socialist realism with reference to the prescribed shift from the proletarianism associated with the Proletkult movement toward the Marxism-Leninism promoted by the Comintern. Yet the recourse to normative aesthetics obscures the more troubling problem, extensively discussed in the Soviet Union (and later in the United States), that the literature of the working class was gradually being reduced to the literature of the Communist Party. In the late Weimar Republic, the almost compulsory calls for more militancy in art and life also indicated a growing dependence on culture as a

---

6 Karl August Wittfogel, "Proletarische Kampfkultur," *Die Rote Fahne*, 7 June 1925. The article was part of a series that includes "Über proletarische Kultur," *Die Rote Fahne*, 31 May 1925 and "In Kampf mit welchen Elementen entwickelt sich die proletarische Kultur?," *Die Rote Fahne*, 21 June 1925. On the idea of a religion of *Kampf*, see his "Die proletarische Religion," *Platz dem Arbeiter! Erstes Jahrbuch* (1924): 213–215. Many writings have been reprinted in Karl August Wittfogel, *Zur Frage einer marxistischen Ästhetik: Abhandlung* (Cologne: Kölkkalkverlag, 1973).

7 For new research on the Weimar KPD, see Norman La Porte and Rolf Hofrogge, *Weimar Communism as Mass Movement 1918–1933* (Chadwell Heath: Lawrence & Wishart, 2017). Assessments of German communism in the larger context of modern German history can be found in Eric D. Weitz, *Creating German Communism, 1890–1990: From Popular Protests to Socialist State* (Princeton: Princeton University Press, 1997) and, together with David E. Barclay, eds., *Between Reform and Revolution: German Socialism and Communism from 1840 to 1990* (New York: Berghahn, 1998).

substitute for revolutionary action – a point confirmed by the KPD's unwillingness to form viable alliances with other leftist groups and their declining appeal among the working classes (instead of the mass of unemployed).

The discussions among KPD functionaries about the most suitable genres and styles for creating a more militant culture reproduced familiar ideological differences (e. g., with the left communists) and often took place along generational lines. Gertrud Alexander (born in 1882), the feuilleton editor of *Die Rote Fahne* and a leading cultural critic, had repeatedly claimed communist ownership of the bourgeois heritage since her intervention in the 1920 Art Scoundrel Debate. Her veneration of the great works as a source of critical insight informed both her belief in the artist as a mediator between classes and her opposition to modernism as a phenomenon of bourgeois decadence. Promoting the classics as an eternal source of aesthetic pleasure, Alexander insisted that, despite capitalist exploitation, "culture has always existed, and immortal things were created. The new culture will not and cannot develop so fast that the worker, the new man, could not and should not take pleasure in the beautiful things of the past."[8]

Founded in 1928 by a group of younger writers (all born during the 1890s), the Bund proletarisch-revolutionärer Schriftsteller (BPRS, Association of Proletarian Revolutionary Writers) announced a clear break with this traditional narrative of great art existing beyond or outside class. Inspired by the worker-correspondents movement in the Soviet Union, the BPRS set out "to transform proletarian revolutionary literature so that it conquers, cultivates, and organizes the hearts and minds of the working class and the large working masses for the task of class struggle and the goal of proletarian revolution."[9] In developing strategies for turning workers into readers and, ultimately, thinkers, KPD functionaries took their cues from Lenin who famously demanded that workers not limit their education to "'*literature for workers*' but learn to master *general literature*."[10] Through the journal *Die Linkskurve* (1929–1932, literally: left turn), the BPRS operated as part of various cultural initiatives coordinated after 1929 by the short-lived Interessengemeinschaft für Arbeiterkultur (IfA, Alliance of Workers Culture Groups). BPRS writers published their works with Wieland Herzfelde's legendary Malik publishing house, which launched the inexpensive Rote-Eine-

---

8 Gertrud Alexander, "Herrn John Heartfield und George Grosz," *Die Rote Fahne*, 9 June (1920).
9 Quoted in Gerhard Friedrich, *Proletarische Literatur und politische Organisation. Die Literaturpolitik der KPD in der Weimarer Republik und die proletarisch-revolutionäre Literatur* (Frankfurt am Main: Peter Lang, 1981), 21.
10 Vladimir Ilyich Lenin, "What Is to Be Done?" (1902), http://www.marxists.org/archive/lenin/works/1901/witbd/ii.htm, 1 March 2017.

Mark Roman (Red-One-Mark Novel) series; the Neue Deutsche Verlag, which functioned as the publishing arm of Willi Münzenberg's Internationale Arbeiterhilfe (IAH, International Workers' Aid); and the Greifenverlag in Rudolstadt/ Thuringia, which maintained an idiosyncratic catalogue of progressive and alternative books.[11]

Hailed during the 1970s for producing both "the only truly Marxist conception of literature of its time" and the proletarian-revolutionary literature that "must be considered a foundation of Marxist literary theory to this day,"[12] *Die Linkskurve* published critical essays, book reviews, conference reports, and short opinion pieces. Its editorial collective included an editor in chief, plus Kurt Kläber (1897–1959), Erich Weinert (1890–1953), Ludwig Renn (1889– 1979), and the already mentioned Johannes R. Becher and Hans Marchwitza. Most contributors insisted that only the "right" definition could give rise to the ideal proletarian novel and that only the "correct" application of Marxist theory would bring about a revolutionary situation. Confirming the international character of these debates on the "literature of the world revolution," articles by Oto Biha (i.e., Oto Bihalji Merin) and others were translated and discussed by proletarian authors and communist critics as far away as the United States and Japan.[13] In the journal's first issue, Becher, who had previously edited a *Proletarische Feuilleton-Korrespondenz* (1927–1929), called for the transformation of all of literature into a *Kampfgebiet* (combat zone). With his typical hyperbole, he de-

---

[11] On the BPRS, see Friedrich Albrecht and Klaus Kändler, *Bund proletarisch-revolutionärer Schriftsteller Deutschlands 1928–1935* (Leipzig: VEB Bibliographisches Institut, 1978). For the larger context, see Rüdiger Safranski and Walter Fähnders, "Proletarisch-revolutionäre Literatur," in *Literatur der Weimarer Republik 1918–1933*, ed. Bernhard Weyergraf (Munich: Hanser, 1995), 174–231; and Rob Burns, "Theory and Organisation of the Revolutionary Working-Class Literature in the Weimar Republic," in *Culture and Society in the Weimar Republic*, ed. Keith Bullivant (Manchester: Manchester University Press, 1977), 122–149.
[12] Frank Rainer Scheck, ed., *Erobert die Literatur! Proletarisch-revolutionäre Literaturtheorie und -debatte in der "Linkskurve" 1929–1932* (Cologne: Kiepenheuer & Witsch, 1973), 10. The second reference appears in Helga Gallas, *Marxistische Literaturtheorie: Kontroversen im Bund proletarisch-revolutionärer Schriftsteller* (Neuwied: Luchterhand, 1971), 12. *Die Linkskurve* has been reprinted in 1970 by Detlev Auvermann in Glashütten im Taunus. When the West-Berlin-based-KPD-ML-affiliated Oberbaumverlag republished the Reihe proletarisch-revolutionärer Romane, *Die Zeit* called the books "agitational aids in struggle for socialism in the Federal Republic and West Berlin." Quoted by Christian Schultz-Gerstein, "Wie aus der Pistole geschossen," 18 April 1975, ZeitOnline, http://www.zeit.de/1975/17/wie-aus-der-pistole-geschossen, 1 March 2017.
[13] Oto Biha advanced the cause of the proletarian mass novel in "Der proletarische Massenroman," *Die Rote Fahne*, 2 August 1930. His internationally known essay is "On the Question of Proletarian-Revolutionary Literature in Germany," *Literature of the World Revolution* 1.4 (1931): 88–105.

scribed a literature borne of the drumfire of war and the street battle of revolution. Stationed in an important section on the front in the larger battle between communism and capitalism, the new types of writers-soldiers were

> amazing fellows who seethe with impatience, who hammer their sentences until their language bursts but who also can be so disciplined and matter-of-fact in their hearts that they make sober calculations and construct their language worlds like machinists. The most important event in the field of literature is the emergence of a proletarian-revolutionary literature, a literature that sees the world from the perspective of the revolutionary proletariat.[14]

Turning literature into a battlefield meant actively promoting the new work of BPRS members such as Kläber, Renn, and Marchwitza as well as Willi Bredel and Ernst Ottwalt. It meant rejecting what Becher dismissively called *Arbeiterdichter* (worker poets) in the folk tradition of Max Barthel and distinguishing themselves from the *Linkeleuteliteratur* (left-sympathizer literature) written by so-called fellow travelers such as Alfred Döblin, Kurt Tucholsky, and Leonard Frank.[15] For an important genre like the novel, this meant developing a distinctly proletarian aesthetic in critical dialogue with the established traditions of the social novel and the educational novel, on the one hand, and with new forms such as the reportage novel and the modernist novel, on the other. And as regards concurrent attempts at separating the tradition of the novel from the confines of national literature, this meant developing the proletarian novel in critical dialogue with new literary experiments in the Soviet Union and as part of international networks of exchange that, to give just one example, led to the translation of all Upton Sinclair novels by the Malik publishing house.[16]

The ideal proletarian novel, as F. C. Weiskopf and Kurt Hirschfeld insisted, stood out through its correct political *Gesinnung* (stance) and *Tendenz* (tendency). In a sharp departure from the earlier insistence on authentic voices, coming from the working class was no longer regarded a prerequisite of legitimate authorship. Thus liberated from the constraints of economic determinism, the proletarian novel could focus on its primary task as a laboratory of political emotions and become an essential part of class discourse and the collective

---

14 Johannes R. Becher, "Unsere Front," *Die Linkskurve* 1.1 (1928): 1.
15 Johannes R. Becher, "Einen Schritt weiter!," *Die Linkskurve* 2.1 (1930): 1–5. In the Soviet Union, the preferred term was fellow traveler.
16 For a comparative perspective, including on the reception of German communist writers and critics in the US, see Anthony David Dawahare, *American Proletarian Modernism and the Problem of Modernity in the Thirties* (Ann Arbor, MI: UMI Press, 1996).

imaginary.[17] With these larger questions in mind, Hermann Duncker proposed that proletarian writers once and for all jettison the belief in individual agency and personal freedom that until now had kept them beholden to bourgeois values.[18] For Karl Grünberg the main goal of proletarian literature was a kind of emotional reeducation, namely "to prepare those parts of the front for battle where our heavy artillery of editorials, lectures, and informational brochures has failed and do so through poems or reportages, short stories or novels, agitprop scenes or dramas."[19] Using an even more aggressive tone, Becher called on proletarian-revolutionary writers to draw inspiration from their "active hatred of everything that oppresses human beings from the outside and the inside, of everything that hinders the free development and growth of human faculties, hatred of all forms of laziness, freeloading, superficiality, as personified by various opportunists and good for nothings."[20]

Two literary congresses played an important part in the formulation of *Die Linkskurve's* official position in line with ongoing developments in the Soviet Union. The First International Conference of Proletarian and Revolutionary Writers in Moscow in 1927 had led to the founding of the BPRS in October 1928 at a time when Germany was considered the center of world communism outside the Soviet Union. The 1930 Kharkov Conference, attended by Grünberg and Marchwitza, affirmed dialectical materialism as the foundation of proletarian literature but within a narrower definition of socialist realism. Henceforth, clear rules guided the literary treatment of the relationship between objective and subjective reality and the forms of mediation establishing individual and society as mutually constitutive terms. It was left to journals like *Die Linkskurve* to enforce the literary rules and conventions that could protect the working class from the double threat of bourgeois psychologism and modern formalism. The discourses of tendency and partiality provided the main criteria for evaluating proletarian-revolutionary literature along these lines, with the originally favored "tendency" even-

---

[17] F. C. Weiskopf and Kurt Hirschfeld, "Über den proletarischen Roman," in *Zur Tradition der deutschen sozialistischen Literatur: Eine Auswahl von Dokumenten*, ed. Alfred Klein (Berlin: Aufbau, 1979), 210–219.

[18] Hermann Duncker, "Schriftsteller und Weltanschauung," reprinted in Klein, *Zur Tradition der deutschen sozialistischen Literatur*, 206–210.

[19] Karl Grünberg, "Was wir wollen," reprinted in *Zur Tradition der deutschen sozialistischen Literatur*, 178–179.

[20] Johannes R. Becher, "Unser Bund," reprinted in *Zur Tradition der deutschen sozialistischen Literatur*, 115–116.

tually dismissed as too mechanistic and replaced by "partiality" as the aesthetically and politically more productive term.

August Wittfogel published a series of articles in *Die Linkskurve* in 1931 and 1932 in response to the writer and critic Lu Märten (1879–1970) that insisted on the incommensurability of proletarian literature and literary modernism and confirmed the KPD's antagonistic course in literary and political matters.[21] Today Wittfogel, whose early literary experiments included an expressionist play, *Rote Soldaten* (1921, Red Soldiers), is best known for his scholarly work on the Asiatic mode of production – and the rabid anticommunism of his later years in the US. The unjustly neglected Märten had earlier published a highly original historical-materialist treatise, titled *Wesen und Veränderung der Formen/ Künste* (1924, About the Nature and Transformation of Forms/ Arts), that examined the transformation of artistic forms since the industrial revolution with a view toward the radical potential unleashed by this process. In the short *Linkskurve* article on Marxist aesthetics that caught Wittfogel's attention, Märtens once again argued for the primacy of artistic form over content and insisted on the interrelatedness of modes of production and aesthetic styles.[22] Articulating a critique of the autonomy of art that foregrounded the concept's historical connection to the rise of capitalism and the industrial revolution, she called for a materialist aesthetic at once based on the communal modes of production prevalent during the medieval period and informed by the most advanced media and technologies available in the present. Only a programmatic rejection of autonomous art in favor of the collectivist practices modeled by Proletkult and others could give rise to new art forms and functions in the age of mechanical reproducibility. For Märtens, the compatibility of Marxism and modernism provided both the means and the ends in setting into motion such a truly materialist revolutionary process.

Aware of other modernist sympathizers in the radical left but singling out Märtens by name, Wittfogel obviously felt compelled to defend the BPRS's preoc-

---

21 The discussion began with Karl August Wittfogel, "Zur Frage der marxistischen Ästhetik," *Die Linkskurve* 2.5 (1930): 6–7 and "Weiteres zur Frage einer marxistischen Ästhetik," *Die Linkskurve* 2.8 (1930): 15–17.
22 Lu Märten, "Zur Frage einer marxistischen Ästhetik, " *Die Linkskurve* 3.5 (1931): 15–19. For the response by Wittfogel, see "Antwort an die Genossin Lu Märten," *Die Linkskurve* 3.6 (1931): 23–26. The debate between Märtens and Wittfogel has been reprinted in *Zur Frage einer marxistischen Ästhetik: Abhandlung* (Cologne: Kölnkalkverlag, 1973). The writings by Märtens have been reprinted in *Formen für den Alltag. Schriften, Aufsätze, Vorträge*, ed. Reinhard May (Dresden: VEB Verlag der Kunst, 1982), including the 1929 article "Kunst und Proletariat" (109–116).

cupation with the question of tendency. Demanding that all true art reflect the contradictions of the age, including art in capitalist societies, he asserted that, "the proletarian work of art alone is capable of doing that. And for that reason, only the latter can become a true work of art. It is tendency."[23] For Wittfogel, two powerful historical forces, the accumulation of capital and the heroism of the proletariat, had produced conditions befitting Hegel's description of a heroic age distinguished by great art and great men. Aware of the transformative power of art especially under such circumstances, he defended contemporary efforts to create a proletarian culture before the advent of the revolution by comparing its beginnings under capitalism to those of bourgeois culture under feudalism.[24] "The proletarian work of art, unlike the bourgeois one, does not have to be ashamed of its tendency," he concluded: "On the contrary, it becomes an original, great, and true work of art simply by giving expression to fundamental and essential class experiences and class positions (always: in the sphere of sense perception) and simply by possessing the courage of proletarian tendency."[25]

Georg Lukács's contributions to *Die Linkskurve* offer a more nuanced reiteration of Wittfogel's basic argument, beginning with the reframing of the problem of modernism in light of his own earlier theoretization, in *History and Class Consciousness*, of the proletariat as the true subject of history. Published in 1932, "Tendency or Partiality?" marks the culmination of a long debate on proletarian culture that, especially given its underlying assumptions about political emotions, can be traced back to the so-called tendentious art debate from the early 1910s. This debate will therefore be used on the remaining pages to draw attention to the similarities and continuities between SPD and KPD positions on socialist literature and proletarian culture, despite the obvious differences between their respective models of *Gemeinschaftskultur* und *Kampfkultur*.[26] Primar-

---

[23] Karl August Wittfogel, "Noch einmal zur Frage einer marxistischen Ästhetik," *Die Linkskurve* 2.10 (1930): 22.

[24] Karl August Wittfogel, "Entwicklungsstufen und Wirkungskraft proletarisch-revolutionärer Kulturarbeit," *Die Linkskurve* 3.1 (1931): 17–23.

[25] Wittfogel, "Noch einmal zur Frage einer marxistischen Ästhetik," 22–23.

[26] Georg Lukács, "Tendenz oder Parteilichkeit?," *Die Linkskurve* 4.6 (1932): 13–21, in English as "'Tendency' or Partisanship?," in *Essays on Realism*, ed. Rodney Livingstone (Cambridge: MIT Press, 1981), 33–44. For the larger context, see David Pike, *Lukács and Brecht* (Chapel Hill: University of North Carolina Press, 1985), especially the chapter on Berlin; and Eugene Lunn, *Marxism and Modernism: An Historical Study of Lukács, Brecht, Benjamin, and Adorno* (Berkeley: University of California Press, 1984). The key text here is "Erzählen oder Beschreiben?," reprinted as "Narrate or Describe?," in *Writer and Critic and Other Essays*, ed. and trans. Arthur Kahn (London: Merlin Press, 1970), 110–148. Brecht, Bloch, and Benjamin continued to debate the political, aesthetic, and emotional legacies of modernism under the conditions of exile (i.e., in rela-

ily concerned with the relationship between literature and politics, the participants in the original tendentious art debate set out to clarify unresolved questions about artistic quality and political tendency, the function of socialist art under capitalism, and the working class's debt to bourgeois traditions, including the classics. About twenty years later, the official KPD position on proletarian literature presented tendency and partiality as alternative models of literary production (and, by extension, reception) and did so through arguments first developed in the SPD party press.[27] Only now, tendency was denounced on account of its superficial understanding of aesthetic critique and partiality introduced as the formally and politically more radical category.

The tendentious art debate had begun with several articles by the Dutch dramatist Herman Heijermans (1864–1924) writing under the pseudonym Heinz Sperber that, between 1910 and 1914, appeared in the SPD party newspaper *Vorwärts* and related publications. Against the defenders of the literary canon, Sperber had denounced the promotion of great works and eternal values as misguided, insisted that all works had a political tendency, and argued for the development of a strong and vibrant socialist art in the present. The proletarian class instinct, he insisted, should be the sole measure of the quality of art, and tendency the guiding principle for all artistic practices and critical evaluations.[28] Sperber's reference to instinct, with its implicit assumptions about class and character, and his formulation of what detractors ridiculed as "the doctrine of the callous fist (*schwielige Faust*)" provoked strong counterarguments. One included the defense of aesthetic autonomy and literary quality that, for instance, included a denunciation of naturalist writers and other modernists. Heinrich Ströbel (1869–1944), soon to become the editor of *Vorwärts*, objected in particular to Sperber's willful reduction of proletarian art to specific themes and views and, worse, an evaluation of aesthetic qualities based solely on rather subjective measures of tendency. He reminded his readers that a proletarian class position only guaranteed a certain "*susceptibility* for socialist ideology" that needed to be cultivated. For that reason, socialist *Tendenzkunst* (tendentious art) had to be developed in conjunction with the aesthetic education of the workers.[29] Aware of the dearth of suitable works, Friedrich Stampfer (1874–1957), another *Vorwärts*

---

tion to expressionism) and, in response to the threat of fascism, presented arguments that would later inspire the distinction between progressive and reactionary modernism.
27 The main texts of the tendentious art debate have been reprinted in Tanja Bürgel, ed., *Tendenzkunst-Debatte 1910–1912: Dokumente zur Literaturtheorie und Literaturkritik der revolutionären deutschen Sozialdemokratie* (Berlin: Akademie, 1987).
28 Heinz Sperber, "Tendenziöse Kunst," reprinted in Bürgel, *Tendenzkunst-Debatte*, 10–14.
29 Heinrich Ströbel, "Eine ästhetische Werttheorie," *Die Neue Zeit* 29.1 (1911): 598.

journalist, offered a compromise solution that allowed for the temporary inclusion of a few classic works in an evolving socialist canon: "Hail to tendentious art if the tendency is ours and the art work in question great art. But tendency alone is not art and cannot take the place of art in a drama."[30] Accused by Stampfer of mistaking class instinct for aesthetic judgment, Sperber responded that progress in literary and political terms could only be made once the class instinct had been strengthened and the art of the ruling class thoroughly rejected.[31] For reasons discussed in great detail in chapter 8 on the discourse of culture and education, Sperber's position remained a minority position among Social Democrats, but his insistence on tendency established an early model for the KPD's enlistment of literature in a highly confrontational *Kampfkultur* organized around the radicalizing effects of partiality.

Identifying the BPRS proletarian writers with what was now called (bad) tendency allowed Lukács in "Tendency or Partiality?" at once to promote the nineteenth-century realist novel as a superior model for contemporary literature and to denounce modernist experimentation as a symptom of social and cultural decay. The realist novel, he would later expound in his main contribution to a Marxist aesthetic, represented a modern version of the traditional epic and provided privileged access to the grand narratives of history. These qualities were presumably missing from the novels by BPRS authors, given their preference for typical stories of typical workers and their choice of description over narration as an appropriate mode of fiction. In contrast to the false immediacy promised by modernism as a style and technique, the formal complexities of the realist novel according to Lukács offered a fictional mode in which individuals functioned as embodiments of social contradictions and, in so doing, reaffirmed the ability of the Hegelian dialectics to capture objective reality in its totality.

Lukács's denunciation of literary tendency and his attack on literary modernism may have been informed by idealist philosophy as channeled through Mehring, but his political interventions in the early 1930s are inseparable from the KPD's confrontational course in political and artistic matters during the final years of the Weimar Republic. The debates in *Die Linkskurve* established the terms under which normative aesthetics and communist orthodoxy could become one, not least through the competing emotional and aesthetic techniques called tendency and partiality. Scholarly assessments have evaluated these de-

---

30 Friedrich Stampfer, "Kunst und Klassenkampf," reprinted in Bürgel, *Tendenzkunst-Debatte*, 56.
31 See Friedrich Stampfer, "Klasseninstinkt und Kunstverständnis," in Bürgel, *Tendenzkunst-Debatte*, 61–64 and Heinz Sperber, "Klasseninstinkt und Kunstverständnis," in Bürgel, *Tendenzkunst-Debatte*, 64–67.

bates in the context of Marxist aesthetics and Comintern strategy but ignored the continuities in the underlying assumptions about identification, attachment, and commitment. Particularly relevant to this study are the intense struggles over two very different emotional models, the communitarian culture promoted by the cultural socialists in the SPD and the militant culture advocated by the leading literary theorists in the KPD. As the next two chapters argue, the related struggles between a humanist model grounded in nineteenth-century concepts of subjectivity and a Soviet-inspired model of emotional engineering can be reconstructed through two case studies on the education of the proletarian child and the liberation of proletarian sexuality that further expand the meaning of proletarian culture.

Chapter 15
The Emotional Education of the Proletarian Child

> The proletarian child is born into his class – more precisely, into the next generation of his class. [...] This situation, like life itself, takes possession of him from the first moment – indeed, while he is still in the womb. Contact with it is wholly aimed at sharpening his consciousness, from an early age, in the school of poverty and suffering.
>
> Walter Benjamin, "A Communist Pedagogy"

Children are the future; this simple fact (or banal truth) has been especially relevant to social movements that express an unwavering belief in the betterment of all human beings. At no time were the dreams brighter and the expectations higher that during what Ellen Key, the Swedish reform pedagogue, called "the century of the child."[1] Around 1900, youth – in the sense of generation, attitude, program, and metaphor – emerged as a driving force behind turn-of-the-century art and literature (e. g., Jugendstil) and inspired bold dreams of social transformation in the context of the life reform movement and, later, the expressionist movement. The popular Wandervogel groups offer but one example of the availability of youth discourse to competing political ideologies and cultural sensibilities. From Montessori kindergartens to Waldorf schools, educators set out to prepare the young for the challenges of life under conditions of modernity.[2] Reform pedagogues, too, aligned their educational theories with a broader critique of nationalism and militarism and treated the raising of the next generation as an integral part of the larger fight for equality, freedom, and democracy. All these various movements and initiatives, including the socialist and communist groups discussed in this chapter, celebrated the young as the embodiment of the future and, by implication, a better society.

---

[1] The reference is to Key's most influential work, *Barnets århundrade* (1900, *The Century of the Child*). On the trope of youth in modern German culture, see Thomas Koebner, Rolf-Peter Janz, and Frank Trommler, eds., *"Mit uns zieht die neue Zeit." Der Mythos Jugend* (Frankfurt am Main: Suhrkamp, 1985).

[2] On the connection between literature and emotional education, see Ute Frevert et al., eds., *Learning How to Feel: Children's Literature and Emotional Socialization, 1870–1970* (Oxford: Oxford University Press, 2014). The anthology includes chapters on individual emotions such as fear, compassion, shame, boredom, and so forth, with Jan Plamper's discussion of bravery in a Russian children's novel about the civil war (191–208) of particular relevance to this discussion.

As it turned out in 1918/19, youth also meant life after war and empire and, most relevant to this study, life in revolutionary times. Socialist and communist educators responded to these challenges with increased activism, from organizing children's summer camps and starting workers' youth groups to promoting proletarian children's literature. In the socialist lifeworld, the defining conflict was rarely with the parental generation and focused instead on the ruling class and its institutions. All initiatives had two goals in common, to compensate children for the fate of being born into the next generation of their class (to paraphrase Benjamin) and to introduce them to a different kind of living, being, and feeling as proletarians. This included dealing with the problem of *Minderwertigkeitsgefühl* (feeling of inferiority) and building up their *Gemeinschaftsgefühl* (feeling of community) through a combination of educational, recreational, and cultural initiatives.[3] Socialist and communist children's activists agreed that the injuries sustained in what Benjamin, in the epigraph above, calls "the school of poverty and suffering" required the building of counterpublics and the telling of counternarratives.[4] Aligning pedagogy and politics subsequently meant making working-class children aware of the realities of class society – and drawing heavily on psychological theories to develop their class consciousness. To compensate for the pervasive feelings of shame, anxiety, insecurity, and hopelessness so widespread among working-class youth, socialist activists focused on strengthening children's sense of community and belonging. This included introducing them to models of radical democracy far removed from the oppressive morality of institutionalized Christianity and the authoritarian structure of the bourgeois *Klassenschule* – that is, a school system created to preserve class hierarchies. The new approaches to teaching and learning spearheaded by reform pedagogies proved crucial to all initiatives that treated education as socialization into the modern culture of democracy and citizenship. But they proved especially relevant, even in their reliance on bourgeois models, for the initiation of the next generation of socialists into the political culture of SPD and KPD (or their Austrian counterparts). This chapter examines the growing attention to emotional education among socialist writers and activists and traces its relevance to the making of proletarian identifications in the parallel projects of socialist peda-

---

[3] In the scholarly literature, *Minderwertigkeitsgefühl* has been translated as "feeling of inferiority" and "inferiority feeling;" both are to be distinguished from inferiority complex, given the latter's suggestion of psychological disorder.
[4] Walter Benjamin, "A Communist Pedagogy," in *Selected Writings, 1927–1930*, ed. Michael William Jennings Howard Eiland, and Gary Smith, trans. Rodney Livingstone (Cambridge, MA: Belknap Press of Harvard University Press, 2005), 273–274. In the same volume, see Benjamin's reflections on "Program for a Proletarian Children's Theater," 201–206.

gogy and proletarian children's literature. In line with the expanded definition of culture presented in this book, the turn toward two categories often excluded from aesthetic discourse, namely the useful and the instructional, is bound also to expand the discussion of aesthetic and political emotions and establish new connections between the concrete proposals for socialist education and the fictional solutions to the problems of proletarian youth. The writings by Austrian psychologist Alfred Adler (1870 – 1937) on class society and feelings of inferiority will consequently be used to identify the prevailing modes of identification, forms of attachments, and values and beliefs associated with the project of socialist education and proletarian mobilization during the 1920s and early 1930s. The chapter's second part presents three types of literary texts – an agitprop skit for youth groups, a puppet play for small children, and a novel for young adults – to reconstruct the didactic elements of a thus defined emotional culture of class with a special emphasis on the therapeutic functions and agitational effects of fictional solutions.

At least since the publication of Jean Jacques Rousseau's *Emile*, the child in western culture has functioned as an embodiment of the innate potential in human beings and a conduit to the emancipatory project of humanism. No matter whether childhood is treated as a preparatory or exceptional life stage or whether it is seen as a period of freedom or discipline, the very concept has given educators, writers, and philosophers a generative framework for testing competing ideas about human nature and the civilizing effect of education. Educating the next generation has been inseparable from broader discourses of folk, community, society, and nation (or empire) and often been enlisted in the imagination of different societies and better worlds. However, these changing conceptions of childhood cannot be analyzed outside the official institutions of family, church, and nation and the historical articulations of class, gender, and race. Whereas the idealization of childhood as a state of innocence is inseparable from the rise of the middle class and the culture of bourgeois individualism after the French Revolution, the making of the modern masses during the industrial revolution cannot be understood without the public policies, social services, and educational models that conceive of youth as the beneficiary of discipline as well as punishment. The connections between youth and power are nowhere more apparent than in the coordinated efforts by state and local agencies since the Wilhelmine Empire to at once protect and control poor children through labor, truancy, and vagrancy laws and to rely on the youth welfare system as an instrument of social control (e. g., through state homes and youth prisons).[5]

The young democracies formed after the cataclysm of World War I offered many new opportunities for translating psychological insights into pedagogical practices geared toward the children of the working class. On 13 November 1923, the Reichsarbeitsgemeinschaft der Kinderfreunde (RAG, Friends of Proletarian Children) was founded in Berlin as an association committed to the program of education for democracy. Their goal, in the words of founder Kurt Löwenstein (1885–1939), was the institutionalization of what he called "collective self-confidence"[6] in preparation for a proletarian revolution. Under his leadership, the Kinderfreunde became part of an elaborate network of SPD-affiliated organizations and publications that included the Sozialistische Arbeiterjugend and the Vienna-based journal *Die sozialistische Erziehung* (1921–1934) edited by Otto Felix Kanitz (1894–1940). Envisioning a better future for working-class youth in opposition to bourgeois society and commercial culture, these educators remained fully aware of the powerful influence of old religious traditions and new mass diversions. To offer an attractive alternative to the Christian rite of Confirmation, for instance, the socialists conceived of the *Jugendweihe* as a secular initiation ritual complete with poems, songs, and *Sprechchöre*.[7] As for more mundane amusements, socialist educational primers and youth group manuals provided detailed suggestions for child-appropriate ball games, singing games, and dancing games, published sample programs for successful group events with enticing lectures and musical performances, and gave practical advice on everything from building maypoles, pennants, and garlands to sewing special banners and uniforms and decorating youth club houses.

By the end of the 1920s, more than one hundred thousand children had joined Kinderfreunde groups in Germany alone. Their recreational activities nurtured children's personalities in nonhierarchical, antiauthoritarian settings and emphasized the experiential quality of socialism as a political commitment. Following the model of their Austrian comrades, the German Kinderfreunde divided children into different age groups called Jungfalken (Young Falcons) und Rotfalken (Red Falcons); some camps even included toddler groups known as Nestfalken (Nest Falcons). Beginning with the legendary 1927 Children's Republic

---

[5] For a historical overview, see Sven Steinacker, *Der Staat als Erzieher. Jugendpolitik und Jugendfürsorge im Rheinland vom Kaiserreich bis zum Ende des Nazismus* (Stuttgart: Ibidem, 2007).
[6] Kurt Löwenstein, *Die Aufgaben der Kinderfreunde* (Berlin: Arbeiterjugend-Verlag, 1931), 8.
[7] See Siegfried Wolf, "Revolutionär-proletarische Jugendweihen und Vorbereitungskurse in den ersten Jahren der Weimarer Republik. Ein Beitrag zur weltanschaulichen Bildung und Erziehung der proletarischen Jugend" (PhD diss., Pädagogische Hochschule Zwickau, 1984).

Seekamp near Kiel, annual summer camps for thousands of working-class children modeled the organization of these tent cities on the principles of parliamentary democracy (see figure 15.1).[8] Under the motto "working-class children conquer the world!," these children's republics created a utopian space in which everything from daily rituals, chores, and physical exercises to evening entertainments and coed sleeping arrangements was designed to instill a strong sense of class pride in their young citizens.[9] In the words of Anton Tesarek, the influential pedagogue active in the SPÖ (Social Democratic Party of Austria), these socialist summer camps and related children's festivals offered compelling proof, against the miseries of working-class life, of "the right to be joyful" – that is, as a human being. Of course, he was well aware that until the revolution, "every proletarian festivity will suffer under the weight of oppression that weighs down on the entire proletarian class."[10]

Fig. 15.1 Kinderrepublik Seekamp 1927, photograph. With permission of Schilksee-Archiv Pieper-Wöhlk.

---

8 Anton Tesarek, "Die Kinderrepublik Seekamp—Ihr Sinn und Auftrag," *Sozialistische Erziehung* (1927/28): 33–34. For a contemporary account, see Andreas Gayk, ed., *Die rote Kinderrepublik. Ein Buch von Arbeiterkindern für Arbeiterkinder* (Berlin: Arbeiterjugend-Verlag, 1928); the book was reprinted in 1976.
9 See Andreas Gayk, *Arbeiterkinder erobern die Welt!* (Berlin: Reichsarbeitsgemeinschaft der Kinderfreunde, 1930).
10 Anton Tesarek, *Feste der Arbeiterkinder* (Vienna: Jungbrunnen, 1927), 4.

In preparing the next generation for the classless society of the future, the children's republics insisted on shared work responsibilities and total equality between the sexes and, through group activities, trained new group behaviors in line with core socialist values, such as tolerance, nonviolence, and international solidarity. During the last years of the Weimar Republic, the Kinderfreunde also worked hard to distinguish their holistic socialist pedagogy from the more agitational, militaristic approaches taken by KPD-affiliated groups. It was in response to these larger developments that Löwenstein, who was on the school board in Berlin-Neukölln, repeatedly characterized working-class children as (socialist) builders of society rather than (communist) destroyers of society and concluded that

> our children are the living testament and expression of their proletarian existence. This proletarian existence means inferiority as long as we do not create the opposite effect through a new *community*, through a *different* reality. And that is exactly what we do with our groups. Here our children are not proletarians, but Red Falcons; here they are *not* belittled and cast to the side. Instead they make decisions for themselves, build a happy and fulfilling life together, make plans and carry them out, and in their children's republic, already experience a new socialist state.[11]

Equally concerned with the special problems of working-class children, but with greater emphasis on their psychological preparation for class struggle, the KPD by 1919 had already founded a competing Kinderverband that agitated in the schools and disseminated its ideas through the journal *Das proletarische Kind*. The Rote Jungpioniere (ages ten to fourteen), too, had their own weekly newspaper titled *Jung-Spartakus* and, later, *Die Trommel*.[12] Edwin Hoernle (1883–1952), the author and editor of several works of communist pedagogy, became a leading figure in the children's group movement and actively promoted the transformation of schools into centers of political agitation. His influence can be traced all the way to the proletarian moment in Japan.[13] Arguing against the poisonous effects of bourgeois high culture and the empty rhetoric of liberal educational re-

---

[11] Kurt Löwenstein, *Freie Bahn den Kinderfreunden* (Berlin: Reichsarbeitsgemeinschaft der Kinderfreunde, 1930), 41. On his conception of childhood, also see *Das Kind als Träger der werdenden Gesellschaft*, sec. rev. ed. (Vienna: Jungbrunnen, 1928).
[12] See Heiko Müller, *"Kinder müssen Klassenkämpfer werden!" Der Kommunistische Kinderverband in der Weimarer Republik (1920–1933)* (Marburg: Tectum, 2013). For the larger historical context, also see Peter D. Stachura, *The Weimar Republic and the Younger Proletariat: An Economic and Social Analysis* (New York: Palgrave Macmillan, 1989).
[13] See Samuel Perry, *Recasting Red Culture in Proletarian Japan: Childhood, Korea, and the Historical Avant-garde* (Honolulu: University of Hawaii Press, 2014), 14–15.

form, Hoernle advocated building class consciousness by encouraging children's participation in mass rallies and propaganda campaigns – if need be, against the will of their apolitical mothers. The ultimate goal was the integration of children and adolescents into a united front of the revolutionary working class. For Hoernle, class-conscious, working-class parents had only one responsibility: *"To recruit and educate our children for our class, to fill them with proletarian solidarity, communist sense of community, and revolutionary fighting energy – this is the first and foremost task that the revolutionary proletariat now owes their children."*[14] Hoernle was well aware that "the struggle for the soul of the proletarian child" was bound to encounter considerable obstacles in individual character traits and personal needs and desires. Nonetheless, for him, class pride offered the best emotional defense against the daily humiliations experienced by all proletarians in capitalist society. In line with official KPD directives, developing class pride meant above all developing an attitude of militancy:

> What should we do then? Should we, the fighting class, go without telling our children why we are fighting, why they too must become fighters? Can a mother refrain from telling her starving child why he is starving? Can we sit in shameful silence when our children ask us, "Why are you fighting? Mother, why are you going to the demonstration? Brother, why are you unemployed?" Should we pretend to be impartial when children report the lies and smears of their bourgeois friends? Should we tell them that they are too young to understand when they read the lies and defamations in the newspapers and ask us about them? No! We will tell our children: Be proud of your striking, protesting parents, siblings, and friends, who are thrown into prison and struck down in street battles. Be proud when someone calls you a Spartacist child. Do not be afraid to be called a communist and act like a communist.[15]

The unbridgeable gap between the romanticized views of childhood in bourgeois culture and the great hardships suffered by the children of the working class was used by various educational initiatives and debates across the leftist spectrum to both uncover the deceptions of dominant ideology and prove the superiority of Marxist analyses. However, their emphasis on class-based analyses and collective solutions could not account for the fact that psychological injuries and deformations were always suffered individually. Redefining the process of class socialization consequently required special attention to the emotional aspects of

---

14 Edwin Hoernle, *Die Arbeiterklasse und ihre Kinder. Ein ernstes Wort an die Arbeitereltern* (Berlin: Sieber, 1921), 12. Lutz von Werder and Reinhart Wolff republished Hoernle's *Grundlagen der proletarischen Erziehung* (1929) in 1969 as a contribution to then ongoing discussions about socialist education and political emancipation.

15 Hoernle, *Die Arbeiterklasse und ihre Kinder*, 15–16.

growing up working class, beginning with the feelings of inferiority mentioned in many workers' life writings and extensively discussed in most socialist educational manuals. Their conclusion that these feelings of inferiority had to be treated in class-specific terms attests to the considerable influence of Alfred Adler, the founder of individual psychology who, after founding the first clinic for child psychology in Vienna in 1920, became actively involved in education reform and child advocacy.[16] One of the original members of the Psychoanalytic Society, Adler eventually broke with Freud over the decisive role the latter attributed to the unconscious and the drives. Adler began developing a more holistic view of the individual that emphasized his or her unique sense of self and world, with the experience of *Gemeinschaftsgefühl* treated as an integral part of this process. His interest in the social causes of mental and physical illness and his belief in the improvability of human nature attest to his intellectual debts to Enlightenment thought and the modern project of social reform. Concerned with the external and internal obstacles to individual self-realization, Adler throughout his career paid special attention to the problem of low self-esteem and its long-term consequences. His distinction between the universal human experience of *Minderwertigkeitsgefühl* (feeling of inferiority) and the clinical etiology of *Minderwertigkeitskomplex* (inferiority complex) allowed him to develop the key categories of what became known as individual psychology in line with its original commitment to a socialist humanism. Adler was acutely aware of the daily insults and small resentments that prevented working-class children from developing a strong sense of community and partaking in the socialist culture of solidarity that could sustain them through personal struggles. At the same time, he regarded feelings of inferiority also as a powerful resource in the fight for social justice and the rise of the workers' movement – a point indirectly confirmed by the political memoirs and workers' life writings discussed in chapters 3 and 7.

Building on the work of Adler, who was widely known in Viennese socialist circles, socialist educators and children's activists used the diagnosis of feelings of inferiority to gauge the psychological consequences of economic exploitation and social discrimination. This conceptual opening toward a class-based understanding of emotions enabled them to conceive of therapeutic experiences of community tailored specifically to the needs of working-class children. Karl Korn, the editor of *Arbeiter-Jugend*, for example, observed that one can "mobilize young people for socialism, but it must be a socialism that takes into account the

---

[16] The main works to be considered in this context are Alfred Adler, *Die andere Seite. Eine massenpsychologische Studie über die Schuld des Volkes* (Vienna: Leopold Heidrich, 1919) and the very influential and frequently reprinted *Menschenkenntnis* (Leipzig: S. Hirzel, 1927).

unique nature of their state of consciousness. In other words, a socialism that appeals to the emotions; the sense of camaraderie; the concept of honor; the young's sense of justice; and the ideals of freedom, equality, and fraternity capable since ancient times of enflaming mainly the youthful soul."[17] Oskar Drees, a well-known sport functionary, echoed Korn's heartfelt sentiments when he called for more coordinated efforts "to overcome those feelings of inferiority anchored in the soul of proletarian youth and build up their self-esteem and self-confidence."[18]

Beyond the shared belief in the main goals of socialist pedagogy, considerable disagreements existed concerning the role of individual personality in definitions of class and its implications for the making of proletarian identifications. Convinced of the radicalizing effects of suffering, the left-radical activist Otto Rühle described the political awakening of (a male) proletarian youth as "a process by which the fate of his class is repeated and redefined through him. The experience of humiliation awakens strong impulses of opposition and resistance deep within him. Hardship and sorrow are transformed into insight and action."[19] However, these negative experiences rarely proved sufficient to start a movement or build a party. It was only radical changes in the institutions of learning such as the introduction of the so-called *Einheitsschule* (comprehensive school) that could provide the appropriate structure for the development of a new socialist morality. "Freedom, independence, truthfulness, solidarity – these are the foundations and pillars of the education to socialism,"[20] the prolific Rühle concluded. Adding a more controversial public health perspective on the psychology and pathology of class society, Austrian educator Otto Felix Kanitz observed that the children of the working class were not only doubly oppressed by the patriarchal family and the class system but also born with diminished mental and physical faculties due to their prenatal exposure to alcohol; these disadvantages, he insisted, continued in their often futile daily struggles against hunger, poverty, and criminality. Disproving any romanticized views about an innate sense of community and solidarity among the working class, these dire circumstances, according to Kanitz, often gave rise to

---

17 Karl Korn, *Die Arbeiterjugendbewegung*, 3 vols. (Berlin: Arbeiterjugend-Verlag, 1923), 3: 379–80.
18 Oskar Drees, quoted in Jörg Wetterich, *Bewegungskultur und Körpererziehung in der sozialistischen Jugendarbeit von 1893 bis 1933. Lebensstile und Bewegungskonzepte im Schnittpunkt von Arbeitersportbewegung und Jugendbewegung* (Münster: Lit, 1993), 278.
19 Otto Rühle, *Das proletarische Kind. Eine Monographie* (Munich: Albert Langen, 1922), 372.
20 Otto Rühle, *Erziehung zum Sozialismus. Ein Manifest* (Berlin: Verlag Gesellschaft und Erziehung, 1919), 22.

a pronounced culture of resentment, with some workers wishing others to be treated as badly as they had been. Drawing perhaps on his work with the Austrian Kinderfreunde, he called this compensatory fantasy "a more dangerous enemy of socialism today than all the actual capitalists in the world."[21]

By addressing the problem of childhood and adolescence in class terms, socialist educators not only dismantled the myths of apolitical education upheld by many bourgeois reformers but also confronted persistent petty-bourgeois attitudes prevalent among working-class parents. Taking very different approaches to this persistent problem, SPD-affiliated organizations promoted educational initiatives to further class allegiance, while KPD-affiliated organizations were primarily interested in enforcing party allegiance. In general, Social Democrats avoided the overt politicization of childhood, emphasizing instead the development of individual personalities within the humanistic models of sociability found in class as community. Communists, by contrast, took an openly instrumental approach and treated children and adolescents as the first line of attack in a coordinated political mobilization of the working class. Educational historians have examined these different conceptions of childhood through the political schisms and rivalries in the Weimar left.[22] While these differences cannot be ignored, they should not be read as direct expressions of opposing party programs. Awareness of the embeddedness of socialist educational theory and praxis in the larger humanistic discourses of childhood is equally important when it comes to the discursive role assigned to emotions in these various contexts. Socialist and communist pedagogies shared the same overarching concerns with the proletarian child's initiation into the community or the collective, with both terms still used interchangeably. Moreover, the building of imaginary communities around the figure of the child and the myth of youth involved complicated processes of projection that cannot be reconstructed through educational manuals and treatises alone and that require the unique insights gained from the emotional scenarios imagined by proletarian children's literature.

In recent years, Sven Steinacker, Heiko Müller, and Sabine Andresen have published comprehensive studies on socialist and communist pedagogies in the German context. By contrast, the proletarian children's literature of the 1920s has been more or less ignored since the historical groundwork done by GDR scholars Ingmar Dreher, Hansgeorg Meyer, Horst Kunze, and Heinz Wege-

---

[21] Otto Felix Kanitz, *Das proletarische Kind in der bürgerlichen Gesellschaft* (Jena: Urania, 1925), 34.

[22] For an introduction to the pedagogical concepts of SPD and KPD, see Sabine Andresen, *Sozialistische Kindheitskonzepte. Politische Einflüsse auf die Erziehung* (Munich: Ernst Reinhardt, 2006), 34–119.

haupt during the 1970s and 1980s.[23] The enduring disregard for didacticism in literature is one reason for the neglect of children's literature in general; another involves the disciplinary blind spots that have prevented more interdisciplinary approaches to the educational initiatives, pedagogical theories, and literary representations concerned with childhood and adolescence. In fact, even some socialists early on questioned the need for, and value of, a proletarian children's literature and defended the tradition, embraced by reform pedagogy, of using literature exclusively for the cultivation of fantasy worlds set apart from everyday life. However, their growing frustration with the existing children's literature and its promotion of conservative moral values and bourgeois behavioral norms through picture books and cautionary tales compelled more and more activists to look for alternatives, whether in the form of socialist appropriations of classic tales or proletarian versions of folk characters. Meanwhile, the authors of proletarian children's literature took advantage of the technological advances in publishing that made possible the democratization of reading and writing and allowed them to reach children through the unique didactic powers of fiction.

Ruth Fischer, the sister of Hanns Eisler, once described the shared goal of socialist authors, educators, and activists as follows: "We describe what we know. [...] We describe what everyone should know."[24] While socialist and communist pedagogy remained firmly in male hands, some of the most successful authors of proletarian children's literature were women – evidence of a gendered division of labor that often aligned imaginary worlds with female perspectives. The works produced under such uneven conditions covered a wide range of genres, from Hermynia zur Mühlen's socialist fairytales (with illustrations by George Grosz) in *Was Peterchens Freunde erzählen* (1921, What Little Peter's Friends Tell)

---

23 The standard works are Ingmar Dreher and Hansgeorg Meyer, *Die deutsche proletarisch-revolutionäre Kinder- und Jugendliteratur zwischen 1918 und 1933* (Berlin: Kinderbuchverlag, 1975) and Horst Kunze and Heinz Wegehaupt, *Spiegel proletarischer Kinder- und Jugendliteratur, 1870–1936* (Berlin: Kinderbuchverlag, 1985). Historical materials on the topic have been reprinted in Manfred Altner, ed. and intr., *Das proletarische Kinderbuch. Dokumente zur Geschichte der sozialistischen deutschen Kinder- und Jugendliteratur* (Dresden: VEB Verlag der Kunst, 1988). For a recent assessment, see Helga Karrenbrock, "Sozialistische Kinder- und Jugendliteratur," in *Die Kinder- und Jugendliteratur in der Zeit der Weimarer Republik*, 2 vols., ed. Norbert Hopster (Frankfurt am Main: Peter Lang, 2012), 2: 587–608. For an English-language account, see Luke Springman, *Comrades, Friends, and Companions: Utopian Projections and Social Action in German Literature for Young People, 1926–1934* (New York: Peter Lang, 1989). For a comparative perspective, see Julia L. Mickenberg, *Learning from the Left: Children's Literature, the Cold War, and Radical Politics in the United States* (Oxford: Oxford University Press, 2006).
24 Ruth Fischer and Franz Heimann, *Deutsche Kinderfibel* (Düsseldorf: W. Schroeder, 1986) n. p. First published in 1933.

to Berta Lask's Marxist world history of *Auf dem Flügelpferde durch die Zeiten: Bilder vom Klassenkampf der Jahrtausende* (1925, On the Winged Horse of Time: Scenes from the Class Struggle throughout the Millenniums) to Lisa Tetzner's successful novel and play, *Hans Urian. Die Geschichte einer Weltreise* (1929 and 1931, Hans Urian: The Story of a Trip around the World). Several works landed on the Nazis' list of banned books, evidence that the emotional education of socialist children was perceived as a serious threat to more restrictive models of folk community. Others played a key role in the internationalism of proletarian children's literature, with zur Mühlen's proletarian folk tales translated into English and Japanese.

Proletarian children's literature built on existing genres, including fairytales, historical novels, and morality plays, and employed familiar figures, themes, and motifs in order to provide inspirational stories of working-class empowerment. The recourse to tradition and convention allowed their authors to uncover the visible and invisible hierarchies that sustained capitalist societies and make their devastating effect on working-class life intelligible to young readers. Identification played a central role in the intended process of agitation in the political and emotional sense. Serving as a laboratory of emotions, proletarian children's literature was brought in alignment with official SPD and KPD positions through the selective appropriation of older cultural traditions and modes of address. Accordingly, the bourgeois belief in the autonomous individual had to be adapted to the collective narratives of class unity and solidarity. The moral messages from folk culture were frequently referenced but without their emphasis on social harmony and faith in authority, and the Christian ideal of brotherly love redefined to fit the new political goals of equality, freedom, and democracy. Even the formative role of reading and writing in the making of the public sphere was fundamentally redefined, with the cult of inwardness in bourgeois culture replaced by the ethos of collective action in working-class culture.

In presenting typical emotional situations and offering appropriate behavioral solutions from a class perspective, the authors of proletarian children's literature usually employ three distinct but interrelated strategies: a didactic one that defines the project of moral education in class-specific terms; an agitational one that explains the world through Marxist categories; and a therapeutic one that, based on the diagnosis of feelings of inferiority, builds up children's sense of self-worth. The initial acknowledgment of individual pain and suffering is usually followed by the integration of such isolating feelings into a collective narrative of class empowerment. The emotional and cognitive work to be performed always requires conscious rejection of the ideology of individualism in bourgeois society and willing acceptance of the working class as the ideal model of the community/collective. Moments of observation and acts of imitation are essential to this socialization into class consciousness; the same holds true for the emotional processes involved in training a class habitus based on solidarity.

The following three literary lessons use different forms and genres to stage paradigmatic scenes of proletarian identification and achieve surprisingly similar emotional effects. First lesson: always talk and act together with others, and you will overcome feelings of powerlessness and worthlessness. This is the simple message of Otto Müller's *Der Wagen* (1922, The Cart), an agitprop skit written by a twenty-year-old mechanic active in the Socialist Workers' Youth. The closing scene features a sixteen-year-old working-class boy named Fritz who needs help with a heavy cart but only gets condescending lectures from a pastor, professor, and policeman and sneering comments from passersby representing a cross section of Weimar class society. This is the moment when two young communists, Robert and Gertrud, enter the stage:

> *Robert:* I saw the whole spectacle from the window. At least four to five people walked by you and nobody helped you.
> *Gertrud (comes from the other side of the square):* Robert, what are you doing here? Where are you going?
> *Robert:* Oh Gertrud, I just wanted to help bring the cart around.
> *Gertrud:* I'll help too!
> *Robert:* OK, then one, two, three, and we're out!
> *Fritz:* At last, a few people who don't just tell stories, but actually take charge (*zugreifen*)!
> *Robert:* Yes, if we proletarians don't help each other, no one else will.
> *Gertrud:* Oh, the bourgeois, away with them; they only tell pious stories and other than that let us do the drudgework (*schuften*) for them. (*"for them" is stressed*)
> *Fritz:* Tell me now, who are you that you take action and offer your help?
> *Robert:* We're young proletarians like you.
> *Gertrud:* And we belong to the Communist Youth.
> *Fritz:* Oh, r-r-r-really?
> *Robert:* Well, let's go! We'll tell you more on the way.
> *Robert and Gertrud:* Let's take the cart, onward, here we go! (*Without effort the three take the cart and exit.*)[25]

The brief exchange combines two equally important lessons, a moral one (i.e., helping others) and a practical one (i.e., getting things done). Significantly, the object that brings these two lessons together is a handcart, a telling metaphor both of the power of mobility and the drudgery of physical labor. The

---

[25] Otto Müller, *Der Wagen. Beinah ein Putsch aus dem Leben junger Proletarier* (Berlin: Verlag der Jugendinternationale, 1922), n. p. For an overview of proletarian children's theater, see Gerhard Eikenbusch, *Sozialdemokratisches und kommunistisches Kinder- und Jugendtheater in der Weimarer Republik* (Frankfurt am Main: Peter Lang, 1997).

above scene presents Fritz's struggles from the point-of-view of the two young communists who watch from a distance and then approach him to present their analysis of the problem (i.e., the cart is too heavy) and their proposal for a solution (i.e., to combine the strength of three people). Their separate arrivals have the additional benefit of showing the habitus of solidarity as one of observation, identification, and imitation, with the girl modeling her behavior on the other boy's initial intervention. "Telling stories" meanwhile is denounced as counterproductive and the value of action affirmed through the linguistic shift from a submissive *schuften* (i.e., toil for someone) to the activist *zugreifen* (i.e., to grasp, seize, take hold of something). Not surprisingly, the scene ends offstage, with the arrival of the emboldened trio at a meeting of the KJD (Communist Youth of Germany).

Fig. 15.2 Kinderfest der Sozialistischen Arbeiterjugend (SAJ) 1928, photograph. With permission of Archiv der deutschen Jugendbewegung, Witzenhausen, AdJb, F 1 Nr. Seriennr. 297/Bildnr 02.

Second lesson: do not accept things as they are – question everything and everyone, including parents; there is no better way of overcoming feelings of inferiority. This is main message conveyed by a beloved puppet known as Red Kasper (see figure 15.2). His exploits were featured prominently in *Der rote Kasper*, a series of short puppet plays published in Leipzig by the SPD-affiliated Arbeiter-Theater-Verlag Jahn; his communist counterpart appeared in the KPD's Proletarisches Kasperletheater series by the Berlin-based A. Hoffmann Verlag.[26] A famous character from the German puppet theater tradition, Kasper (or Kasperle) is usually described as an irreverent jester-figure in the tradition of Pulcinella from the Italian *commedia dell'arte*. Loud, frank, cheeky, and equipped with a slapstick, he embodies the liberating effect of aggression and the subversive power of laughter. At the same time, his affinities for the exaggerated and the grotesque come with an enduring belief in the importance of moral distinctions and ethical principles. Red Kasper, his young socialist offspring, regularly fights modern-day versions of the old kings and robbers, effecting a reversal of the moral order that in the traditional puppet plays makes king, prince, and princess the sole objects of respect and desire. Confronted with their modern reincarnations, the spirited young champion of the proletariat simply tells them to get lost: "Yes, my dear old hero from the 'good old times,' your days are numbered. The working-class children don't need wondrous tales with all that dusty stuff of 'good fairies and beautiful princesses.'"[27] Time and again the Red Kasper shows children how to mistrust authorities, challenge hierarchies, and stand up for the common people. Moreover, his physical tricks and verbal tirades offer plenty of evidence that social reality can indeed be changed and that knowledge is, in fact, power. Acknowledging the puppet's irreverent spirit, Fritz Blaszovsky describes him as "a trustworthy helper of the oppressed, always rebelling against those who abuse their authority and power. His project is the fight against all forms of injustice."[28]

In *Revolte im Kasperhaus* (1929, Revolt in Kasper's House), a puppet play by SPD reform pedagogue Ernst Heinrich Bethge (1878–1944) who wrote under the pseudonym Lobo Frank, Comrade Kasper is once again busy preventing wrongdoings and modeling solutions. In the scene cited here, he uses indignation and irreverence to instill a militant watchfulness in his young fans that can be practiced even on their parents. He demonstrates how to catch capitalists hiding their

---

[26] For extensive documentation, see Ernst Friedrich Suhr and Gina Weinkauff, eds., *Revolte im Kasperhaus. Ein Lesebuch mit Dokumenten und Bildern zum Puppentheater der Arbeiterjugendbewegung* (Cologne: Prometh, 1983). For a historical overview, also see Gina Weinkauff, *Der Rote Kasper. Das Figurentheater in der pädagogisch-kulturellen Praxis der deutschen und österreichischen Arbeiterbewegung von 1918–1933* (Bochum: Deutsches Institut für Puppenspiel, 1982).
[27] J. Heisser, "Der proletarische Kasper," *Das proletarische Kind* 11.4/5 (1931): 83.
[28] Quoted in Franz Studynka, *Der rote Kasperl. Anleitung zum Kasperlspielen* (Vienna: Jungbrunnen, 1929), 11.

sacks of money, stop kings from returning to their castles, and resist the temptations of the "booze devil" and the "beer witch." After witnessing a particularly dysfunctional Reichstag session, he turns to his impressionable audience with clear instructions:

> *Kasper:* Children, children, here we just saw a very sad but very true example of the unity of the proletarian masses. Sure, they sang "The Internationale" with conviction, but they still managed, at all costs ...
> *Children (interrupting him):* to get into a fistfight.
> *Kasper:* Thank you. And now go home and tell all the big people: Kasper has gotten his stick back. They need to set a better example for the future; otherwise, Kasper will shellac them good. Goodbye, kiddies.
> *Children:* Goodbye, Kasper.[29]

The rhetorical strategies employed by Red Kasper build on the close connection between the emotional tone of socialist agitation and the performative quality of proletarian identifications: the invitation to a shared position of knowledge (i.e., "we just saw") by someone with authority; the reversal of hierarchies through which children are charged with educating their parents (i.e., "now go home"); and the justification of violence (i.e., shellacking) as an appropriate form of conflict resolution. Moreover, the dialogic structure of the scene, with the children finishing Kasper's sentences, provides a critical model for diagnosing the shortcomings of parliamentary democracy and, implicitly, validating the Marxist notion of dictatorship of the proletariat and the Leninist model of the revolutionary vanguard party. Their spirited exchanges with the Red Kasper suggests that the children already possess many of the cognitive skills to be tested in future confrontations both personal and political. The agitational work to be completed by the puppet play then lies in modeling the emotional resilience required in the struggle for a future society yet to come.

The third and final lesson: understand that feelings – feelings of exclusion, anger, and fear – are an important part of class struggle; this is the main message of one of the most successful proletarian children's books of the Weimar period, *Ede und Unku* (1931), "a novel for boys and girls" published by Malik with photographs from the studio of John Heartfield and translated into English in 1935 as *Eddie and the Gipsy*.[30] For its author, Grete Weiskopf (1905–1966), who

---

29 Lobo Frank (i.e., Ernst Heinrich Bethge), *Revolte im Kasperhaus oder Alles steht uff'm Kopp. Ein schnafftes Puppenspiel für Sozialisten und Freidenker* (Leipzig: Alfred Jahn, 1929), n. p.
30 Rahel Rosa Neubauer makes this point in "John Heartfield und die Kinderbücher des Malik-Verlags," in *Alex Wedding (1905–1966) und die proletarische Kinder- und Jugendliteratur*, ed. Susanne Blumesberger and Ernst Seibert (Vienna: Praesens, 2007), 143–154.

published under the pen name Alex Wedding, writing for children meant "to write for our future" and, through fictional settings and scenarios, to model the attitudes and behaviors necessary for the project of radical change.[31] Whereas Erich Kästner, in the surprisingly similar story of *Pünktchen and Anton* (1931, in English as *Annaluise and Anton*), solves the problem of economic inequality through the promise of social reconciliation, Weiskopf emphasizes the need for class unity as a prerequisite of effective political action. By presenting the main character as a figure of doubt and hesitation, she is able to model the necessary emotional transition from isolation to solidarity in ways reminiscent of the young men in the novels about the Ruhr Uprising discussed in chapter 9.

Set in a Berlin working-class neighborhood, the story of *Ede and Unku* is constructed around two best friends: Ede Sperling, whose father loses his job in a factory and briefly becomes a strikebreaker, and Max Klabunde, the son of a KPD member and Ede's main guide into the world of proletarian thinking and feeling. Adding a touch of exotic otherness, a young Sinti girl from the fairground called Unku is introduced to mediate between these two male positions. Toward the end of the novel, a still hesitant Ede can be found watching the other children play a game of demonstration, with one group cast as workers and another as riot police. Several of the children seem highly skilled in the art of street battle with guns featuring prominently in their game plan:

> One could see Max run back into the trucking company and come back with a long stick upon which the children pinned a piece of red cloth. Then Ede watched how they arranged themselves in two rows of four. Max led the way and waved the flag through the air. And they all sang, "Left, left, left, Red Wedding is on the March." Ewald blew on a small comb. "It's the workers' wind orchestra," Orje announced expertly. Ede would much rather have marched with the other boys. But Gustav held him back and said that things were about to start. Now the others marched to an empty building site; Max jumped onto a crate, ran his hand through his hair, and shouted: "Comrades!" "Let's go!" cried Orje and ran out of the gate. And the boy with the balloon cap [i.e., Ede] thought he'd much rather be a worker, and the next time he would no longer be so stupid.[32]

The scene can be read as an almost paradigmatic scene of proletarian identifications, beginning with its subject matter, a group of working-class children playing class struggle. Once again, the spectacle of resistance is presented from the outside, but here it involves two outside perspectives, that of the characters

---

[31] Quoted in Blumesberger and Seibert, *Alex Wedding (1905–1966)*, 23. Grete Weiskopf was the wife of the communist journalist Franz Carl Weiskopf.
[32] Alex Wedding (i.e., Grete Weiskopf), *Ede und Unku. Ein Roman für Jungen und Mädchen* (Berlin: Malik, 1931), 112–123.

(e.g., "Ede watched") and that of the intended reader (e.g., "one could see"). From this bifurcated perspective, the reader is invited at once to watch the scene and watch Ede watching and, in so doing, become part of a compelling scene of interpellation. In addition, the rules of the game have Ede stand on the side with a few other children cast as riot police waiting for their cue to beat up the workers. A brief moment of inaction allows them to make appreciative comments on the fictional workers' high level of organization and their effective use of songs and symbols. In light of the fact that the dreams of revolution have always been articulated in homosocial terms, the loving description of a resplendent Max running his hand through his hair should not be dismissed as gratuitous. In fact, this moment of intimacy within the performance of communist militancy functions as an integral part of the larger scene of ideological seduction. Not surprisingly, at the end of this passage, Ede, "the boy with the balloon cap," would rather find himself on the other side of the spectacle, together with the comrades. At last, the sharpening of consciousness that, for Benjamin, made proletarian childhood a "school of poverty and suffering" can provide the kind of emotional education that promotes class unity and solidarity.

To conclude, the competing approaches to education taken by SPD and KPD educators and children's groups (and their Austrian counterparts) reproduce the growing differences between the two main leftist parties in the postwar years. At the same time, they reveal the enduring influence of psychoanalytically inspired theories, including Adler's concept of feelings of inferiority, even as the behaviorist theories developed in the Soviet Union found wider acceptance especially among the practitioners of agitprop and the communist educators who would have agreed with Stalin's characterization of cultural workers as human engineers of the soul. This chapter has shown that individual psychology, socialist pedagogy, and proletarian literature rely on surprisingly similar assumptions both about the transformational potential of imagining alternative forms of society and sociability and about the key role of emotions in forming proletarian identifications and attachments. The same assumptions about the conditions of the working class and the difficulties of class mobilization that informed approaches to childhood and adolescence can be extended to adulthood, and the question of working-class sexuality in particular. As the next chapter sets out to prove, the controversial work of Wilhelm Reich offers the best introduction to the socialist project of sex education and sexual liberation during the Weimar years and the inevitable clash between the competing models of free sexuality identified with Freudian and Marxist theories of repression.

Chapter 16
Wilhelm Reich and the Politics of Proletarian Sexuality

> In sexual relations and sexual intercourse, the man is the bourgeois and the woman the proletarian.
>
> Otto and Alice Rühle, *Sexualanalyse*

Since the October Revolution, the proletarian fantasy has been haunted by the problem of sex: as a source of competing interests, a distraction from political commitments, and a threat to the strength and unity of the working class. But what if sexual desire could be seen not as a problem but a solution to the problem of class consciousness? What if the promise of sexual fulfillment would become inseparable from the fight for a classless society? This was precisely the political strategy suggested by Wilhelm Reich (1897–1957), the controversial Austrian-born psychoanalyst, sex reformer, and communist activist. Enlisting the Freudian theory of libido in an analysis of class society, Reich formulated his theories while working as a trained analyst, sex educator, and political activist in Vienna and, later, Berlin where he started the so-called Sex-Pol (or Sexpol) movement. Against communist calls for discipline and self-control, he insisted on the productive quality of what he called *Lust* (lust), an all-encompassing term that signifies desire, pleasure, and joy in their widest senses. And against the social reformers' diagnosis of widespread sexual misery in the working class, he promised the panacea of full genital health. Through the convergence of sexuality and politics in Sex-Pol, he insisted, proletarians could be released from the double lack of sexual desire and class consciousness. Moreover, lust, in both the narrowly sexual sense that betrays Reich's background in psychoanalysis and the expanded sense that attests to the influence of *Lebensphilosophie* (or vitalism), could be turned into a driving force behind the larger project of revolution.

Reich's calls for a liberated proletarian sexuality and his gendered theories of sexual and political repression draw attention to a frequently neglected aspect in the making of the proletarian dream and are bound to increase awareness of its libidinal sources, including through the project of sociosexual liberation that accounts for the later reception of his writings in the United States and Western Europe. The above epigraph by Otto and Alice Rühle, two influential Weimar sex activists, confirms the pervasive influence of Marxist theory and socialist praxis on post-World War I discussions on class and sexuality.[1] At the same time, Reich's extensive revisions of his theories in American exile point to the easy transferability of the discourse of sexual pleasure to various 1960s and 1970s liberation movements. Given this complicated process of readings and rereadings, the politicization of sexuality since the 1920 cannot be separated from the bourgeois projections onto the imagined body of the working class – with the resultant displacement of political fantasy into sexual fantasy making the proletariat the subject and object of a very different kind of individualized body politics.

In ways that anticipate later criticisms of Freudo-Marxism, the relationship between Reich and the KPD proved difficult from the beginning. Rejecting the standard rhetoric of personal sacrifices in the name of party discipline, Reich's arguments for political emancipation through sexual liberation encountered strong resistance among the leadership. In the fall of 1933, he was expelled from the KPD, having recently joined following his move to Berlin in 1930. Living in Copenhagen at the time, Reich had just published *Massenpsychologie des Faschismus. Zur Sexualökonomie der politischen Reaktion und zur proletarischen Sexualpolitik* (1933, Mass Psychology of Fascism: On the Sexual Economy of Political Reaction and on Proletarian Sexual Politics), which included a blunt assessment of the KPD's mistakes in the final years of the Weimar Republic. Even worse, the book challenged the Marxist belief in the primacy of economics and offered a psychoanalytically grounded analysis of the sexual foundation of fascism as a populist mass movement with authoritarian structures. In November, the Communist Party of Denmark likewise expelled (nonmember) Reich from its ranks in response to allegations that the political refugee had proposed turning communist youth organizations into hotbeds of licentiousness.[2] The coupling of communism and psychoanalysis would have to wait for the revival of Freudo-Marxism during the student movement to realize its full emancipatory potential, though by that time, the proletariat (at least in the sense used in this study) had already disappeared from the world historical stage.

In their hostile reactions to Reich, the Communists were not that different from the Nazis whose 1933 media campaign against this alleged corrupter of German youth had forced the infamous sexologist to leave Germany, first for Den-

---

[1] Otto und Alice Rühle, *Sexual-Analyse. Psychologie des Liebes- und Ehelebens* (Rudolstadt: Greifenverlag, 1929), 13. Challenging Reich's assumption of greater natural sexual potency in the working class, they note higher rates of frigidity among proletarian women (77–78).
[2] Wilhelm Reich, *Listen, Little Man!*, trans. Ralph Manheim (New York: Farrar, Straus & Giroux, 1974), 75.

mark and, in 1939, for the United States.³ Too much sex – or the wrong kind of sex – was the main objection made by party propagandists on the left and the right. Reich's professional colleagues in Vienna, where he had studied and worked with Freud, used a different explanation – too political – when they expelled him from the International Psychoanalytic Association in 1934. His greatest offense in their view was that he had politicized psychoanalysis by placing the problem of libido at the center of all progressive social and political movements.

As Elizabeth Ann Danto has shown, Red Vienna not only gave rise to public housing estates, socialist educational initiatives, and a form of democratic socialism known as Austro-Marxism but also made possible the reconceptualization of modern subjectivity in explicitly collectivist terms.⁴ What Danto describes as a flourishing of civil society after the collapse of empire included the long overdue recognition of the urban masses as a subject of critical inquiry, a process that included a psychological aspects of massification examined by Alfred Adler through the concept of *Gemeinschaftsgefühl* (sense of community) introduced in chapter 15. A prominent figure in psychoanalytic circles, Reich during his Vienna years participated in the discovery of a psychology of the working class by starting to see patients at the Ambulatorium, which provided free mental health and sex advice. He also worked as a counselor at the Sexualberatungsklinik für Arbeiter und Angestellte (Sex-Hygiene Clinic for Workers and Employees). These initiatives exposed him for the first time to the sexual miseries of the working class: married women and men suffering from sexual dysfunction, young people ignorant about the basic facts of sexual reproduction, and the crowded living quarters and long working hours that left few opportunities for privacy and intimacy.

His writings from those early years often combine the dialogic format of sex advice in doctor-patient conversations with informative sections on contraception, masturbation, venereal diseases, and premarital sex. Meanwhile, his membership in the Sozialistische Gesellschaft für Sexualberatung und Sexualforschung (Socialist Society for Sexual Advice and Sexual Research) allowed him

---

3 A good example of the Nazi vilification of Reich as a seducer of German youth can be found in Gesamtverband deutscher antikommunistischer Vereinigungen, ed., *Ein Kampf um Deutschland* (Berlin: n.p., 1933), 18.

4 On the Viennese period, see Elisabeth Ann Danto, *Freud's Free Clinics: Psychoanalysis and Social Justice, 1918–1938* (New York: Columbia University Press, 2005). On the larger context for Reich's continuing problems in Berlin, see Veronika Fuechtner, *Berlin Psychoanalytic: Psychoanalysis and Culture in Weimar Republic Germany and Beyond* (Berkeley: University of California Press, 2011).

to gather rich empirical data for a later study on the authoritarian character structure. Unlike his wife, Annie Reich (1902–1971), whose own work with children convinced her that, "only the liberation of the proletariat from its oppressors will bring about the liberation of sexuality,"[5] Reich firmly believed that the experience of sexual fulfillment could be enlisted productively in the process of political radicalization. Eventually his more controversial theories led to the decisive break with Freud, with Reich rejecting his former mentor's belief in repression as a function of the reality principle and insisting on full orgiastic genitality as the foundation of a truly free society.

Red Vienna, the city of Reich's academic training and intellectual formation, provided the formative experiences that made possible the discursive coupling of "proletarian" and "sexuality." Demonstrations, strikes, and uprisings played a key role in his concomitant political radicalization. Chapters 1 has shown that the spectacle of the revolutionary masses was frequently experienced as a moment of libidinal discharge by participants as well as observers and described along these lines in scientific accounts as well as literary treatments. Most psychoanalysts at the time would have interpreted these highly sexualized scenarios as an expression of pre-Oedipal fears about being overwhelmed and losing control, but for many socialists, these situations also confirmed the possibility of alternatives to bourgeois individualism in the form of collective agency and, by extension, orgasmic potency. Like countless fellow Viennese, Reich witnessed the 15 July 1927 burning of the Palace of Justice. This "practical course in Marxist sociology" profoundly influenced his later views on the psychology of the masses – as it did, with very different implications, for Elias Canetti and Hermann Broch. The sight of policemen shooting workers in cold blood triggered what Reich later called his political awakening: *"Machine men!* This thought was clear and irrefutable. Since then it has never left me; it became the nucleus for all my later investigations of man as a political being."[6] The inhuman treatment of the workers by the police to him appeared as a symptom of the capitalist assault on *Lebensenergie* (life energy) – a process first examined through the notion of character armor as a bourgeois defense against overwhelming emotions and developed further through the diagnosis of the authoritarian personality in his influential analysis of fascism.

---

[5] Annie Reich, *Wenn dein Kind dich fragt. Gespräche, Beispiele und Ratschläge zur Sexualerziehung* (Berlin: Verlag für Sexualpolitik, 1932), 32.
[6] Wilhelm Reich, *People in Trouble*, trans. Philip Schmitz (New York: Farrar, Straus and Giroux, 1976), 27.

"Psychoanalysis is the mother and sociology [i.e., Marxism] the father of sex-economy. *But a child is more than the sum total of his parents.*"[7] The child in question turned out to be Sex-Pol, officially called Deutscher Reichsverband für proletarische Sexualpolitik (German Federal Association for Proletarian Sexual Politics). Founded in Berlin in 1930, the association soon renamed itself the Einheitsverband für proletarische Sexualreform und Mutterschutz (Confederate Association for Proletarian Sex Reform and the Protection of Mothers) to signal its active contribution to the broader fight for reproductive rights.[8] The association provided working-class men and women with sex-positive information, education, and counseling. Incorporating what Marxist theorists used to call the subjective factor into an objective analysis of class society under capitalism, Sex-Pol's ultimate goal was to "turn individual sexual education into a mass action."[9] This included a critical examination of the historical role of church and family in using sexual repression as an instrument of social control. What distinguished Sex-Pol from other leftist groups was its explicit rejection of the repressive morality of the culture of shame and hypocrisy that kept Social Democracy beholden to petty-bourgeois values.

During the Weimar years, the sex reform movement functioned as an integral part of the proletarian lifeworld, opening public clinics that provided free contraceptives and marriage counseling and supporting public campaigns against Clause 218, the paragraph banning abortion, and Clause 175, the paragraph criminalizing homosexuality. Part of larger international developments, sexological research played a key role in the fight for women's rights and sexual freedom, whether in relation to birth control (Helene Stöcker, Margaret Sanger), homosexual rights (Magnus Hirschfeld, Havelock Ellis), or the calls for free love (Clara Zetkin, Alexandra Kollontai) that proclaimed the full compatibility of communism and feminism. Historians Atina Grossmann and Dagmar Herzog have rightly emphasized the contribution of sex reform to the demands for reproductive rights and gender equality and the initiatives for a decriminalization of homosexuality and prostitution. They have also drawn attention to the contradic-

---

[7] Wilhelm Reich, Introduction, *The Mass Psychology of Fascism*, trans. Theodore P. Wolfe (New York: Orgone Institute Press, 1946), xxiii.
[8] On the Einheitsverband, see Marc Rackelmann, "Wilhelm Reich und der Einheitsverband für proletarische Sexualreform und Mutterschutz. Was war die Sexpol?" *Emotion. Beiträge zum Werk von Wilhelm Reich* 11 (1994): 56–93.
[9] Wilhelm Reich, *Die Massenpsychologie des Faschismus. Zur Sexualökonomie der politischen Reaktion und zur proletarischen Sexualpolitik*, sec. ed. (Copenhagen: Verlag für Sexualpolitik, 1934), 255. Because of extensive revisions in the English translations published by Orgone Institute Press, all German works by Reich will be translated from the original unless noted otherwise.

tions within sexology as a modern science promoting eugenics in the name of social hygiene and public health – the kind of biopolitics soon to be perfected in the Nazi racial state.[10]

From Reich's perspective, the project of sex reform offered little more than temporary relief from the psychosexual deformations caused by capitalism and ultimately failed to realize the radical nature of Marxist and psychoanalytic thought. His controversial defense of healthy genitality as the sign of a fully developed adolescent personality led to sharp disagreements with the socialist physician Max Hodann (1894–1946) who headed the public health department in Berlin-Reinickendorf. Counseling working-class youth had convinced Reich that "class consciousness and active, responsible political engagement invariably change the attitude toward sexuality – for they offer solutions to sexual difficulties and the overstimulation of sexual impulses by using up sexual energy and, at the same time, facilitating a satisfying sex life."[11] Concerned about possible misunderstandings, Hodann at one point warned his colleague: "The naive reader might interpret this to mean [...] get rid of sexual inhibitions, let people have as much sex as they want, and then they will automatically join the class struggle."[12] Reich, in fact, encouraged such interpretations as he boldly asserted that, "the will of youth toward the joy of life will be the most powerful force of the revolution"[13] and eventually turn young workers into a sexual and political vanguard. Hodann continued to insist that a new proletarian morality in line with the principles of Sex-Pol would be the opposite of the sexual depravity so widespread in bourgeois society, for "it is beneath us to let ourselves be defined by our drives alone." As he explained, "sexual drives characterize the beginning of friendship and love. But we can only approve of these impulses, justify them to ourselves, once they have withstood the critical force of our own reasoning."[14]

---

10 On the sex reform movement, see Atina Grossmann, *Reforming Sex: The German Movement for Birth Control and Abortion Reform, 1920–1950* (Oxford: Oxford University Press, 1995). On the continuities of sex reform in the Third Reich, also see Dagmar Herzog, *Sex after Fascism: Memory and Morality in Twentieth-Century Germany* (Princeton: Princeton University Press, 2005).
11 Wilhelm Reich, *Der sexuelle Kampf der Jugend* (Berlin: Verlag für Sexualpolitik, 1932), 51.
12 Hodann, quoted in Wilfried Wolff, *Max Hodann (1894–1946). Sozialist und Sexualreformer* (Hamburg: von Bockel, 1993), 136.
13 Reich, *Die Massenpsychologie des Faschismus*, 11.
14 Max Hodann, *Bub und Mädel. Gespräche unter Kameraden über die Geschlechterfrage* (Rudolstadt: Greifenverlag, 1928), 22–23. Because of the controversial nature of sex education, Hodann's *Sexualelend und Sexualberatung. Briefe aus der Praxis* (1928) and *Geschlecht und Liebe in biologischer und gesellschaftlicher Beziehung* (1932) were banned by the Weimar censors.

If Reich's views on adolescent sexuality scandalized many professionals involved in socialist youth work, his masculinist attitudes set him apart from socialist activists with a more egalitarian view of gender and sexuality. To give just two examples, the prolific Otto Rühle used the critique of traditional marriage and gender roles to declare that "in the rejection of, and liberation from, the hegemony of male-oriented sexuality lies the rebirth of eroticism"[15] and to call for a new sexual ethics in the spirit of socialism – a very different project of sexual liberation indeed. Meanwhile, the young Elfriede Friedländer (née Eisler, and later known as Ruth Fischer, 1895–1961), in a short 1920 pamphlet on the sexual ethics of communism, conceded that complete sexual freedom could not be achieved during periods of political struggle and, moreover, that everyone should have the right to be promiscuous, polygamous, or monogamous. Her explanation, "because sexual life in all of its manifestations is solely the choice of each individual," not only confirmed the irreducibility of desire to social or economic determinations, but also it refused to make any empty promises of sexual gratification.[16]

Sex-Pol, as conceived by Reich, represented both a public repudiation of bourgeois prejudices about the moral depravity of the working class and a decidedly masculinist alternative to the new communist morality advocated by Rühle and Hodann. *"Why no happiness on earth, why should not pleasure (Lust) be the content of life?"*[17] Reich at one point asked provocatively. And if all human yearning and striving aimed at the "realization of happiness on earth,"[18] he concluded, these desires needed to be taken into account by every social movement. Translated into Marxist terminology, this meant that, "the affirmation of life in its subjective form as the affirmation of sexual lust and in its objective social form as the socialist planned economy must be advanced to reach subjective consciousness and objective realization. The fight for the affirmation of life must be organized."[19] In other words, if capitalism required sexual repression

---

15 Otto Rühle, *Die Sozialisierung der Frau* (Dresden: Am anderen Ufer, 1924), 49 and 56. After all, he concludes, happier marriages make happier families resulting in more children and, hence, more socialists.

16 Elfriede Friedländer, *Sexualethik des Kommunismus. Eine prinzipielle Studie* (Vienna: Neue Erde, 1920), 49.

17 Reich, Die Massenpsychologie *des Faschismus*, 198.

18 Wilhelm Reich, *Die Sexualität im Kulturkampf. Zur sozialistischen Umstrukturierung des Menschen*, expanded ed. (Copenhagen: Sexpol-Verlag, 1936), xv. The additional chapters in the expanded edition discuss the fight for sexual liberation in the Soviet Union. Note again the different English title for the 1945 and 1974 editions, *The Sexual Revolution: Toward a Self-Governing Character Structure*.

19 Reich, *Die Sexualität im Kulturkampf*, 246 (original entirely in italics).

for its functioning, the Sex-Pol movement had to fight for sexual liberation through the institutions of education, medicine, and the law.

In 1920s Vienna and 1930s Berlin, the parallel projects of sexual and communist revolution gave rise to proletarian sexuality as a liberatory discourse; it also produced the contradictions that would continue to haunt later adaptations. The constitutive tension between a postindividual ethos of masses and multitudes and an antibourgeois individualism with Nietzschean overtones made Reich's radical interventions part of a larger intellectual formation that included Franz Jung and his literary experiments with collective agency. At the same time, Sex-Pol established a theoretical model based on which the emancipatory movements of the 1970s and beyond pursued their own experiments with lust in, and for, life. In ways that will prove important for the remaining pages, Reich's rediscovery as a key figure of Freudo-Marxism and his reassessment as part of a Foucauldian biopolitics has drawn renewed attention to his long-standing interest in somatic approaches to the body.[20] In its most (in)famous manifestation known as orgone energy, Reich's fascination with the preindividual, life-affirming force called life energy developed out of his intellectual debt to *Lebensphilosophie* and Nietzscheanism, including their enlistment in an aestheticization of masculinist positions. Before 1933, the combination of psychoanalytic, Marxist, and vitalist concepts allowed Reich to equate proletarian subjectivity with male heterosexual genitality. After 1935, he began to revise his sex political theories in line with a decidedly American philosophy of individualism. In light of such strategic adjustments to changing circumstances, Reich's sexual politics might be described best through what psychoanalysts Sebastian Hartmann and Siegfried Zepf call nineteenth-century biologism masking as (Marxist) materialism.[21]

The coupling of sex and politics in Reich was achieved through a contradiction, the superior genital health of the (male) proletariat and the deep sexual misery of the working class. In his writings, he repeatedly emphasized the con-

---

[20] Examples of the renewed interest in Reich include the 2007 exhibition at Vienna's Jüdisches Museum called "Wilhelm Reich—Sex! Pol! Energy!" which produced the catalog *Wilhelm Reich Revisited*, ed. Birgit Johler (Vienna: Verlag Turia+Kant, 2008), and the biopic by Antonin Svoboda, *Der Fall Wilhelm Reich* (2012), with Klaus Maria Brandauer in the title role; the latter was released together with the documentary *Wer hat Angst vor Wilhelm Reich?*

[21] Sebastian Hartmann and Siegfried Zepf, "Sankt Wilhelm oder die wahre Wahrheit eines 'wahren' Sozialisten," in *Der "Fall" Wilhelm Reich. Beiträge zum Verhältnis von Psychoanalyse und Politik*, ed. Karl Fallend and Bernd Nitzschke (Frankfurt am Main: Suhrkamp, 1997), 223–248. For two very different biographies, see Wilhelm Burian, *Psychoanalyse und Marxismus. Eine intellektuelle Biographie Wilhelm Reichs* (Frankfurt am Main: Makol, 1972) and Myron R. Sharaf, *Fury on Earth: A Biography of Wilhelm Reich* (New York: St. Martin's Press, 1983).

nection between class society and sexual repression and advocated relentlessly for the individual's right to sexual happiness, including through the separation of sexuality from procreation. According to Reich, the denial of infantile sexuality and the suppression of adolescent sexuality had a detrimental impact on the development of healthy genitality. However, his subsequent calls for sexual liberation in the spirit of heterosexual genitality were predicated on a double exclusion in the sexual and political realm. On one side, the exultation of communist potency required the denial of those oral and anal desires that Freud and others call polymorphous perverse and the pathologization of those sexual variants that for Magnus Hirschfeld, founder of the Wissenschaftlich-humanitäres Kommittee (Scientific-Humanitarian Committee), include homosexuality. On the other side, the affirmation of masculinity as the normative model of a healthy sexuality reduced the problem of femininity to a condition of lack. Within this logic, women had access to sexual and political agency only within the terms of masculinity, an argument that had profound consequences for their assigned role in the workers' movement.

Reich's scenarios of sexual and political revolution were based on timeworn clichés about the greater sexual prowess and healthier sexual appetites of the lower classes that had fueled the literary imagination since the French Revolution. These fantasies translated deep-seated fears about the power of the masses into highly sexualized terms. With proletarians thus cast as modern primitives, Reich, partly under the influence of the anthropologist Bronislaw Malinowski, freely speculated about "that part of natural sexuality that distinguishes the members of the exploited class from those of the ruling class and that has gradually been destroyed in the process of 'democratization' without ever disappearing altogether."[22] Lacking the economic goals and opportunities of the middle class, the workers presumably had no need to control their sexual urges and to comply with bourgeois conventions of marriage and family life. Despite the very real problems caused by poverty and hardship, proletarians presumably were less neurotic overall, with Reich concluding that "genitality is all the more unrestrained, the worse the material living conditions are."[23] Accordingly, the ideal-typical revolutionary distinguished himself through a specific sociosexual habitus (i.e., open, direct, simple) against which everything and everyone

---

[22] Reich, *Die Massenpsychologie des Faschismus*, 144. Reich draws on an anthropological perspective (indebted to Malinowski) on sexuality in primitive communist societies to buttress his argument for sexual liberation in *Der Einbruch der Sexualmoral. Zur Geschichte der sexuellen Ökonomie*, sec. ed. (Copenhagen: Verlag für Sexualpolitik, 1935).

[23] Wilhelm Reich, *Die Funktion des Orgasmus. Zur Psychopathologie und zur Soziologie des Geschlechtslebens* (Leipzig: Internationaler Psychoanalytischer Verlag, 1927), 169.

else could be described as artificial, excessive, and degenerate. "How does one recognize the character traits of the true revolutionary?" Reich asked in 1934, sounding almost like a party functionary: "Plain outer composure, ability to engage directly with people, simple, natural demeanor in sexual matters, ordinary, no posing or ranting, not only an emotional but primarily a rational commitment to socialism, no calcification of the party apparatus, no patriarchal attitude toward women and children."[24]

The difficulties of reconciling Reich's original program of a transgressive proletarian sexuality with this normative description of the true revolutionary as communist ascetic cannot be explained through the different political situations in Red Vienna and Reich's Copenhagen exile or through the changing priorities of an international antifascist Popular Front. Instead both positions will be used here to reveal continuities in Reich's thought from early observations about the unbounded sexuality of the modern masses to later reflections on the protoplasmic flows that represent the somatic source of life itself. Translated into Marxist terms, these life energies are the main concern of what Reich, during the Weimar years, calls the sex economy, the system of libidinal blockages and ossifications that organizes sexual repression under conditions of monopoly capitalism. Many of these ideas were first presented in *Die Funktion des Orgasmus* (1928, *The Function of the Orgasm*), an influential pamphlet about the importance of orgasmic potency for emotional health and the transformative quality of what he calls full-body genital orgasm. His bioenergetic approach allows Reich to combine the politics of sex and the economics of desire in what, at the time, appeared as the most compelling model of explanation for their shared sources and energies – namely Freudo-Marxism; it also accounts for his main disagreements with the psychoanalytic concept of (bourgeois) subjectivity. The theoretical program of sexual economy acknowledges the close connection between the historically determined structure of the drives, beyond the given amount of somatic energy, and the social and economic conditions of working-class life, including emotional life, under capitalism. Yet his heavy use of economy as a metaphor eventually shifts the argument to another model of bioenergetic flows and exchanges that extends the analysis to precapitalist times and includes, rather surprisingly, a critique of patriarchy. His surprising turn to anthropological perspectives reflects the recognition that the problem of what he calls self-subjugation is older than capitalism and must in fact be locat-

---

24 Ernst Parell [i.e., Wilhelm Reich], *Was ist Klassenbewußtsein? Ein Beitrag zur Diskussion über die Neuformierung der Arbeiterbewegung* (Copenhagen: Verlag für Sexualpolitik, 1934), 68–69. The treatise was first published in *Zeitschrift für politische Psychologie und Sexualökonomie*, the journal of the Sex-Pol movement.

ed in the structure of patriarchal societies. Making these insights available to class analysis allows Reich to propose a model of sexual economic self-regulation that, in contrast to the moral prohibitions in repressive societies, develops its ethical standards with a view toward the sociosexual health of the collective. Of course, the proposed integration of nature and culture, and of individual and society, into another kind of human history whose ultimate goal nonetheless remains communism further highlights the unresolvable tensions between liberationist and authoritarian tendencies in Reich's thought that would become only more pronounced during his life and work in the United States.

No passage captures his belief in communist revolution and his bioenergetic view of life better than the conclusion of *Was ist Klassenbewußtsein?* (1934, What is Class Consciousness?), a short treatise that calls on the workers to "learn not how to reject the personal but to politicize it."[25] Their most powerful weapons against the forces of political reaction, Reich insists once more, are the individual pursuit of happiness and the collective demand for satisfaction of their needs and desires. Given the centrality of the personal and political to his communist and postcommunist commitments, the final list of demands, offered in the spirit of antifascism, but already moving toward the language of psychotherapy, deserves to be quoted at length:

> The class consciousness of the masses is not knowledge of the historical and economic laws that govern the life of human beings, but it is:
> 1. knowledge of one's own vital needs in all areas;
> 2. knowledge of the means and possibilities of satisfying them;
> 3. knowledge of the obstacles that a social order based on private property puts in the way of their satisfaction;
> 4. knowledge of one's own inhibitions and anxieties that prevent one from understanding the necessities of one's life; [...]
> 5. knowledge that individuals unified as the masses make an invincible force against the power of the oppressors.[26]

Removed from the organizational and ideological frameworks that had inspired and sustained Sex-Pol during the Weimar years, Reich's emancipatory project in exile became entirely focused on the individual, with the radicalizing force of lust now limited to the therapeutic project of self-discovery within capitalist society. Without the mutually constitutive analysis of political and sexual economy,

---

[25] Wilhelm Reich, "Reforming the Labor Movement," in *Sex-Pol Essays: 1929–1934*, ed. Lee Baxandall, intro. Bertell Ollmann, trans. Anna Bostock (New York: Random House, 1972), 367.
[26] Reich, *Was ist Klassenbewußtsein?*, 65. Translated into English as "What is Class Consciousness?," in *Sex-Pol Essays*, 275–358.

the proletarian fantasy gave way to the individual credo of self-maximization. Evidence of the process of adaptation to American conditions, the German word *Kenntnis*, which denotes both consciousness and cognition, is reduced to the more limited "knowledge" in the English translation of the passage cited above. Phrases like "the power of the oppressors" still retain the sound of communist agitation. However, references to "satisfaction" or "inhibitions and anxieties" already announce Reich's conceptual shift from collective to individual liberation.

Confirming such readings, the subtitle "On the Sexual Economy of Political Reaction and on Proletarian Sexual Politics" was deleted from the first English translation of *The Mass Psychology of Fascism* (1946) distributed by the Orgone Institute Press. Together with the subtitle, all references to proletarian culture and the Sex-Pol movement were likewise expunged to make room for what Reich in the new introduction calls the more inclusive model of work-democracy. He even explains his self-editing: "There are no class distinctions when it comes to character. For that reason, the purely economic concepts of 'bourgeoisie' and 'proletariat' were replaced by the concepts 'reactionary' and 'revolutionary' or 'free-minded,' which relate to man's character and not to his social class. These changes were forced upon us by the fascist plague."[27] By declaring the project of proletarian revolution a victim of fascism, the late Reich was able to salvage the project of sexual revolution for contemporary appropriations. However, this meant sacrificing the proletariat, that group of men and women who in the early 1920s inspired his radical theories about sexuality and class and who provided the collective body recognized in his provocative calls for sexual and political revolution.

As this chapter has shown, Wilhelm Reich played a key role in the discovery of Freudo-Marxism by the student movement and was venerated as an intellectual forefather of various New Left movements and countercultural groups during the 1970s. Another famous Weimar contemporary, John Heartfield, was also rediscovered during that turbulent time, namely as the originator of political photomontage and an aesthetic habitus of rage perfected in the fight against fascism. It is unclear whether Reich and Heartfield crossed paths during their years in Berlin, but it is fairly easy to see how their intellectual (or artistic) biographies played a key role in their political radicalization and why they at times succumbed to the attractions of communist orthodoxy and heteronormative masculinity. Moreover, based on earlier discussions of the representation of collective bodies by the Cologne Progressives and the performance of embodied ideology in com-

---

27 Reich, *The Mass Psychology of Fascism*, xxiv.

munist agitprop, it should not surprise that the radicalizing effects of photomontage can be analyzed with particular clarity through one recurring visual motif in Heartfields's photomontages, the hand that becomes a fist.

Chapter 17
John Heartfield's Productive Rage

> John Heartfield today *knows how to salute beauty*. He knows how to create those images which are the very beauty of our age since they represent the cry of the people. [...] His art is art in Lenin's sense for it is a weapon in the revolutionary struggle of the proletariat. [...] He knows no signpost other than dialectical materialism, none other than the reality of the historical process, which he, filled with the anger of battle (*rage du combat*), translates into black and white.
>
> Louis Aragon, "John Heartfield and Revolutionary Beauty"

Anger and rage are powerful artistic weapons. No Weimar artist was more aware of their strategic function than the famous *photomonteur* John Heartfield (1891–1968), and no fellow communist knew this better than the French writer Louis Aragon whose paean to revolutionary beauty singles out Heartfield for uniting aesthetics and politics in the name of the proletariat.[1] During the Weimar years, Heartfield systematically developed further the connection between aesthetic and political emotions that chapters 10 and 11 have examined under the heading of proletarian modernism.

Defined less by any specific artistic form or style than by its class-based, interventionist approach to formal innovation, proletarian modernism emerged at the intersection of avant-garde movements and left-wing radicalisms in close dialogue with new media technologies and cultural theories. The main proponents faced many challenges in asserting their socialist commitments, among them the antimodernist positions prevalent among KPD critics, the enduring preference of Social Democrats for nineteenth-century forms and styles, and the mass-produced attractions offered by the culture industry and realized in the democratic modalities of what Miriam Hansen has called vernacular modernism. Like the writer Franz Jung (discussed in chapter 10) and the artist Franz Wilhelm Seiwert (discussed in chapter 11), Heartfield set out to expose the power structures in capitalist societies by rejecting conventional notions of realism as verisimilitude, and like the others, he aimed to strengthen class-based attachments without recourse to traditional forms of identification. Choosing photomontage as his preferred artistic medium, Heartfield though was unique in draw-

---

[1] Louis Aragon, "John Heartfield and Revolutionary Beauty" (1935), cited in Wendy Ann Parker, "Political Photomontage: Transformation, Revelation, and 'Truth'" (PhD diss., University of Iowa, 2011), Appendix A, 129–130.

ing on a singular emotion – what his brother Wieland Herzfelde called *produktiver Jähzorn* (productive rage) – and making its formal manifestations the organizing principle behind his approach to political photomontage.[2]

In this chapter, the term "productive rage" will be used to approach the making of proletarian identifications through the language of embodied ideology and one particular visual motif, that of hands and fists. When Herzfelde used the term in a 1962 biography of the younger brother, he explained his all-consuming rage in psychological terms, that is, the result of having been abandoned by their parents – in Heartfield's case, at the age of seven. This traumatic experience, Herzfelde concluded, fueled the strong sense of injustice that Heartfield channeled into his fervent belief in the future of communism.[3] It would be easy, all too easy, to rely on psychobiography to explain both his need for artistic innovation and his tendency toward political dogmatism. In fact, many of the socialists and communists mentioned in this book suffered parental abandonment or neglect, endured lifelong illnesses and disabilities, and, as a consequence of their political activism, experienced economic hardship, political persecution, as well as years of imprisonment and exile. These individual experiences, in ways that cannot be elaborated here, contributed to the making of collective imaginaries – but in Heartfield's case, through the discourse of rage (i.e., *rage du combat*, *produktiver Jähzorn*) that assumed a central place in the emotional regimes associated with proletarian modernism. With the exception perhaps of George Grosz, no other Weimar artist employed modernist techniques with such visceral contempt and disgust: contempt for the political elites and disgust with the hypocrisies of bourgeois life. The degree to which the aggressive gestus of photomontage served as protection against a very different set of emotions – fear, despair, and powerlessness – can only be raised as a question, since pursuing this line of inquiry with regards to Heartfield's relationship to the KPD would require a psychobiographical discussion of communist militancy and Weimar masculinity.

Confirming the destructive energies inherent in photomontage, the surviving originals for the posters, fliers, and magazine covers that Heartfield created for the KPD and affiliated organizations often resemble battlefields marked by cuts,

---

2 Wieland Herzfelde, *John Heartfield: Leben und Werk. Dargestellt von seinem Bruder* (Dresden: VEB Verlag der Kunst, 1976), 18. In her analysis of the relationship between the brothers, Nancy Roth translates the phrase as "high-energy temper;" see "Heartfield's Collaboration," *Oxford Art Journal* 29.3 (2006): 395–418.

3 Herzfelde, *John Heartfield*, 12. After the war, the psychobiographies of Weimar-era communists would become part of the selective reclamation in the GDR of Weimar modernism for the socialist heritage; as to be expected, fear and shame have no place in these accounts.

tears, erasures, and inscriptions. Unlike Kurt Schwitters or Hannah Höch, Heartfield never had any interest in exploring the ambiguity and multivalence revealed through such textual rupturing and suturing. Rhetorically his photomontages are either for or against, animated by complete opposition or full agreement; his default emotional style always involves struggle. Not surprisingly, photomontage for him was synonymous with partisanship, a vehicle for channeling painful experiences into a singular outward emotion, rage, and translating deep-seated antagonisms into simple political slogans. Heartfield's unique contribution to the proletarian dream can therefore be described as two-fold: as a historical case study on how a communist artist employs the discourse of rage to forge proletarian identifications – and does so against a long Social Democratic tradition emphasizing peace and harmony; and as a methodological reflection on the relationship between political emotion and artistic technique that reevaluates the propagandistic potential of photomontage outside the familiar binaries of manipulation and critique.

Nothing is better suited to retrace the formal manifestations of Heartfield's productive rage than his sustained interest in the most symbolically charged part of the working-class body and the proletarian body politic: the hand. In fact, Sergei Tretyakov was the first to note the photomonteur's preoccupation with hands, concluding that, "in Heartfield, the hand plays an even more important role in the composition than the face. Rarely does an artist manage so well to convey the appearance of a person through the representation of the hand."[4] The nineteenth-century workers' movements had made the raised fist their official salute, a practice that continues in civil rights and liberation movements to this day. Working within these traditions, Heartfield repeatedly used hand images to address questions of labor and industry and juxtapose the conditions of production in capitalist and communist societies. Toward the end of the Weimar Republic, hands and fists were enlisted primarily to express his full support for the Communists and organize his unrelenting attacks on the National Socialists.

---

4 Sergei Tretyakov, reprinted in Roland März, ed., *John Heartfield: Der Schnitt entlang der Zeit. Selbstzeugnisse Erinnerungen Interpretationen, Eine Dokumentation* (Dresden: Verlag der Kunst, 1981), 311.

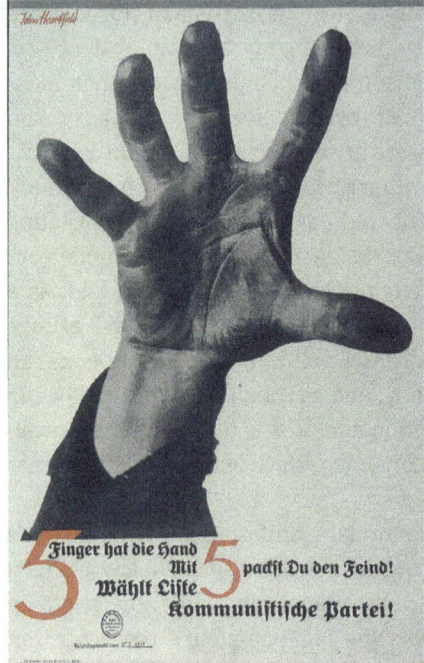

Fig. 17.1 John Heartfield, *5 Finger hat die Hand/Five Fingers Has the Hand* (1928), KPD election poster, Bundesarchiv-Bildarchiv. Copyright 2017 The Heartfield Community of Heirs/Artists Rights Society (ARS), New York/VG Bild-Kunst Bonn.

Fig. 17.2 Heartfield's KPD election poster on the streets of Berlin, photograph. With permission of Bundesarchiv-Bildarchiv.

For the KPD election campaign in 1928, the Dada provocateur-turned-communist propagandist designed a well-known poster, *5 Finger hat die Hand* (Five Fingers Has the Hand), the first of several works included in later exhibitions as perfect exemplars of politically committed art. Capturing the gestus of dissent in a simple gesture, Heartfield's contribution can almost be treated as a political primer on the representational practices through which "hand" and "fist" came to function as contingent and consecutive terms (see figure 17.1). The sense of urgency conveyed by the election poster may even have swayed some voters in cities such as Berlin to vote for the Communists. On 20 May 1928, the day of the Reichstag election, the KPD received a surprising 10.6 percent of the vote (up 1.7 percent), while the SPD remained the strongest party with 29.8 percent. Meanwhile the NSDAP had to content itself with a meager 2.6 percent. Emboldened, the KPD leadership interpreted declining support for the established parties and widespread disaffection with democracy as confirmation of their Moscow-endorsed confrontation course with the SPD. In reality, the proletarian dream was already being appropriated, if not hijacked, by a very different kind of socialist revolution. Five years later, the KPD was banned and Heartfield forced into exile in Prague and, later, London. His postwar reputation as the inventor of political photomontage would not come from his extensive work for the KPD, but from the antifascist photomontages that appeared on the covers of *Arbeiter-Illustrierte-Zeitung* (*AIZ*, Workers Pictorial Newspaper) during the early 1930s and in exile publications such as *Volk-Illustrierte* (*VI*) throughout World War II.[5]

A deceptively simple design, *Five Fingers* depicts a man's open hand against a neutral white background, with the fingers slightly curled and the lines of the palm clearly visible. The hand's size and shape, together with the dark cuff of the boilersuit, suggest an industrial worker, with the shaded areas on the left evoking the dirt and grime of manual labor. As was his practice, Heartfield retouched the original photograph, in this case in order to intensify the gesture of grasping and seizing. The intended message is one of confidence and determination, but in light of the interrelatedness of rage and fear, the raised hand might also suggest a man (and a party) pleading for help. In fact, the oddly long index finger is reminiscent of Christian hand signs and an established iconography of sacrifice that the communist ethos of party discipline repeatedly referenced. The artist's signature in the upper left and the number five are drawn in bright red. This centrally placed "5" appears as part of two slogans, "With 5 You Seize the Enemy" and "Vote List 5 Communist Party." The slippage, in the mode of address, from the second person singular ("You Seize") to the plural imperative ("Vote"), prefigures the necessary move from individual to collective agency that presumably will produce a successful election outcome – if need be, through violent action. Lest there be any doubts about the implied relationship between hand and fist, it was Ernst Thälmann, the leader of the KPD, who personally approved the poster and, in another context, allegedly said: "You can break one finger, but five fingers make a fist."[6]

---

5 For a historical perspective on the 1928 electoral campaign, see Eric D. Weitz, *Creating German Communism, 1890–1990: From Popular Protests to Socialist State* (Princeton: Princeton University Press, 1997), 62–99.

6 Original: "Einen Finger kann man brechen, aber fünf Finger sind eine Faust." The often-quoted sentence appears in Kurt Maetzig's two-part biopic *Ernst Thälmann, Sohn seiner Klasse* (1954). On Thälmann's reaction to the poster, see the memo by Gertrud Heartfield reprinted in März, *John Heartfield*, 51.

Fig. 17.3 John Heartfield, *Die Rote Fahne*, 20 May 1928, cover, Deutsches Historisches Museum. Copyright 2017 The Heartfield Community of Heirs/Artists Rights Society (ARS), New York/VG Bild-Kunst Bonn.

In May 1928, on the streets of Berlin and elsewhere, Heartfield's posters could be found on apartment buildings, underpasses, and construction fences where they took on the appearance of artist's multiples, with their rows of raised hands suggesting an almost religious form of supplication (see figure 17.2). One week before the election, *Five Fingers* appeared again on the front page of *Die Rote Fahne*, the daily newspaper of the KPD, with the fingertips now reaching across its masthead, a telling indication of the infiltration of writing by more aggressive impulses. On election day, the number "5" (i.e., the number under which the KPD was listed on the ballot) acquired an even more dangerous quality when the newspaper's front page showed five Weimar politicians, including a member of the SPD, hanging from nooses attached to these numbers, a shocking illustration of the KPD's social fascism thesis (see figure 17.3).[7] One year later, the

---

[7] Cover of *Die Rote Fahne*, 20 May 1928. The "victims" are Chancellor Wilhelm Marx, Foreign Minister Gustav Stresemann, Interior Minister Walther von Keudell (spelled Keudel here), former Interior Minister Wilhelm Külz, SPD politician Arthur Crispien, and NSDAP leader Adolf Hitler.

influential 1929 *Film und Foto* exhibition in Stuttgart opened with an entire section devoted to Heartfield that displayed *Five Fingers* under the above-mentioned motto of "Benütze Foto als Waffe" (see figure 17.4). And two years after that, the poster was exhibited in the Pushkin Museum in Moscow, amid works by George Grosz and others, but now under a banner declaring, "Glory to the Soviet Union. Glory to the Dictatorship of the Proletariat."[8] Given the various political and artistic contexts in which *Five Fingers* appeared during the Weimar years, its arrival in the Soviet Union at the height of Stalinism cannot be seen as anything but a logical extension of its originating emotional and political impulses.

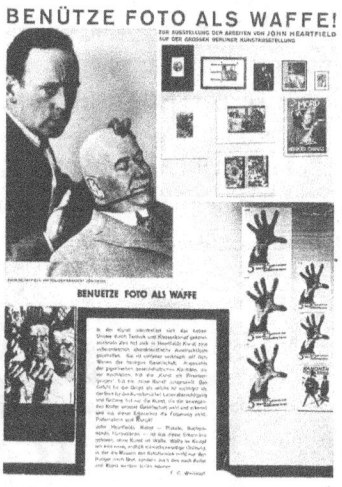

Fig. 17.4 John Heartfield, 1920 self-portrait, photograph, Akademie der Künste Archiv, Berlin. Copyright 2017 The Heartfield Community of Heirs/Artists Rights Society (ARS), New York/VG Bild-Kunst Bonn.

Fig. 17.5 1929 *Film und Foto* Exhibition in Stuttgart, John Heartfield exhibit "Benütze Foto als Waffe! Use photography as a weapon!" *AIZ* 29.37 (1929): 17. This includes his 1929 self-portrait with Police Commissioner Zörgiebel. Akademie der Künste Archiv, Berlin.

Confirming this point, on two occasions in the 1920s, Heartfield used his own hands to establish the gestus of photomontage as one of emphatic appeal as well as violent assault. Both self-portraits corroborate Andrés Mario Zervigón's

---

8 My thanks to Mark Smith for the translation from the Russian.

description of Heartfield's photographic practice as "an emotional rather than a rational means of communication."[9] Establishing his public persona as a Dada artist, an early self-portrait from 1920 features the artist in profile, with sharp, tight facial features and his hands raised plaintively (see figure 17.4). Eerily reminiscent of later portraits of Nazi propaganda minister Joseph Goebbels, his self-representation combines aspects of the figure of the angry artist with that of the skilled agitator.[10] A second self-portrait appears as part of a photomontage in *AIZ* 7.37 (1929) together with the command to "Use Photography as a Weapon" (see figure 17.5). Significantly, Heartfield inserts himself into the picture frame in order to complete the transition from political artist to activist. He literally cuts off the head of SPD Police Commissioner Zörgiebel and, in so doing, demonstrates how a primal emotion can be translated into an artistic technique and how the latter, in turn, can give rise to a revolutionary movement. Emphasizing this connection, Franz Carl Weiskopf, in the accompanying text, describes Heartfield's cutting as "a weapon in the struggle for a new, truly humane society where the workers are able not just to satisfy their hunger for bread but for culture and art as well."[11]

By the end of the industrial revolution, hands had become a convenient shorthand in visual representations of modern industry, technology, capitalism, and the working class.[12] New mass movements, including the workers' move-

---

[9] Andrés Mario Zervigón, *John Heartfield and the Agitated Image: Photography, Persuasion, and the Rise of Avant-garde Photomontage* (Chicago: University of Chicago Press, 2012), 6.

[10] In this early Dada self-portrait, Heartfield not only looks uncannily like Goebbels; his expressive hand gestures also resemble the oratorical poses developed by Hitler in collaboration with his personal photographer Heinrich Hoffmann. For a close reading of the later image, see Sabine Kriebel, "John Heartfields Selbstporträt von 1929," in *John Heartfield: Zeitausschnitte Fotomontagen 1918–1938*, ed. Freya Mülhaupt (Ostfildern: Hatje Canz, 2009), 64–73. Interestingly, the poster for Helmut Herbst's film essay *John Heartfield Fotomonteur* (1977) also features images of hands with and without scissors in different positions.

[11] The occasion for the publication in *AIZ* was an article about the 1929 Greater Berlin Art Exhibition.

[12] For a discussion of the rich symbolism of the clenched fist, see Gottfried Korff, "Rote Fahnen und geballte Faust. Zur Symbolik der Arbeiterbewegung in der Weimarer Republik," in *Fahnen, Fäuste, Körper. Symbolik und Kultur der Arbeiterbewegung*, ed. Dietmar Petzina (Essen: Klartext, 1986), 27–60. Korff links these symbols to the experience of loss of utopia, with (pseudo)religious images and ideas replaced by concrete political programs. For the continuities between Communist and Nazi uses of the fist as a political symbol, see Sherwin Simmons, "'Hand to the Friend, Fist to the Foe': The Struggle of Signs in the Weimar Republic," *Journal of Design History* 13.4 (2000): 319–339. For a comparative history of the fist in the larger context of totalitarian politics, also see Steven Heller, *Iron Fists: Branding the 20th-Century Totalitarian State* (London: Phaidon, 2008).

ment, had appropriated the hand – raised or extended, offered or withheld – as a powerful symbol of political unity and strength. As Barbara McCloskey has shown, Grosz's contribution to this emerging communist iconography became an important inspiration for Heartfield.[13] It can also be assumed that he was familiar with the 1917 cartoon "The Hand that Will Rule the World," published in *Solidarity*, the journal of the International Workers of the World (IWW), known as Wobblies. After the October Revolution, this gesture acquired a more violent charge on communist election posters, such as the 1920 "Vote for Spartakus" (i.e., the precursor of the KPD), which depicts a bright red (bloody) fist smashing an ineffectual Reichstag. A comparison to Lucian Bernhard's famous 1915 poster for a war bond drive indicates that this symbolism of the fist was part and parcel of a broader militarization of civil society during and after the war. The same can be said about later Nazi propaganda posters depicting muscular German workers crushing the representatives of parliamentary democracy and global finance capital. The graphic quality and simple visual message of these political posters clearly influenced Heartfield's design of the circular logo for the RFB (Alliance of Red Front Fighters), the paramilitary group affiliated with the KPD, that features a massive raised fist, knuckles directed outward, set against the backdrop of a mass demonstration. It is not known whether the KPD adopted the raised fist as its official salute after Heartfield created the Rotfront logo, as Aragon claims in the above-cited paean to "revolutionary beauty" (see figure 17.6). However, it stands to reason that the anticapitalist and antidemocratic sentiments shared by KPD and NSDAP made it increasingly difficult to promote the fist as a valid gestural alternative to the Nazi salute, given its proliferation on Nazi election posters from 1929 onward that, with exhortations like "Put an End to Corruption! Vote National Socialists!," show large red fists crushing so-called Jewish-Bolshevik conspiracies.

Hands and fists were part of a widespread preoccupation, if not obsession, in Weimar visual culture – inseparable from the modern body discourses that rejected the bourgeois cultivation of psychological interiority in favor of the physicality of manual labor, sports, and sexuality. From the sinewy hands in the expressionist portraits of Oskar Kokoschka and the surrealist hand photograms by László Moholy-Nagy to the famous posters for Fritz Lang's *M* (1931), with its ominous red letter inscribed in the murderer's palm, hands offered a convenient way of affirming the values of individualism while exploring the new languages of collective bodies. Avant-garde artists and photographers used men's hands to re-

---

[13] See Barbara McCloskey, *George Grosz and the Communist Party: Art and Radicalism in Crisis, 1918 to 1936* (Princeton: Princeton University Press, 1997), 101.

Fig. 17.6 John Heartfield, Rotfront logo, cover of *Der rote Stern* 11 (May 1928), Deutsche Nationalbibliothek Leipzig. Copyright 2017 The Heartfield Community of Heirs/Artists Rights Society (ARS), New York/VG Bild-Kunst Bonn.

flect on the crisis of modern subjectivity. Meanwhile, in countless cigarette ads, well-groomed women's hands became emblems of the new culture of mass diversion. The popular pseudoscience of chiromancy promised access to the soul of modern man through the reading of palms. The practice of fingerprinting in modern criminology used similar assumptions about the readability of the body for the disciplinary regimes of the modern penal code.[14] Meanwhile, in modern factories and industries, the problem with hands – that is, the need to control and ultimately replace them – was to be addressed through radical innovations in the forms of scientific management known as Taylorism and the modes of industrial production associated with Fordism.

Trained in advertising and graphic design, Heartfield was familiar with the advanced methods and techniques that, in early twentieth-century visual culture, made marketing and propaganda almost coextensive terms. In turning individual hands into symbols of collective strength, he relied heavily on modern typography to transform a vague sense of indignation into more targeted expressions of class hatred, beginning with his graphic approach to captions and slo-

---

[14] It might be productive to consider the surrealist elements in Heartfield through a comparison to another famous hand associated with the communist avant-garde, the hand crawling with ants in Luis Buñuel's *Un Chien Andalou* (1929).

gans. His mode of address always involves imperatives, and his exhortations always refer to struggle and confrontation. For instance, on the cover of the KPD's 1927 May Day *Festzeitung*, Heartfield pairs the image of three male workers raising their fists with the closing line from *The Communist Manifesto*, "Proletarians of all countries, unite!" An election poster from 1930 enlists a male and female worker holding up a hammer and sickle to implore voters to "Fight with us." Captions from *AIZ* covers include appeals and declarations such as "Hit hard, proletarian! So that a new world emerges from misery and pain," "We all only know one enemy, the class of exploiters," or "All fists clenched into one, show the fascists your power!"[15] The combination of images and texts invariably aims at cognitive clarification and emotional intensification. Thus the word "hit" in "Hit hard, proletarian!" is placed above a hammer forging a white-hot piece of iron, and the caption of "We only know one enemy" appears right next to the fists of a white and a black man.

Nothing captures Heartfield's agitational method better than the slogan *Foto als Waffe* (photography as a weapon), which was displayed prominently in several exhibitions of his work during the last years of the Weimar Republic. This militaristic terminology marked a sharp departure from the aspirational discourse on culture and education (discussed in chapter 8) and the belief in aesthetic experience as self-actualization in the humanist tradition. Following Friedrich Wolf's announcement that "art is a weapon!"[16] the old distinctions between purposeless enjoyment and purposeful instruction no longer served any purpose for a new generation of communist photographers and graphic designers. Photography came to occupy a central place in the ensuing battle over images and imaginaries, with Adolf Behne describing photomontages as "photography plus dynamite"[17] and Kurt Tucholsky calling on all communists to "fight in league with photography."[18] The large gun on the Heartfield cover for Franz Jung's *The Conquest of the Machines* confirms that the reference to "weapon" in these contexts can be understood in very literal terms. In *Die Rote Fahne*, even

---

15 The captions are from *AIZ* 9.52 (1930), 13.36 (1934), and 13.49 (1934). A number of these images have been reprinted in David King and Ernst Volland, *John Heartfield: Laughter Is a Devastating Weapon* (London: Tate Publishing, 2015).
16 See Friedrich Wolf, *Kunst ist Waffe! Eine Feststellung* (Berlin: Arbeiter-Theater-Bund Deutschland, 1928).
17 Ignaz Wrobel [i.e., Kurt Tucholsky], "Die Tendenzphotographie," *Die Weltbühne* 21 (17 April 1925): 637.
18 Adolf Behne, "Die Kunst als Waffe," *Die Weltbühne* 27.34/35 (1931): 301–304. Behne's assertion is taken from the 1931 article "John Heartfield (Künstler des Proletariats)," reprinted in März, ed., *John Heartfield*, 185–187.

Durus declared montage a "Marxist method of artistic creation" ideally suited for uncovering the contradictions in social reality. Indeed, his advice to photomonteurs, "to hammer the truth into people's brains over and over again – the truth of exploitation, of the degrading capitalist system, of the conditions of the liberation of the proletariat – and thus to agitate and propagandize the masses as effectively as we possibly can"[19] reads very much like a description of Heartfield's own use of hands, often in combination with tools, in unleashing the emotional forces of class struggle.

Five Fingers is a typical example of Heartfield's work for the KPD, but it does not fit easily into prevailing views of photomontage as a form of resistance and an exercise in dissent. As a propagandist for the KPD, Heartfield obviously could not draw on the corrosive force of biting satire and absurdist humor that animated his famous antifascist photomontages and inspired what art historian Sabine Kriebel appropriately calls "left-wing laughter." His KPD allegiances have been impossible to ignore ever since Sergei Tretyakov, in the first monograph on the artist, declared that, "his photomontages cannot be separated from his party work. In fact, they are a history of the Communist Party of Germany."[20] A member of the KPD since the day of its founding on 30 December 1918, Heartfield continues to this day to cause methodological problems because of the constitutive tension in his Weimar-era work between political dogmatism and artistic innovation. It is easy to claim his antifascist photomontages for the cause of democratic modernism and to celebrate his modernist montage as critical intervention; it is much more difficult to draw the same conclusions about the antidemocratic positions in his work for the KPD. If photomontages are indeed forms of assault – sharp shots, in Tretyakov's phrase – what can be concluded about their intended targets and effects? More specifically, what does Heartfield's productive rage suggest about the role of emotions in the making of proletarian identifications?

These questions require some critical reassessment of what Kriebel describes as the contested status of photomontage as a technique of either rupture (i.e., the standard interpretation) or suture, a term adapted from Lacanian-inspired

---

19 Durus [i.e., Alfred Kemény], "Photomontage, Photogram," trans. Joel Agee, in *Photography in the Modern Era: European Documents and Critical Writings, 1913–1940*, ed. Christopher Phillips (New York: Metropolitan Museum of Art, 1989), 184. For a later argument on the affinity between photomontage and proletarian identifications, see Eckhard Siepmann, "Was hat das Proletariat mit der Fotografie, die Fotografie mit der Montage und die Montage mit dem Proletariat zu tun?," in *Politische Fotomontage*, ed. Jürgen Holtfreter (Berlin: Elefanten Press, 1971), 25–33.
20 Tretyakov, cited in Herzfelde, *John Heartfield*, 332. Interestingly, Tretyakov's book also features *Five Fingers* on its cover.

film theory that in her view best captures the integrative, illusionist tendencies in Heartfield's work.[21] The scholarship on Heartfield, she rightly notes, has privileged elements of shock and conflict in order to maintain photomontage's status as an artistic technique well suited for the democratic narratives of modernism prevalent during the Cold War. Examining the more elusive but equally important processes of suturing, of "being stitched into" fictional worlds and, by extension, ideological configurations, brings into closer view those constellations when critical detachment is not needed and adherence to political doctrine required. In other words, how does Heartfield's productive rage complicate the conceptual alternatives of rupture and suture posited by Kriebel in her revisionist reading of photomontage?

At first glance, a KPD poster like *Five Fingers* can easily be read as an example of suture, with the hand on the poster becoming the hand in the voting booth. Here interpellation occurs quite literally through what Louis Althusser, in his definition of the term, compares to the act of hailing. In identifying with, and as, a worker, the subject thus hailed acts out the desired identity of proletarian and communist. By the same token, the *AIZ* covers where Heartfield cuts and pastes to unmask the representatives of the ruling class may be seen as typical examples of rupture, with the contradictions in society made visible through the clash between decontextualized and recontextualized images or between images and texts. However, the rhetorical use of contrast and contradiction in transforming anger into laughter does not necessarily justify the automatic equation of rupture with critique. After all, in the photomontages that focus on the class enemy, the proletarian subject remains beyond the framework, with Heartfield deconstructing the world of appearance but also constructing new classed subjects in line with KPD doctrine. For the same reason, photomontages that conceal the fact that they are made up of reality fragments are no more manipulative or less self-reflexive than ones that rely on multiperspectivism in their compositional approach. Formalist readings that argue otherwise cannot in the final analysis account for the constitutive tension between defensive dogmatism and aggressive irreverence in Heartfield's Weimar-era work. The dynamics of rupture and suture, including their respective formal techniques and propagandistic effects, can only be evaluated within the larger ideological contexts that made the identity of class and party a prerequisite and intended outcome of these in-

---

21 Sabine Kriebel, *Revolutionary Beauty: The Radical Photomontages of John Heartfield* (Berkeley: University of California Press, 2014); early versions of two chapters were published as "Manufacturing Discontent: John Heartfield's Mass Medium," *New German Critique* 36.2 (2009): 53–88 and "Photomontage in the Year 1932: John Heartfield and the National Socialists," *Oxford Art Journal* 31.1 (2008): 97–127.

terpellative effects. Reevaluated in that way, the corresponding artistic techniques represents above all a politically motivated division of labor, with the first reserved for various capitalist, bourgeois, and fascist others and the second performed on the collective body of the imaginary proletariat itself.

Despite the simple design, the meaning of the open hand in *Five Fingers* is far from unambiguous after all: Must the gesture be interpreted as an act of aggression, as suggested by the command "Seize the Enemy"? If so, who is the enemy? Conservative bourgeois parties, such as the German National People's Party and the Catholic Center Party, or the KPD's rivals on the left and right, the so-called "social fascists" (e. g., SPD) and the National Socialists? Or is the gesture a demand to be counted and heard – a demand made to the institutions of Weimar democracy in response to the countless anticommunist measures passed since the fateful days of January 1919? Can the curled fingers be understood as an invitation, directed at the workers themselves who are to be seized by this display of political strength? Or, as yet another possibility, must the extended hand be read as a desperate gesture to save communism from state violence and Nazi aggression? Answering these questions requires at least some consideration of the long history of hands as symbols of divine and human creation and the much shorter history of hands as symbols of the workers' movement.

Hands have figured prominently in religious and secular art ever since Leonardo da Vinci's *Study of Hands* (1474), the inspiration for *The Creation of Adam* in the Sistine Chapel, and Albrecht Dürer's famous etching *Praying Hands* (1508) established their relevance to discourses of faith and work. Intricately drawn hands allowed artists to demonstrate their familiarity with basic human anatomy and their mastery of artistic tools and techniques: paint, pencil, brush, or, in this case, scissors, masks, and retouching ink. Praying and working hands remained a ubiquitous reference point even as the medieval dictum of *ora et labora* (pray and work) was adapted to the decidedly modern regimes of class struggle and industrial labor. The ritualized gestures of supplication, instruction, and argumentation that endowed hands with spiritual qualities continued to inspire the visual archives for the representation of communist faith. It might even be argued that the tradition of the emblem – that is, the pictorial image of a concept with clear didactic functions – had a profound impact on Heartfield's approach to image-text relations, and did so in ways that indirectly confirm the close links between didactic and propagandistic functions and between religious and political traditions in the registers of proletarian modernism. Accordingly, in *Five Fingers*, the emblem's three-part structure returns in the *pictura*, which refers to the visual component of the emblem (i.e., the hand); the *inscriptio*, which makes an ethical demand or conveys a political message ("Five fingers has the hand/ with five fingers you seize the enemy"); and the *subscriptio*, which further clarifies the relationship between *inscriptio* and *picture* ("Vote for list 5/Vote for the Communists").

The gestural codes of communist rage were at once informed by, and mobilized against, the rich imagery of hands in Western art and the attendant discourse of faith and work that had sustained it since the Renaissance. A similar argument about strategies of appropriation can be made with regard to the gendered nature of hands in Heartfield's photomontages. Their contribution to the habitus of proletarian masculinity, which has already been discussed in chapters 10 and 14, is easily confirmed through a comparison with the very different hands – pleading, caressing, and protecting – in the woodcuts and drawings of Käthe Kollwitz. Her mothers and children serve to invite empathic identification with the working class. Even the men and women in the lithograph *Solidarität* (1932, Solidarity), created in celebration of the fifteenth anniversary of the October Revolution, stand for a compassionate version of communism that announces its social values through the highly symbolic gesture of joining hands.

In terms of emotional regimes, proletarian modernism involved a rejection of the sentimentality of nineteenth-century socialism (discussed in chapter 3) and the culture of empathy advocated by humanist socialists like Kollwitz or Otto Nagel, for that matter. Accordingly, Heartfield channeled the productive force of rage to the working-class recipient and, in the process, gave form to the historical subject-to-be, the proletariat under the leadership role of the KPD. His reliance on montage as an artistic technique for advancing the habitus of *Kampfkultur* took place across visual media and in active dialogue between the artistic and political avant-gardes, especially in the Soviet Union. In line with the collaborative nature of proletarian modernism, this process meant close cooperation with the Malik publishing house run by Wieland Herzfelde and the IAH (International Workers' Aid), Willi Münzenberg's communist media empire. Advancing the goals of communist internationalism, it meant extensive exchanges with Tretyakov, the most influential mediator between Berlin and Moscow, and creative encounters with El Lissitzky, Alexander Rodchenko, and Gustavs Klutsis. Above all, it meant embracing the decidedly masculinist vision of the New Soviet Man promoted by the Bolsheviks and celebrated by the photographers associated with Lef. Heartfield's photomontages have sometimes been described as techniques of demystification, but his works in support of the Soviet Union attest even more to his considerable skills at remystification – or, to use Kriebel's preferred term, suturing. On the remaining pages, these qualities will be examined through the return of an aesthetic form and didactic mode seemingly at odds with the shock and rupture of photomontage, namely allegory.

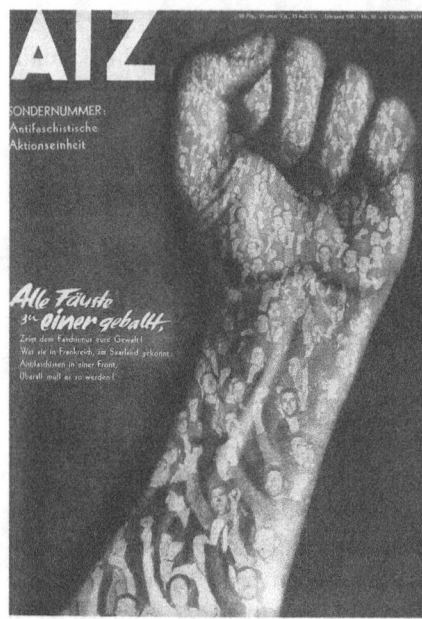

Fig. 17.7 John Heartfield, "Alle Fäuste zu einer geballt/All Fists Clenched into One," *AIZ* 13.49 (1934), photomontage, cover image. Copyright 2017 The Heartfield Community of Heirs/Artists Rights Society (ARS), New York/VG Bild-Kunst Bonn.

Fig. 17.8 Gustav Klutsis, "Workers! Everyone Must Vote in the Election of Soviets" (1930), photomontage, The Art Institute of Chicago. Copyright 2017 Estate of Gustav Klutsis Artists Rights Society (ARS), New York.

By the early 1930s, allegory once again offered itself as the aesthetic modality best suited for reconciling social reality and ideological fantasy while maintaining the emotional intensity that in the late 1910s had initially brought Heartfield to Dada Berlin. The rhetorics of allegory signaled a retreat from the referentiality of photography and added yet another layer of meaning to the indexicality of hands. In several photomontages made for the Association of the Friends of the New Russia, the hammer and sickle are no longer just workers' tools; the material objects are now reduced to communist symbols. Similarly, the hands holding these objects no longer belong to a male worker or a female peasant but to the disembodied standard bearers of world communism as defined by the Comintern. These allegorical tendencies became even more pronounced after the defeat of the KPD in 1933 and the projection of all hopes for revolution onto the Soviet Union, a process that aligned Heartfield's visual language even more closely with that of Klutsis. His cover for "A New Year!" *AIZ* 9.52 (1930) still refers to the material world of labor and industry – the steel is forged and the impact, as measured by the sparks, is profoundly physical. The accompanying text establishes a direct link between the blacksmith's daily work and the proletariat's historical mission: "A new year! A new year like every other? No!! It must not be! So that a new world can arise out of misery and pain: hit hard, proletarian!" However, on the cover of *AIZ* 13.36 (1934), the promise of communist victory already requires a surfeit of symbolism, from the four raised fists and a fifth hand holding the red flag with hammer and sickle on the left to Thälmann's head floating saint-like on the right. Finally, a special *AIZ* 13.40 (1934) issue promoting the Antifaschistische Aktionseinheit announces, "All fists clenched into one" (see figure 17.7) with its stylized fist made up of many men and women raising their fists.[22] Interestingly, Heartfield's visualization of the antifascist struggle is modeled on a 1930 photomontage by Klutsis that pairs a similar composite arm and fist with slogans like "Workers! Everyone must vote in the election of Soviets" and "Let's fulfill the plan of great works" (see figure 17.8).[23]

The unifying effect of productive rage behind Heartfield's consistent use of hands as an index and an icon of political mobilization could even be used to explain his surprising return to religious imagery during the London exile years – imagery that refers back to the Weimar period and the hidden connections, in life and art, between rage and suffering. Heartfield acknowledges as much when, for the March 1942 cover of the German anti-Nazi monthly *Freie deutsche Kultur*, he chooses a hand nailed to a cross-like Swastika that, even in this moment of greatest pain, preserves the defiant spirit of *Five Fingers* (see figure 17.9). These Christian references could be read as adaptation to the conditions of exile, as disillusionment with the project of communism, or as yet another example of the power of hands in managing political emotions across iconographic traditions and ideological positions. What is beyond doubt, however, is the central role of emotions as heuristic devices and organizing principles during that brief historical alliance between modern art and class politics called proletarian modernism. This is true even for a Heartfield friend and collaborator from the communist lifeworld of Weimar Berlin and, later, East Berlin usually associated with critical detachment and, most famously, the estrangement effect, Bertolt

---

22 Several other examples can be cited to support this argument about the centrality of the hand/fist motif in Heartfield: the black and white fists raised in solidarity in *AIZ* 10.26 (1931), the hands in front of the machine cogs announcing the new popular front policy in *AIZ* 15.20 (1936), and the raised hand, surrounded by electric sparks, that stands in for an underground radio station as the voice of freedom in *VI 16* (1937).
23 On the Heartfield-Klutsis connection, see Maria Gough, "Back in the USSR: John Heartfield, Gustavs Klucis, and the Medium of Soviet Propaganda," *New German Critique* 36.2 (2009): 133–183.

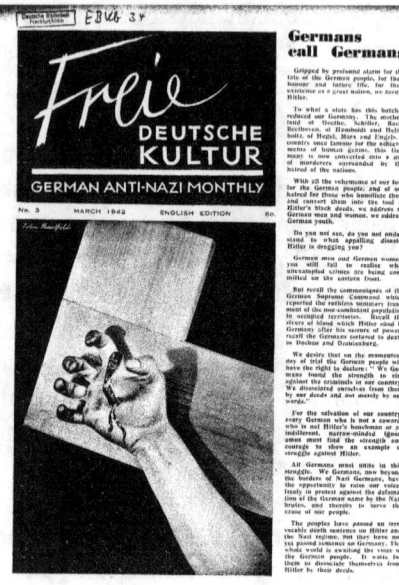

Fig. 17.9 John Heartfield, cover of *Freie Deutsche Kultur* 3 (March 1942), Deutsche Nationalbibliothek, Deutsche Exilarchiv 1933–1945. Copyright 2017 The Heartfield Community of Heirs/Artists Rights Society (ARS), New York/VG Bild-Kunst Bonn.

Brecht. In the larger context of this book, his involvement with *Kuhle Wampe*, that classic of leftist filmmaking from the late Weimar years, offers the perfect final case study both for the long history and the enduring relevance of proletarian identifications.

Chapter 18
Kuhle Wampe and "Those Who Don't Like It"

Brecht: Both Tretyakov and I agreed – in opposition to the bourgeois aesthetic of "entering into the spirit of things" – that works of art should be designed as models, analogous to those used in science. I hope I'll be able to discuss these ideas with other Soviet colleagues when we get to Moscow.
Eisenstein [Looks up]: You really believe that stuff? It sounds like a chemistry lesson. Chemistry without the magic.
Brecht [Lights his cigar butt]: When you get a chance to see our experiment, *Kuhle Wampe*, you'll –
Eisenstein [Brusquely]: I've already seen it. And that's exactly what's wrong with it. *Man merkt die Absicht.*

Lars Kleberg, "The Aquarians"

The pointed exchange between Bertolt Brecht and Sergei Eisenstein on a train somewhere between Berlin and Moscow never took place.[1] However, their argument concerns a real point of contention in Weimar-era debates on proletarian culture, namely the tension between artistic practices that define aesthetic experience as disinterested pleasure and the politically committed art that calls for more didactical, interventionist modes. The object of contention, *Kuhle Wampe, oder Wem gehört die Welt?* (1932, *Kuhle Wampe, or Who Owns the World?*), continued the formal experiments started by Jung, Seiwert, and Heartfield (see chapters 10, 11, and 17) in the quintessential modern mass medium of film. Often identified with Brecht and his theory of epic theater, this classic of leftist filmmaking draws on aspects of what Sergei Tretyakov (1892–1937), the influential Soviet writer and translator, calls operativity and will consequently be read as an example of operative filmmaking. Against the gendered divides that continued to dominate communist imaginaries, *Kuhle Wampe* mobilized a very different model of proletarian identifications. The filmmakers did so by using a young woman to announce the workers' desire to change the world because they, in her words, "don't like it." In the process, the filmmakers redefined the

---

[1] Lars Kleberg, "The Aquarians," in *Starfall: A Triptych*, trans. Anselm Hollo (Evanston, IL: Northwestern University Press, 1988), 4. Eisenstein refers to the Goethe quote "Man merkt die Absicht, und man ist verstimmt." Brecht and Dudow did indeed go to Moscow for the May 1932 premiere of *Kuhle Wampe*, but it is doubtful that Eisenstein would have been able to watch the film beforehand.

very terms of politically engaged art, including the relationship between aesthetic emotions and political emotions.

Operativity in Tretyakov refers to the ability of the work not only to reflect but also to intervene in social reality. "The attention of constructors of our life," he explains, "must be focused not upon perfect works of art, but upon the perfect individual, full of organizational skill and the will to overcome the obstacles that lie along the path to the total mastery of life."[2] Understood in this way, operativity involves the montage of raw materials, or facts, for the purpose of cognitive and emotional stimulation – in *Kuhle Wampe* through the montage of locations, situations, activities, and Berlin workers for what Tretyakov would call a "film made of facts." Mass media such as newspaper, photography, and film proved especially suited for this kind of operative method, given their technical availability to collective modes of production and reception and their thematic affinity for everyday materials taken from modern life. The ultimate goal of operative literature according to Tretjakov was to make writers and readers active participants in the transformation of social reality; the same can be said about *Kuhle Wampe* as an example of operative filmmaking.

Rereading *Kuhle Wampe* from the perspective of operativity also moves the conception of political filmmaking beyond two aesthetic paradigms, often seen as mutually exclusive: the aesthetics of rupture and critique, associated with montage, and the aesthetics of continuity and immersion, associated with classical narrative. As if anticipating later leftist positions in favor of a cinema of distanciation, Tretyakov emphatically promoted both, "cinema as an intellectualizer and cinema as an emotionalizer: these are the two ways that cinema serves to actively construct our new reality."[3] Confirming his point, *Kuhle Wampe* draws on the entire range of cognitive and emotional faculties as it models the conditions under which the habitus of "not liking it" amounts to more than a statement of opinion. Specifically, the film provides a dialectical model for engaging the emotional and cognitive faculties that, through their mutual articulation, in-

---

[2] Sergei Tret'iakov, "Art in the Revolution and the Revolution in Art," *October* 118 (2006): 18. This book uses the more traditional spelling of his name but reproduces the different spellings in the citations from the English and the German. Tretyakov was acquainted with many of the participants in the *Kuhle Wampe* project. He traveled repeatedly to Berlin during the early 1930s and translated German literature into Russian, wrote short portraits of Eisler and Brecht, and published the first biography of Heartfield. For an appreciative critical assessment, see Walter Benjamin, "The Author as Producer," in *Selected Writings, Vol. 2, 1927–1934*, trans. Rodney Livingstone et al., ed. Michael W. Jennings, Howard Eiland, and Gary Smith (Cambridge, MA: The Belknap Press of Harvard University Press, 1999), 768–782.

[3] Sergei Tret'iakov, "Our Cinema," *October* 118 (2006): 36.

vite proletarian identifications – and do so through from the point of view of a woman.

Fig. 18.1 *Kuhle Wampe*, DVD capture. Male worker on the train: "And who will change the world?"

Fig. 18.2 *Kuhle Wampe*, DVD capture. Female worker on the train: "Those who don't like it!"

At the end of *Kuhle Wampe*, a young working-class woman looks straight into the camera as the high angle lighting bathes her in a halo of light. To an older middle-class man's question from offscreen, "And who will change the world?" she replies: "Those who don't like it! (*Denen sie nicht gefällt*)" (see figure 18.1 and 18.2). The tone is assertive and, like the Ernst Busch songs and Rote Sprachrohr skits that precede her, has a percussive quality that promises more confrontational situations for the future. The choice of the intransitive verb (*nicht*) *gefallen* – to (not) like, enjoy, or approve – suggests an attitude that, in the context of a heated political argument, sounds strangely constrained, especially compared to the more common portrayal of communist workers through the habitus of aggressive militancy. Yet read as an example of Brechtian gestus, the acting technique that expresses social relations through physical gestures, the woman's response can be interpreted as a reenactment of the film's politics of emotions – that is, an expression of dissent that reflects on its own conditions of enunciation. The connotative meaning of "not liking it" places the speaker in an enunciatory position of moral or aesthetic judgment – but not necessarily of revolutionary action. However, by giving the last word to a confident young woman, the film's final scene in fact identifies the discursive position from which the habitus of power can already be tested, and this precisely is the meaning of operativity.

Fig. 18.3 *Kuhle Wampe*, DVD capture. The Bönike family: mother and son.

Fig. 18.4 *Kuhle Wampe*, DVD capture. The Bönike family: father and son.

Fig. 18.5 *Kuhle Wampe*, DVD capture. The Bönike family: father and daughter.

Fig. 18.6 *Kuhle Wampe*, DVD capture. Anni and Fritz at the workers' sport festival.

The conditions for operativity in *Kuhle Wampe* are established through a bifurcated structure that combines fiction and documentary in mutually illuminating ways. In the first half, the story of the Bönike family is told as a familiar social drama that begins with a heated lunchtime discussion about unemployment and the suicide of the unemployed son, continues with the eviction of the family to a tent city near Müggelsee, and culminates in the daughter's rushed engagement, brief breakup, and eventual reconciliation with her boyfriend (see figure 18.3, 18.4, 18.5, and 18.6). Introduced as a counterpoint to the wish fantasies perpetuated by classical genre cinema, the documentary sequences in the film's second half introduce a compelling alternative to these experiences of lack of choice, namely the sense of unity and solidarity found in communist party work and workers' sport. Operativity, in that sense, means to persuade the fictional characters in the storyline, the extras in the documentary sequences, and the movie-theater audiences to agree on one simple point: the urgent need to change the world.

The articulation of a revolutionary strategy, however, required the kind of mass support available only in Berlin, the center of proletarian mobilization during the Weimar Republic. Moreover, it depended on the extensive exchanges that allowed leftist artists and writers to look for new models of cultural production in the Soviet Union. Inconceivable without the traffic in ideas between Moscow and Berlin, *Kuhle Wampe* was the product of a unique collaboration involving directors Bertolt Brecht and Slatan Dudow (1903–1963), composer Hanns Eisler, and screenwriter Ernst Ottwalt (1901–1943), who were either KPD members or sympathizers at the time of the film's production. Brecht's experiments with new media technologies such as radio and film and his legal battles with the UFA studio had resulted in his penetrating analysis of the culture industry and intensified his search for a materialist aesthetic based on new conceptions of character, role, and performance. Especially his development of *Lehrstücke* had made him explore new acting and staging techniques that could turn audiences into political actors. The Bulgarian-born Dudow had already addressed the problem of working-class housing in the documentary short *Zeitprobleme: Wie der Arbeiter wohnt* (1930, How the Berlin Worker Lives) and, after the war, would continue to make feature films for the East German DEFA studio. Meanwhile, Eisler, a student of Arnold Schönberg turned frequent Brecht collaborator, had abandoned the twelve-tone system in favor of the more agitational tones and hybrid musical styles that distinguished the *Kampflied* (see chapter 4) and later led to his selection as the composer of the GDR national anthem. A different kind of convert, Ottwalt had joined the KPD and BPRS after a youthful episode in the Freikorps, which he recounted in the autobiographical novel *Ruhe und Ordnung* (1929, Law and Order).

Descriptions of the collective involved in the making of *Kuhle Wampe* often fail to mention Hertha Thiele (1908–1984), the Berlin-based stage actress who had just appeared in Leontine Sagan's *Mädchen in Uniform* (1932, *Girls in Uniform*), the lesbian cult classic. In *Kuhle Wampe*, her friendship with her work colleague and fellow communist Gerda (played by Marta Wolter) is easily the most stable and supportive relationship in the narrative. Here Thiele is cast as Anni Bönike, who is the only member of her working-class family with a paying job as a spot welder and who helps her evicted family find temporary refuge in a tent settlement outside Berlin. She gets engaged to her boyfriend Fritz (played by Ernst Busch) because of an unplanned pregnancy and later breaks this engagement and has an abortion (alluded to in scenes cut from the censored version). She then moves in with her best friend and joins the workers' sport movement. With a short blond bob parted on the side, practical dark skirt, and white blouse with tie, Thiele is the very embodiment of the New Woman. Already her first appearance in the film establishes her status as the complete opposite of her mother, the type of older, worn-out working-class woman familiar from the works of Käthe Kollwitz and Heinrich Zille. Despite similarities in body type and attire, Anni has also little in common with her brother, the kind of slender, sensitive young man often depicted in Weimar films about the dangers of the big city. Her way of walking, of entering and exiting the frame perfectly captures the confidence and determination that informs all of her actions, including in the montage sequence about her agonizing decision in favor of abortion. Unlike other Weimar-era female protagonists confronted with an unwanted pregnancy, including in Martin Berger's *Kreuzzug des Weibes* (1926, Woman's Crusade) and Friedrich Wolf's *Cyankali* (1931, Cyanide), Anni is never punished for her sexual desires; on the contrary, her experiences with an unsupportive boyfriend, family, and public health system only end up radicalizing her.

How is the gestus of "not liking it" articulated in filmic terms in the opening and closing sequences? Titled "One Unemployed Less," the opening sequence begins with quick images of groups of men looking for work, and it ends with an eerily silent suicide scene and the recognition that the consequences of mass unemployment are always suffered individually. Formally reminiscent of Walter Ruttmann's *Berlin, die Sinfonie der Großstadt* (1927, *Berlin, Symphony of a Big City*), the sequence captures the legendary energy of labor and industry in Weimar Berlin: large factory complexes, wide city streets, and endless tenements with inner courtyards. Yet in *Kuhle Wampe*, the young men do not rush to their workplaces; they gather in the early morning to read the want ads and then speed away on their bicycles. Accompanied by a dissonant, frantic musical score, the closeups of peddling feet and turning wheels convey the men's growing sense of desperation. "No hiring," the notice at the factory gate says. The transition from montage to narrative continuity – and, concomitantly, from what is presented as reality to what is known to be fiction – occurs when the camera follows one young man as he arrives home in his working-class neighborhood. This is how Eisler, under the heading "Movement as a Contrast to Rest," later describes his score for the opening sequence:

> A slum district of drab, dilapidated suburban houses is shown in all its misery and filth. The atmosphere is passive, hopeless, depressing. Providing critical commentary, the music is brisk, sharp, a polyphonic prelude of a *marcato* character, and its strict form and stem tone, contrasted with the loose structure of the scenes, acts as a shock deliberately aimed at arousing resistance rather than sentimental sympathy."[4]

---

4 Theodor W. Adorno and Hanns Eisler, *Composing for the Films* (London: Continuum, 2007), 17. On the role of music, see Bertolt Brecht, "Über gestische Musik," in *Schriften zum Theater. Über eine nicht-aristotelische Dramatik* (Frankfurt am Main: Suhrkamp, 1993), 252–255. For an overview of discussions on music and gestus, also see Friedemann J. Weidauer, Bernadette Grubner, and Stephen Brockmann, eds., *Das Brecht Jahrbuch / The Brecht Yearbook 33: Gestus—musik—*

This description involves nothing less than a definition of gestus in music, that is, an attitude of resistance that requires a particular set of emotions. Musically, the shift to interiority, which also means to more empathetic modes of spectatorship, is announced by a sentimental tune played by street musicians, which completes the transition to the inside of the apartment and, by extension, the world of private feelings brought out into the open as the Bönike family sits down for lunch. Discussing the dire economic situation, the parents spout platitudes, such as "Industrious people always succeed" and "Unemployed and impolite, too? No one can afford this!" Anni questions their stubborn belief in individual responsibility and declares: "There simply is no work!" Cutaways to shots of cyclists in the morning sun corroborate her position, whereas the mother's selfless service prompts an ironic visual commentary in the cut to a popular saying on the tea towel above the kitchen sink: "Do not bemoan the morning that brings toil and work. It is its own reward to care for the people you love." Throughout, the (unnamed) son says nothing and sits hunched forward averting his eyes. Once the others have left, he gets up and walks toward the window. The camera follows and moves closer as he takes off his watch and lays it on the sideboard – a perfect illustration of Tretyakov's biography of the object (with its implicit critique of psychologism). Anni's brother first moves a flowerpot and then climbs on the windowsill. The camera cuts to the mother coming up the stairs with a shopping bag, followed by a closeup of his hand on the window frame and then a loud scream offscreen, followed by closeups of the flowerpot and his watch as inanimate witnesses to his jump to death.

Very similar in its formal structure, the closing sequence starts with a series of long shots celebrating modern industry and technology, but instead of a cacophony of dissonant sounds, the rousing theme from Eisler's famous "Solidarity Song" is heard. Significantly, the song is still without words since the workers have not yet found their voice. The conditions that allow them to announce themselves as the legendary proletariat of *The Communist Manifesto* are established through the small gestures of camaraderie and cooperation during preparations for the workers' sport festival. The determination of the young workers is acknowledged in the well-known lyrics now added, with the refrain "Forward, and never to forget/ what our strength consists of!/ When starving or when eating,/ forward, never to forget/ solidarity!" Every scene that follows adds another level of agency to the meaning of "not liking it." The newsreel footage of workers marching in formation through Berlin's working-class neighborhoods gives way

---

text =Gestus—music—text (Madison: University of Wisconsin Press, 2008), especially Darko Suvin, "Emotion, Brecht, Empathy vs. Sympathy" (53–67).

(via the sounds of whistling and roaring engines) to a montage sequence depicting various athletic competitions. Notwithstanding the superficial similarities with the weekend sequences in *Berlin, Symphony of a Big City* and *Menschen am Sonntag* (1930, *People on Sunday*) by Billy Wilder and Robert Siodmak, these scenes of workers bicycling, running, swimming, and rowing serve a fundamentally different purpose. They show not what Marx calls the reproduction of labor power in the name of profit maximization but the training of the proletarian body for the overthrow of the capitalist system. As the cold, hard voice of Ernst Busch in the "Sport Song" admonishes the contestants: "Come together in one body/ to fight together./ And learn to win!"

The workers' sport festival is the final destination for the characters in the diegesis, but it is also the place where private desires become part of public events and where the operative method in *Kuhle Wampe* is at its most powerful and (perhaps unsurprisingly) least apparent. The documentary sequences, shot without original soundtrack and edited in the manner of a compilation film, are presented here as the locus of reality and truth; they also function as the source of the greatest emotional intensities in the diegesis. The lengthy sequence even includes an agitprop skit on housing discrimination performed by the Rote Sprachrohr as a direct commentary on the eviction of the Bönike family. As Theodore Rippey has noted, the spectacle of class mobilization serves as emotional compensation for the matter-of-fact treatment of the central couple's romance. In fact, the formation of the collective could be described as the film's true love story.[5] The juxtaposition of fictional and documentary modes is established through the corresponding techniques of continuity editing, which relies on invisible cuts for creating a time-space continuum and guaranteeing emotional engagement, and of analytical editing, which, in the form of montage sequences, breaks time-space continuity to create sensory or cognitive effects. Meanwhile, the movement of the main characters between both worlds, the world of family drama and the world of class politics, defines the terms of engagement and brings forth the possibility of collective agency precisely through the operative nature of these formal differences. The point of contact between two paradigms – analytical editing and continuity editing, documentary and fiction, and reality and ideology – is openly thematized when a shot of workers discussing Hegel on the shores of the Müggelsee is followed by one of Fritz and Anni renewing their friendship based on shared political beliefs.

---

5 Theodore F. Rippey, "*Kuhle Wampe* and the Problem of Corporeal Culture," *Cinema Journal* 47.1 (2007): 3–25.

In the final scene on the crowded tram back to Berlin, the workers get a first chance to test their new rhetorical skills in discussions with several middle- and lower-middle class passengers. Their competing interpretations of a sensational newspaper story about the burning of twenty-four million pounds of coffee in Brazil connect the problems of ordinary Berliners to the movements of global capital. The filmic presentation equates the proposed solutions with specific class positions (bourgeois, petty bourgeois) and reactionary ideologies (nationalism, colonialism, militarism). Drawing on the typology of class perfected by George Grosz and Otto Dix, the confrontation between middle-aged burghers and (silent) plump matrons, on the one side, and young, slender, and articulate male and female workers, on the other, stages the class divides in explicitly corporeal and sartorial terms. Significantly, the question of who will change the world is answered through the equation of communism with youth as the embodiment of a better future. Marching into the underpass and toward the light, the workers return to Berlin accompanied by a rousing rendition of the "Solidarity Song" and its increasingly probing question, "Who owns the world?"

So far, key sequences have been used to reconstruct the simultaneously destabilizing and radicalizing effects of the female perspective on a "typical" story of unwanted pregnancy and an "atypical" story of broken engagement. The insertion of this female perspective into a conventionally male script of proletarian mobilization perfectly illustrates the operative method: that is, an intervention into social reality through a scrambling of the discourses – fiction versus documentary, private versus public, and emotional immersion versus critical detachment – that define classical narrative in the cinema. The same can be concluded about the film and its particular mode of production. On the formal level of editing and montage, Brecht and Dudow established their own position of "not liking it" through a two-pronged strategy: the critical insights gained from the tension between fictional and documentary material and the emotional intensities generated through the tension between analytical and associative editing.

Kuhle Wampe satisfies Tretyakov's definition of operativity – the choice of the right subject matter (*sujet*), the analysis of the fact in its concrete manifestations, and the conditions conducive to transforming facts into arguments – even as regards the last criterion, "the participation in the life of the subject itself."[6] Brecht and Dudow may not have joined the workers in the factories or the tenements, the literary strategy advocated by the BPRS, but they did, in fact, inter-

---

6 Sergej Tretyakov, "Der Schriftsteller und das sozialistische Dorf," in *Die Arbeit des Schriftstellers. Aufsätze Reportagen Porträts*, ed. Heiner Boehncke, trans. Karla Hielscher (Reinbek: Rowohlt, 1972), 120. This lecture was first given in Berlin in January 1931.

vene actively in the organization of the Berlin working class. According to producer Georg Hoellering, a thousand Fichte worker athletes, members of the world's largest communist sport club, were recruited to appear in the competitions.[7] In 1930, the communist workers' sport groups had been excluded from the Arbeiter- Turn- und Sportbund (ATSB, Workers' Gymnastics and Sports Federation) and, together with the KPD's Naturfreunde, started the Arbeitersportverein (ASV) Fichte as a model for the union of sport and revolution under the slogan of Rotsport (Red Sports).[8] Brecht was fully aware of the implications of staging a public event for a film production when he noted: "Naturally, the organisation of the work was a much greater effort for us than the (artistic) work itself, i.e., we came more and more to treat organisation as an essential component of artistic labour. This was only possible because the work as a whole was political work."[9] Hiring worker-athletes to play themselves at a staged sports event to be included in a feature film about the working class: nothing better describes the goal of the operative filmmaker to turn audiences into political actors and intervene directly into social reality.

Exceeding the filmmakers' expectations, the responses to *Kuhle Wampe*, complete with several censorship decisions, continued this operative method in the divided terms of film reception. Fourteen thousand Berliners saw what conservative critics denounced as a dangerous *Tendenzfilm* (tendentious film) after its long-awaited German release on 30 May 1932 in the Atrium Theater. The world premiere, which had taken place sixteen days earlier in Moscow, was the reason for the train trip undertaken by Brecht in the fictional conversation quoted in the epigraph.[10] Presumably fearing a mass uprising, the Prussian censors concluded in their second censorship decision on 9 April 1932 that, "the overall attitude of this moving picture [is] capable of endangering public order

---

7 On the Fichte club, see Herbert Dierker, "'Größter Roter Sportverein der Welt'. Der Berliner Arbeitersportverein Fichte in der Weimarer Republik," in *Illustrierte Geschichte des Arbeitersports*, ed. Hans Joachim Teichler and Gerhard Hauk (Berlin: Dietz, 1987) 93–107. On the workers' sport movement as a "sport political movement," see Fritz Wildung, *Arbeitersport* (Berlin: Bücherkreis, 1929) and André Gounot, *Die Rote Sportinternationale, 1921–1937: Kommunistische Massenpolitik im europäischen Arbeitersport* (Münster: Lit, 2002).
8 Ben Brewster, "Making *Kuhle Wampe*. An Interview with Georg Hoellering," *Screen* 15.4 (1974): 71–79. For recollections about location shooting, also see the short article by Ernst Busch published in *Welt am Abend*, 16 March 1932.
9 Bertolt Brecht et al., "Collective Presentation," *Screen* 15.2 (1974): 43.
10 This number is taken from the advertisement in *Lichtbildbühne*, 7 June 1932.

and the vital interests of the state."[11] The Nazis banned the film for good in March 1933 because of its communist tendencies.

If staging a sporting event with Fichte members functioned as an integral part of operative filmmaking, the filmmakers' meetings with the Prussian censorship board served similar effects. In ways already laid out in Brecht's famous lawsuit against Nero-Film over Georg Wilhelm Pabst's 1931 film adaptation of *Die Dreigroschenoper* (*The Threepenny Opera*), the censors' arguments ended up confirming every aspect of Brecht and Dudow's innovative approach to political filmmaking. In his analysis of the earlier lawsuit, Brecht had described the confrontation with the studio as a critical intervention into the conditions of artistic production under capitalism. The *Kuhle Wampe* project can be similarly characterized as a testing of the limits within which expressions of political dissent were possible. In recalling the meeting, Brecht expressed delight about the censors' objections to the overly mechanical way in which the son's suicide was portrayed. Channeling their voices, he concluded: "The audience will not even want to stop [the son], as it were, which would be the expected reaction in an artistic, humane, warm-hearted representation. Good God, the actor does it as if he were showing how to peel cucumbers. [...] Leaving the building, we [i.e., Brecht and Dudow] did not conceal our admiration for the astute censor."[12] Clearly, from Brecht's perspective, the censors had performed their assigned part in a very public debate on realism, modernism, and the politics of identification.

Film reviewers ended up playing similar roles by basing their arguments on the political function of emotion. Their juxtaposition of the "bad" emotion manufactured by the UFA dream factory and the "good" cognition trained in the much-admired Soviet films established the basis for later scholarly readings that automatically equated emotion with cooptation. Leftist filmmaking for many contemporaries meant moving beyond the victim mentality of the so-called Zille films, named after the famous portraitist of Berlin's urban poor, Heinrich Zille, and rejecting the surfeit of melodrama in social problem films like Piel Jutzi's *Mutter Krausens Fahrt ins Glück* (1929, Mother Krause's Journey to Happi-

---

11 "Erstes Verbot des Films, Film-Oberprüfstelle, 31 March 1932," rpt. in Bertolt Brecht, *"Kuhle Wampe:" Protokoll des Films und Materialien*, ed. Wolfgang Gersch and Werner Hecht (Frankfurt am Main: Suhrkamp, 1969), 110. A second ban on 9 April confirmed the first, with final approval of a revised cut version given on 21 April 1932. The collection includes the censorship protocols, including those pertinent to the abortion story.
12 Bertolt Brecht, "Short Contribution on the Theme of Realism," rpt. in *Brecht on Film and Radio*, ed. and trans. Marc Silberman (London: Methuen, 2000), 209. The book contains a very useful scene segmentation of the film (209–258).

ness).¹³ For that reason, several critics welcomed what they saw as more dispassionate tones, with Herbert Ihering praising *Kuhle Wampe* as "unsentimental and, for that reason, righteous,"¹⁴ and with Heinz Lüdeke speaking approvingly of "succinct, unsentimental scenes."¹⁵ The few comments that acknowledged the film's emotional appeal focused on its musical score, with Benjamin von Brentano singling out "Eisler's forward whipping, rousing music."¹⁶ While film critics insisted that montage was an effective agitational method, the workers themselves (to the degree possible) expressed a clear preference for less mediated images of contemporary problems. For instance, the opening sequence prompted one young metal worker in a union paper to complain: "Over and over again the same images of cyclists looking for work! Repeat these images once, fine! Anything more makes matters worse. And then the question: Does every unemployed have a bike?"¹⁷

Almost forgotten after its final ban by the Nazis in 1933, *Kuhle Wampe* was rediscovered in the 1970s through the convergence of Western Marxism, Brechtianism, and academic film studies. However, its new status as a model of political filmmaking did not resolve the conceptual tension between the emotional and cognitive aspects of political mobilization – on the contrary. The 1974 special issue of *Screen* on *Kuhle Wampe* may have established the film's importance for leftist film culture, but it also evaluated its artistic contribution through the Marxist orthodoxies of the times. Once again, emotions served as an indicator of wrong political attitudes or formal choices. James Pettifer, for instance, faulted the filmmakers for their ultra-leftist utopianism, complained about residues of petty-bourgeois consciousness, and criticized Eisler's score for achieving little

---

13 For an introduction to the leftist film culture of the Weimar Republic, see Jürgen Berger et al., eds., *Erobert den Film! Proletariat und Film in der Weimarer Republik* (Berlin: Neue Gesellschaft für Bildende Kunst, 1977); Jürgen Kinter, *Arbeiterbewegung und Film (1895–1933): Ein Beitrag zur Geschichte der Arbeiter- und Alltagskultur und der gewerkschaftlichen, sozialdemokratischen Kultur- und Medienarbeit* (Hamburg: Medien-Pädagogik-Zentrum, 1986); and Bruce Murray, *Film and the German Left in the Weimar Republic: From "Caligari" to "Kuhle Wampe"* (Austin: University of Texas Press, 1990).

14 Herbert Ihering, "Die verbotene *Kuhle Wampe*," rpt. in Brecht, *"Kuhle Wampe:" Protokoll*, 143.

15 Heinz Lüdeke, "Der Fall Weekend *Kuhle Wampe*," rpt. in Brecht, *"Kuhle Wampe": Protokoll*, 154.

16 Bernard von Brentano, "Der verbotene *Film Kuhle Wampe*," rpt. in Brecht, *"Kuhle Wampe": Protokoll*, 174.

17 Review of *Kuhle Wampe* in *Metallarbeiter-Jugend*, qtd. by Jürgen Kinter, *Arbeiterbewegung und Film (1885–1933): Ein Beitrag zur Geschichte der Arbeiter- und Alltagskultur und der gewerkschaftlichen und sozialdemokratischen Kultur- und Medienarbeit* (Hamburg: Medienpädagogik Zentrum, 1986), 326.

more than "simple empathetic emotional effects."[18] Equally opposed to anything tainted by emotions, Bernard Eisenschitz limited his definition of montage in a properly leftist film to "the very process by which a new dramatic art relocates actors and story within a chain of causality, and the spectator's interest is no longer aroused by harmonising with his emotions, but through recognition – of reality – and of what is at stake in that reality."[19]

The politics of emotion has continued to haunt the film in its status as an exemplar of radical film practice. Following the 1974 Screen issue, a Brechtian reading of *Kuhle Wampe* by Martin Walsh found fault with its presumably conventional (i.e., emotional) qualities, compared to Brecht's more innovative work in the theater and the impact of his theoretical writings on the "Brechtian" filmmaking of Jean-Luc Godard as well as Jean-Marie Straub and Danièle Huillet.[20] More recent contributions acknowledge the film's redistribution of emotional and cognitive elements across the public-private, male-female divides. The privileging of rupture as a more properly leftist mode still prevails in Marc Silberman's description of the film's model of spectatorship as one based on dramatized acts of cognition and intent on "awakening the spectator's recognition of the possibility for change."[21] Meanwhile her analysis of sound-image prompts Nora Alter to describe *Kuhle Wampe* as a "fully dialectical film that operates on the interstices between identification and distanciation."[22] And in an insightful reading that addresses the difficulty of representing proletarian identifications in the act of becoming, Gal Kirn draws on Rancière's notion of the event to aptly summarize the problem as follows:

> The actual process that is at work in Brechtian politics is the thinking of the (im)possibility of the proletarian subject, a subject that is always-already present, but is invisible to the dominant order (capitalism) and subjected to the dominant (liberal, petit-bourgeois) ideol-

---

18 James Pettifer, "Against the Stream: *Kuhle Wampe*," *Screen* 15.2 (1974): 56.
19 Bernard Eisenschitz, "Who Does the World Belong to? The Place of a Film," *Screen* 15.2 (1974): 70.
20 Martin Walsh, *The Brechtian Aspect of Radical Cinema* (London: British Film Institute, 1981), 10. For a critique of Brechtianism and its affirmation of the emotion-cognition divide, see Murray Smith, "The Logic and Legacy of Brechtianism," in *Post-Theory: Reconstructing Film Studies*, ed. David Bordwell and Noël Carroll (Madison: University of Wisconsin Press, 1996), 130–48.
21 Marc Silberman, "Whose Revolution? The Subject of *Kuhle Wampe* (1932)," in *Weimar Cinema: An Essential Guide to Classic Films of the Era*, ed. Noah Isenberg (New York: Columbia University Press, 2009), 327.
22 Nora M. Alter, "The Politics and Sounds of Everyday Life in *Kuhle Kampe*," in *Sound Matters: Essays on the Acoustics of Modern German Culture*, ed. Nora M. Alter and Lutz P. Koepnick (New York: Berghahn, 2004), 87.

ogy of the society. On an empirical level, the working class is subjected to the dominant ideology and its practices (such as alcoholism, escapism, petit-bourgeois mentality) and therefore cannot constitute the revolutionary class as such, but only an empirical entity. But the famous utterance that calls for the subject of change does not call upon an already formed political entity. The subject that is already present will have to be formed during the political process of subjectivisation.[23]

The shared goal of Tretyakov's operative literature and Brecht's notion of *Umfunktionierung* (functional transformation) according to Benjamin was to "make the literary [or in this case, filmic] products accessible to an immediately social, and therefore materialist, analysis." With the author or director functioning as a producer of new meanings and new situations, montage, the quintessential modernist technique, could finally be used to provide "the dialectical starting point from which the unfruitful antithesis of form and content can be surpassed" and, in so doing, "achieve the correct determination of the relation between tendency and quality."[24] Benjamin's reading of Tretyakov in "The Author as Producer" provides a useful model for thinking beyond the conceptual binaries – montage versus continuity, shock versus suture, modernism versus realism – that divided the Weimar left and continue to trouble the scholarly assessment of formally innovative and politically engaged art from the period. In fact, strategies of rupture and immersion both have a legitimate place in Brecht's definition of realism as "showing up the dominant viewpoint as the viewpoint of the dominators" and his insistence on "writing from the standpoint of the class which has prepared the broadest solutions for the most pressing problems afflicting human society."[25] The difference between continuity editing and analytical editing (or montage) opens up a space for the articulation of alternatives to class society precisely by at once reproducing the public-private divide and revealing it as a major obstacle to class mobilization. The relationship between reality and fiction and their different claims on the real within the diegesis define the terms under which the operative method can be applied to the "facts" of Berlin's working-class life and communist activism.

The cultural and artistic practices deployed in the name of operativity established even the conditions under which proletarian dreams can survive in contemporary forms and modalities – most recently in the "reimagining, retracing,

---

23 Gal Kirn, "*Kuhle Wampe*, Politics of Montage, De-montage of Politics?," *Film-Philosophy* 11.1 (June 2007): 42.
24 Benjamin, "The Author as Producer," 770.
25 Bertolt Brecht, "The Popular and the Realistic," in *Brecht on Theatre: The Development of an Aesthetic*, ed. and trans. John Willett (London: Methuen, 1992), 109.

remixing, reenacting, and reloading" of *Kuhle Wampe* in Berlin of the 2010s.[26] In that sense, the dismissive comment by Eisenstein that "one senses the intention" has proven to be the surest guarantee of the film's continuing relevance. The ways in which the scholarship about working-class culture and the history of socialism has followed similar patterns of forgetting and rediscovery, and engaged in comparable forms of operativity, will be considered in the book's afterword. It is the purpose of what normally would be called an overview of the scholarship to have a similar effect: to appreciate the legacies of the past, to use it to shed light on the present, and to find the critical questions and tools to ask new questions about the future.

---

26 See the 2011 Audio Visual Research Workshop "*Kuhle Wampe* Revisited," http://www.labor berlin-film.org/kuhle-wampe-revisited/, 1 March 2017, with its slogan "We want to reimagine, retrace, remix, reenact, and reload *Kuhle Wampe*" as a very contemporary example of operativity. For an account of the project, see Giulia Palladini, "The Weimar Republic and its Return: Unemployment, Revolution, or Europe in a State of *Schuld*," in *Performances of Capitalism, Crises, and Resistance: Inside/Outside Europe*, ed. Marilena Zaroulia and Philip Hager (New York: Palgrave Macmillan, 2015), 17–54.

Afterword:
A Historiography of the Proletarian Dream

> Historical fissures – crises, war, capitulation, revolution, counterrevolution – denote concrete constellations of social forces within which a proletarian public sphere develops. Since the latter has no existence as a ruling public sphere, it has to be reconstructed from such rifts, marginal cases, isolated initiatives. To study substantive attempts at a proletarian public sphere is, however, only one aim in our argument: the other is to investigate the contradictions emerging within advanced capitalist societies for their potential for a counterpublic sphere.
>
> Oskar Negt and Alexander Kluge, Public Sphere and Experience

In their influential study on *Öffentlichkeit und Erfahrung. Zur Organisationsanalyse von bürgerlicher und proletarischer Öffentlichkeit* (1972, in English as *Public Sphere and Experience: Toward an Analysis of the Bourgeois and Proletarian Public Sphere*), Oskar Negt and Alexander Kluge introduce "proletarian" and "public sphere" with the same political interests that, more than one hundred years earlier, prompted Marx and Engels to distinguish between the descriptive and analytical term "working class" and the politically and emotionally charged term "proletarian." Making productive use of that distinction, Negt and Kluge conceptualize a critical position from which to acknowledge the long history of working-class struggles and to imagine alternatives to the bourgeois public sphere in the Federal Republic. Yet in order for these potentials to be realized, they acknowledge, the proletarian public sphere has to be reconceived – which also means, it has to be rediscovered through the interpretative practices that distinguish the humanities from the social sciences and that connect new social movements to the class mobilizations of the past. Few studies from the 1970s express so clearly as Negt and Kluge's do the theoretical, academic, and political goals that propelled a diverse group of scholars and activists to claim working-class culture as a subject of critical inquiry and, ultimately, an example of *Gegenöffentlichkeit* (counterpublic sphere). And few contributions associated with Critical Theory and the New Left are as insistent in using what the authors call the first historical "attempts at a proletarian public sphere"[1] to communicate the

---

[1] Oskar Negt and Alexander Kluge, *Public Sphere and Experience: Towards an Analysis of the Bourgeois and Proletarian Public Sphere*, foreword Miriam Hansen, trans. Peter Labanyi, Jamie Owen Daniel, and Assenka Oksiloff (London: Verso, 2016), xliii. For a continuation of these arguments, see, by the same authors, *History and Obstinacy*, trans. Richard Langston et al., ed. Devin Fore (New York: Zone, 2014). For an early contribution on debate on a proletarian counterpublic

sense of urgency and possibility with which the problem of cultural hegemony and class society can, and must, be addressed.

Negt and Kluge's pronouncement that "We believe it is wrong to allow words to become obsolete before there is a change in the objects they denote"[2] not only offers a compelling argument for studying the working-class writers and artists and socialist theorists and activists presented in the previous eighteen chapters. For the purposes of this afterword, their warning against forgetting also opens up a space for acknowledging the generations of literary scholars, labor historians, and cultural theorists on both sides of the Atlantic who, in the 1970s, rediscovered the forgotten culture of the working class and the workers' movement. Like their historical subjects, most of the studies from the period have either been forgotten or declared irrelevant to contemporary research interests. In awareness of the complicated relationship between social struggles in history and the history of these struggles, rereading these works cannot be separated from a broader assessment of Critical Theory and the New Left and their profound impact on new social movements and the humanities since the 1970s. This tumultuous period has now become historical itself. With the end of the Cold War and the demise of Western Marxism, the insights and blind spots of these years have added yet another layer of attachments to the proletarian dream. They have introduced new ways of thinking about class, culture, and society, especially in the context of (British) cultural studies. But they have also created new impasses, whether through nostalgia for socialism and retreat to theory or through various critical interventions, from the discredited embourgeoisement thesis to the ubiquitous diagnosis of a postindustrial, postclass society, made to prove the obsolescence of class-related perspectives and categories.[3]

The forgotten works, minor genres, flawed arguments, and obsolete styles presented in this book have made it possible to address questions and uncover connections that were ignored by the scholarship from the 1970s and 1980s and that have been marginalized by the cultural studies paradigms prevalent since the 1990s. The introduction established the book's main research questions by highlighting the insufficient consideration of aesthetic questions in cultural studies; the limited attention to collective identifications and imaginaries; the urgent relevance of more historical perspectives on political emotions in social

---

sphere, see Werner Eisner and Wolfgang Eggersdorfer, "Arbeiterliteratur und proletarische Gegenöffentlichkeit," *alternative* 104 (1975): 217–227.

2 Negt and Kluge, *Public Sphere and Experience*, xlv.

3 For a critique of the concept of *Verbürgerlichung* in the context of postwar sociology see Birgit Mahnkopf, *Verbürgerlichung. Die Legende vom Ende des Proletariats* (Frankfurt am Main: Campus, 1985).

movements; and, above all, the unique qualifications of German working-class culture for a series of case studies on historical emotions and emotions in history. With the proletarian dream functioning both as the main topic and as the organizing device, the process of rediscovery had to involve a clear separation between collective imaginary and working-class reality and an equally careful distinction between Marxist, socialist, and communist positions on culture, and actual visual, literary, and musical practices.

The main findings can be summarized in a number of ways, beginning with their conceptual significance for future research in this area. To begin with, the case studies have shown the proletarian dream as an extension of, and an alternative to, working-class reality and Marxist theory. By taking the chosen texts seriously as aesthetic phenomena, the readings were able to confirm working-class culture as a semiautonomous public sphere. The introduction of political emotions as an important but understudied force in social movements, and the workers' movement in particular, has not only uncovered new aspects of working-class culture but also expanded the area of inquiry to include seemingly competing traditions and countervailing tendencies. These include the enduring influence of religion and religiosity in the culture of socialism; the belief in the bourgeois heritage and the formative quality of culture and education; the resonances of the culture industry in socialist versions of mass culture; the unique status of proletarian modernism as part of international developments; the profound rupture marked by World War I and the Revolution of 1918/19; and the considerable debts of the proletarian dream to nineteenth-century discourses of community, folk, and cultural nationalism.

Four propositions with particular relevance to the second volume can be highlighted: First, the central term that propelled the proletarian dream from the first songs and treatises written during the *Vormärz* era to the Weimar-era offerings of cultural socialism was that of community – and specifically the emotional communities imagined through words, stories, songs, and images. Before its appropriation by the Nazis, community and related terms such as people, folk, and mankind functioned as the main category of proletarian identifications and socialist commitments, projecting shared understandings of precapitalist forms of belonging, harmony, and unity into utopian communitarian conditions. Despite the strong theoretical commitment to internationalism in the workers' movement and the many border crossings involving socialist leaders, groups, and texts, the proletarian imagination before World War I remained largely confined by local and provincial perspectives on a thus defined community. As part of the complicated German history of socialism and nationalism, the internationalist, collectivist positions cultivated in the *Kampfkultur* of the Weimar KPD remained the exception. Nonetheless the famous artists, writers, and thinkers associated with the Weimar left in the wider sense attracted much of the scholarly attention as the proponents of a formally innovative and politically committed art. Rereading the lesser socialist poems, plays, images, and songs produced over the course of almost seventy years and concerned primarily with preserving, restoring, or dreaming about community has brought into sharp relief the emotional affinities between socialism and nationalism, especially in the languages of revolution. Closely related, the intersecting discourses of class, folk, and nation have confirmed the significance of cultural appropriation – over the insistence on originality and innovation as key characteristics of modern art movements – in either adapting the promises of community to the conditions of modern class society and mass culture or providing lines of flight into distant pasts and futures.

Second, the proletarian dream was from the beginning sustained by a cult of masculinity that originated in established patterns of homosocial sociability, that remained beholden to capitalist models of manual and industrial labor, and that acquired a decidedly militant tone after World War I. These gendered divides are reproduced in the emotionally charged terms that inform the distinction between mass discourse and class theory, the critical evaluation of bourgeois literary genres and styles, the approaches to socialist pedagogy and sex education, and the forms of identification shared by proletarian novels and mass spectacles. In more surprising ways, continuities in the gendered narratives of class have brought attention to the very different emotional regimes that defined masculinity in the late nineteenth century, including the culture of male sentimentality that found expression in emotional socialism. The homosocial lifeworld created by Wilhelmine Social Democracy, the sexism and misogyny of the workers' movement in its various forms, and the promotion of a decidedly male ethos of order and discipline shared by communism and National Socialism will remain central concerns in the second volume on the Third Reich and the German Democratic Republic.

Third, the dependence of the proletarian dream on well-established aesthetic registers and artistic traditions has revealed the continuing relevance of Enlightenment thought and Weimar classicism for the workers' movement. This includes the belief in the emancipatory power of the aesthetic, the enlistment of aesthetic emotions as political emotions, the promotion of culture as a model of national identity, and the considerable debts to earlier discourses of folk, community, and the people. The individual case studies have shown how the bourgeois heritage informed all aspects of working-class culture, including the belief in *Kultur* and *Bildung*; how bourgeois notions of interiority were appropriated for the habitus of community and collectivity; and how idealist aesthetics, including its most normative categories, continued to inform the socialist approach to modernity, modernism, and the historical avant-gardes. Despite international (ist) connections and commitments, the culture of the workers' movement before World War I remained under the influence of local perspectives in its cultural practices and of national traditions in its aesthetic theories. Despite the close connections between Austrian and German Social Democracy, and despite the Jewish contribution to Marxist theory and the history of the KPD, Prussianism and Protestantism remained important influences on the emotional regimes developed in the name of proletarian culture. For these reasons, the second volume on the workers' states will pay special attention to the constellations of nationalism and socialism conjured in the name of the working class and the subterranean currents of antisemitism that continued to resonate in later critiques of liberalism and modernism.

Fourth and last point: Taking seriously the emancipatory and prefigurative functions of the proletarian dream and considering its compensatory and disciplining effects makes it possible, finally, through the introduction of emotion as both a major theme and a heuristic device, to leave behind the unproductive binaries that have constrained academic studies on working-class culture and the culture of socialism and communism. Unlike previous approaches that treat socialist art and literature as a reflection of social reality or evaluate the texts' formal and thematic choices against the criteria of Marxist theory or bourgeois high culture, *The Proletarian Dream* has approached these proliferating, heterogeneous, and often undistinguished texts as founding sites for the convergence of political emotion and aesthetic emotion, as laboratories of imagined emotional communities, and as incubators for class-based emotional regimes. Departing from the diagnosis of the modern masses as the embodiment of dangerous irrationality, the most important models of proletarian mobilization have been introduced through their respective emotional cultures, including the emotional socialism of the nineteenth century and the cold stream of Marxism of the early twentieth century. The reconstruction of these emotional archives has not been limited to literary genres, art forms, performance practices, and visual styles – that is, definitions of culture in the narrow sense. Attentive to Williams's definition of culture as a whole way of life, the proletarian dream has also been analyzed through the select socialist and communist appropriation of concepts from modern psychology and sociology, the refunctionalization of bourgeois notions of selfhood, subjectivity, and interiority; and the gradual opening toward mass cultural forms of celebrity culture and multimediality. The introduction of emotions into the historical constellations of class and culture has brought into sharp relief the generative and transformative power of political emotions in defining the terms of individuality, sociability, and community. The resultant focus on political emotions and the politics of emotion has moved the debate beyond older distinctions that evaluate the desired convergence of socialism and working-class culture primarily as a function of theory or ideology and without sufficient attention to the unique qualities of the aesthetic. The overview of the scholarship on working-class culture on the remaining pages indicates continuing resistance to emotion – this time as a category of cultural history. At the same time, the scholars' own emotional investment in the subject matter indirectly confirms the inseparability of politics and emotions in the study of social movements.

I

The existing body of research on working-class culture in German history, literature, and related disciplines deserves to be recognized on its own terms but can also be reread in light of its complicated relationship to the subject of inquiry. Because of the distinct cycles of remembering and forgetting shared by these researchers and their historical subjects, such rereadings cannot follow the standard conventions of what is typically called a review of the scholarship. Instead the resonances of the proletarian dream in academic registers will be used here as yet another way of accessing the emotional archives of a social movement that played a formative role during the rise of modern capitalism, class society, and democracy and that continued in the very different social movements of the 1960s and beyond. Few research areas have been as susceptible to the dominant narratives about capitalism and democracy, justice and equality, and progress and crisis, as the study of working-class culture. And for reasons that confirm many of the findings of this study, few scholarly debates are as profoundly marked by the participants' own investments, both personal and political, in the conditions of their terms of engagement. The multi-volume archival projects on workers' literature or socialist theater completed during the GDR may be saturated with Marxist-Leninist terminology but they nonetheless include valuable sources and documents to be used by future generations. The contested nature of the working class as a category of critical inquiry is just as apparent in contributions by West German historians and sociologists that insist on scientific objectivity as they set out to prove the obsolescence of class as a valid category of inquiry. Meanwhile, the scholars most invested in the working-class culture as an alternative or oppositional culture use these forgotten traditions to challenge basic assumptions about culture and society and propose more expansive and inclusive approaches. Yet they, too, reproduce the blind spots – concerning the role of gender and sexuality, the influence of religion and folk tradition, and the affinities between socialism and nationalism – that characterized the workers' movements and the socialist and communist parties of the late nineteenth and early twentieth centuries.

These dynamics are especially apparent in light of the profound social and cultural transformations set into motion in the wake of "1968." Their resonances in the scholarship, including changes in academic disciplines and intellectual cultures, may be used productively to understand the initial enthusiastic reclamation (and gradual marginalization) of working-class history and culture since the 1970s. This might include the following questions: Can the rediscovery of the working class, inside and outside academia, also be seen as a form of mourning for the demise of traditional class society and the changing nature of work in postindustrial society? In what ways are the subsequent waves of scholarly interest and disinterest also a manifestation of the changing fortunes of Marxism after the death of communism? And to what degree are these rereadings motivated by the continuing search for new models of social movements and counterpublics?

As this book has shown, from the early 1870s to the early 1930s, the proletarian dream emerged as the product of extensive textual productivity and intensive cultural activity focused on empowering the working class and establishing their active role in dramatic social and economic transformations and major world historical events. The stories, images, figures, symbols, and rituals created under these conditions conjured the vision of a revolutionary class united in the fight against oppression and injustice and emboldened by dreams of a better, happier future. The extensive, but short-lived scholarly engagement with working-class culture during the 1970s and 1980s and its resonances in the new social and cultural histories can be read in similar terms, as a process of identification and projection. Looking back, it would be easy to disqualify many early studies because of their Marxist orthodoxies, New Left pieties, and social romantic fantasies of class and revolution. Especially the more dogmatic and polemical contributions have not stood up to the test of time, with their predictions about the imminent demise of capitalism invalidated by later political developments and their evaluation of socialist writers and thinkers marred by fealty to some "correct" version of communism or "better" Marxist theory. A recurring argument made in these studies can be summarized as follows: political mistakes were made; if parties had only pursued the right course of action, if theorists had only analyzed the situation correctly, if workers had only been better organized, or if intellectuals had only been more supportive. In these scenarios, symbolic practices bear much of the blame – if artists and writers had only rejected the bourgeois heritage, returned to the classical forms and models, fully embraced avant-garde techniques, or joined the workers in the factories and on the streets.

For about a decade, the history of the working class produced a wealth of academic and journalistic treatments, including in the form of local histories. Brought back into public awareness through book publications and museum exhibitions, the Weimar Republic provided heroic stories of labor strikes and revolutionary actions as well as idyllic scenes of class solidarity and working-class life. Throughout the 1970s, the search for historical and political precursors colored the choice of subject matter and method of interpretation. In West Germany, the intense debates in journals, anthologies, and exhibition catalogues compensated for the historical defeat of the working class in 1933 by establishing Weimar as the model of a formally innovative and politically committed art henceforth identified with the names of Lukács, Brecht, Bloch, and Benjamin. In East Germany, the idealization of the revolutionary working class and the Weimar KPD served largely legitimizing purposes in the context of state socialism and official heritage culture. Questioning (or affirming) the relevance of the Marxist critique of capitalism and class society remained an important part of the scholarship published by small leftwing publishing houses in the West and well-funded state archives and academies in the East. Similar conditions made possible the revisionist histories of the workers' movement written in the political milieu of the parties still acting in their names, the SPD, SED, KPD, and DKP, plus the various left wing splinter groups forming after the student movement.[4]

The existing scholarship on working-class culture could be classified in conventional ways and distinctions be made between East and West German scholars, West German and Anglo-American scholars, or social, labor, cultural, and literary historians. Such categories would track the ongoing transformations of an emerging interdisciplinary field through its positions at the center and the margins of humanities research more generally and through its subsequent responses to the challenges posed by poststructuralism and various linguistic, visual, spatial, material, and emotional turns. In this particular case, however, the internal logic of academic disciplines – the introduction of new areas of inquiry or research questions, the establishment of a corpus of works, and the call for more differentiated accounts or different interpretations – involves strong theoretical and emotional attachments that find privileged expression in relation to (working-class) culture and its utopian promises and emancipatory potentials. For that reason alone, a historiography of the proletarian dream might be reconstructed best through the international and interdisciplinary dialogues devel-

---

4 For a useful historical overview, see Helga Grebing, *Geschichte der deutschen Arbeiterbewegung. Von der Revolution 1848 bis ins 21. Jahrhundert* (Berlin: Vorwärts, 2007), an earlier version was translated into English by Edith Körner as *The History of the German Labour Movement: A Survey* (London: Berg, 1985).

oped through the critical engagement with questions of working-class, proletarian, socialist, and communist culture, with the inevitable conceptual slippages treated as an integral part of the findings.

British labor historians set the discussion into motion, beginning with Eric Hobsbawm who decided to rewrite what he called the long nineteenth century from the perspective of laboring men.[5] Focusing on the birthplace of early capitalism and the industrial revolution, two other historians came to be identified with influential critical traditions, E. P. Thompson as the representative of a humanist Marxism and Raymond Williams through his culturalist perspectives on class society and politics. Thompson and Williams emphasized the importance of romantic anticapitalism to the early socialist movements. Both also acknowledged the crucial role of bourgeois mediators (teachers, publishers, agitators), old and new forms of mediation (allegory, satire, caricature), and various places of mediation (clubs, associations) in the emergence of working-class culture. Thompson set the tone in his path-breaking 1963 study on the making of the British working class when he famously announced his intention to rescue individual workers from "the enormous condescension of posterity."[6] Rejecting the available top-down histories, he approached class as a historical phenomenon based in human relationships and articulated "in the raw material of experience and in consciousness." Thompson's notion of lived experience profoundly changed the conceptualization of class and culture, moving it away from the traditional base-superstructure model and toward a more dynamic understanding of culture. This is how he defined the latter: "The class experience is largely determined by the productive relations into which men are born – or enter involuntarily. Class consciousness is the way in which these experiences are handled in cultural terms: embodied in traditions, value-systems, ideas, and institutional forms. If the experience appears as determined, class consciousness does not."[7]

---

[5] See Eric Hobsbawm, *Labouring Men: Studies in the History of Labour* (London: Weidenfeld and Nicolson, 1965). Also see the two recent volumes from his monumental history of the long nineteenth century, *The Age of Revolution: 1789–1848* (New York: Vintage Books, 1996) and *The Age of Capital: 1848–1875* (London: Weidenfeld and Nicolson, 2010).

[6] E. P. Thompson, *The Making of the English Working Class* (London: Victor Gollancz, 1963), 12. For an example of the extensive reception of Thompson in Germany, see Michael Vester, *Die Entstehung des Proletariats als Lernprozess. Die Entstehung antikapitalistischer Theorie und Praxis in England 1792–1848* (Frankfurt am Main: Europäische Verlagsanstalt, 1970) and Heiko Geiling, *Die moralische Ökonomie des frühen Proletariats. Die Entstehung der hannoverschen Arbeiterbewegung aus den arbeitenden und armen Volksklassen bis 1875* (Frankfurt am Main: Materialis, 1985).

[7] Thompson, *The Making of the English Working Class*, 9–10.

The momentous shift from class as a structure to class as a relationship turned working-class culture into a privileged site for studying the practices and processes that produced class identifications. In an equally influential 1958 study on culture and society, Raymond Williams offered an expanded definition of culture that, given its etymological roots (e. g., in agricultural cultivation), aims to encompass "a whole way of life, material, intellectual and spiritual," and extend from institutions and artifacts to rituals, values, and beliefs.[8] Unlike bourgeois culture with its emphasis on the autonomous individual, working-class culture for him was founded on, and sustained by, community and solidarity as core organizing principles and consequently found privileged expression in specific structures of feeling. His belief in the formative power of culture allowed Williams furthermore to conceive of class as a learning process that included political victories and defeats and that continuously reaffirmed its original commitments through what he called the moral economy, the kind of values and virtues examined in this book through terms such as emotional regimes and emotional practices. His later reflections on keywords like class, culture, hegemony, and revolution allowed Williams to develop further his approach to cultural materialism against the structuralism of Louis Althusser and others and to lay the foundation for what would eventually become (British) cultural studies.

The groundbreaking work by Hobsbawm, Thompson, and Williams and the social and cultural transformations associated with the New Left has had a powerful effect on British and American historians specializing in modern Germany. Richard J. Evans, who has contributed several studies on the German working class and the women's movement, and Geoff Eley, who has written about the making of German democracy and the transnational history of the European left, have each used categories of class to revisit core assumptions about the parallel processes of democratization and modernization. For Evans, this has meant moving beyond the almost habitual equation of working class with workers' movement and toward a greater emphasis on the role of mass culture and leisure practices in the articulation of oppositional views and alternative forms of protest. For Eley, this has involved affirming the role of the workers' movement in the difficult German path toward democracy and of the New Left in developing new forms of solidarity in dialogue with new social movements.[9] His insistence

---

8 Raymond Williams, *Culture & Society: 1780–1950* (New York: Columbia University Press, 1958), xvi. Also see his *Marxism and Literature* (Oxford: Oxford University Press, 1977).
9 For references, see Richard J. Evans, *The German Working Class 1888–1933: The Politics of Everyday Life* (Totowa, NJ: Barnes & Noble, 1982) and *Proletarians and Politics: Socialism, Protest and the Working Class in Germany before the First World War* (New York: Harvester Wheatsheaf, 1990), as well as Geoff Eley, *Forging Democracy: The History of the Left in Europe, 1850–2000*

that "working class" and "Social Democracy" not be treated as identical terms and their respective histories written with awareness of their complicated relationship became an integral part of the subsequent process of remapping and revisiting.[10]

Reclaiming the forgotten history of working-class culture during those decades often included arguments over terminologies and methodologies – arguments that concerned the difficulty of thinking class within or outside a Marxist (and what kind of Marxist?) critical framework and, more generally, theorizing the relationship between class, culture, and society beyond the terms established during the late nineteenth century. The various proposals by West German scholars for defining the relationship between "working class" and "culture" and, closely related, between "working class" and "socialism" served different theoretical, methodological, and disciplinary interests but shared the conviction that such discussions were useful and necessary. To give a few examples, in a 1979 survey of the state of historical research, Jürgen Kocka addressed the problem of historical continuities and called for a clearer distinction between working-class culture and the legacies of *Volkskultur* (popular culture, folk culture).[11] Helga Grebing and Matthias Winter introduced the term *Arbeiterbewegungskultur* (culture of the workers' movement) to highlight the close connection between working-class culture and workers' movement.[12] Some scholars advanced the

---

(Oxford: Oxford University Press, 2002) and, with Keith Nield, *The Future of Class in History: What's Left of the Social?* (Ann Arbor: University of Michigan Press, 2007). Since the early interventions by Evans, the local histories presented by David Crew, Mary Nolan, and Lynn Abrams and the introduction of gendered perspective by Carole Elizabeth Adams and Kathleen Canning have further complicated discussions of class, labor, and culture. For references, see David F. Crew, *Town in the Ruhr: A Social History of Bochum, 1860–1914* (New York: Columbia University Press, 1979); Mary Nolan, *Social Democracy and Society: Working Class Radicalism in Düsseldorf, 1890–1920* (Cambridge: Cambridge University Press, 1981); Lynn Abrams, *Workers' Culture in Imperial Germany: Leisure and Recreation in the Rhineland and Westphalia* (London: Routledge, 1992); Carole Elizabeth Adams, *Women Clerks in Wilhelmine Germany: Issues of Class and Gender* (Cambridge: Cambridge University Press, 1988); and Kathleen Canning, *Languages of Labor and Gender: Female Factory Work in Germany, 1850–1914* (Ithaca, NY: Cornell University Press, 1996).
10 Geoff Eley, "Joining Two Histories: the SPD and the German Working Class, 1860–1914," *From Unification to Nazism: Reinterpreting the German Past*, ed. Geoff Eley (London: Allen & Unwin, 1986), 171–199.
11 Jürgen Kocka, "Arbeiterkultur als Forschungsthema. Einleitende Bemerkungen," *Geschichte und Gesellschaft* 5.1 (1979): 5–11.
12 See Helga Grebing, "Von der Klassenkultur zur Massenkultur? Drei Fragen zur Arbeiterbewegungskultur," in *Arbeit und Kultur*, ed. Gerd Köhler und Matthias N. Winter (Freiburg im Breisgau: Dreisam, 1989), 119–123, 142–143, und 160–161 and Michael Grüttner, "Arbeiterkultur versus Arbeiterbewegungskultur. Überlegungen am Beispiel der Hamburger Hafenarbeiter 1888–1933," in

more descriptive category of *Arbeiterkultur* (workers' culture) in order to include groups and milieus outside the highly politicized world of socialist parties and labor unions. Other scholars noted the limitations of class as an analytical category with an inbuilt affinity for antagonistic interpretations and pointed to the greater importance of cultures of social integration over cultures of social conflict in liberal (i.e., Western) democracies. The various attempts at developing a shared critical vocabulary by combining elements from theories of class formation and social stratification can be seen, among other things, in Gerhard Albert Ritter's all-inclusive characterization of *Arbeiterkultur* as "the whole set of relations of a way of life specific to a social stratum, which finds its expression not only in artistic manifestations of the workers and in their educational activities, but in their social and political behavior, in their value systems, and in their own institutions."[13]

Working-class history and the history of the socialist movement benefitted greatly from the critical interventions that profoundly changed the discipline of history during the 1970s and 1980s and contributed to the introduction of social history and cultural history as the dominant paradigms. The close connection between political culture and historical research in the Federal Republic can be tracked from the earliest studies on the workers' movement (e.g., by political scientist Wolfgang Abendroth) to the voluminous tomes devoted to Social Democracy and its cultural institutions.[14] While some studies reproduced the ideological divisions between Old and New Left, others used the historical find-

---

Studien zur Arbeiterkultur, ed. Albrecht Lehmann (Münster: Coppenrath, 1984), 244–282. For a literary perspective on these questions, see Wilfried van der Will and Rob Burns, *Arbeiterkulturbewegung in der Weimarer Republik. Texte, Dokumente, Bilder*, 2 vols., (Frankfurt am Main: Ullstein, 1982).

13 Gerhard Albert Ritter, "Arbeiterkultur im Deutschen Kaiserreich. Probleme und Forschungsansätze," in *Arbeiterkultur*, ed. Gerhard Albrecht Ritter (Königstein/Taunus: Athenäum, 1979), 15–39. Also see Gerhard Albrecht Ritter and Klaus Tenfelde, *Arbeiter im Deutschen Kaiserreich 1871 bis 1914* (Bonn: Dietz, 1992). For a Weberian approach, see Josef Mooser, *Arbeiterleben in Deutschland 1900–1970. Klassenlagen, Kultur und Politik* (Frankfurt am Main: Suhrkamp, 1984). For a Marxist approach, see Manfred Scharrer, *Arbeiterbewegung im Obrigkeitsstaat. SPD und Gewerkschaft nach dem Sozialistengesetz* (Berlin: Rotbuch, 1976); *Kampflose Kapitulation: Arbeiterbewegung 1933* (Reinbek: Rowohlt, 1984); and *Arbeiter und die Idee von den Arbeitern 1848 bis 1869* (Cologne: Bund, 1990).

14 See Wolfgang Abendroth, *Einführung in die Geschichte der Arbeiterbewegung*, 2 vols. (Heilbronn: Distel, 1985). Representative works by GDR historians include Jürgen Kuczynski, *Die Geschichte der Lage der Arbeiter unter dem Kapitalismus*, 40 vols. (Berlin: Akademie, 1960–72); Hartmut Zwahr, *Proletariat und Bourgeoisie in Deutschland. Studien zur Klassendialektik* (Cologne: Pahl-Rugenstein, 1980) and, as editor, *Die Konstituierung der deutschen Arbeiterklasse von den dreißiger bis zu den siebziger Jahren des 19. Jahrhunderts* (Berlin: Akademie, 1981).

ings to advance sociological perspectives on social stratification over explicitly Marxist definitions of class. Aside from a few exceptions, the Marxist approaches taken by British historians and the social history approaches favored by German historians produced starkly different accounts of nineteenth century working-class culture. In the Federal Republic, the 1980s and 1990s were dominated by detail-rich social histories inspired by the new critical social sciences, with some scholars publishing comprehensive overviews of particular periods, as did Heinrich August Winkler in his enormous three-volume history of the Weimar Republic, and with others focusing on particular regions, as did Klaus Tenfelde in his studies on provincial Bavaria and the Ruhr region.[15] As the best-known representative of the Bielefeld School, Jürgen Kocka contributed voluminous studies on the history of wage labor and class formation in the nineteenth and early twentieth centuries.[16] The process of proletarization, usually defined as downward mobility, allowed Kocka and others to study class formations at the intersection of work and life and to follow their ongoing transformation in new social structures and forms of sociability. Similar processes have been examined through the changing nature of family, neighborhood, and urban life and extended to the tastes and attitudes that exist outside the working world. One perhaps unintended consequence of this abundance of case studies has been a growing difficulty of demarcating the conceptual terrain identified with the working class.

The new social history promoted by the Bielefeld School since the 1970s has relied heavily on modernization theory to arrive at a more dynamic understanding of modern class society and used the rich study of social movements to support or disprove some of the arguments made in conjunction with the debate about a German *Sonderweg* (unique path) of historical development. By contrast, the project of *Alltagsgeschichte* (history of everyday life) initiated by Alf Lüdtke has drawn attention to the lifeworld of the working class, making everything, from daily diets and furnishings to group sports and annual festivals, a subject

---

15 For references, see Heinrich August Winkler, *Arbeiter und Arbeiterbewegung in der Weimarer Republik*, 3 vols: Vol. 1: *Von der Revolution zur Stabilisierung, 1918 bis 1924* (Berlin: Dietz, 1984); Vol. 2: *Der Schein der Normalität, 1924 bis 1930* (Berlin: Dietz, 1985); Vol. 3: *Der Weg in die Katastrophe, 1930 bis 1933* (Berlin: Dietz, 1987). For two local studies, see Klaus Tenfelde, *Proletarische Provinz. Radikalisierung und Widerstand in Penzberg/Oberbayern 1900–1945* (Munich: Oldenbourg, 1982) and *Sozialgeschichte der Bergarbeiterschaft an der Ruhr im 19. Jahrhundert* (Bonn: Verlag Neue Gesellschaft, 1981).

16 See Jürgen Kocka, *Lohnarbeit und Klassenbildung: Arbeiter und Arbeiterbewegung in Deutschland 1800–1875* (Berlin: Dietz, 1983); *Arbeitsverhältnisse und Arbeiterexistenzen: Grundlagen der Klassenbildung im 19. Jahrhundert* (Bonn: Dietz, 1990); and *Klassengesellschaft im Krieg: Deutsche Sozialgeschichte 1914–1918*, sec. ed. (Göttingen: Vandenhoeck & Ruprecht, 2011).

of scholarly interest and theoretical value. *Alltagsgeschichte* played an important role in the establishment of a new public history through its interest in local knowledges and affinity for oral histories. The popular history workshops with their emphasis on history from below and the musealization of the age of industrialization (e. g., European Route of Industrial Heritage) are inconceivable without these shifts in perspective. By validating individual voices and everyday concerns, *Alltagsgeschichte* posed a fundamental challenge to both the master narratives of class and the structural categories favored by social historians. Against the privileging of labor as the basis of class identities and the assumption of a linear process of class socialization, Lüdtke introduced the notion of *Eigensinn* (usually translated as obstinacy) "to make visible the diverse and contradictory and, above all, not-connected forms of individual behavior behind the myth of the 'proletariat.'"[17]

II

Historians continue to publish innovative research on the German working class, and often do so in dialogue with the theoretical interventions made by feminist theory, new historicism, postcolonial studies, and so forth. By contrast, working-class culture and the culture of socialism have more or less disappeared from German cultural studies in the Anglo-American context, and even more so, in Germany where traditional philology, literary history, and philosophical, formalist, and theoretical approaches predominate. The fact that the monographs written in the name of a highly politicized *kritische Germanistik* have left almost no traces in current research questions confirms the essentially conservative nature of the university as an institution and attests to the discipline's hegemonic function and, closely related, to its almost obligatory crises of legitimacy. Anglo-American German studies have followed a slightly different pattern that has resulted in cultural studies adaptations of ideology critique in the tradition of the Frankfurt School and under the influence of theories of hegemony, resistance, and subversion developed by British cultural studies. With similarly problematic consequences, the transformation of the humanities in response to various social movements and larger cultural developments has resulted in the proliferation of simultaneously essentialist and constructivist discourses of identity and a relat-

---

17 Alf Lüdtke, *Eigen-Sinn: Fabrikalltag, Arbeitererfahrungen und Politik vom Kaiserreich bis in den Faschismus* (Hamburg: Ergebnisse, 1993), 13. For a critical response, see Detlev Peukert, "Arbeiteralltag: Mode oder Methode?," in *Arbeiteralltag in Stadt und Land. Neue Wege der Geschichtsschreibung*, ed. Heiko Haumann (Berlin: Argument, 1982), 8–39.

ed preoccupation with symbolic politics as the main site of contestation and affirmation in a globalized world dominated by new social media and the very different collective imaginaries organized through them.

Notwithstanding the almost habitual invocation of class as part of the conceptual trinity of gender, race, and class, serious engagement with questions of class remains rare even in the current theoretization of intersectionality and positionality, the discussions about cultural hybridity and multiculturalism, and the mapping of a transnational German literature through the lens of multilingual literacies and cosmopolitan sensibilities. Similarly, the productive insights gained at the intersection of German studies with gender studies, postcolonial studies, and critical race studies have yet to be applied to the cultural articulation of class differences in the historically developed structures of social and economic inequality and the discourses of folk, community, and nation. And with special relevance to the study of emotions in social movements, it would be difficult to imagine a greater divide separating the breadth and depth of political and aesthetic emotions mobilized in the name of the proletariat – ranging from suffering, indignation, and pathos to rage, hatred, and pride – and the much more limiting equation of the human condition with the positions of victim and perpetrator and with the experience of trauma and loss in contemporary identity discourses.

Despite the seemingly insurmountable distance separating these identity discourses from the early Marxist studies on working-class culture, both lines of inquiry can be traced back to the emergence of the New Left in the mid-1960s and the social movements of the 1970s. A product of these developments, the rediscovery of workers' literature and socialist literature subsequently took place as part of a larger critique of bourgeois culture and society: the critique of the culture industry and the insistence on the utopian function of art; the emergence of a formally advanced and politically engaged aesthetics associated with the names of Brecht and Benjamin; the turn to mass culture and popular culture as potential sites of resistance and subversion; and the critical self-reflection of the humanities and their historical role in the defense of high culture and the invention of national literature. In West Germany, the leftists' claims on a radically democratic tradition of culture associated with socialism and the working class not only placed them in opposition to bourgeois high culture but also to Marxist-Leninist interpretations of class and culture developed in East Germany and fully in line with the policies of the workers' and peasants' state.

In the Federal Republic, the reclamation and, perhaps, reinvention of a forgotten working-class culture resulted in the discovery of rich histories and traditions purged from the archives, museums, and libraries during the Third Reich. Often published by small leftist publishers, numerous reprints, new editions, and annotated anthologies made socialist, communist, and anarchist texts again available to interested readers and contributed to a growing interest in local and regional history that included the interrelated histories of industry, labor, and technology. These developments even extended to the voices of contemporary workers, as evident in the founding of the Werkkreis Literatur der Arbeitswelt (Working Group on Literature of the Working World) and the revival of workers' film and photography modeled on Weimar-era initiatives. The key terms employed in this process of critical reclamation – opposition, resistance, and subversion – not only speak to the underlying search for aesthetic modalities and collective imaginaries that could prove valuable to then-contemporary forms of protest, but they also attest to a painful awareness of the rapid disappearance of traditional industries, labor parties, and forms of resistance and, with them, theoretical models for understanding power and change. Aware of these contemporary perspectives, Germanist Wolfgang Emmerich described the new research as a critical intervention into the political culture of the Federal Republic: against the loss of historical awareness in the workers' movement and the political apathy of the workers but also against the fetishization of the proletariat by the student movement.[18]

Engaging in a broader critique of *Germanistik* as a discipline in the double sense of the word, Emmerich, together with Frank Trommler, Bernd Witte, and others, subsequently introduced the designations "worker" and "socialist" into existing literary histories and, in the process, radically expanded conventional definitions of canon, period, and genre and established terms of literary analysis. In the years that followed, Trommler's comprehensive history and Simone Barck's lexicon of socialist literature as well as Heinz Ludwig Arnold's two-part primer and Gerald Stieg and Bernd Witte's short study guide on workers' literature identified key authors and works, examined prevailing forms and themes, and evaluated literary movements in relation to the structures of class society, the institutions of dominant culture, and the connection to socialist and communist parties.[19] Since then, more specialized studies have covered top-

---

[18] Wolfgang Emmerich, *Proletarische Lebensläufe. Autobiographische Dokumente zur Entstehung der zweiten Kultur in Deutschland*, 2 vols. (Reinbek: Rowohlt, 1980), 1: 9–35.

[19] For references in chronological order, see Gerald Stieg and Bernd Witte, *Abriß einer Geschichte der deutschen Arbeiterliteratur* (Stuttgart: Klett, 1973); Frank Trommler, *Sozialistische Literatur in Deutschland. Ein historischer Überblick* (Stuttgart: Kröner, 1976); Martin H. Ludwig, *Arbeiterliteratur in Deutschland* (Stuttgart: Metzler, 1976); Heinz Ludwig Arnold, *Handbuch zur deutschen Arbeiterliteratur*, 2 vols. (Munich: edition text + kritik, 1977); and Simone Barck et al., eds., *Lexikon sozialistischer Literatur. Ihre Geschichte in Deutschland bis 1945* (Stuttgart: Metzler, 1994).

ics ranging from Wilhelmine workers' choral societies to the Weimar *Sprechchor* movement that confirm these groups' heavy debts to bourgeois culture and folk culture but, in the lifeworld dominated by the KPD, also show the strong influence of developments in the Soviet Union. Throughout the heavy emphasis on literary theories and debates has offered further evidence of the inordinate significance attributed to criticism as a (surrogate) public sphere at the time. More problematically, these research interests point to the continued overvaluation of ideas (rather than emotions) in the assessment of workers' literature and socialist literature today.

The heated arguments over the best definition of *Arbeiterliteratur* (workers' literature) – namely, as literature by, for, or about workers, or as literature about labor conditions and the workers' movement – became an integral part of the entire process of rediscovery and reevaluation. The same holds true for the conceptual tension between "socialist literature" and "working-class literature" and many scholars' continued reliance on an idealist aesthetic complete with unquestioned assumptions about appropriate forms, genres, and styles. Sometimes this revisionist process extended to movements excluded from the dominant leftwing narrative of class mobilization, as was the case for the left radicalism studied by Walter Fähnders.[20] At other times, the goal was to move beyond conventional poetological categories and genre distinctions and to radically rethink the social function of literature, a process that proved most successful in the close attention to modernist forms and the opening toward new mass media. Arguing along these lines, Bernd Witte (under the influence of Tretyakov) proposed to redefine workers' literature as a functional literature, namely "the attempt of developing a class literature through which the proletariat gains a sense of self and asserts itself against the cultural hegemony of the bourgeoisie."[21]

A brief comparison to the research conducted in East Germany during the same time period helps to further clarify the political significance of the scholarly discovery of working-class culture in West Germany, Great Britain, and the United States. Obviously, the steady flow of monographs, editions, and anthologies published in Berlin (East) and Leipzig, a historical center of Social Democ-

---

20 See Walter Fähnders and Martin Rector, *Linksradikalismus und Literatur. Untersuchungen zur Geschichte der sozialistischen Literatur in der Weimarer Republik*, 2 vols. (Reinbek: Rowohlt, 1974) and *Anarchismus und Literatur: Ein vergessenes Kapitel deutscher Literaturgeschichte zwischen 1890 und 1910* (Stuttgart: Metzler, 1987). Both authors also served as editors of *Literatur im Klassenkampf. Zur proletarisch-revolutionären Literaturtheorie, 1919–1921: Eine Dokumentation* (Frankfurt am Main: Fischer, 1974).
21 Stieg and Witte, *Abriß einer Geschichte der deutschen Arbeiterliteratur*, 12.

racy, would not have been possible without the investment of vast resources by the SED leadership in a subject matter of greatest relevance to the future of socialism during the Cold War. Ambitious editorial projects such as the twenty-five volumes of *Textausgaben zur frühen sozialistischen Literatur in Deutschland* (1963–1986), edited by Ursula Münchow and published by the Deutsche Akademie der Wissenschaften, made forgotten socialist authors and texts available again. With their extensive bibliographical annotations, these editions remain essential for anyone working on the period.[22] A similar collaborative project from the 1970s, titled *Beiträge zur Geschichte der deutschen sozialistischen Literatur im 20. Jahrhundert*, focused specifically on the continuities between Weimar Republic and GDR and added an internationalist orientation by including several volumes on the Soviet Union.[23] Today these publications, from facsimile reprints to critical anthologies to specialized bibliographies, also document the patterns of exclusion (e. g., regarding the perspectives of anarcho-syndicalism and council socialism) that made these socialist archives fully compatible with Marxist-Leninism and the ideology of state socialism. East German literary and cultural historians had two not always compatible assignments, to write the history of the revolutionary working class on the basis of political orthodoxies that were always subject to revision and, secondly, to provide historical and political legitimacy for the GDR's role as the first German workers' state and the SED's position as the party of socialist unity. If there is one area in which East German research institutes were ahead of their West German counterparts, it was in the inclusion of socialist and communist artists in the history of modern art and a historiography of modernism that paid close attention to socialist realist traditions. Thus the class-based art history that produced the permanent exhibition at Otto-Nagel House in East Berlin already established a visual archive for collective imaginaries and socialist histories when many of the artists included had never been mentioned in West German overviews of modern German art – a shortcom-

---

22 Other projects coordinated by Ursula Münchow include *Aus den Anfängen der sozialistischen Dramatik*, 5 vols. (Berlin: Akademie, 1964–73), as well as *Frühe deutsche Arbeiterautobiographie* (Berlin: Akademie, 1973) and *Arbeiter über ihre Leben: Von den Anfängen der Arbeiterbewegung bis zum Ende der Weimarer Republik* (Berlin: Dietz, 1976). Other editorial projects include Helmut Barth, *Zum Kulturprogramm des deutschen Proletariats im 19. Jahrhundert: Eine Sammlung kulturpolitischer und ästhetischer Dokumente* (Dresden: Verlag der Kunst, 1978).
23 Typical titles from that series include Friedrich Albrecht, *Deutsche Schriftsteller in der Entscheidung. Wege zur Arbeiterklasse 1918–1933* (Berlin: Aufbau, 1970); Alfred Klein, *Im Auftrag ihrer Klasse. Weg und Leistung der deutschen Arbeiterschriftsteller 1918–1933* (Berlin: Aufbau, 1976); Ursula Münchow, *Arbeiterbewegung und Literatur 1860–1914* (Berlin: Aufbau, 1981), and several other volumes on debates and developments in the Soviet Union.

ing soon to be rectified by the Marxist art history that would emerge in the 1970s on both sides of the Atlantic.²⁴

In *Germanistik*, the study of working-class literature and socialist literature opened up new ways of thinking about aesthetics, politics, and emotion under the influence of Critical Theory and as part of the project of ideology critique. The fact that many contributions, perhaps as part of an argument for disciplinary legitimacy, remained beholden to traditional literary criteria does not invalidate their significance at the time, but instead highlights the dialogic process by which the provocation of the proletarian dream, including its heterogeneous aspects and contradictory elements, was continuously forgotten and remembered, denounced and celebrated. The Social Democratic infatuation with the bourgeois heritage especially during the Wilhelmine years sometimes posed a problem for younger scholars socialized into the (Weimar-era) equation of radical politics with formal innovation. Unable to fit older sensibilities – especially the affinity for melodrama and sentimentality – into the available histories of avant-garde art and literature, literary scholars proposed a number of conceptual openings. Seeking a solution within traditional literary terms, Witte proposed to define the workers' literature of the Wilhelmine period as a fourth literary tradition in addition to symbolism, naturalism, and trivial literature.²⁵ Meanwhile, cultural anthropologists working at the intersection of literary studies and cultural history explored the connections between working-class culture and popular culture, especially in relation to *Heimatkunst* (regional art) and *Volkskunst* (folk art). One welcome result of this productive dialogue between the disciplines was greater attention to "the other cultures," sometimes forgotten in the preoccupation with working-class culture, which continue to represent very different oral traditions, preindustrial communities, and anticapitalist sensibilities.²⁶ Last but not

---

24 For example, see Albrecht Dohmann, *Bild der Klasse: Die deutsche Arbeiterklasse in der bildenden Kunst* (Berlin: Tribüne, 1971); Hubertus Gaßner and Eckhart Gillen, eds., *Zwischen Revolutionskunst und sozialistischem Realismus. Realismus: Dokumente und Kommentare: Kunstdebatten in der Sowjetunion von 1917–1934* (Cologne: Du Mont, 1979); and Renate Hartleb and Dietulf Sander, eds., *Worin unsere Stärke besteht: Malerei Graphik Plastik Fotografie: Kampfaktionen der Arbeiterklasse im Spiegel der bildenden Kunst* (Leipzig: Das Museum, 1986). A typical exhibition catalogue is F. Weidemann, *Otto-Nagel-Haus: Abteilung proletarisch-revolutionärer und antifaschistischer Kunst der Nationalgalerie. Führer durch die Ausstellung* (Berlin: Staatliche Museum zu Berlin, 1984).
25 Bernd Witte, "Literatur der Opposition. Über Geschichte, Funktion und Wirkmittel der frühen Arbeiterliteratur," in *Handbuch zur deutschen Arbeiterliteratur*, ed. Heinz Ludwig Arnold (Munich: edition text + kritik, 1977), 1: 7–45.
26 See Helmut Fielbauer and Olaf Bockhorn, eds., *Die andere Kultur: Volkskunde, Sozialwissenschaften und Arbeiterkultur: Ein Tagungsbericht* (Vienna: Europaverlag, 1982); Dietrich Mühlberg

least, the study of new mass media and their impact on the traditional arts allowed a new generation of film and media scholars to reassess working-class culture in relation to the culture industry and, with special attention to the workers' photography and workers' radio movements, further expand the fields of inquiry toward a truly materialist approach to the study of cultural production and consumption in the technological age.[27]

Given the widespread tendency for presentist approaches, the scholarship on socialist literature frequently reproduced unchallenged assumptions that equated the "worker" automatically with revolutionary causes and reduced the "proletariat" to its radicalizing effects. In developing more complex models, some scholars proposed reconceptualizing German working-class culture by moving beyond national boundaries, for instance in the form of comparative studies, or by focusing on the Wilhelmine years as the most crucial period of class formation. Building on Lenin's theory of two cultures, Emmerich introduced the relational term of a "second culture" to identify the socialist elements that in all societies arise seemingly naturally from the working and living conditions of the people and that are always mobilized against dominant bourgeois culture.[28] Against the privileging of the skilled industrial workers and their reformist positions, the social historian Karl Heinz Roth uncovered the voices of the "other" worker's movement consisting of unskilled workers and presented them as the truly revolutionary movement.[29] Adding to the understanding of class culture as fluid and contested, labor historian Erhard Lucas studied the historical narratives of proletarization as a two-pronged process that involved the

---

and Rainer Rosenberg, eds., *Literatur und proletarische Kultur: Beiträge zur Kulturgeschichte der deutschen Arbeiterklasse im 19. Jahrhundert* (Berlin: Akademie, 1983), especially Dietrich Mühlberg, "Literatur in der Arbeiterklassenkultur: Bemerkungen zu Ansätzen kulturhistorischer Forschung" (17–44); and, by the same author, *Proletariat: Kultur und Lebensweise im 19. Jahrhundert* (Vienna: Böhlau, 1986). For very personal recollections on East German scholarship on working-class culture, see Horst Groschopp, "Auf der Suche nach dem historischen Subjekt für sozialistische Kultur. Erinnerungen an die Arbeiterkulturforschung in der DDR," *Kulturation, Online Journal für Kultur, Wissenschaft und Politik* 29.7 (2006), 15 pp.

27 For the Weimar period, examples include Joachim Büthe, *Der Arbeiter-Fotograf. Dokumente und Beiträge zur Arbeiterfotografie, 1926–1932* (Cologne: Prometh, 1978) and Bruce Murray, *Film and the German Left in the Weimar Republic: From "Caligari" to "Kuhle Wampe"* (Austin: University of Texas Press, 1990).

28 Emmerich, *Proletarische Lebensläufe: Autobiographische Dokumente zur Entstehung der zweiten Kultur in Deutschland*, 1: 30–35.

29 See Karl Heinz Roth, *Die "andere" Arbeiterbewegung und die Entwicklung der kapitalistischen Repression von 1880 bis zur Gegenwart: Ein Beitrag zum Neuverständnis der Klassengeschichte in Deutschland* (Munich: Trikont, 1974); and Dieter Kramer, *Theorien zur historischen Arbeiterkultur* (Marburg: Verlag Arbeiterbewegung und Gesellschaftswissenschaft, 1987).

deskilling of craftsmen and artisans and the movement of rural laborers from the country to the city.[30] Cultural anthropologist Wolfgang Kaschuba also offered a critique of normative accounts of class when he drew attention to the so-called subbourgeois classes and what he called *Arbeiteralltagskultur*, a workers' culture of everyday life distinguished through "its own meeting places and spaces of communication, with specific forms of sociability and living conditions, with its own image of society and set of values."[31]

The personal and political investments that made this kind of cultural historical research a battlefield for larger theories of culture and politics are most apparent in the debates on working-class culture as an alternative culture, oppositional culture, or subculture and, in closing, can be used to return to the original questions about political emotions laid out in the introduction. After all, the preoccupation with the otherness of working-class culture did not begin and end with the hallucination of a mass soul in nineteenth-century mass discourse and the dream of socialist community shared by *Vormärz* utopian socialists and Weimar-era cultural socialists. More contemporary version of emotional socialism survived in scholarly debates that, from the perspective of today, seem equally blind to the presuppositions of their times. Very often, the resulting debates involved arguments over appropriate names and definitions. In an early contribution, sociologist Guenther Roth introduced the notion of subculture to present Social Democracy during the Wilhelmine years as a "study in working-class isolation and national integration."[32] Because of its inward-looking group identity and hostile stance toward mainstream culture, Social Democracy according to Roth, who used the term synonymously with working class, ultimately failed to challenge existing hierarchies and, through the compensatory function of its lifeworld, helped to stabilize social structures and political institutions. Twen-

---

30 Erhard Lucas, *Arbeiterradikalismus. Zwei Formen von Radikalismus in der deutschen Arbeiterbewegung* (Frankfurt am Main: Roter Stern, 1976).
31 Wolfgang Kaschuba, *Lebenswelt und Kultur der unterbürgerlichen Schichten im 19. und 20. Jahrhundert* (Munich: Oldenbourg, 1990), 31. For an East German perspective, see Wolfgang Jacobeit and Ute Mohrmann, eds., *Kultur und Lebensweise des Proletariats: Kulturhistorische und volkskundliche Studien und Materialien* (Berlin: Akademie, 1973). For an Austrian perspective, see Helmut Fielhauer and Olaf Bockhorn, eds., *Die andere Kultur: Volkskunde, Sozialwissenschaften und Arbeiterkultur: Ein Tagungsbericht* (Vienna: Europaverlag, 1982).
32 Guenther Roth, *The Social Democrats in Imperial Germany: A Study in Working Class Isolation and National Integration*, preface Reinhard Bendix (Totowa, NJ: Bedminster, 1963). A good discussion of Roth can be found in Evans, *The German Working Class*, 15–53. For a comparative study through the perspective of German labor migration, see Hartmut Keil and John B. Jentz, eds., *German Workers in Chicago: A Documentary History of Working-Class Culture from 1850 to World War I* (Urbana: University of Illinois Press, 1988);

ty years later, historian Vernon Lidtke offered a very different account that emphasized social conflict and segmentation rather than social cohesion and integration. Accordingly, he described the labor movement "as an alternative culture in which organized workers could fulfill their needs for companionship, sociability, recreation, learning, and aesthetic satisfaction; partake in the community forming effects of associations, clubs, festivals, and songs; and cultivate what he described as the core socialist values of freedom, equality, and brotherhood."[33] Treating the social-cultural milieu of the worker's movement as part of a heterogeneous culture held together by internal contradictions, Lidtke concluded that "the socialist labor movement offered the vision and, in considerable part, the actuality of an alternative culture in the midst of the social realities of Imperial Germany [...] an alternative that appealed not only to workers, but to many others who took seriously its broad humanitarianism."[34]

Within their respective subfields but no longer part of a larger political or intellectual project, scholars continue to introduce additional layers, new perspectives, and productive complications to the study of working-class culture by focusing specifically on questions related to artistic medium, literary genre, and forms of cultural consumption and by revisiting cultural practices through various theories of visuality, spatiality, and performativity.[35] However, as the summary of the debates on working-class culture as an oppositional or alternative culture illustrates, the research questions from the 1970s and 1980s do not translate easily into contemporary perspectives and concerns. Moreover, the initial identification of the proletarian dream with an emancipatory project has been rarely challenged – not with regards to its traditional gender politics during the Wilhelmine years, its nationalist commitments during World War I, its authoritarian tendencies in the Weimar KPD, or its continuities in the cult of the worker after 1933. Perhaps the contemporary configurations of politics and emotion described in the book's introduction will finally make it possible to liberate the proletarian dream from mainstream condescension and leftist nostalgia and

---

[33] Vernon L. Lidtke, *The Alternative Culture: Socialist Labor in Imperial Germany* (Oxford: Oxford University Press, 1985), 3. A good discussion of the book can be found in chapter 4 of Evans, *Proletarians and Politics* (72–92).

[34] Lidtke, *The Alternative Culture*, 201.

[35] Examples include W. L. Guttsman, *Art for the Workers: Ideology and the Visual Arts in Weimar Germany* (Manchester: Manchester University Press, 1997); Hans-Joachim Schulz, *German Socialist Literature 1860–1914: Predicaments of Criticism* (Columbia, SC: Camden House, 1993); Richard Bodek, *Proletarian Performance in Weimar Berlin: Agitprop, Chorus, and Brecht* (Columbia, SC: Camden House, 1997); and Carol Poore, *The Bonds of Labor: German Journeys to the Working World, 1890–1990* (Detroit: Wayne State University Press, 2000).

take seriously its historical and theoretical challenges to dominant culture and hegemonic practices.

To return to the epigraph, in defining the proletarian public sphere as a counterpublic sphere, Negt and Kluge in 1972 responded to a profound legitimation crisis caused by the disappearance of traditional class society, the crisis of liberal democracy, the weakening of the nation-state, and the rise of modern mass media.[36] Kluge would later expand on their critical intervention by highlighting the power of emotions as a productive force, beginning with his characterization of politics as an intensification of everyday feelings and, more generally, as part of a materialist theory of experience. With special relevance for *The Proletarian Dream*, Negt and Kluge's argument for the importance of counterpublic spheres, proletarian or otherwise, finds powerful expression in their insistence not to "allow words to become obsolete before there is a change in the objects they denote." It is in the same spirit that this book has reconstructed the proletarian dream across late-nineteenth and early-twentieth century German history and through the cultural practices that imagined the revolutionary working class as an emotional community.

---

[36] For an early reflection on these connections, see Alexander Kluge, "The Political as Intensity of Everyday Feelings," trans. Andrew Bowie, *Cultural Critique* 4 (1986): 119–128.

Select Bibliography

(This selected bibliography is limited to German and English-language monographs and anthologies; primary texts and more specialized works can be found in the footnotes of individual chapters.)

Abrams, Lynn, *Workers' Culture in Imperial Germany: Leisure and Recreation in the Rheinland and Westphalia* (London: Routledge, 1992).

Akademie der Künste, ed., *Textausgaben zur frühen sozialistischen Kultur in Deutschland*, 25 vols. (Berlin: Akademie, 1964–87).

Albrecht, Friedrich, *Deutsche Schriftsteller in der Entscheidung: Wege zur Arbeiterklasse 1918–1933* (Berlin: Aufbau, 1970).

Altner, Manfred, *Das proletarische Kinderbuch: Dokumente zur Geschichte der sozialistischen deutschen Kinder- und Jugendliteratur* (Dresden: Verlag der Kunst, 1988).

Arnold, Heinz-Ludwig, and Manfred Bosch, *Handbuch zur deutschen Arbeiterliteratur*, 2 vols. (Munich: edition text + kritik, 1977).

Barclay, David E., and Eric D. Weitz, *Between Reform and Revolution: German Socialism and Communism from 1840 to 1990* (New York: Berghahn, 1998).

Barth, Helmut, *Zum Kulturprogramm des deutschen Proletariats im 19. Jahrhunderts. Eine Sammlung kulturpolitischer und ästhetischer Dokumente* (Dresden: Verlag der Kunst, 1978).

Berger, Stefan, *Social Democracy and the Working Class in Nineteenth and Twentieth Century Germany* (New York: Longman, 2000).

Berger, Jürgen, *Erobert den Film! Proletariat und Film in der Weimarer Republik* (Berlin: Neue Gesellschaft für Bildende Kunst, 1977).

Bodek, Richard, *Proletarian Performance in Weimar Berlin: Agitprop, Chorus, and Brecht* (Columbia, SC: Camden House, 1997).

Bogdal, Klaus-Michael, *Schaurige Bilder: Der Arbeiter im Blick des Bürgers am Beispiel des Naturalismus* (Frankfurt am Main: Syndikat, 1978).

Bollenbeck, Georg, *Zur Theorie und Geschichte der frühen Arbeiterlebenserinnerungen* (Kronberg/Taunus: Scriptor, 1976).

Brauneck, Manfred, ed., *Die Rote Fahne: Kritik, Theorie, Feuilleton 1918–1933* (Munich: Wilhelm Fink, 1973).

Brown, Timothy Scott, *Weimar Radicals: Nazis and Communists between Authenticity and Performance* (New York: Berghahn, 2009).

Canning, Kathleen, *Languages of Labor and Gender: Female Factory Work in Germany, 1850–1914* (Ithaca, NY: Cornell University Press, 1996).

Dohmann, Albrecht, *Bild der Klasse: Die deutsche Arbeiterklasse in der bildenden Kunst* (Berlin: Tribüne, 1971).

Eley, Geoff, *Forging Democracy: The History of the Left in Europe, 1850–2000* (Oxford: Oxford University Press, 2002).

Emig, Brigitte, *Die Veredelung des Arbeiters: Sozialdemokratie als Kulturbewegung* (Frankfurt am Main: Campus, 1980).

Emmerich, Wolfgang, *Proletarische Lebensläufe: Autobiographische Dokumente zur Entstehung der zweiten Kultur in Deutschland*, 2 vols. (Reinbek: Rowohlt, 1980).

Evans, Richard J., *Proletarians and Politics: Socialism, Protest, and the Working Class before the First World War* (New York: St. Martin's, 1990).

Evans, Richard J., *The German Working Class 1888–1933: The Politics of Everyday Life* (Totowa, NJ: Barnes & Noble, 1982).
Fähnders, Walter, and Martin Rector, *Linksradikalismus und Literatur. Untersuchungen zur Geschichte der sozialistischen Literatur in der Weimarer Republik*, 2 vols. (Reinbek: Rowohlt, 1974).
Fähnders, Walter, *Anarchismus und Literatur: Ein vergessenes Kapitel deutscher Literaturgeschichte zwischen 1890 und 1910* (Stuttgart: Metzler, 1987).
Fähnders, Walter, and Martin Rector, eds., *Literatur im Klassenkampf. Zur proletarisch-revolutionären Literaturtheorie, 1919–1923: Eine Dokumentation* (Frankfurt am Main: Fischer, 1974).
Feidel-Mertz, Hildegard, *Zur Ideologie der Arbeiterbildung* (Frankfurt am Main: EVA, 1972).
Fielbauer, Helmut, and Olaf Bockhorn, eds., *Die andere Kultur: Volkskunde, Sozialwissenschaften und Arbeiterkultur: Ein Tagungsbericht* (Vienna: Europaverlag, 1982).
Fischer, Jürgen, and Peter Michael Meiners, *Proletarische Körperkultur und Gesellschaft. Zur Geschichte des Arbeitersports* (Giessen: Achenbach, 1973).
Friedrich, Gerhard, *Proletarische Literatur und politische Organisation: Die Literaturpolitik der KPD in der Weimarer Republik und die proletarisch-revolutionäre Literatur* (Frankfurt am Main: Peter Lang, 1981).
Fülberth, Georg, *Proletarische Partei und bürgerliche Literatur: Auseinandersetzungen in der deutschen Sozialdemokratie der II. Internationale über Möglichkeiten und Grenzen einer sozialistischen Literaturpolitik* (Neuwied: Luchterhand, 1972).
Gallas, Helga, *Marxistische Literaturtheorie: Kontroversen im Bund proletarisch-revolutionärer Schriftsteller* (Neuwied: Luchterhand, 1971).
Gamper, Michael, *Masse lesen, Masse schreiben: Eine Diskurs- und Imaginationsgeschichte der Menschenmenge 1765–1930* (Munich: Wilhelm Fink, 2007).
Guttsman, W. L., *Art for the Workers: Ideology and the Visual Arts in Weimar Germany* (Manchester: Manchester University Press, 1997).
Hardt, Yvonne, *Politische Körper: Ausdruckstanz, Choreographien des Protests und die Arbeiterkulturbewegung in der Weimarer Republik* (Münster: Lit, 2004).
Hein, Anna Elisabeth, and Peter Ulrich Hein, *Kunstpolitische Konzepte der deutschen Arbeiterbewegung: Eine Darstellung am Beispiel Literatur und Theater* (Münster: Lit, 1983).
Hoffmann, Ludwig, and Klaus Pfützner, *Theater der Kollektive: Proletarisch-revolutionäres Berufstheater in Deutschland 1928–1933: Stücke, Dokumente, Studien* (Berlin: Henschel, 1980).
Hoffmann, Ludwig, *Deutsches Arbeitertheater 1918–1933*, sec. exp. ed. (Munich: Rogner & Bernhard, 1973).
Hoffrogge, Ralf, *Sozialismus und Arbeiterbewegung in Deutschland: Von den Anfängen bis 1914* (Stuttgart: Schmetterling, 2011).
Hornauer, Uwe, *Laienspiel und Massenchor: Das Arbeitertheater der Kultursozialisten in der Weimarer Republik* (Cologne: Prometh, 1985).
Jacobeit, Wolfgang, and Ute Mohrmann, eds., *Kultur und Lebensweise des Proletariats: Kulturhistorische und volkskundliche Studien und Materialien* (Berlin: Akademie, 1973).
Kaschuba, Wolfgang, *Lebenswelt und Kultur der unterbürgerlichen Schichten im 19. und 20. Jahrhundert* (Munich: Oldenbourg, 1990).

Keil, Hartmut, ed., *German Workers Culture in the United States, 1850 to1920* (Washington DC: Smithsonian Institution Press, 1988).
Kelly, Arthur, ed., *The German Worker: Working-Class Autobiographies from the Age of Industrialization* (Berkeley: University of California Press, 1987).
Kinter, Jürgen, *Arbeiterbewegung und Film (1885–1933): Ein Beitrag zur Geschichte der Arbeiter- und Alltagskultur und der gewerkschaftlichen, sozialdemokratischen Kultur- und Medienarbeit* (Hamburg: Medienpädagogik-Zentrum, 1986).
Klenke, Dietmar, Peter Lilje, and Franz Walter, *Arbeitersänger und Volksbühnen in der Weimarer Republik* (Bonn: Dietz, 1992).
Kocka, Jürgen, *Arbeitsverhältnisse und Arbeiterexistenzen: Grundlagen der Klassenbildung im 19. Jahrhundert* (Bonn: Dietz, 1990).
Kocka, Jürgen, *Klassengesellschaft im Krieg: Deutsche Sozialgeschichte 1914–1918*, sec. ed. (Göttingen: Vandenhoeck & Ruprecht, 2011).
Kocka, Jürgen, *Lohnarbeit und Klassenbildung: Arbeiter und Arbeiterbewegung in Deutschland* (Berlin: Dietz, 1983).
Kramer, Dieter, *Theorien zur historischen Arbeiterkultur* (Marburg: Verlag Arbeiterbewegung und Gesellschaftswissenschaft, 1987).
Lammel, Inge and Ilse Schütte, eds., *Hundert proletarische Balladen, 1842–1945* (Berlin: Verlag Tribüne, 1985).
Lammel, Inge, *Arbeiterlied – Arbeitergesang: Hundert Jahre Arbeitermusikkultur in Deutschland* (Berlin: Hentrich & Hentrich, 2002).
Lammel, Inge, *Arbeitermusikkultur in Deutschland 1844–1945: Bilder und Dokumente* (Leipzig: Deutscher Verlag für Musik, 1984).
Lidtke, Vernon L., *The Alternative Culture: Socialist Labor in Imperial Germany* (Oxford: Oxford University Press, 1985).
Lucas, Erhard, *Arbeiterradikalismus. Zwei Formen von Radikalismus in der deutschen Arbeiterbewegung* (Frankfurt am Main: Roter Stern, 1976).
Ludwig, Manfred H., *Arbeiterliteratur in Deutschland* (Stuttgart: Metzler, 1976).
Mallmann, Klaus Michael, *Kommunisten in der Weimarer Republik: Sozialgeschichte einer revolutionären Bewegung* (Darmstadt: Wissenschaftliche Buchgesellschaft, 1996).
Mühlberg, Dietrich, and Rainer Rosenberg, eds., *Literatur und proletarische Kultur: Beiträge zur Kulturgeschichte der deutschen Arbeiterklasse im 19. Jahrhundert* (Berlin: Akademie, 1983).
Mühlberg, Dietrich, *Proletariat: Kultur und Lebensweise im 19. Jahrhundert* (Vienna: Böhlau, 1986).
Münchow, Ursula, *Arbeiter über ihre Leben: Von den Anfängen der Arbeiterbewegung bis zum Ende der Weimarer Republik* (Berlin: Dietz, 1976).
Münchow, Ursula, ed., *Aus den Anfängen der sozialistischen Dramatik*, 5 vols. (Berlin: Akademie, 1964–73).
Petzina, Dietmar, ed., *Fahnen, Fäuste, Körper: Symbolik und Kultur der Arbeiterbewegung* (Essen: Klartext, 1986).
Poore, Carol, *The Bonds of Labor: German Journeys to the Working World, 1890–1990* (Detroit: Wayne State University Press, 2000).
Ritter, Gerhard Albrecht, and Klaus Tenfelde, *Arbeiter im Deutschen Kaiserreich 1871 bis 1914* (Bonn: Dietz, 1992).
Ritter, Gerhard Albrecht, ed., *Arbeiterkultur* (Königstein im Taunus: Athenäum, 1979).

Rohrwasser, Michael, *Saubere Mädel, starke Genossen. Proletarische Massenliteratur?* (Frankfurt am Main: Roter Stern, 1975).

Roth, Lynette, *Painting as a Weapon: Progressive Cologne, 1920–1933: Seiwert Hoerle Arntz* (Cologne: Walther König, 2008).

Rülcker, Christoph, *Zur Ideologie der Arbeiterdichtung 1914–1933. Eine wissenssoziologische Untersuchung* (Stuttgart: Metzler, 1970).

Saage, Richard, ed., *Solidargemeinschaft und Klassenkampf. Politische Konzeptionen der Sozialdemokratie zwischen den Weltkriegen* (Frankfurt am Main: Suhrkamp, 1986).

Scharrer, Manfred, *Arbeiter und die Idee von den Arbeitern 1848 bis 1869* (Cologne: Bund, 1990).

Scharrer, Manfred, *Arbeiterbewegung im Obrigkeitsstaat: SPD und Gewerkschaft nach dem Sozialistengesetz* (Berlin: Rotbuch, 1976).

Scheck, Frank Reiner, *Erobert die Literatur! Proletarisch-revolutionäre Literaturtheorie und -debatte in der "Linkskurve" 1929–1232* (Cologne: Kiepenheuer & Witsch, 1973).

Schmidt, Christoph, *Vom Messias zum Prolet: Arbeiter in der Kunst* (Stuttgart: Franz Steiner, 2010).

Schulz, Hans-Joachim, *German Socialist Literature, 1860–1914: Predicaments of Criticism* (Columbia, SC: Camden House, 1993).

Springman, Luke, *Comrades, Friends and Companions: Utopian Projections and Social Action in German Literature for Young People, 1926–1934* (New York: Peter Lang, 1989).

Steenson, Gary P., *"Not One Man! Not One Penny!" German Social Democracy, 1863–1914* (Pittsburgh: University of Pittsburgh Press, 1981).

Stieg, Gerald, and Bernd Witte, *Abriß einer Geschichte der deutschen Arbeiterliteratur* (Stuttgart: Klett, 1973).

Suhr, Ernst-Friedrich, and Regina Weinkauff, eds. *Revolte im Kasperhaus. Ein Lesebuch in Dokumenten und Bildern zum Puppentheater der Arbeiterjugendbewegung* (Cologne: Prometh, 1983).

Tenfelde, Klaus, *Die Ausbreitung der deutschen Arbeiterbewegung* (Göttingen: Vandenhoeck & Ruprecht, 1987).

Tenfelde, Klaus, *Sozialgeschichte des deutschen Kommunismus* (Göttingen: Vandenhoeck & Ruprecht, 1995).

Trommler, Frank, *Sozialistische Literatur in Deutschland: Ein historischer Überblick* (Stuttgart: Kröner, 1976).

Türk, Klaus, *Arbeit und Industrie in der bildenden Kunst. : Beiträge eines interdisziplinären Symposiums* (Stuttgart: Franz Steiner, 1997).

Ueberhorst, Horst, *Frisch, frei, stark und treu. Die Arbeitersportbewegung in Deutschland 1893–1933* (Düsseldorf: Droste, 1973).

Weber, Hermann, *Die Wandlung des deutschen Kommunismus: Die Stalinisierung der KPD in der Weimarer Republik* (Frankfurt am Main: EVA, 1969).

Weber, Richard, and Rolf Henke eds., *Arbeiterbühne und Film* (Cologne: Henke, 1974).

Weber, Richard, *Proletarisches Theater und revolutionäre Arbeiterbewegung 1918–1925* (Cologne: Prometh, 1978).

Weitz, Eric D., *Creating German Communism, 1890–1990: From Popular Protests to Socialist State* (Princeton, NJ: Princeton University Press, 1997).

Welskopp, Thomas, *Das Banner der Brüderlichkeit: Die deutsche Sozialdemokratie vom Vormärz bis zum Sozialistengesetz* (Bonn: Dietz, 2000).

Will, Wilfried van der, and Rob Burns, *Arbeiterkulturbewegung in der Weimarer Republik: Texte, Dokumente, Bilder*, 2 vols., (Frankfurt am Main: Ullstein, 1982).

Winkler, Heinrich August, *Arbeiter und Arbeiterbewegung in der Weimarer Republik*, 3 vols. 1: *Von der Revolution zur Stabilisierung, 1918–1924* (Berlin: Dietz, 1984); 2: *Der Schein der Normalität, 1924 bis 1930* (Berlin: Dietz, 1985); and 3: *Der Weg in die Katastrophe, 1930 bis 1933* (Berlin: Dietz, 1987).

Witte, Bernd, ed., *Deutsche Arbeiterliteratur von den Anfängen bis 1914* (Stuttgart: Reclam, 1977).

Wunderer, Hartmann, *Arbeitervereine und Arbeiterparteien; Kultur- und Massenorganisationen in der Arbeiterbewegung (18

Index

Abendroth, Wolfgang 345
Abrams, Lynn 163–164
Abusch, Alexander 194
Adelberg, Elfriede 55
Adler, Alfred 272, 277, 287, 290
aesthetics 5, 16, 20, 24, 61, 65, 109, 118, 155, 166, 168, 171, 210, 256, 260, 265, 268, 320, 337, 348, 352
Agitationsredner, Der (1926) 246
Agitator, Der (1928) 244
Agitator, Der (1931–32) 253
Agitator, Der/Otto Rühle spricht (1920) 236, 244–246, 253
Agitator/Volksredner (1920) 245–246
agitprop 97–99, 239–247 241–243, 247–251
Aktion, Die 213, 218
Alexander, Gertrud 148, 182, 199, 207, 261
allegory 10, 12, 13, 99, 101–119, 146, 207, 209, 316, 342
Allgemeine Arbeiter-Union (AAUE) 217
Allgemeiner Deutscher Arbeiterverein (ADAV) 90, 93, 122, 125, 126, 236,
Alten und die Neuen, Die (1884) 70, 129
Althusser, Louis 58, 230, 313, 343
Am Webstuhl der Zeit (1873) 129
Anderson, Benedict 16, 17
Anderson, Evelyn 196
Anti-Socialist Laws 28, 77, 81, 86, 103, 126, 143, 156, 163, 165, 236, 258
Aragon, Louis 301, 309
Arbeiter-Illustrierte-Zeitung (AIZ) 305, 311, 313, 316, 317
"Arbeiter-Marseillaise" (1864) 34, 88, 93, 126
Arbeiter-Theaterbund Deutschlands (ATBD) 260
Arbeiter Thomas (1930) 198
Arbeiterfrage, Die (1912) 138, 147
Arbeiterfriede (1922) 198, 203
Arbeiterschicksale (1906) 151
Arnold, Heinz Ludwig 349
Arntz, Gerd 209, 212, 214–215, 217–221

Arp, Hans 205
Assoziation revolutionärer bildender Künstler (ASSO) 245
Audorf, Jacob 88, 93, 126
Auf dem Flügelpferde durch die Zeiten: Bilder vom Klassenkampf der Jahrtausende (1925) 281
Aus dem Klassenkampf (1894) 100, 111
Aus der Gedankenwelt einer Arbeiterfrau, von ihr selbst erzählt (1909) 152
Aus der Tiefe. Arbeiterbriefe: Beiträge zur Seelen-Analyse moderner Arbeiter (1909) 138, 141, 145, 147
Aus meinem Leben (1910–14) 64, 68–69

Baader, Franz von 37
Baader, Ottilie 154
Backes, Dirk 214–215
Badiou, Alan 182
Baluschek, Hans 209, 215
Barck, Simone 349
Barrikaden an der Ruhr (1925) 180
Barth, Emil 77–78
Barthel, Max 234, 263
Bebel, August 64, 66–69, 72, 76, 81, 127, 133, 158
Becher, Johannes R. 233, 253, 262–264
Beethoven, Ludwig van 95, 110
Behne, Adolf 311
Beier, Gerhard 156
Benjamin, Walter 3, 19, 79, 104, 112, 256, 270–271, 287, 332, 341, 348
Benus, Benjamin 219
Bergarbeiter (1909) 236
Berger, Martin 324
Berking, Helmuth 44
Berlin, die Sinfonie der Großstadt (1927) 324, 326
Bernhard, Lucian 309
Bernhardt, Sarah 134
Bernstein, Eduard 60–61, 71
Bethge, Ernst Heinrich (pseud. Lobo Frank) 226, 284–285

Biedermann, Friedrich Karl 37
Biha, Oto 262
Bismarck, Otto von 125, 127, 131
Blanqui, Louis-Auguste 51
Blaszovsky, Fritz 284
Bloch, Ernst 79, 129, 244, 266, 341
Blumtritt, Max 247
Böcklin, Arnold 110, 115–116
Bodek, Richard 241
Bogdal, Klaus-Michael 117–118
Bogdanov, Alexander 243
Bohnen, Uli 214
Bollenbeck, Georg 145, 170–172
Bosse, Friedrich 236
Bourdieu, Pierre 239
bourgeois culture 5, 16, 20, 145, 158–159, 163, 168–172, 227, 256, 266, 276, 343, 348, 350, 353
Brandstetter, Gabriele 250
Brauer, Erwin 182, 189
Brecht, Bertolt 8, 98, 195, 201, 207, 234, 240, 318–320, 323–325, 327–332, 341, 348
Bredel, Willi 263
Brennende Ruhr (1929) 180–191
Brentano, Benjamin von 330
Briefs, Goetz 46
Briefe über die ästhetische Erziehung des Menschen (1794, Letters on the Aesthetic Education of Man) 94, 169
Broch, Hermann 291
Broda, Rudolf 140
Bröger, Karl 234
Bromme, Moritz William Theodor 127, 149–151
Bronner, Ferdinand 236
Broßwitz, Conrad 226
Broué, Pierre 178
Buber, Martin 42
Buch der Freiheit (1893) 111
Bulthaupt, Heinrich 236
Bund der Kommunisten (Communist League) 70
Bund proletarisch-revolutionärer Schriftsteller (BPRS) 179, 183, 194, 198, 199, 261–268, 323, 327
Bürgel, Bruno Hans 151

bürgerliche Gesellschaft, Die (1861) 39
Burstein, Andrew 25
Busch, Ernst 321, 323, 326, 328
Buttinger, Joseph 82–83
Büttner, Heinrich 121, 128–131, 136

Canetti, Elias 291
Canning, Kathleen 344
Cavalier und Arbeiter (1850) 235
Chor der Arbeit (1923) 252–253
Christus im Ruhrgebiet (1922) 217
Chytry, Josef 20
Colberg, Eckard 132
Cologne Progressives 204, 206, 208, 211–215, 219–221, 238, 299
Comintern 8, 97, 101, 195, 242, 260, 269, 316
communism 15, 17, 29, 50, 57, 70, 83, 99, 183, 188, 195–199, 217, 245, 263 214, 254, 289, 294, 298, 302, 314–317, 327, 337–338
Corinth, Lovis 245
Courths-Mahler, Hedwig 185
Crane, Walter 107, 113–114
Cyankali (1931) 324

Daheim (1894) 236
Danto, Elizabeth Ann 290
Delacroix, Eugène 115, 209
Demonstration (1925) 209–211, 213, 217–218, 245
Demonstration (1930) 209
Denkwürdigkeiten und Erinnerungen eines Arbeiters (1903) 148–149
Deutsch, Julius 140
Deutsche Arbeiter-Sänger Zeitung 95
Deutscher Arbeiter-Sängerbund (DAS) 95–96
Diederichs, Eugen 149
Diktatur des Proletariats, Die (1918) 60
Dilthey, Wilhelm 65
Dix, Otto 205, 244, 327
Döblin, Alfred 263
Doesburg, Theo van 205, 207
Dohna, Herrmann Graf zu 38
Dönniges, Helene von 123, 125, 131, 137
Drees, Oskar 278

Dreher, Ingmar 279–280
Drei Monate Fabrikarbeiter und Handwerksbursche (1891) 148
Dreigroschenoper, Die (1931) 329
Dreyhaus, Hermann 185
Dudow, Slatan 319, 323, 327, 329
Duncker, Hermann 264

Eagleton, Terry 18, 20
Ede und Unku (1931) 285–287
education 59, 142, 154, 161–166, 257, 268, 270–281, 287, 290, 192, 295, 336–337
Eichhorn, Friedrich 111
Ein Schlingel (1867) 236
Ein Standpunkt zur Vermittlung socialer Mißstände im Fabriksbetriebe (1843) 38
Ein steiniger Weg (1921) 67, 154
Ein verunglückter Agitator oder die Grund- und Bodenfrage (1874) 236
Eisenstein, Sergei 319, 333
Eisler, Hanns 98, 195, 252, 280, 320, 323–325, 330
Eisner, Kurt 71
Eley, Geoff 343–344
Ellis, Havelock 292
Emig, Brigitte 165
Emmerich, Wolfgang 145, 349, 353
emotional community 8, 13, 46, 60, 65, 79, 82, 356, 86, 99, 101, 173, 222–223, 356
Engels, Friedrich 14, 36, 49–51, 54–61, 69–71, 104, 122, 135, 161, 168, 334
Erinnungen eines Proletariers aus der revolutionären Arbeiterbewegung (1913) 154
Eroberung der Maschinen, Die (1923) 194–197, 199–201
Evans, Richard J. 343–344

Fähnders, Walter 199, 350
Familie Wawroch (1899) 236
Felixmüller, Conrad 216, 244, 254
Ferdinand Lassalle, Der Held des Volkes oder: Um Liebe getödtet! Socialer Roman (1892) 121, 128–132
Fischer, Carl 148–151
Fischer, Franz Louis 151

Fischer, Ruth (née Elfriede Eisler, pseud. Elfriede Friedländer) 280, 294
folk culture 16, 103, 105, 119, 145, 155, 172, 225, 228, 258, 281, 350
Frank, Leonard 263
Franz von Sickingen (1859) 170
Frau und der Sozialismus, Die (1878) 68
Fraser, Nancy 212
freien Arbeiter im preußischen Staat, Die (1847) 38
Freiligrath, Ferdinand 52, 93, 131
Freud, Sigmund 41, 45, 47, 128, 226, 277, 289–291, 296
Frölich, Paul 127
Fuchs, Eduard 100–111
Fünf Finger hat die Hand (1928) 304–307, 312–317
Funktion des Orgasmus, Die (1928) 296

Gamper, Michael 40–41
Geiger, Theodor 36, 45–47
Gemeinschaft 16, 43, 46, 97, 227, 232, 260, 266, 271, 277, 290, 1
(German) Revolution of 1848 89, 115, 123, 235
German Revolution of 1918/19 12, 45–48, 77, 136, 179–180, 212, 217, 259, 336
Gerstenberger, Katharina 14
Gerster, Ottmar 226
Geschichte und Klassenbewußtsein (1923) 61, 266
gespaltene Mensch, Der (1927) 223, 234
gewerbliche Proletariat, Das (1926) 46
Goebbels, Joseph 308
Goethe, Johann Wolfgang von 101, 110–110, 165
Göhre, Paul 138, 141, 148–151, 153–154
Golgatha (1908) 236
Gotsche, Otto 177, 193, 197
Graf, Herbert 226
Gramsci, Antonio 28, 158, 228–229
Grebing, Helga 344
Gregorovius, Ferdinand 84
Griebel, Otto 209
Gronostay, Walter 234
Groschopp, Hans 164
Grossmann, Atina 182, 292

Großstadt (1923)   234
Grosz, George   205, 211, 217, 244, 280, 302, 307, 309, 327
Grote, Heiner   122
Grünberg, Karl   180–187, 190, 264
Gumperz, Julian   177
Günther, Siegfried   96–97
Guttmann, Alfred   95–96

Hans Urian. Die Geschichte einer Weltreise (1929)   281
Hardt, Yvonne   225
Harkort, Friedrich   33
Hart, Heinrich   156
Hartig, Valtin   257–258
Hatzfeldt, Countess Sophie von   123
Hauptmann, Gerhart   73, 180, 235
Heartfield, John   8, 195, 199–200, 205, 216–217, 261, 285, 299–320
Hegel, Georg Wilhelm Friedrich   56–58, 109, 266, 326
Heilbut, Kurt   258
Heine, Heinrich   54, 90, 131, 135
Heinz, Hellmuth   245
Henckell, Karl   111
Herder, Johann Gottfried   20, 85, 144, 155, 172
Herwegh, Georg   90, 126
Herzfelde, Wieland   206, 261, 302, 315
Herzig, Arno   132
Herzog, Dagmar   292
Heynen, Robert   241
Hickethier, Knut   117
Hirschfeld, Kurt   263
Hirschfeld, Magnus   292, 296
Hirth, Georg   53
Hobsbawm, Eric   16–17, 73, 342–343
Höch, Hannah   303
Hodann, Max   293
Hoellering, Georg   328
Hoelz, Max   195–196
Hoerle, Heinrich   211–212, 214–216
Hoernle, Edwin   90, 275–276
Hoffmann, Adolf   235, 284
Holek, Wenzel   150–151
Honneth, Axel   211–212
Höppener, Hugo (Fidus)   106

Hornauer, Uwe   234
Hoym, Carl   90

Ihering, Herbert   330
Im Hinterhaus (1903)   236
Im Kampf (1892)   236
Ins Leben hinein (1929)   234
Interessengemeinschaft für Arbeiterkultur (IfA)   261
Internationale, Die (1928–30)   209
"Internationale, The"   194, 252, 285
Internationale Arbeiterhilfe (IAH)   242, 262, 315

Jaspers, Karl   45
Johannesson, Adolf   232
Jones, Gareth Stedman   23, 74
Jonsson, Stefan   40–41
Jugendgeschichte einer Arbeiterin, Die (1909)   152–153
Jung, Franz   8, 192, 194–204, 295, 301, 311, 319
Jutzi, Piel   329

Kampf um die Arbeitsfreude, Der (1927)   140, 229
Kampf um Kohle (1931)   183
Kampf vor den Fabriken (1926)   194
Kampfgemeinschaft der Arbeitersänger (KdAS)   97, 260
Kampfgenoss   260
Kanitz, Otto Felix   273, 278–279
Kaschuba, Wolfgang   354
Kästner, Erich   286
Kautsky, Karl   60–61, 66, 71–73, 105, 153, 168
Kautsky, Minna   70–71, 129, 143
Kemény, Alfred (pseud. Durus)   97, 312
Key, Ellen   270
Kharkov Conference (1930)   184, 264
Kirn, Gal   331–332
Kläber, Kurt   180–181, 262–263
Klein, Julius Leopold   235
Klinger, Max   110
Kluge, Alexander   4, 334–335, 356
Klutsis, Gustav(s)   315–317
Kocka, Jürgen   344, 346

Kokoschka, Oskar 217, 309
Kollontai, Alexandra 292
Kollwitz, Käthe 180, 205, 215, 238, 246, 315, 323
Kommunistische Arbeiter-Partei Deutschlands (KAPD) 195
Kommunistische Jugend Deutschlands (KJD) 283
Kommunistische Partei Deutschlands (KPD) 7, 10, 13, 28, 62, 63, 78, 96–98, 127, 166, 178–183, 189, 192, 194–197, 209, 222, 235–237, 238–247, 250–254, 256–269, 271, 275–276, 279, 286–289, 301–306, 309, 311–316, 323, 328, 336–338, 341, 350, 355
Kommunistischer Jugendverband Deutschlands (KJVD) 241
Könnemann, Erwin 182
Korff, Gottfried 117
Korn, Karl 277–278
Korsch, Karl 50, 61
Kosstrin, Hannah 239
Kracauer, Siegfried 3, 45, 65
Kreuzzug des Weibes (1926) 324
Kriebel, Sabine 312–315
Kriege, Hermann 70
Krusche, Hans-Joachim 182
Kuhle Wampe, oder Wem gehört die Welt? (1932) 251–252, 318–324, 326–333
Kultur 16, 142, 155, 163, 167, 226, 257–258, 268, 315, 336–337, 344–345
Kulturwille: Monatsblätter für Kultur der Arbeiterschaft 257–260
Kun, Béla 195
Kunze, Horst 279

Lage der arbeitenden Klasse in England, Die (1845) 55–56
Landauer, Gustav 216
Lang, Fritz 309
Lask, Berta 193, 199, 281
Lassalle, Ferdinand 12, 81, 93, 104, 120–131, 133–137, 142, 168, 170
Lassalle: Ein Leben für Freiheit und Liebe (1902) 136
Lava (1921) 185
Lavant, Rudolf 148

Le Bon, Gustave 34–35, 41–42, 45, 47, 65
Leben eines Landarbeiters, Das (1911) 150
Lebensgang eines deutsch-tschechischen Handarbeiters (1909) 150
Lebensgeschichte eines modernen Fabrikarbeiters (1905) 149
Lebensgestaltung und Klassenkampf (1928) 220–221
Ledebour, Georg 78
Lenin, Vladimir Ilyich Ulyanov 55, 59–61, 98, 145, 178, 197, 242, 261, 301, 353
Lepenies, Wolf 170–172
Lessing, Gotthold Ephraim 169
Lethen, Helmut 207–208
Leuna 1921 (1927) 193–194
Levenstein, Adolf 138–142, 145, 147, 154
Lex-Nerlinger, Alice 205
Libertas/Helvetia (1891) 115
Liberty Leading the People (1830) 209
Lidtke, Vernon 355
Liebknecht, Karl 217
Liebknecht, Wilhelm 66, 67, 77, 81, 125, 158–162
Liebknecht Luxemburg Lenin (1927) 233
Lilien, Ephraim Moses 115–116
Linkskurve, Die 180, 252, 254, 257, 261–266, 268
Lipinski, Richard 235
Lissitzky, El 315
Liszt, Franz 110
Lorbeer, Hans 233
Lotz, Max 141–142, 145, 147
Löwenstein, Kurt 273, 275
Lucas, Erhard 182, 353–354
Lüchow, Johann Christian 90
Lüdeke, Heinz 330
Lüdemann, Susanne 40–41
Lüdtke, Alf 346–347
Lukács, Georg 50, 61, 201, 266, 268, 341
Luxemburg, Rosa 197, 217, 259

M (1931) 309
Mai-Festzeitung 106, 113–116
Malinowski, Bronislaw 296
Man, Hendrik de 222, 224, 226–230, 234, 237, 259, 289, 315, 319

Manifesto of the Communist Party (1848) 51–52, 69
Mann, Thomas 180, 228
Mann im Beton (1932) 234
March Action (1921) 177, 179, 192–197, 200
Marchwitza, Hans 180–185, 190–192, 253, 262–264
Marcus, George E. 25
Märten, Lu 236, 265
Marx, Karl 14, 24, 36, 40, 45, 49–52, 54–61, 69–70, 74, 90, 111–112, 122, 127, 135–136, 161, 164, 168–170, 257–258, 326, 334, 338, 340, 342
Marxism 1, 49–53, 69, 77, 79, 111, 113, 118, 127, 136, 144, 157, 164, 167, 230, 244, 260, 284
Marxismus und Philosophie (1923) 61
Märzstürme (1933) 177, 197
Maschinenstürmer, Die (1922) 237
masculinity 57–58, 64–68, 82, 86, 98–99, 101, 104, 110, 152–153, 177–191, 211, 225, 250, 259, 296, 299, 315, 337,
Masereel, Frans 219
Masse. Ein Beitrag zur Lehre von den sozialen Gebilden, Die (1930) 46
Masse Mensch (1921) 237
Masse und ihre Aktion, Die (1926) 46–47
Massenpsychologie des Faschismus (1933) 289, 292–294, 296
mass psychology 4, 6, 34–35, 41–45, 59, 65, 289, 299
mass discourse 33–35, 38–52, 337
Mehnert, Paul 236
Mehring, Franz 73, 124, 153, 168–170, 207, 268
Merson, Allen 156–157
Meyer, Gustav William 97
Meyer, Hansgeorg 279
Meyer, Joseph 162
Mihaly, Jo 238, 247–250
moderne Proletariat, Das (1910) 34, 140
modernism 8–9, 194–195, 203–215, 225, 234, 250, 261–268, 301, 312–315, 317, 332, 336, 338, 350
Moholy-Nagy, László 309

Moreau, Gustave 110
Most, Johann 44, 49, 90–91
Mühlen, Hermynia zur 280–281
Münchow, Ursula 144, 351
Münzenberg, Willi 262, 315
Mutter Krausens Fahrt ins Glück (1929) 329

Nagel, Otto 205, 315, 351
Napoleon Bonaparte 134
nationalism 18, 19, 28, 60, 62, 85, 119, 127, 134, 155, 170, 223, 327, 336–340
Nationalsozialistische Arbeiterpartei (NSDAP) 220
Naturgeschichte des Volkes als Grundlage einer deutschen Social-Politik, Die (1854–1869) 38
Naumann, Friedrich 151
Negt, Oskar 4, 334–356
Neue Welt, Die 73
Neue Zeit, Die 126–127, 168
Neumann, Bernd 149–150
Neurath, Otto 214, 219–221
Nietzsche, Friedrich 197
Nussbaum, Martha 25

October Revolution 61–62, 78, 154, 173, 198, 207, 255, 259, 288, 309, 315
Ortega y Gasset, José 45
Osterroth, Nikolaus 154
Ostwald, Hans 147–148
Otto-Walster, August 129, 143, 236
Ottwalt, Ernst 263, 323

Pabst, Georg Wilhelm 329
Paris Commune 38, 44, 259
pathos 13, 76, 98, 101, 108–109, 118, 198, 202, 208, 215, 244, 348
Paul, Bruno 106
Perthaler, Alois Freiherr von 38
Pestalozzi, Johann Heinrich 165
Peuckert, Will-Erich 39
Peukert, Josef 154, 156
Pfemfert, Franz 218
Piscator, Erwin 242, 249
Plekhanov, Georgi 242
Pohl, Klaus-Dieter 117

Popp, Adelheid 142, 152–153
populism 6, 19, 26, 29, 30, 86, 130, 134, 223, 289
Pottier, Eugène 88
Preczang, Ernst 236
Preußentum und Sozialismus (1919) 66
proletarian culture 158, 161, 166, 171–172, 215–220, 227, 241–243, 254, 258, 266, 269, 299, 319, 338
proletarian identification 3, 5, 7–16, 37, 47, 68–71, 78, 89, 98, 103, 111–112, 135, 137, 139, 140, 146, 179, 215, 218, 221, 230, 233, 240, 256, 271, 278, 282, 285–287, 302–303, 318, 321, 331, 336
proletarian literature 72, 158, 168, 173, 188, 204, 255, 264–267, 287
Proletariat, Das (1906) 42–43
Proletarier (1920) 198
Proletarier-Liederbuch (1873) 90–93
Proletarier singe! Kampf- und Volkslieder (1919) 90
Proletarische Feuilleton-Korrespondenz 262
proletarische Kind, Das 275
Proletkult 97, 241–242, 260, 265
Prometheus 100–115
Prüfer, Sebastian 132
Psychologie des foules, La (1895) 34, 41
Psychologie du socialisme (1899) 34

Querner, Curt 205, 209, 238, 244–245, 249, 254

Radbruch, Gustav 227
Rancière, Jacques 26–27, 331
Rector, Martin 199
Reddy, William 3, 23–24
Reger, Erik 185
Rehbein, Franz 150–151
Reich, Annie 291
Reich, Wilhelm 229, 239, 288–299, 337, 348
Reinisch, Marion 249
religion/religiosity 67, 77, 79, 87, 105, 121, 124–128, 133, 135–136, 149, 157, 166, 217, 225, 245–246, 273, 306, 314, 317, 336
Renn, Ludwig 262

Renner, Karl 79
Revolte im Kasperhaus (1929) 284–285
Revolutionary Association of Proletarian Writers (RAPP) 184
Rheinische Zeitung 111
Riehl, Wilhelm Heinrich 36, 38–40
Rippey, Theodore 326
Ritter, Gerhard Albert 345
Rocker, Rudolf 69
Rodchenko, Alexander 315
Rohrwasser, Michael 188
Rosenberg, Alfred 228
Rosenow, Emil 236
Rosenwein, Barbara 23
Rote Erde (1928) 234
Rote Fahne, Die 96, 195, 261–262, 306, 308, 311
Rote Lieder (1924) 90
Rote Soldaten (1921) 265
rote Sprachchor, Das (agitprop troupe) 251
rote Sprachrohr, Das (journal) 238, 250–253, 321, 326
Rote Woche, Die (1921) 198
Roter Frontkämpferbund (RFB) 241, 309
Roth, Karl Heinz 353
Roth, Lynette 214
Rousseau, Jean Jacques 24, 142, 272
Ruhe und Ordnung (1929) 323
Rühle, Otto 238, 243–244, 247, 254, 278, 288–289, 294
Rühle-Gerstel, Alice 288
Ruhr Uprising (1920) 179–182, 189, 192, 194, 196, 217, 286
Ruttmann, Walter 324

Sagan, Leontine 323
Sanger, Margaret 292
Schapper, Karl 70
Scherchen, Hermann 97, 229
Schiller, Friedrich 19–20, 73, 94–95, 109–110, 118, 130, 134, 146, 169–170, 250
Schiller, ein Lebensbild für deutsche Arbeiter (1905) 170
Schirokauer, Alfred 136
Schirokauer, Arno 137
Schönberg, Arnold 98, 323

Schönlank, Bruno 223–224, 232, 234
Schweitzer, Johann Baptist von 236
Schwitters, Kurt 205, 303
Scriabin, Alexander 110
Seid geweiht! (1927) 234
Seiwert, Franz Wilhelm 8, 195, 204–206, 208–218, 221, 301, 319
sentimentality 13, 23, 25, 65–68, 79–82, 99, 103, 118, 127–129, 156, 164, 203, 207–208, 215, 253, 315, 325, 330, 337, 352
Severing, Carl 179
Sewell, Sara Ann 182
sexuality 134, 152, 180–185, 189, 269, 287, 288–299, 229
Shelley, Percy Bysshe 110
Sighele, Scipio 42
Silberman, Marc 240, 331
Simmel, Georg 65
Simplicissimus 105
Slevogt, Max 106, 113–114
Sloterdijk, Peter 143, 208
Smith, Adam 24
Sombart, Werner 36, 42–43, 47
Sontzeff, Sophie von 131
Sozialdemokratische Arbeiterpartei Deutschlands (SDAP) 158
Sozialdemokratische Partei Deutschlands (SPD) 28, 40, 60–64, 73, 77–80, 87, 90–93, 103–106, 111–113, 124, 127, 151, 163–168, 178, 227, 235, 237, 237, 250, 252–260, 267, 269, 271, 273, 279, 281, 284, 287, 305, 308, 314
Social Democracy 3, 8,10–11, 60, 65–69, 77–80, 83, 99, 104–105, 114–117, 122, 132–137, 148–154, 158, 165–170, 223–235, 255, 292, 337–338, 344–345
Sozialismus und Communismus des heutigen Frankreich, Der (1842) 36
Sozialismus und soziale Bewegung (1908) 43
socialist culture 5, 7, 17, 66, 100, 107, 119, 129, 168, 227, 235, 277
Sozialistische Arbeiterjugend Deutschlands (SAJ) 283
Sozialistische Erziehung, Die 274
Sozialistische Republik 187, 208–211

Spengler, Oswald 45, 66, 214
Spethmann, Hans 189
Stalin, Josef 242, 287
Stearns, Peter N. and Carol Z. 23
Stein, Lorenz von 35–38, 40, 47
Steinacker, Sven 279
Steinberg, Hans-Josef 157
Steinberg, Marc 166
Stemmle, R. A. 234
Stieg, Georg 349
Stirner, Max 197
Stöcker, Helene 292
Strodtmann, Adolf 90
Sturm auf Essen (1930) 180–184, 190, 192
Süddeutscher Postillon 100, 103–107, 114, 127
Sue, Eugène 54
Suvin, Darko 240

Tag des Proletariats (1925) 233
Tarde, Gabriel 42
Tenfelde, Klaus 346
Tesarek, Anton 274
Tetzner, Lisa 281
Thälmann, Ernst 178, 305, 317
Theweleit, Klaus 188–189
Thiele, Hertha 323
Thompson, E.P. 342–243
Tillich, Paul 45
Toller, Ernst 233, 237, 249, 255–256
Tönnies, Ferdinand 228
Treitschke, Heinrich 34
Tretyakov, Sergei 303, 312, 315, 319–310, 325, 327, 332, 350
Trommel, Die 275
Trommler, Frank 349
Tucholsky, Kurt 263, 311

Ulk 115–116
Unabhängige Sozialdemokratische Partei Deutschlands (USPD) 179, 196, 226
Uthmann, Gustav Adolf 97

Vallentin, Maxim 251–253
Vereinigte Kommunistische Partei Deutschlands (VKPD) 195
Vierkandt, Alfred 46

Vleugel, Wilhelm 46
Volk-Illustrierte (VI) 305
Volkskunde des Proletariats (1931) 39–40
Volpedo, Giuseppe Pellizza da 209
Vom Arbeiter zum Astronomen (1919) 151–152
Vom Beter zum Kämpfer (1920) 154
Vorwärts 71, 106, 111, 267–268, 341

Wagner, Richard 135
Wahre Jacob, Der 101–102, 105
Walter, Franz 157, 165, 233
Walzwerk 183
Wangenheim, Gustav von 242, 252–253
Warburg, Aby 250
Warstat, Matthias 225
Was ist Klassenbewußtsein? 297–299
Was Peterchens Freunde erzählen 280
Weber, Die 73, 235
Weber, Max 43–44, 120, 140
Weidt, Jean 238, 247–250, 254
Weimann, Richard 155–156
Weinert, Erich 262
Weisenborn, Günther 234
Weiskopf, Franz Carl 286, 308
Weiskopf, Grete (pseud. Alex Wedding) 263–286
Weitling, Wilhelm 52, 69, 120
Weitz, Eric 182
Weitz, Ulrich 104
Werner, Julius 34
Wesen und Veränderung der Formen/ Künste (1924) 265
Wie ein Pfarrer Sozialdemokrat wurde (1900) 148
Wieland, Christoph Martin 20
Wiese, Leopold von 46
Williams, Raymond 16, 74–76, 82, 160, 338, 342–343
Winkler, Heinrich-August 346

Winter, Matthias 344
Wir! Ein sozialistisches Festspiel 224–230
"Wissen ist Macht" (1872) 159
Witte, Bernd 144–145, 349, 350
Wittich, Manfred 84
Wittfogel, Karl August 259, 265–266
Wolf, Friedrich 273, 292, 311, 324
Wolter, Marta 323
workers' associations 14, 69, 80, 82, 86, 112, 123, 129, 156–157, 160, 163–165, 179, 257
workers' life writings 139, 141–154, 277
workers' movement 58, 65, 68, 72, 76–80, 85, 88, 94, 104, 107, 118, 121, 126–127, 136, 139, 143, 146, 151–154, 163, 167, 171–173, 209, 225, 247, 277, 296, 303, 314, 335–338, 343–350
workers' songs 84, 96–97
workers' sports 97, 157, 231, 240, 247, 252, 322–328
working-class culture 3–7, 10, 14, 17, 22, 22–29, 63, 73, 75, 83, 85, 116, 129, 145, 157–160, 167, 172, 218, 220, 259, 281, 333–355
Wundt, Wilhelm 65
Wurm, Emanuel 87

Zeitprobleme: Wie der Arbeiter wohnt (1930) 323
Zeller, Magnus 238, 245–246
Zeller, Ursula 117
Zervigón, Andrés Mario 307–308
Zetkin, Clara 78–79, 207, 292
Zille, Heinrich 215, 323, 329
Zimmermann, Otto 227, 232–233
Zörgiebel, Karl 307–308
"Zu Trutz und Schutz" (1871) 159
Zur Psychologie des Sozialismus (1927) 229–230